Personality Disorder and Community Mental Health Teams

Personality Disorder and Community Mental Health Teams

A Practitioner's Guide

Edited by

Mark J. Sampson and Remy A. McCubbin
Manchester Mental Health and Social Care Trust

Peter Tyrer
Imperial College London

John Wiley & Sons, Ltd

Chichester • New York • Weinheim • Brisbane • Singapore • Toronto

Copyright © 2006   John Wiley & Sons Ltd, The Atrium, Southern Gate, Chichester,
West Sussex PO19 8SQ, England

Telephone (+ 44) 1243 779777

Email (for orders and customer service enquiries): cs-books@wiley.co.uk
Visit our Home Page on www.wiley.com

Other Wiley Editorial Offices

John Wiley & Sons Inc., 111 River Street, Hoboken, NJ 07030, USA

Jossey-Bass, 989 Market Street, San Francisco, CA 94103-1741, USA

Wiley-VCH Verlag GmbH, Boschstrasse 12, D-69469 Weinheim, Germany

John Wiley & Sons Australia Ltd, 42 McDougall Street, Milton, Queensland 4064, Australia

John Wiley & Sons (Asia) Pte Ltd, 2 Clementi Loop #02-01, Jin Xing Distripark, Singapore 129809

John Wiley & Sons Canada Ltd, 22 Worcester Road, Etobicoke, Ontario, Canada M9W 1L1

Wiley also publishes its books in a variety of electronic formats. Some content that appears in print may
not be available in electronic books.

Library of Congress Cataloging-in-Publication Data
Personality disorder and community mental health teams: a practitioner's
  guide/edited by Mark J. Sampson, Remy A. McCubbin, and Peter Tyrer.
    p. cm.
  Includes bibliographical references and index.
  ISBN-13: 978-0-470-01171-3
  ISBN-10: 0-470-01171-8
    1. Personality disorders. 2. Personality disorders–Treatment.
    3. Community mental health services. 4. Crisis intervention (Mental health services)
    I. Sampson, Mark J. II. McCubbin, Remy A. III. Tyrer, Peter J.
    [DNLM: 1. Personality Disorders. 2. Personality Disorders–therapy.
    3. Community Mental Health Services. 4. Patient Care Team. WM 190 P46703 2006]
  RC554.P457 2006
  362.196′8581–dc22   2005024801

British Library Cataloguing in Publication Data
A catalogue record for this book is available from the British Library

    ISBN-13 978-0-470-01171-3 (hbk)   0-470-01171-8 (hbk)
    ISBN-10 978-0-470-01172-0 (pbk)   0-470-01172-6 (pbk)

Typeset 11/13pt Times by Thomson Press (India) Limited, New Delhi
Printed and bound in Great Britain by TJ International Ltd, Padstow, Cornwall, UK
This book is printed on acid-free paper responsibly manufactured from sustainable forestry
in which at least two trees are planted for each one used for paper production.

Contents

SECTION TWO   TREATMENT AND MANAGEMENT IN COMMUNITY MENTAL HEALTH TEAMS

About the Editors

Mark Sampson works as a clinical psychologist in two Community Mental Health Teams (CMHTs) in South Manchester. He has been a part of these teams for the past five years and during this time developed experience and expertise in working with patients with personality disorder. He originally trained as a general and psychiatric nurse before studying psychology, obtaining a doctorate in clinical psychology from the University of Manchester in 1999. He uses integrative approaches to working with patients with personality disorders, but is strongly influenced by cognitive and cognitive analytic therapies.

Remy McCubbin first studied Biology at Southampton University, graduating in 1987. He went on to study for a MA in Psychology at Nottingham University, graduating in 1993, before working on an evaluation of three CMHTs in the Midlands. In 1998 he completed a doctorate in clinical psychology, since which time he has worked across several community teams in South Manchester. This has inspired an interest in personality disorder, and has led to a recognition of the importance of such difficulties in the response to treatment of many people seen by these services. He has an interest in several forms of therapy, and the potential advantages of integrating various approaches within multi-disciplinary interventions. Away from personality disorder, he has an interest in the role of affective avoidance in the maintenance of various Axis I and Axis II disorders.

Peter Tyrer is the Head of the Department of Psychological Medicine at Imperial College, London, Honorary Consultant in Rehabilitation Psychiatry, Central North West London Mental Health NHS Trust, and Honorary Consultant in Assertive Outreach (IMPACT team) in West London Mental Health Trust. He obtained his medical qualifications at the University of Cambridge at St Thomas's Hospital London in 1965 and trained in psychiatry at the Maudsley Hospital and Institute of Psychiatry, London. He has carried out research into personality disorder since he was a medical student and has published two books and over 100 original articles on the subject. He is the founder president of the British and Irish Group for the Study of Personality Disorders and the Co-Chair of the Section on Personality Disorders of the World Psychiatric Association. He is a Fellow of the Academy of Medical Sciences, of the Faculty of Public Health, of the Royal College of Physicians, and of the Royal College of Psychiatrists. He is the Editor of the *British Journal of Psychiatry* and on the editorial board of seven other journals. Despite his academic interests he still regards himself primarily as a 'coal-face' psychiatrist, who has learnt most from his patients—and among the most stimulating and challenging of these have been those with personality disorder.

LIST OF CONTRIBUTORS

Nic Alwin   Consultant Clinical Psychologist, Roch House Therapy Centre, Fairfield General Hospital, Rochdale Road, Bury Old Road, Bury, BL9 7TD, UK.

Dawn Bennett   Consultant Clinical Psychologist, Clinical Psychology Service, St Ives House, Accrington Road, Blackburn, BBI 2EG, UK.

Lara Bennett   Clinical Psychologist, Department of Clinical Psychology, Laureate House, Wythenshawe Hospital, Manchester, M23 9LT, UK.

Ron Blackburn   Emeritus Professor of Clinical and Forensic Psychological Studies, Division of Clinical Psychology, University of Liverpool, L69 3GB, UK.

Tom Burns   Professor of Social Psychiatry, University of Oxford, Department of Psychiatry, Warneford Hospital, Oxford, OX3 7JX, UK.

Kate Davidson   Honorary Professor of Clinical Psychology, Glasgow Institute of Psychosocial Interventions, NHS Greater Glasgow and University of Glasgow, Glasgow, UK.

Mark Evans   Consultant Psychiatrist in Psychotherapy, Psychotherapy Service, Gaskell House, Swinton Grove, Manchester, M13 0EU, UK.

Janet Feigenbaum   Senior Lecturer in Clinical Psychology, University College London, Consultant Clinical Psychologist, NELMHT, Sub-Dept Clinical Health Psychology, London, WC1E 6BT, UK.

Rex Haigh   Consultant Psychiatrist in Psychotherapy, Berkshire Health-care Trust, Berkshire, UK.

Kate Hellin   Consultant Clinical Psychologist, Therapeutic Community Service North, Victoria Avenue, Crewe, CW2 7SQ, UK.

Eddie Kane   Director Keer Consulting and member of the DH and Home Office Expert Advisory Group, Department of Psychological Medicine, Imperial College, St Dunstan's Road, London, W6 8RP, UK.

Ian B. Kerr   Consultant Psychiatrist and Psychotherapist, Sheffield Care Trust, and Hon. Senior Lecturer, School of Health and Related Research (ScHARR), University of Sheffield, Michael Carlisle Centre, Osbourne Road, Sheffield, S11 9BF, UK.

Remy McCubbin   Clinical Psychologist, Department of Clinical Psychology, Laureate House, Wythenshawe Hospital, Manchester, M23 9LT, UK.

James Moorey   Consultant Clinical Psychologist, Rawnsley Building, Manchester Royal Infirmary, Oxford Road, Manchester, M13 9WL, UK.

Giles Newton-Howes   Specialist Registrar in General Adult Psychiatry on the Charing Cross rotation, London, UK.

Mark J. Sampson   Clinical Psychologist, Department of Clinical Psychology, Laureate House, Wythenshawe Hospital, Manchester, M23 9LT, UK.

Mary Shinner   Consultant Clinical Psychologist, Psychology Services, Bolton, Salford and Trafford Mental Health Trust, Bury New Road, Prestwich, Manchester, M25 3BL, UK.

Gary L. Sidley   Consultant Clinical Psychologist, Psychology Services, Bolton, Salford and Trafford Mental Health Trust, Prestwich, Manchester, M25 3BL, UK.

Preface

In the UK, recent government proposals have emphasised that people with personality disorder are seen as 'legitimate business' for generic mental health services and, therefore, for community mental health teams (CMHTs). These proposals have been welcomed by many working in the field, and should in time help to prevent people with such difficulties being excluded from mental health services.

However, many practitioners working in CMHTs are currently unsure how best to support patients with these types of problem. The idea for this book came from observing and experiencing the struggles that CMHTs can go through when trying to develop effective care plans for people with personality disorder.

It is our hope that the book accurately conveys a sense of the considerable distress that is often associated with personality disorder—distress not only for the patient, but also for their friends and family, and for those working in services trying to help them. We then hope to provide useful ideas about how CMHT practitioners can work more effectively, to support each of these groups. The book has deliberately been aimed at the 'non-specialist' CMHT practitioner, i.e. someone who does not already have a detailed knowledge of the literature relating to these patients. For those who do wish to read further, however, each chapter also provides an overview of key references contained in the wider literature.

The book is divided into two sections. In the first section, recent government initiatives relating to personality disorder are outlined, and ideas underlying psychological and biological treatments are introduced. The second section focuses specifically on the particular roles and functions of the CMHT, in trying to support patients with these disorders.

Figuratively speaking, the 'tent' for personality disorder is set up in Chapters 1 and 2, and the theoretical concepts pinning it to the ground (by not particularly sturdy guy ropes) are described in Chapters 3 and 4. Each guy rope relates to a specific treatment or group of treatments, and the nature of each is set out in Chapters 5–7. It is important for the reader to realise that the accounts contained in these chapters present their 'product' in the best possible light, and do not always take account of the problems that are encountered in practice. These problems are illustrated in Section Two, which emphasises the importance of the fundamental concepts of 'engagement' and 'alliance' and that there is no simple formula or protocol that provides all the answers.

This book does, however, contain a framework around which CMHTs are able to structure their thinking. The evidence base for many of the interventions used for personality disorder is at present a small and unstable one. Because we have so little that is really solid—there is, for example, no intervention effective enough to be published in a NICE guideline—it is tempting to clutch at the favourable results that are published and make as much of them as we can. In such a climate, there can be an incentive to exaggerate the evidence for certain approaches. This would be unfortunate and, ultimately, unhelpful. While we should not be pessimistic about our efforts in CMHTs to tackle personality disorder effectively, we should acknowledge that much of what we describe is 'patient-based evidence'. This is useful, but it is only a beginning. There is an old Ghanaian proverb, 'a man does not know how far he has to go until he starts walking'; this book represents the start of what is likely to be a long march.

Some comments should also be made regarding the terminology used in this book. While acknowledging the difficulties associated with a diagnostic approach and the term 'personality disorder', this terminology is at present the one most widely used and most readily understood, and as such allows for the clearest communication of ideas. We have also chosen to use the term 'patient' rather than, for example, 'client' or 'service user'. While this might seem peculiar—especially when many of the challenges for services arise *because* people with these difficulties do not easily fit with an 'illness' model of care—we do believe it is helpful to be reminded that CMHTs operate in a psychiatric system heavily influenced by a medical model of 'illness'.

Personality disorder has been largely ignored or denied in much of psychiatric practice, which has typically hidden behind terms such as 'resistant depression' and 'simple schizophrenia', instead of acknowledging that it is personality factors that are responsible for much of the variation in clinical response and outcome that we see in practice. Practitioners who have been puzzled by this variation (often to the point of questioning their own competence) will hopefully be encouraged to realise that much of this variation can be put down to personality in all its aspects and that these factors can be amenable to intervention. In our view, patients with personality disorder are an extremely rewarding group of people to work with. We hope this book will help to inspire interest and confidence in such work among CMHT practitioners.

Mark Sampson

Remy McCubbin

Peter Tyrer

SECTION ONE
Theoretical Background

1

Personality Disorder: New Initiatives in Staff Training

EDDIE KANE

INTRODUCTION

A good deal is already known about personality disorders. There is also an increasing understanding of what is helpful and unhelpful for people with these disorders. It is therefore important to communicate this knowledge to the increasing numbers of staff, in a wide range of agencies, with whom they come into contact.

With a few notable exceptions, clinicians have for years tended to avoid involvement in the treatment and support of people with personality disorders. Tolerance of these attitudes is rightly declining. This change in attitude has been well supported by new Guidance from the National Institute for Mental Health in England (NIMHE, 2003a, 2003b) developed in the wake of the National Service Framework for Mental Health (Department of Health, 1999). Relatively small sums of new national money have been used to stimulate the growth of new and sometime novel services. As well as service development, training for staff is becoming a higher priority.

Despite these encouraging developments and changes in attitude there is a long way to go. People with personality disorders are still one of the most socially excluded groups in our society. Their experience of services from a wide range of agencies demonstrates a lack of tolerance and awareness of their issues and of them as individuals. Other chapters in this book aim to help redress the situation by offering readers an opportunity to be more aware of personality disorders, the people who experience them and the techniques and support systems that can help them.

BACKGROUND

Recent initiatives from the UK government to improve services for people with a personality disorder have raised the profile and the importance of staff training for a wide range of staff engaging with patients with these problems. No longer can training be the preserve of a minority of interested professionals. Rather, it will need to move centre stage for a much wider range of people, in many different agencies. An appreciation of current thinking and the development of best practice is important for anyone involved in delivering community-based services. In particular, working with people with personality disorders is likely to become an essential area of required expertise for Community Mental Health Team (CMHT) members.

The competencies required for working with people with personality disorders are in many respects similar to those needed to work with other individuals with a range of mental disorders. However, there are some clear differences. Direct professional involvement in the area of personality disorders demands a high degree of personal resilience, the ability to maintain good boundaries and manage hostility and conflict. Individual members of staff also need to be multi-disciplinary team players and be able to appreciate the value of team working and support. Just as important is the ability to tolerate and manage the emotional impact on the multi-disciplinary team's functioning that intensive working with people with a personality disorder can create.

Recent work by the National Institute for Mental Health England (NIMHE) has begun to firm up the agenda for staff training and suggests an integrated 'Skills Escalator' as the most effective framework for staff training and development.

This chapter will:

- discuss the context for the recent government and NIMHE initiatives to improve services for people with personality disorders
- outline these initiatives, particularly those related to staff training
- reflect on how these initiatives could help CMHTs work more effectively.

Taking this training and development framework forward is perhaps one of the most critical areas of mental health services in which progress needs to be made nationally. Without such progress, people with personality disorders will remain one of the most excluded groups of individuals, will be denied relevant and sensitive services, and will continue to be vulnerable in our society. This is a future that ought not to be contemplated in 21st century Britain.

A FRAMEWORK FOR REFORM

The National Service Framework for Adult Mental Health (NSFMH) (Department of Health, 1999) describes a clear set of responsibilities. These responsibilities focus particularly on the provision of evidence-based and effective services for all people with mental disorders, including those with personality disorders (who are debilitated and excluded as a result). As part of the practical implementation of the NSFMH, in January 2003 the National Institute for Mental Health in England published *Personality Disorder: No Longer a Diagnosis of Exclusion* (NIMHE, 2003a). The guidance was intended to build on standards four and five of the NSFMH, and to ensure the development of specific services for people with personality disorders.

The guidance started from the premise that personality disorders are common and often disabling conditions. Many people with personality disorders are able to manage their lives and relationships successfully on a day-to-day basis. However, there are a significant number of individuals who suffer a great deal of distress. These individuals often receive few or no tailored services and their interactions within their social and their service networks are frequently dysfunctional, and unsatisfactory to themselves and the people to whom they try to relate. Few National Health Service (NHS) organisations and even fewer of the other potential service-providing agencies have specific services for people with personality disorders. In 2002 only 17 per cent of NHS Mental Health Trusts provided a dedicated service for people with a personality disorder (NIMHE, 2003a). The situation is compounded by the fact that even where there is dedicated provision, the services are based on widely varying and occasionally conflicting therapeutic models and approaches. As a result, people are frequently treated or supported at the margins—for example, in Accident and Emergency departments, through inappropriate admissions to psychiatric units, lost in a CMHT's caseload or as frequent and unsatisfied attendees at a GP's surgery.

Underlying this unsatisfactory state of affairs is the belief amongst many mental health and social care professionals that there is nothing that people with a personality disorder can be offered that would help them move towards recovery and an improved ability to cope with everyday life. The guidance also highlighted the danger that the proposed changes in the draft Mental Health Bill would emphasise even further the enormous gap in services and skills by removing the so-called 'treatability test', which has been frequently used as a way of excluding individuals from treatment, particularly by mental health service providers. In effect, some of the most damaged and excluded people in society are refused treatment because individual clinicians make decisions based on their view that people with a personality disorder will not respond to any interventions they have at their disposal. This process of exclusion is legitimised by the current Mental Health Act, which specifies that an individual must be deemed to be treatable before treatment is offered.

Clearly, this was not a position that could continue if the government's commitment to modernise services was to be delivered. Not only was new investment needed in direct service provision, but also a major initiative was required to provide new training opportunities to ensure that not only clinicians and practitioners but also staff in a wide range of agencies had access to training, ranging from 'awareness training' to specific high-level treatment skills.

In summary, *Personality Disorder: No Longer a Diagnosis of Exclusion* (NIMHE, 2003a) recommends that services should:

- Assist people with personality disorder who experience significant distress or difficulty to access appropriate clinical care and management from specialist mental health services.
- Ensure that offenders with a personality disorder receive appropriate care from forensic services and interventions designed both to provide treatment and to address their offending behaviour.
- Establish the necessary education and training to equip mental health practitioners to provide effective assessment and management.

Translating these specific aspirations for personality disorder services into action on the ground has become one of the major challenges for mental health and other services providers, trying to deliver the spirit and the targets set out in the NSFMH. However, the publication of the guidance, the promise of new money and the setting of specific delivery targets for the NHS has led to a focus on these services as areas where performance improvement is expected by the Department of Health, NHS Trusts, Strategic Health Authorities and Primary Care Trusts. This in turn has stimulated a number of developments aimed at improving services, and appears to have introduced tentative discussions about 'recovery', aligning clinical and organisational responses to people with personality disorder to the mainstream of modern mental health policy and development.

Amongst the developments are 11 new, community based services funded by the Department of Health. These new services are very diverse. Some are to be provided within specialist mental health services, others will be run directly by service users and another group will be delivered through local voluntary organisations. The client groups being targeted through these new services are equally diverse. They include young people, adults and those who have severe substance misuse problems. It is hoped that with the establishment of these new services, and their subsequent independent evaluation, there will be a significant shift upwards in the evidence base about what works and what does not work in treating and supporting people with personality disorders. The evaluation of the bids to provide these new services has had close involvement from a national service user reference group. This group was instrumental in making the final choices and their opinions genuinely weighed as heavily as those of their colleagues from the statutory agencies. After such a positive experience, it is hoped that the pattern of closer involvement of service users in developing and evaluating services will become the norm for services to people with personality disorders, which in the past it certainly has not been.

THE TRAINING GAP

The key to delivering new services and transforming the response of existing mainstream mental health and social care services for people with personality disorder is the development of a workforce that is more aware of the issues that affect people with personality disorders and the way they react to them. This should be a *minimum* requirement affecting staff in many agencies, both statutory and voluntary, which provide a wide range of essential services including housing, emergency and primary care, employment and benefits advice. Developing personality disorder awareness is important if staff are to better understand the behaviours and attitudes with which they may be presented from time to time, and be able to respond more effectively. It is also a vital ingredient in challenging the stigma that is associated with the diagnosis of personality disorder. To date, that label has more often than not resulted in the exclusion of people from help and support, and has restricted their ability to participate properly as full members of society. The weight of stigma is still a major obstacle for individuals attempting to seek help with their problems. It is fuelled to a large extent by the absence of personality disorder perspectives in mainstream professional training. This difficult and perverse position is summed up well by the following observation: 'In Britain we have the remarkable phenomenon that large numbers of quite severely disordered people who require considerable therapeutic effort are deemed untreatable' (Gunn, 2000).

Although a vital component of service reform, personality disorder awareness is not of itself sufficient. There is also a need for some staff groups to develop new ways of working with people with personality disorder, drawing on the currently small but expanding evidence base, to find ever more effective interventions and support mechanisms. These staff groups are in a wide range of agencies and often in roles not traditionally associated with delivering services to people with personality disorders. In the background survey work carried out prior to the development of *Personality Disorder: No Longer a Diagnosis of Exclusion*, groups other than those traditionally associated with delivering services to people with a personality disorder emerged as high priorities for new training initiatives. These groups included health visitors, district nurses, junior doctors in Accident and Emergency departments and local authority housing officers. New ways of delivering training to these groups need to emerge and existing training technologies need to be adapted to meet what is a growing need, which will translate into a growing demand for relevant, accessible and high quality training programmes.

TRAINING INITIATIVES: THE NATIONAL CONTEXT

The new service developments for people with personality disorders are taking place in a rapidly evolving mental health training and educational context. This evolving context includes new structures and partnerships, as well as the arrival of new players. Key to these new programmes and partnerships are the Regional Development Centres of NIMHE. Each of the regional offices has the responsibility to work with a broad range of local agencies delivering services to people with personality disorders, and has been given funding to help move the training and development agenda forward.

The regional initiatives already underway comprise a wide range of approaches and objectives. For example:

- pilot 'personality disorder awareness cascade' courses
- mapping of existing training programmes
- development of multi-stakeholder training specifications

- development of CD-ROM and internet-accessed training packages
- tailored training for primary care staff.

In addition to developing tailored training packages that reflect local need, there is much still to be done to embed awareness of personality disorders into the pre- and post-registration education. Key targets are clearly professionals working directly in therapeutic relationships, but also other professionals who come into contact with people with a diagnosis of personality disorder, including GPs and other primary care staff. This breadth of approach is vital if effective and co-ordinated support networks for individuals are to be established.

There is evidence of an encouraging recognition of the need to change both pre- and post-registration training to incorporate the dimension of personality disorder, by several of the key national registration bodies. These include the Royal College of Psychiatrists (RCoP), the British Psychological Society (BPS) and the Nursing and Midwifery Council (NMC). There is also growing enthusiasm from organisations such as the Prison Service, which at any one time has custody of large numbers of people with personality disorders and whose staff are often ill equipped to develop or deliver a productive set of interventions.

It is also important to acknowledge that whilst good quality, multi-disciplinary training is in short supply it does exist. There are some examples of existing good practice, including well established training programmes, manuals and other training materials. These at least represent a foundation for future national, regional and more local developments and consideration needs to be given to how best to apply these tools to new and wider audiences. One possibility which has been discussed is the development of a 'capability benchmark' process for these products and programmes, which would act in the same way as the quality kite mark in ensuring consistent standards. The benchmark process would be led through NIMHE and its education partners. Assessing the quality of existing training programmes and media will be an important first step.

When there so obviously remains a great deal to be done, with new programmes and media to develop, it is easy to start re-inventing the wheel and fragmenting the development programme. Whilst needing to avoid such fragmentation, one area that requires immediate attention is the involvement of service users in the development and operation of training programmes. A key characteristic of the national development programme running through the NIMHE regional offices has been the close involvement of service users. It is important that this pattern is reflected as other agencies and initiatives move into this area of work. The involvement of service users must go far beyond the traditional representational and consultative roles and engage with the training needs of service users themselves and their involvement in the delivery of professional and awareness training.

A NATIONAL TRAINING FRAMEWORK

There is a need for exponential improvements and increases in training availability to secure improved services and learn from new developments and evidence. If this is to be delivered consistently around the country, it requires a framework to which people can refer and through which people can make sense of the various other training initiatives, related to current general mental health service developments. In order to provide such a framework, NIMHE carried out a detailed piece of development work involving a wide range of experts, including service users. The result was the publication of *Breaking the Cycle of Rejection: the Personality Disorder Capabilities Framework* (NIMHE, 2003b). The framework highlights some of the critical capabilities that are appropriate to interactions with people with personality disorders and that are required by staff at all levels and in a variety of agencies. The framework was not designed to be a definitive work. Rather, it describes a process which will be enhanced and changed over time as knowledge expands and services develop. The framework builds on a number of basic principles that are designed to break the 'cycle of rejection', which is the experience of many people with personality disorders. It starts from the premise that developing responsive and sensitive services for people with personality disorder is possible and will promote social inclusion and deliver better outcomes.

The underlying principles of the framework are that training:

- should be based on respect for the human rights of service users and their carers
- programmes should consider how best to reflect the views and experiences of service users and carers
- should be aimed at breaking the cycle of rejection at all levels, including self-rejection, the social support system, practitioners and the wider health and social care systems
- should encourage service user autonomy and the development of individual responsibility
- should be multi-agency and multi-sectoral
- should support team and organisational capacity as well as that of individual practitioners

- should be connected to meaningful life-long learning and skill escalator programmes
- should be based on promoting learning in approaches to treatment and care that are supported by research evidence, where it exists.

These principles were derived from *Personality Disorder: No Longer a Diagnosis of Exclusion* and from the work of an expert advisory group and a service user focus group. The aim of the framework is to identify the specific capabilities required of staff working with people with personality disorders in a range of agencies and delivery settings, and to relate these to the various stages of an individual's career development. The framework is built around identified points of a user pathway. These key points include:

- access and referral routes
- interventions and treatment episodes
- recovery and stepping down from treatment.

The framework looks to staff being able to access training through innovative, multi-disciplinary training courses linked to their career progress. This approach will help to create a workforce with a much better understanding of personality disorders and who are more aware of the impact of these disorders on families, individuals, agencies and the wider society. In turn, the aspiration is that such a workforce will act more appropriately, compassionately and be less judgemental to behaviours that are often hard to understand and difficult to tolerate. This trained workforce should be able to work more confidently with people with a personality disorder in multi-disciplinary teams, delivering increasingly better evidenced interventions and supports. This better trained and more aware workforce will also be able to support and empower those who use services. They will help individuals to achieve their full potential and in so doing break the cycle of rejection which characterises so much of the negative and rejecting attitudes and practices of so many agencies.

The *Personality Disorder Capabilities Framework* describes the qualities and skills required by individuals working in primary, secondary and specialist services and also in the wide range of other community agencies that people may contact. The framework encompasses:

- 'performance'—skills that practitioners need to have and how they need to use them in their work
- 'ethics'—integrating values and social awareness into professional practice

- 'reflective practice'—effectively implementing evidence-based practice and review, and learning from outcomes
- 'commitment to life-long learning'.

The framework is built on the assumption that different staff in different organisations may well need different 'levels' of the same capability, linked to their roles and functions in a given service. To do this, the framework introduces the idea of the 'skills escalator'. This enables the development of valued career pathways in working with people with a personality disorder. It recognises that in common with many other areas of health and social care some of the interaction most valued by service users is undertaken by people with no formal professional qualifications, and indeed by service users themselves. The wide range and complexity of concerns and needs presented by people with personality disorders requires a well co-ordinated multi-disciplinary and multi-skilled approach. Inevitably, some of these staff will work outside the specialist mental health sector, or indeed local authorities and the NHS more generally. These individuals also need an appropriate level of understanding and skills in engaging, communicating with and delivering the services and support of their agencies to people with personality disorders.

The framework also proposes that *managing* teams, and the leadership of organisations providing services to people with personality disorders, is a critical area of capability. In the absence of this leadership capability, there is likely to be a high level of burn-out, absenteeism, sickness and dis-illusionment in teams working with people with personality disorders. The framework outlines the sort of management capabilities required to support staff and sustain services. The framework identifies the capable *organisation* as being key to staff becoming and remaining effective. It defines the capable organisation as being one that requires:

- operational models that can respond to the complexity of the needs presented by service users
- ease of access to appropriate levels of treatment and support
- the development of standards for multi-disciplinary service delivery
- cross-boundary and cross-agency agreements to support the movement of service users away from dependency on services and towards proper social inclusion
- consistent support for staff teams
- access to supervision, education and training.

The framework emphasises that all the above must be underpinned by a culture aimed at sustaining learning. The capable organisational model has implications for the way learning opportunities are delivered and sustained. The boundary between training, practice development and supervision is not a clear one, and each of these dimensions has a role to play in growing and sustaining the professional development of staff.

Probably the most critical aspect of the framework, which, though harrowing, gives cause for optimism, is the fact that it leans heavily on the experiences of people with personality disorder who are contemporary users of the very variable services currently available. It is designed around the user pathway into, through and out of service. It highlights the staff capabilities needed at identified points on the user pathway and it relates the type and level of training required by different staff if they are to develop those capabilities. The framework emphasises that in order to work positively with people with personality disorders, it is essential to have an understanding of the causes and the consequences of these complex conditions. The debate has been clouded over recent years by the close connection made by many politicians and sections of the media between personality disorder and dangerousness. Whilst there clearly are dangerous people who have personality disorders, the numbers are small. It is much more common for people with personality disorder to be highly vulnerable to abuse and the experience of violence, and to self-harm and suicide. 'We have been damaged, often early in life and we have grown up with mistaken beliefs about ourselves. For these reasons we have difficulties with relationships because we often believe that we are unlovable and we are very sensitive to rejection. For that reason we need easier and known access to services' (quote from a service user in *Personality Disorder*; North Essex News, 2003).

The framework starts from this user viewpoint and identifies four domains of capabilities:

- promoting social functioning and obtaining social support
- improving psychological well-being
- assessing and managing risk to self and others
- management and leadership.

Each of these domains is related to four career stages:

- pre-employment
- vocational education
- professional training
- continuing professional development.

The framework details what expectations there should be of the training and skills required to operate as a capable practitioner at each of the career stages and for each of the domains of capability.

THE SKILLS ESCALATOR

The *Capabilities Framework* builds on the concept of the 'Skills Escalator'. Modern NHS human resource practice is predicated on organisations committing to give people without professional qualifications, or who work at relatively low skill levels in the NHS and other heath and social care settings, the opportunity to progress to roles requiring professional levels of training and qualification. The model of the skills escalator puts in place what are termed 'stepping-on points', cadet schemes, role conversion, back-to-work schemes and 'stepping-off points', to enable existing staff to move progressively on to more demanding and complex roles. The escalator approach opens up opportunities for groups of staff whose developmental needs have been overlooked. It acknowledges that life and experiences from other work settings can be just as valuable as more formal pre-professional training and experience. It enables organisations to draw in people with the right personal attitudes and attributes needed for work within new services, rather than focussing exclusively on their professional or academic achievements. It also offers a way out of career ruts for existing staff. The development of a career escalator for work in personality disorder services opens up the opportunity for a more strategic and integrated approach to workforce recruitment, retention and development. It also encourages innovative approaches to recruitment that are more likely to draw in people with the personal attributes required for work within new services for personality disorder rather than the current focus on professional qualifications.

COMMUNITY MENTAL HEALTH TEAMS AND THE CAPABILITIES FRAMEWORK

What relevance do the new initiatives in services for people with personality disorders have for community mental health teams (CMHTs) and their individual staff members? Is there any relevance to CMHTs of the *Capabilities Framework* and the skills escalator? The answer to both questions is, unequivocally, yes. The reason why, and some of the practical applications, are explored in the remainder of this chapter.

CMHTs are at a crossroads in their development and their role in the delivery of modern mental health services. Since the post-NSFMH investments and developments in mental health services, there has been a sharp increase in specialist teams delivering services to some service users and in some of the service areas previously covered by CMHTs and indeed in-patient services. These include:

- assertive outreach
- early intervention in psychosis
- crisis resolution and home treatment
- primary care outreach.

These and other initiatives have expanded the capacity of the mental health services but have also forced a re-appraisal of the role of the CMHTs. The NSFMH and subsequent implementation guidance strongly support the CMHT as the gateway into services. However, despite this assertion there is not even today universal coverage by CMHTs in England. There are clearly defined models and structures for the teams, but there is little consistency in their actual make-up and role on the ground.

Added to the demands on CMHTs is certainly going to be a greater involvement in delivering and co-ordinating services for people with personality disorders. CMHTs should and frequently do operate at the interface with other agencies, delivering services to people experiencing mental distress. No group of people consistently stands at these complex interfaces more than people with personality disorders. In addition, even without the passage of a new Mental Health Act, there is a growing recognition that it is wholly unacceptable that a large group of individuals who have clear, complex and unmet needs for treatment and support can be ignored because of institutional prejudice and the stigmatisation of personality disorder. Given that many if not most of these individuals require support and treatment in the community, the CMHT will inevitably become a key player in delivering expanded services and new approaches to treatment.

How can the *Capabilities Framework* help? There are a number of ways the framework can be used at a team and individual level, both as a capabilities assessment and a training tool and as a staff and career planning methodology. There are also other approaches in the framework, such as reflective practice, which will help improve the functioning of the team and its individual members. These are examined in more detail below.

The framework is initially best used by the CMHT as an assessment tool to:

- Initiate whole team workforce planning for their involvement with their patients with personality disorder.

- Develop targeted training for specific individuals or groups within the team who may take the lead in co-ordinating or delivering the team's work in respect of personality disorder services.
- Align career and training pathways for individuals who wish to become more specialist in this area of work.
- Align the continuing professional development of individuals and the team as a whole.
- Examine and strengthen the team's management capacity.
- Engage service users in a dialogue about service needs and, where possible, find ways of involving them in the training and development of the team.

Application of the framework in this way will stimulate the team to look more closely at its functioning across the board, since much of the analysis of the team's and individual's functioning in respect of services to people with personality disorder will be reflected in attitudes and ways of working with other groups.

A further and equally challenging way of using the framework as an assessment tool is to examine the work and capacity of the team under each of the capability domains, for example the following.

PROMOTING SOCIAL FUNCTIONING AND OBTAINING SOCIAL SUPPORT

- Does the team have a clear understanding of diversity, differences and rights and apply them to people with personality disorders, and support other staff in maintaining positive and respectful attitudes?
- Is the team capable of contributing to the development of positive strategies for challenging stigma and for promoting social inclusion in partnership with service users?
- Is the team geared up to support the personal and social networks of service users and their carers?
- Is the team able to advocate on behalf of service users and their networks in the wider organisation and with other agencies?
- Is the team and its members capable of boundary maintenance and able to support each other in this often challenging area?
- Is the team robust enough to support the challenge of reflective practice?

IMPROVING PSYCHOLOGICAL WELL BEING

- Is the team capable of applying a critical understanding of theories of personality disorder?

- Is the team or at least some of its members capable of the clinical assessment of personality disorders and other mental health needs, using standardised measures and contributing to the formulation of treatment and support plans?
- Is the team capable of applying case formulation techniques?
- Is the team capable of establishing and maintaining productive long term therapeutic relationships with service users with a personality disorder and supporting staff in maintaining demanding therapeutic relationships?
- Is the team and its members capable of tolerating frustration and anxiety?
- Is the team capable of working accountably within its organisation and aware of the impact on the team of working with people with a personality disorder?

ASSESSING AND MANAGING RISK TO SELF AND OTHERS

- Is the team capable of undertaking actuarial risk assessments, particularly understanding the risk of offending behaviour, or harm to self or others?
- Can the team undertake dynamic risk assessments focused on cognitive and inter-personal factors, substance misuse and lifestyle indicators?
- Could the team undertake a family and community risk assessment?
- Is the team capable of collaborating with multi-disciplinary and multi-agency risk management plans?
- Is the team capable of planning and delivering interventions based on case formulation addressing specific risk factors, providing proposals for risk management and for motivating individuals?

MANAGEMENT AND LEADERSHIP

- Is the team capable of bearing hostility and aggression without retaliation?
- Can the team reflect on its own and others' reactions to clients and offer considered responses?
- Can the team maintain personal and professional boundaries?
- Is the management of the team capable of providing professional support and supervision to individuals?
- Can the team provide support and advice to other agencies who are trying to cope with clients with personality disorder?
- Is the team capable of working across agency boundaries to ensure seamless services?
- Is the team capable and willing to embrace service change, develop positive partnerships with service users and promote social inclusion and challenge rather than contribute to stigma?

(taken from *Breaking the Cycle of Rejection: the Personality Disorder Capabilities Framework*, NIMHE, 2003b).

Another way that the framework can be used is to develop reflective practice. People with a personality disorder can behave in ways that seem to invite reaction. They may, for example, appear to think that no help is ever any use, they can be hostile, they may be demanding. At times they will sabotage all attempts at constructive help. These behaviours can be frustrating, particularly for the hard-pressed CMHT member. Particular skills and knowledge are needed to help practitioners understand the reasons for these behaviours and to rise above the frustration and understand the reasons behind the presentation. This means that judgemental and impulsive responses cannot be indulged in, however pressured or testing the situation. The key to moving forward is to reflect calmly and with the support of other team members about what may be happening and what triggers may have been activated. Practitioners who have this capability and level of professional maturity can maintain the critical focus on the underlying needs of the service user. They will also be able to sustain the effort required to assist the individual in developing less destructive ways of managing their difficulties. These skills can be learned and are useful for all staff working in CMHTs, but they are essential for anyone working with people with personality disorders. Without them, staff will be unable to support service users in coming to terms with and managing the range of social and personal resources that are fundamental to good mental health.

CONCLUSION

No mental disorder carries a greater stigma than that of personality disorder. Those diagnosed with a personality disorder feel labelled by professionals, the media and by society at large. Personality disorder is equated in the minds of many professionals with untreatability. Recently, the media and some politicians have almost made the terms 'dangerous' and 'personality disordered' synonymous. Those with personality disorders are often characterised as time-wasters, manipulative and attention-seeking. Their feeling is often that they are blamed for their condition. In this climate, there is a pressing need to drive through the reform and modernisation of society's and service agencies' perceptions of and relationship with individuals with personality disorders.

It was clear from the work underpinning *Personality Disorder: No Longer a Diagnosis of Exclusion* (NIMHE, 2003a) that there are not enough services available for people with personality disorders, nor is there sufficient awareness of their needs and how best to ensure equity of access to other health and social care services. Staff in most health and social care agencies have little or no awareness, experience or training in work with these individuals.

The government, as part of its attempts to modernise mental health services, has published through NIMHE two guidance papers, aimed at kick-starting the process of reform. There has also been new investment in pilot services in community and forensic services and in the acceleration of training initiatives. There is evidence that these investments are beginning to bear fruit, shown by a revived interest from strategic health authorities, NHS trusts and primary care trusts in the enhancement of services targeting people with personality disorders. These developments are of course welcome, but form only the embryos of what will need to be a major programme of training and investment if we are to develop humane, 21st century services.

CMHTs are at the interface of a wide range of services that people with a personality disorder seek to access. To date, the response of many CMHTs has been as described. The advent of new investment in additional specialist community teams has meant that CMHTs need to re-evaluate their role. In doing this, they should acknowledge the pressing case of people with personality disorders. It is inevitable that as the pressing case to improve services to people with personality disorder grows in strength CMHTs will be drawn inexorably into intervening and providing treatment and support for people with personality disorders. Few teams will currently be equipped either from a skills or a team management point of view. The new *Capabilities Framework* gives an excellent starting point for teams to review their current performance and to formulate plans to develop their responses. In addressing the issues that would enhance performance, capacity and skills in respect of personality disorders, CMHTs will find that they are laying the ground for a clearer identity as deliverers of mental health services and as advocates and intermediaries for all their clients. This re-evaluation of each team and individual's role within the overall constellation of health and social care can only lead to improved performance. It is hoped this will lead to a vastly improved experience and outcome for all service users. This is something that is surely the goal of every practitioner and agency delivering health and social care services.

REFERENCES

Department of Health. (1999). *National service framework for mental health: Modern standards and service models.* London: Author.

Gunn, J. (2000). Future directions for treatment in forensic psychiatry. *British Journal of Psychiatry, 176*, 332–338.

National Institute for Mental Health England (NIMHE). (2003a). *Personality disorder: No longer a diagnosis of exclusion.* London: Author.

National Institute for Mental Health England (NIMHE). (2003b). *Breaking the cycle of rejection: The Personality Disorder Capabilities Framework.* London: Author.

North Essex News. (2003). *Personality Disorder.* Issue 24.

2

What is Personality Disorder?

RONALD BLACKBURN

INTRODUCTION

Habitual personal characteristics that produce marked social disability or
dysfunction are currently described as 'personality disorders' in the fourth
edition of the *Diagnostic and Statistical Manual* (DSM-IV: American
Psychiatric Association, 1994) and the International Classification of Diseases (ICD-10: World Health Organisation, 1992). Until recently, 'personality disorder' was frequently a pejorative term. In Britain, it was associated
with Psychopathic Disorder in the 1959 and 1983 Mental Health Acts for
England and Wales, which permits detention of aggressive offenders in
secure psychiatric hospitals. Although this legal category refers to 'a
persistent disorder or disability of mind', clinicians interpreted this as a
disorder of personality, and linked personality disorder to antisocial behaviour.

   Perspectives have since changed significantly. The third edition of the
DSM (DSM-III: American Psychiatric Association, 1980) classified personality disorders on Axis II to distinguish them from the traditional mental
disorders or clinical syndromes of Axis I. Abnormalities of personality are
now recognised to be frequent accompaniments of common problems met in
clinical practice. Associations with antisocial behaviour were emphasised in
the recent administrative category of 'dangerous as a result of severe
personality disorder' (DSPD: Home Office/Department of Health, 1999),
but government policy now also acknowledges the need for services
for personality disorders throughout the mental health system (National
Institute for Mental Health in England, 2003).

Personality Disorder and Community Mental Health Teams: A Practitioner's Guide.   Edited by
M. J. Sampson, R. A. McCubbin and P. Tyrer. © 2006 John Wiley & Sons, Ltd.

It has also been increasingly accepted that personality disorders are abnormal variations of normal personality. This chapter discusses personality disorder in this light. It examines basic concepts of normal and abnormal personality, the origins and utility of the current classification, and the varying ways in which dysfunctional aspects of personality can be construed. Because most attention has focused on the DSM personality disorders, the discussion refers primarily to this classification.

PERSONALITY AND PERSONALITY TRAITS

THE STUDY OF PERSONALITY

Attempts to group people according to their typical attributes go back to physicians in ancient Greece, but the idea of personality as a stable feature of individuals emerged only a century ago. Early concepts encompassed both normal and abnormal personality, guided by descriptive typologies and psychoanalytic theories, but psychiatric and psychological approaches diverged during the 1930s as psychologists began to study healthy individuals. Psychiatrists continued to prefer a clinical and intuitive approach (Tyrer, 2000), while within psychology the study of personality incorporated the quantitative methods of the natural sciences. Although some psychologists studied both normal and abnormal aspects of personality, systematic attempts to integrate these two traditions emerged only recently (Strack & Lorr, 1997).

There is no definition of personality in the DSM, but nor is there a universally agreed definition of personality in the psychology literature. Personality research, like everyday notions of personality, is concerned with individual distinctiveness, but because this can be conceptualised from different perspectives, theorists have offered a variety of definitions. However, definitions are dictated by theory, and an agreed definition is unlikely without an agreed theoretical framework. From a psychological perspective, personality is essentially an area of inquiry, the subject matter of the area being those social, emotional and cognitive consistencies that contribute to a person's distinctiveness, i.e. *traits* or dispositions, and the psychological structures and processes proposed by different theories to account for these consistencies (e.g. motives, defences, cognitive schemata). Different theories emphasise different processes, but the idea of traits as stable tendencies is central to concepts of personality and personality disorder.

Although early theories aspired to account for the uniqueness of the individual person, recent work focuses on differences between individuals.

This approach draws on research with large samples of the general population, derives assessment from psychological measurement (psychometric) theory, and seeks general principles for understanding variations between people. The clinical application of these principles recognises individual uniqueness, but emphasises aspects that individuals share in varying degrees with others.

PERSONALITY TRAITS

Personality traits describe regularities or consistencies of actions, thoughts or feelings, and are the basic unit in the study of personality and in the DSM classification of personality disorders. Traits are part of the common language (e.g. 'sociable', 'methodical', 'energetic'), although many trait terms used in research originate from particular theories (e.g. 'open to experience', 'overcontrolled'). Traits differ from specific acts or temporary mood states in denoting a *tendency* or disposition to behave in certain ways under relevant conditions, and are inferred from observed behaviour or self-descriptions.

Despite the widespread use of trait terms, their conceptual and empirical status have been debated. The 'person–situation' debate addresses the question of how far the behaviours from which traits are inferred are consistent or generalised across situations. Although we assume that the traits we ascribe to people are manifest in many situations, some psychologists have argued that the features we observe are more a product of the specific situation than of personal dispositions. During the 1970s, the utility of trait description came under attack following an influential review by Mischel (1968), who concluded that research findings on the consistency of behaviour across situations did not justify conceptualising personality in terms of 'broad response dispositions'. However, more recent evidence supports assumptions about the cross-situational and long-term stability of traits. For example, personality traits predict significant life outcomes in occupational functioning, health and academic achievement (Costa & McCrae, 1992).

Mischel subsequently revised his position, and this debate has now subsided with the acceptance of both consistency and situational variability in behaviour, but it served to highlight limitations in the use of traits (Johnson, 1997). For example, to describe someone as 'sociable' or 'aggressive' implies only a greater than average *probability* of sociable or aggressive behaviour, not that the person invariably behaves in that way. Traits therefore describe average behaviour over many settings and occasions. Conversely, we cannot justifiably infer a trait from a single act.

However, situations are not wholly independent of persons. Some settings, such as formal meetings, clearly control behaviour because of social roles and norms, but dispositional variation determines the situations people choose and create. Nevertheless, the consistency of behaviour across situations is merely relative. Personality disorders, which are conceptualised in the DSM as 'inflexible' traits, may, in fact, reflect extreme consistency as a result of failure to discriminate between situations and to adjust behaviour accordingly.

THE STRUCTURE OF PERSONALITY

In personality research, the relationship between behaviour, traits and types is traditionally represented by a hierarchical system in which traits are sets of relatively specific behavioural response dispositions and types are patterns or combinations of particular traits. The DSM categories of personality disorder are 'type' concepts of this kind. However, psychologists have been more concerned with how relationships between traits form *dimensions*, using statistical methods (factor analysis). Dimensions are quantitative continua that summarise the inter-relationships between traits lower in the hierarchy, and represent higher-order and more fundamental dispositions. Relationships between the vast number of normal-range traits denoting behavioural, emotional and cognitive dispositions have been found to reflect a few robust dimensions.

Dimensional analyses have followed several directions. The 'interpersonal circle' (Leary, 1957) identifies different interpersonal styles as combinations of two major dimensions of power or control (dominance versus submission) and affiliation (hostility versus friendliness). Another approach assumes that the most salient personality traits are encoded in natural language, and from a compilation of over 17 000 personality descriptors, statistical relationships between traits were shown to be attributable to a few higher-order dimensions. A related approach, represented by Eysenck, aimed to determine the dimensional structure of personality from questionnaires and ratings in normal and clinical samples, while others proposed more theoretical models (see Strack & Lorr, 1997; Eysenck, 1967).

For many years, there was disagreement on the optimal number of dimensions (Watson, Clark & Harkness, 1994). Some workers suggested that three dimensions are sufficient (e.g. Eysenck's Neuroticism, Extraversion and Psychoticism), while others argued for at least seven. However, convergent findings across methods, samples and cultures now indicate that most variation in personality is accounted for by the 'Big Five' factors of Neuroticism, Extraversion, Agreeableness, Conscientiousness, and

Table 2.1 Dimensions and traits of the five-factor model of personality

Dimension (domain)	Traits (facets)
N. Neuroticism versus stability	anxiety, anger, depression, self-consciousness, impulsiveness, vulnerability, versus calmness, equanimity, emotional stability, social ease, tolerance for frustration and stress
E. Extraversion versus introversion	warmth, gregariousness, assertiveness, activity, excitement-seeking, optimism, versus distance, social avoidance, reserve, leisureliness, excitement-avoidance, low exuberance
O. Openness to experience versus conventionality	active fantasy, aesthetic interests, openness to inner feelings, preference for novelty, intellectual curiosity, unconventionality, versus lack of imagination, low aesthetic appreciation, emotional constriction, preference for routine, conventionality, dogmatism
A. Agreeableness versus antagonism	trust, straightforwardness, altruism, compliance, modesty, tender-mindedness, versus cynicism, manipulativeness, lack of empathy, aggressiveness, arrogance, hard-headedness
C. Conscientiousness versus lack of self-discipline	competence, orderliness, scrupulousness, diligence, self-discipline, caution, versus incompetence, untidiness, unreliability, laziness, procrastination, hastiness

Adapted from Costa and McCrae (1992). *Revised NEO Personality Inventory and NEO Five Factor Inventory professional manual.* Odessa, FL: Psychological Assessment Resources.

Openness to Experience (Costa & McCrae, 1992). These dimensions (or domains) summarise the patterns and inter-relationships of traits (or facets) lower in the hierarchy (Table 2.1).

The five-factor model integrates the divergent dimensional models of different theorists. For example, Leary's dominance and friendliness dimensions are equivalent to Extraversion and Agreeableness. Similarly, Eysenck's Neuroticism and Extraversion dimensions coincide with their counterparts in the five-factor model, while Psychoticism combines low Agreeableness and low Conscientiousness (Watson et al., 1994). The five factors represent biologically derived *basic tendencies* influencing attitudes, relationships, self-concept and our interactions with the environment. Because all of us have a standing at some point on each of these dimensions, the more prominent differences we observe between people, for example in interactions with colleagues, leisure preferences or coping with crises, are likely to reflect the expression of one or more of these tendencies. However, as has been emphasised, personality traits are only one source of influence on our behaviour in a particular setting, which also depends on how we perceive the situation, our mood state and goals at the time and how others react to us. Dominant executives, for example, may sometimes be putty in the hands of their family.

THE CLASSIFICATION OF PERSONALITY DISORDERS

One purpose of distinguishing Axis I and Axis II in DSM-III was to recognise the possible effects of enduring personality characteristics on the treatment of more transient clinical states (Frances, 1980), but the basis for distinguishing Axis I and Axis II is not explicit. Foulds (1971) made a conceptual distinction, arguing that mental illness is defined by *symptoms* signalling a breakdown of function and a departure from a person's own psychological norms. Personality disorder is defined by personality *traits* reflecting continuity and a departure from societal norms of interpersonal functioning. This distinction, however, is not absolute because some clinical disorders take on enduring characteristics, and a clear rationale for distinguishing Axis I and Axis II remains elusive (Livesley, 2001).

The distinction between traits and symptoms is nonetheless useful, and generalised traits are the basic units of personality disorder. They are defined as 'enduring patterns of perceiving, relating to, and thinking about the environment and oneself' (American Psychiatric Association, 1994, p. 630). However, traits constitute personality disorder only when they are 'inflexible and maladaptive and cause significant functional impairment or subjective distress'. Personality disorders are defined generically as enduring patterns of cognition, affectivity, interpersonal behaviour and impulse control that are culturally deviant, pervasive and inflexible and lead to distress or social impairment.

Ten patterns or categories of disorder are identified and grouped into three clusters (Table 2.2). Each category is operationally defined by between seven and nine specific criteria, a set number being required to make the diagnosis of each disorder. These categories imply mutually exclusive types, but it is emphasised that they are categories of *disorder*, not types of *people*, and that individuals may meet criteria for more than one disorder. The clustering of disorders into Clusters A, B and C assumes that disorders within clusters are more likely to be found together than with disorders of other clusters.

This classification was the outcome of committee decisions and built on clinical tradition and intuition rather than research evidence that the criteria

Table 2.2 Clusters, categories and trait patterns of the DSM-IV personality disorders

Cluster	Category	Trait pattern
A: odd, eccentric	Paranoid	distrust, suspicion of others' motives
	Schizoid	social detachment, restricted emotional expression
	Schizotypal	social discomfort, cognitive distortions, behavioural eccentricities
B: dramatic, erratic	Antisocial	disregard for and violation of the rights of others
	Borderline	unstable relationships, self-image, and affects, and marked impulsivity
	Histrionic	excessive emotionality, attention-seeking
	Narcissistic	grandiosity, need for admiration, lack of empathy
C: anxious, fearful	Avoidant	social inhibition, feelings of inadequacy, hypersensitivity to negative evaluation
	Dependent	submissive, clinging behaviour, need to be taken care of
	Obsessive–compulsive	preoccupation with orderliness, perfectionism and control

of each disorder represent distinct groupings (Frances, 1980). Nevertheless, although the potential relevance of personality dimensions is only belatedly acknowledged in DSM-IV (American Psychiatric Association, 1994, pp. 633–634), the DSM classification implicitly recognises a hierarchical structure. The diagnostic criteria are the relatively specific response dispositions that define traits, while categories correspond to types defined by constellations of traits. In turn, the A, B and C clusters represent higher-order types. Some similarities will perhaps be noted between the deviant traits of personality disorder and the traits of the five-factor model, particularly those defining Neuroticism, Introversion and Antagonism.

The DSM adopts a categorical, present-or-absent, system of diagnosis. In psychological measurement terms, this represents a dichotomous (nominal) scale rather than a continuous (ordinal, interval) scale—a distinction reflected, for example, in representing people's height dichotomously in terms of 'tall' or 'short' as opposed to continuously in terms of feet and inches. The threshold number of criteria required for diagnosis was also determined by committee decision rather than empirical research, and limitations of the categorical approach are discussed further below. However, one immediate limitation for clinical practice is that there is no way of specifying the degree or severity of disorder. Although 'severe personality disorder' is now a widely used term, for example in the DSPD category (Home Office/Department of Health, 1999), it has at least six different meanings in the literature, and has no agreed definition (Blackburn, 2000). A diagnosis of personality disorder is itself intended to indicate severe impairment, and the need for a further criterion of severity reflects the limitations of an approach that determines simply presence or absence of disorder on the basis of an arbitrary threshold.

HISTORICAL BACKGROUND

Recognition of personality disorders as a generic class is tied up with the changing meaning of 'psychopathic personality' in Europe and the United States (Pichot, 1978). The origin of this term is often traced to the concept of moral insanity introduced in early 19th century British psychiatry. This was 'a morbid perversion of feelings, habits, and moral disposition', and claimed to be a disorder distinct from traditionally recognised mental disorders. Although highly controversial, the concept influenced the 1913 Mental Deficiency Act, which identified 'moral imbeciles' as 'persons displaying permanent moral defect with strong and vicious criminal propensities'. This was the precursor to the Psychopathic Disorder category of the current Mental Health Act. The defining feature of these categories was essentially undesirable and socially damaging conduct (Blackburn, 1988).

In German psychiatry, however, 'psychopathic' denoted biological rather than moral defect, and had the etymologically correct meaning of 'psycho-logically damaged' (as seen in 'psychopathology'), not 'socially damaging'. During the 1920s, Schneider described a generic class of 'psychopathic personalities' (Schneider, 1950), but he excluded antisocial behaviour as a defining characteristic. Anticipating quantitative conceptions of personality, Schneider construed abnormal personality statistically as deviation from average. Psychopathic personalities were those abnormal personalities whose abnormality caused 'suffering' to themselves or the community, and he proposed a typology of psychopathic personalities. While acknowled-ging that this was intuitive, his psychopathic personalities formed the basis for recent classifications of personality disorders. His criterion of causing suffering to self or others is essentially retained in the DSM criterion of causing 'significant functional impairment or subjective distress'.

American psychiatrists such as Cleckley (1941), however, rejected this typology, seeing most of Schneider's types as variants of neurosis or psychosis. Psychopathic personality was narrowed to mean a specific type of socially deviant individual, following the tradition beginning with moral insanity, and the current concept of *psychopathy* (Hare, 1991) is derived from Cleckley. The DSM antisocial category is considered equivalent to psychopathy in this sense, but it omits the traits central to Cleckley's concept, which are more apparent in narcissistic disorder (e.g. grandiosity, lacking empathy). It is therefore paradoxical that Schneider's psychopathic personalities became today's personality disorders, while 'psychopathic' in Britain and America has described a specific antisocial type.

Origins of the specific categories of the current classification are not explicit. DSM-III aimed to provide an atheoretical description of psychiatric disorders, but definitions of concepts always imply theoretical assumptions, and a mixture of clinical traditions can be discerned. Some categories superficially resemble Schneider's types, notably obsessive–compulsive (anankastic), avoidant (sensitive), histrionic (attention-seeking) and anti-social (affectionless). Schizoid and paranoid disorders owe more to a psychiatric tradition of linking abnormal personality to major mental disorders, although evidence for a link is weak. Schizotypal and borderline disorders, however, were introduced to distinguish 'borderline schizophrenia' from 'borderline personality'. Psychodynamic influences are also apparent. The obsessive–compulsive and dependent categories resemble the anal and oral character types of psychoanalytic theory, respectively, while the introduction of narcissistic and borderline categories in DSM-III reflects the influence of contemporary psychodynamic thinkers, notably Kernberg (1975).

The most immediate influence on the DSM-III selection of categories was the classification developed by Millon (1969) in his eclectic biosocial learning theory. This proposed eight basic coping styles and three more severe derivatives (schizotypal, cycloid/borderline, paranoid). Most of Millon's descriptive labels were imported from earlier concepts (e.g. schizoid, cycloid, histrionic), but his avoidant coping style became a new category in DSM-III. Millon's scheme was tabled as a basis for the DSM-III classification, but was eventually changed in several respects.

This mixture of influences, each with its own aetiological assumptions, imposes limitations on the usefulness of the classification. As Frances (1980) noted, the categories selected and the criteria for defining them 'are based only on clinical intuition and impression that has yet to be confirmed by factor analysis or other forms of validation' (p. 1052). They can therefore be regarded at best as *hypotheses* that particular patterns of traits occur together with sufficient frequency to identify a distinguishable type. Evidence that the specific diagnostic criteria are organised into the categories proposed remains limited (Livesley, 2001).

COMORBIDITY

Personality disorders are not uncommon in the community. Epidemiological surveys suggest that 10–15% of the general population meet critera for one or more personality disorders (Mattia & Zimmerman, 2001), and one study identified a quarter of GP surgery attenders as personality disordered (Moran, Jenkins, Tylee, Blizard & Mann, 2000). Surveys indicate a considerably higher prevalence in clinical populations (Dolan-Sewell, Krueger & Shea, 2001). For example, Alnaes and Torgerson (1988) found that 81 per cent of an outpatient sample met criteria for one or more DSM-III personality disorders, and DeJong, van den Brink, Harteveld, & van der Wielen (1993) identified 78 per cent of substance abusers as personality disordered. Many patients being treated for Axis I disorders therefore also have a co-occurring or comorbid Axis II disorder, and the converse also applies. Overall, nearly three-quarters of patients with a personality disorder are likely to have an Axis I disorder (Dolan-Sewell et al., 2001).

Comorbidity as used in general medicine describes the co-occurrence of diseases known to be independent, but in the context of psychopathology, where aetiology is generally unknown, the term denotes *diagnostic co-occurrence*. Extensive evidence indicates that comorbidity is the rule rather than the exception (Clark, Watson & Reynolds, 1995), and that patients with a single 'pure' disorder are rare. Common patterns of co-occurrence are of avoidant and dependent disorders with anxiety and mood disorders, antisocial disorder with substance abuse and borderline personality disorder with post-traumatic stress disorder.

It now seems unlikely that Axis I/Axis II comorbidity occurs randomly or by chance, but several possible models might account for the relationship (Dolan-Sewell et al., 2001). One is that the co-occurrence is an artefact of the diagnostic system and a reflection of similarities in diagnostic criteria, which may account for the frequent co-occurrence of avoidant disorder with social phobia. Another is that the co-occurring disorders share a common cause. For example, experience of abuse in childhood may lead both to the development of borderline personality traits and a propensity to post-traumatic stress disorder. Yet another model is that personality disorders precede, and increase the risk for, particular Axis I disorders. Evidence favouring one or other models is limited, but the view that personality is itself a risk factor for psychopathology is supported by a longitudinal study of a New Zealand community sample that assessed personality at age 18, and Axis I disorders at ages 15, 18 and 21 (Krueger, Caspi, Moffitt, Silva & McGee, 1996). Distinctive patterns of personality were related significantly to all disorders at all ages, and hence not only correlated with Axis I disorders, but also preceded them.

Comorbidity is also common *within* Axis II disorders, and research with a variety of clinical samples indicates that a half or more of patients meet the criteria for at least two, and not uncommonly four or more personality disorders. For example, Stuart et al. (1998) found that two-thirds of those meeting DSM-III-R criteria for one personality disorder also met criteria for other personality disorders. Borderline, passive–aggressive and paranoid disorders overlapped significantly with most disorders. Findings on comorbidity suggest that 'pure' personality disorders in isolation are rare. The significance of diagnostic overlap is discussed further below.

RELIABILITY AND VALIDITY OF THE CLASSIFICATION

The categories of personality disorder are speculative human inventions (constructs) whose usefulness has yet to be demonstrated empirically. Psychological measurement theory provides evaluative standards of reliability and validity, against which to judge the utility of any assessment procedure. The DSM classification needs to meet these standards to be clinically useful.

RELIABILITY

Inter-rater reliability of a diagnostic assessment refers to agreement or consistency between clinicians, and the provision of explicit operational criteria for each category of disorder in the DSM-III aimed to meet the criticism that psychiatric diagnosis was unreliable. Reliability is commonly measured by kappa, a statistic that corrects for chance agreement. Kappa can range from 1.0 (total agreement) to -1.0 (total disagreement), a kappa of at least 0.60 being considered necessary for acceptable reliability.

Findings in the DSM-III field trials suggested that few categories of personality disorder met acceptable criteria of reliability. This was confirmed by Mellsop, Varghese, Joshua and Hicks (1982), who had three psychiatrists allocate 74 patients to the DSM-III categories. The average kappa was 0.41, the highest being 0.49 for antisocial personality disorder, clearly indicating low agreement between clinicians. Diagnoses of personality disorder made by individual clinicians using unstructured judgement are therefore likely to differ from those of other clinicians. Possible reasons for poor clinical reliability include vague terminology in many criteria, and the mixing of the readily observable (e.g. lacks close friends) with the highly inferential (e.g. chronic feelings of emptiness). Whether or not a trait is 'inflexible' also depends on intuitive clinical judgement.

To ensure diagnostic reliability, structured measures involving standardised presentation and scoring are needed, and several semistructured interviews and self-report questionnaires are now available (Zimmerman, 1994; Clark & Harrison, 2001). Zimmerman (1994) reviewed 15 studies on inter-rater reliability using different interviews and found a mean kappa for each disorder of between 0.62 and 0.77, indicating the achievement of an acceptable level of agreement.

VALIDITY

Reliable assessment, however, does not guarantee validity, i.e. that a measure correctly represents the concept of interest. The appropriate psychometric approach to validation of personality measures is *construct validity* (Clark, Livesley & Morey, 1997). This requires demonstrations that a measure of a construct relates to other variables in theoretically meaningful ways. Two aspects of construct validity are *convergent validity* (different measures of the same construct agree with each other) and *discriminant validity* (measures of different constructs are distinguishable from each other).

Studies of convergent validity find that questionnaire measures agree reasonably well with other questionnaires, but less clearly with interviews, while interview measures agree only moderately with other interviews. Convergent validity across methods is strongest for avoidant personality disorder, weakest for obsessive–compulsive personality disorder, and variable for histrionic and narcissistic disorders (Clark & Harrison, 2001). However, overall, agreement on the diagnosis of specific categories is poor, suggesting that different instruments often define the same category in different ways. Reviewing studies comparing two or more assessment procedures, Perry (1992) noted a median kappa across categories of 0.25. This means that 75 per cent of the variation in assessment is due to factors other than patients' personality dysfunction, and as Perry observed 'this is not a scientifically acceptable state of affairs'.

Poor discriminant validity is demonstrated by high levels of overlapping or comorbid diagnoses, suggesting that categories are not independent of each other. Overlap is greater than that to be expected from the A, B and C clustering suggested in the DSM. While it may reflect overlapping criteria, a more likely explanation is that overlapping diagnoses reflect common underlying dimensions. Factor analyses suggest that four higher-order dimensions underlie the DSM-III and DSM-III-R categories. Mulder and Joyce (1997) described these as 'the four As', i.e. *antisocial* (paranoid, antisocial, borderline, histrionic, narcissistic, passive–aggressive), *asocial* (schizoid, schizotypal), *asthenic* (dependent, avoidant) and *anankastic* (obsessive–compulsive). The inadequate validity of the current categories as a representation of personality disorders clearly limits the clinical usefulness of the system.

CATEGORIES AND DIMENSIONS OF PERSONALITY DISORDER

There is a longstanding debate about whether disorders of personality are appropriately represented as categories or discrete types or by dimensions (Clark et al., 1997; Frances, 1980). The diagnostic approach used in DSM-IV 'represents the categorical perspective that Personality Disorders represent qualitatively distinct clinical syndromes' (American Psychiatric Association, 1994, p. 633). This follows a medical model that implies qualitative distinctions between normality and abnormality and clear boundaries between categories. The alternative is a dimensional approach that assumes only quantitative distinctions. A 'dimensional approach', however, has two possible meanings. First, continua or dimensions may be derived simply by summing up the criteria met within each category, an increasing number of criteria implying a greater degree of disorder. This is a measurement issue. A second more specific meaning is to construe personality disorders in terms of the dimensions identified in personality theories and research.

CATEGORICAL VERSUS DIMENSIONAL MEASUREMENT

Most structured instruments provide both categorical and dimensional measures for each personality disorder. Dimensional measurement essentially represents disorders by means of continuous scales rather than by simple dichotomous categories. Categorical description facilitates communication by using familiar labels, and assigning people to categories can be useful for administrative and research purposes. The advantages of dimensional description lie in the retention of more information, recognition of degrees of severity and greater statistical power in research.

Psychiatrists prefer categorical classification, but dimensions can be readily converted into categories by specifying cut-off points. This is implicit in categorical diagnosis, where the cut-off is simply present or absent. Dimensional and categorical descriptions are not in this respect incompatible. However, Widiger and Costa (1994) found that in 13 of 14 studies in which personality disorder criteria had been analysed both categorically and dimensionally dimensional analysis yielded superior reliability and validity data. There are, then, clear advantages to the routine use of dimensional measures, whether or not personality disorders are discrete entities, and dimensional measurement could provide a firmer foundation for establishing appropriate cut-off points for identifying categories (Clark et al., 1997).

The fundamental issue is whether the organisation or structure of personality dysfunctions is best represented by qualitatively distinct categories or quantitatively varying dimensions. The evidence for frequent comorbid diagnoses clearly contradicts the assumption that the DSM-IV personality disorders represent 'discrete clinical syndromes'. The statistical distribution of personality disorder traits has also been found to be continuous rather than bimodal in patient and nonpatient samples (Livesley, 2001). Similarly, statistical analyses fail to support discrete classes except in the case of schizotypal disorder (Widiger & Frances, 2002). Further, the same factors underlying traits of personality disorder in clinical samples are also found in general population samples (see, e.g., Austin & Deary, 2000), suggesting that differences are quantitative rather than qualitative. Moreover, genetic contributions to personality disorders are comparable to those of normal personality dimensions (Livesley, 2001). The evidence therefore overwhelmingly supports a dimensional representation.

PERSONALITY DISORDERS AND THE DIMENSIONS OF PERSONALITY

Given that personality disorders represent quantitatively varying dimensions, there are good grounds for construing the dysfunctional traits of personality disorder as extreme variants of normal traits, and for relating these disorders to dimensions identified through research on the structure of personality. Several theoretical models have linked abnormal personality to 'normal' personality dimensions (Strack & Lorr, 1997). Leary (1957), for example, proposed that personality disorders were extreme and maladaptive expressions of normal interpersonal styles, representing varying combinations of the dimensions of dominance–submission and hostility–friendliness. However, the five-factor model is widely regarded as the dimensional system most relevant to personality disorders.

Although dimensions do not provide a traditional classification, the current classes of disorder can be translated into a dimensional system.

For example, avoidant personality disorder appears to be primarily a combination of extreme Neuroticism and extreme Introversion, while borderline personality disorder represents extreme Neuroticism and low Agreeableness (Widiger & Costa, 1994). The common element of Neuroticism accounts for the finding that many patients meet criteria for both borderline and avoidant disorders. The five-factor model now has good support for describing personality disorders in this way (Clark & Harrison, 2001; Saulsman & Page, 2004).

There is also evidence that the dimensions underlying the DSM personality disorders are related to those underlying normal personality. Mulder and Joyce (1997) found a relatively strong association of the 'antisocial' dimension identified in the DSM-III-R disorders with the Psychoticism dimension of Eysenck's three-dimensional system. Their 'asthenic' dimension was related to both Neuroticism and Introversion. Austin and Deary (2000) also found strong associations of the personality disorder dimensions with Eysenck's dimensions.

Recognition that the same dimensions underlie normal and abnormal personality raises the possibility of using trait-based dimensional measures instead of the current categories. However, normal range inventories may not provide sufficient coverage of extreme personality variation. For example, Widiger and Costa (1994) point to a difference between the extreme of the normal Conscientiousness dimension (striving for excellence in everything) and the maladaptive conscientiousness of obsessive–compulsive personality disorder (perfectionism that interferes with task completion). Measures targeting pathological traits may therefore be more appropriate.

However, the current diagnostic systems provide an international nomenclature and a basis for communication in research and clinical practice. Reference to the current categories therefore seems unavoidable for the time being. Nevertheless, whatever their administrative uses, categorical diagnoses are a limited basis for treatment planning or monitoring because treatment is more concerned with ameliorating dysfunctional traits than with changing abstract categories.

CONCEPTUALISING DISORDER

The identification of personality disorders in terms of dysfunctional traits implies that ameliorating these disorders requires changing these traits. However, neither the DSM classification nor the dimensional alternatives indicate clearly what needs to be changed. How we think about the nature of 'disorder' or 'dysfunction' is critical in helping people to change or modify their problematic personality characteristics.

The term 'disorder' in medicine commonly denotes abnormal or pathological conditions of unknown aetiology (Taylor, 1976), but with regard to behaviour or mental illness there are no absolute or culture-free criteria of abnormality. Behaviour may be considered abnormal if it is statistically unusual or rare, socially inappropriate or undesirable, subjectively distressing, deviates from optimal social or psychological functioning or fails to meet some ideal standard of health. Most of these enter conceptions of personality disorder, but the most common criteria are the statistical and the functional.

The DSM definition of personality disorders as inflexible and maladaptive traits that cause significant functional impairment or subjective distress is a functional definition of abnormality. However, the DSM-IV criteria are inconsistent in whether they indicate dysfunction or statistical abnormality. For example, 'shows arrogant or haughty behaviours or attitudes' (narcissistic disorder) and 'lacks close friends or confidants other than first degree relatives' (schizoid and schizotypal disorders) are behavioural indicators of traits that may be statistically unusual, but that do not preclude adequate functioning in some contexts. In contrast, 'shows perfectionism that interferes with task completion' (obsessive–compulsive disorder) refers to the conditions under which an extreme trait is dysfunctional.

Psychologists generally adopt a statistical approach, seeing normality and abnormality on a quantitative continuum. A trait is abnormal when its manifestation is extreme, relative to the population average. In these terms, disorders of personality are statistical extremes of normal personality, and can hence be described by reference to the dimensions of personality. This equates inflexibility and dysfunction with extremeness. For example, an extreme level of Introversion implies a limited repertoire of social skills and strategies that are reproduced rigidly across a variety of situations for which they may be inappropriate.

However, although extreme traits seem *necessary* to define abnormalities of personality, they may not be *sufficient* to identify disorder or dysfunction, as indicated by failures to perform social and occupational roles. Dysfunction is not necessarily expressed in extreme traits, because it depends on the context. Some people may have extreme traits but function adequately because their characteristics are not an impediment for a particular role or setting. This is recognised in the notions of *discordant personality* (Foulds, 1971) or *personality accentuation* (Tyrer, 2000), which fall short of disorder. Some writers therefore argue that the dysfunctional component of personality disorder may to some extent be independent of extremes of personality. There is a clear parallel with learning disability, which is not identified by low intelligence alone but by dysfunctional adaptation under conditions requiring intellectual ability.

Livesley (2001) notes that Schneider's distinction between 'abnormal personalities' and 'those that cause suffering to self or others' also implied that statistical abnormality is not sufficient to identify functional impairment. He argues that both the DSM and the five-factor model focus on what personality *is*, but that to understand the nature of dysfunction we also need to ask what personality is *for*. Adopting an evolutionary perspective, he proposes that the functions of personality are to attain the universal life tasks or projects of (a) developing a stable self-system (identity, representations of self and others), (b) interpersonal functioning (attachment, intimacy, affiliation) and (c) forming societal and group relations (prosocial, co-operative behaviour). Personality disorders can hence be understood as extreme variations of personality associated with failure to develop the psychological structures necessary to attain these goals. Livesley proposes that classification should dispense with the current categories, and that Axis II should comprise clinically relevant personality dimensions reflecting dysfunction.

Livesley's analysis seems consistent with the distinction made in personality research between surface and source traits (Johnson, 1997). Surface traits *describe* observable regularities in behaviour that permit prediction of likely future behaviour, but they do not *explain* behaviour. Source traits refer to 'deep' structures and processes posited by theorists that are not directly observable but provide more fundamental causal explanations. In these terms, describing abnormal traits is simply the first step in understanding personality disorder. We need to go beyond these surface manifestations to consider the motivational, cognitive and affective processes that may be responsible for dysfunction.

Most theoretical models developed to guide the treatment of personality disorders have so far been concerned more with these theoretical structures and processes than with the surface traits defining personality disorders. Attempts to improve the classification of personality disorders by reference to the dimensional structure of personality traits have therefore had only a limited impact on strategies for treating these disorders. An integration of trait description and theories of personality is crucial if the classification of personality disorders is to assist clinicians.

REFERENCES

Alnaes, R. & Torgerson, A. (1988). DSM-III symptom disorders (Axis I) and personality disorders (Axis II) in an outpatient population. *Acta Psychiatrica Scandinavica*, 78, 348–355.

American Psychiatric Association. (1980). *Diagnostic and statistical manual of mental disorders* (3rd ed.). Washington, DC: Author.

American Psychiatric Association. (1994). *Diagnostic and statistical manual of mental disorders* (4th ed.). Washington, DC: Author.

Austin, E. J. & Deary, I. J. (2000). The 'four As': A common framework for normal and abnormal personality? *Personality and Individual Differences, 28,* 977–995.

Blackburn, R. (1988). On moral judgements and personality disorders: The myth of the psychopathic personality revisited. *British Journal of Psychiatry, 153,* 505–512.

Blackburn, R. (2000). Treatment or incapacitation? Implications of research on personality disorders for the management of dangerous offenders. *Legal and Criminological Psychology, 5,* 1–21.

Clark, L. A. & Harrison, J. A. (2001). Assessment instruments. In W. J. Livesley (Ed.), *Handbook of personality disorders: Theory, research, and treatment* (pp. 277–306). New York: Guilford.

Clark, L. A., Livesley, W. J. & Morey, L. (1997). Personality disorder assessment: The challenge of construct validity. *Journal of Personality Disorders, 11,* 205–231.

Clark, L. A., Watson, D. & Reynolds, S. (1995). Diagnosis and classification of psychopathology: Challenges to the current system and future directions. *Annual Review of Psychology, 46,* 121–153.

Cleckley, H. (1941). *The mask of sanity.* St Louis: Mosby.

Costa, P. T. & McCrae, R. R. (1992). *Revised NEO personality inventory and NEO five factor inventory professional manual.* Odessa, FL: Psychological Assessment Resources.

DeJong, C. A. J., van den Brink, W., Harteveld, F. M. & van der Wielen, G. M. (1993). Personality disorders in alcoholics and drug addicts. *Comprehensive Psychiatry, 34,* 87–94.

Dolan-Sewell, R. T., Krueger, R. F. & Shea, M. T. (2001). Co-occurrence with syndrome disorders. In W. J. Livesley (Ed.), *Handbook of personality disorders: Theory, research, and treatment* (pp. 84–104). New York: Guilford.

Eysenck, H. J. (1967). *The biological basis of personality.* Springfield, IL: Thomas.

Foulds, G. A. (1971). Personality deviance and personal symptomatology. *Psychological Medicine, 1,* 222–233.

Frances, A. (1980). The DSM-III personality disorders section: A commentary. *American Journal of Psychiatry, 137,* 1050–1054.

Hare, R. D. (1991). *The Hare psychopathy checklist—revised.* Toronto: Multi-Health Systems.

Home Office/Department of Health. (1999). *Managing dangerous people with severe personality disorder: Proposals for policy development.* London: Department of Health.

Johnson, J. A. (1997). Units of analysis for the description and explanation of personality. In R. Hogan, J. Johnson & S. Briggs (Eds), *Handbook of personality psychology* (pp. 73–93). New York: Academic.

Kernberg, O. E. (1975). *Borderline conditions and pathological narcissism.* New York: Aronson.

Krueger, R. F., Caspi, A., Moffitt, T. E., Silva, P. A. & McGee, R. (1996). Personality traits are differentially linked to mental disorders: A multitrait–multi-diagnosis study of an adolescent birth cohort. *Journal of Abnormal Psychology, 105,* 299–312.

Leary, T. (1957). *Interpersonal diagnosis of personality: A functional theory and methodology for personality evaluation.* New York: Ronald.

Livesley, W. J. (2001). Conceptual and taxonomic issues. In W. J. Livesley (Ed.), *Handbook of personality disorders: Theory, research, and treatment* (pp. 3–38). New York: Guilford.

Mattia, J. I. & Zimmerman, M. (2001). Epidemiology. In W. J. Livesley (Ed.), *Handbook of personality disorders: Theory, research, and treatment* (pp. 107–123). New York: Guilford.

Mellsop, G., Varghese, F., Joshua, S. & Hicks, A. (1982). The reliability of Axis II of DSM-III. *American Journal of Psychiatry, 139*, 1360–1361.

Millon, T. (1969). *Modern psychopathology.* Philadelphia, PA: Saunders.

Mischel, W. (1968). *Personality and assessment.* New York: Wiley.

Moran, P., Jenkins, R., Tylee, A., Blizard, R. & Mann, A. (2000). The prevalence of personality disorder among UK primary care attenders. *Acta Psychiatrica Scandinavica, 102*, 52–57.

Mulder, R. T. & Joyce, P. R. (1997). Temperament and the structure of personality disorder symptoms. *Psychological Medicine, 27*, 99–106.

National Institute for Mental Health in England. (2003). *Personality disorder: No longer a diagnosis of exclusion: Policy implementation guidance for the development of people with personality disorder.* London: Department of Health.

Perry, J. C. (1992). Problems and considerations in the valid assessment of personality disorders. *American Journal of Psychiatry, 149*, 1645–1653.

Pichot, P. (1978). Psychopathic behaviour: An historical overview. In R. D. Hare & D. Schalling (Eds), *Psychopathic behaviour: Approaches to research* (pp. 55–70). Chichester: Wiley.

Saulsman, L. M. & Page, A. C. (2004). The five-factor model and personality disorder empirical literature: A meta-analytic review. *Clinical Psychology Review, 23*, 1055–1085.

Schneider, K. (1950). *Psychopathic personalities* (9th ed.). London: Cassell (English translation, 1958).

Strack, S. & Lorr, M. (1997). The challenge of differentiating normal and disordered personality. *Journal of Personality Disorders, 11*, 105–122.

Stuart, S., Pfohl, B., Battaglia, M., Bellodi, L., Grove, W. & Cadoret, R. (1998). The co-occurence of DSM-III-R personality disorders. *Journal of Personality Disorders, 12*, 302–315.

Taylor, F. K. (1976). The medical model of the disease concept. *British Journal of Psychiatry, 128*, 588–594.

Tyrer, P. (2000). *Personality disorders: Diagnosis, management and course* (2nd ed.). Oxford: Butterworth-Heinemann.

Watson, D., Clark, L. A. & Harkness, A. R. (1994). Structures of personality and their relevance to psychopathology. *Journal of Abnormal Psychology, 103*, 18–31.

Widiger, T. A. & Costa, P. T. (1994). Personality and personality disorders. *Journal of Abnormal Psychology, 103*, 78–91.

Widiger, T. A. & Frances, A. J. (2002). Toward a dimensional model for the personality disorders. In P. T. Costa & T. A. Widiger (Eds), *Personality disorders and the five-factor model of personality* (2nd ed.) (pp. 23–44). Washington, DC: American Psychological Association.

World Health Organisation. (1992). *The ICD-10 classification of mental and behavioural disorders.* Geneva: World Health Organisation.

Zimmerman, M. (1994). Diagnosing personality disorders: A review of issues and research methods. *Archives of General Psychiatry, 51*, 225–245.

3

The Causes of Personality Disorder

NIC ALWIN

INTRODUCTION

John, a 35-year-old man with a five-year psychiatric history, sat slumped in the chair looking defeated and angry. Speaking with a mixture of rage and fear he said 'Why can't I cope with this? Why do I want to die? Why do people hate me?'. We had worked together in therapy for 18 months at this point, during which time John had tried to hang himself twice, had taken three life-threatening overdoses, was a regular self-harmer and had battled with anorexia and drug abuse. John had spent most of the last five years in and out of hospital. Professionals working with him found him unreasonable, demanding and personally insulting. He had experienced a physically abusive and emotionally neglectful childhood with few effective boundaries around his behaviour. As a young adult he had been involved in violence, petty crime and drug abuse, but in his mid-20s had settled down with a partner and started a family. Unfortunately, this relationship broke down acrimoniously and he was convicted of assault upon his partner and physical abuse of his child. John was refused access to his child and at this point experienced his first major breakdown.

Histories such as this are strikingly commonplace among patients with personality disorder. Patients such as John regularly present to services, displaying high levels of anxiety/depression/anger/suicidal intent. Patients with these types of difficulty challenge accepted approaches to mental health

Personality Disorder and Community Mental Health Teams: A Practitioner's Guide. Edited by M. J. Sampson, R. A. McCubbin and P. Tyrer. © 2006 John Wiley & Sons, Ltd.

as their distress does not appear to respond to the general treatment approaches used by professionals and they often do not engage with services, tending to present regularly in crisis but to disengage once the crisis has resolved. Quite predictably, working with these patients is often perceived as unrewarding, emotionally draining and frustrating.

To understand the presentation of these patients and respond more effectively to their needs, it is important to understand how and why personality disorders develop. A review of the literature gives a clear indication that these disorders result from multiple adverse psychological and social experiences, combined with an underlying biological vulnerability to develop a personality disorder. Put another way, these disorders reflect the cumulative effect of a number of difficult life events that have reacted with underlying biological predispositions, to create a way of interpreting and responding to other people that is self-destructive and/or destructive to others.

In a mental health system focused upon common mental health problems (such as anxiety and depression) and psychosis, it has been the norm for professionals to focus upon identifying particular symptoms/illnesses and providing appropriate treatment. This approach works well for many patients, but for those with multiple problems that have affected their personality their problems often do not respond to general treatments. This has resulted in frustrating experiences for staff, patients and carers. In my work with personality disordered patients it has been necessary to help both staff and patients to make sense of how any one individual has developed the problems evident in their presentation. To aid this process I have developed a clinical model (see Figure 3.1) designed to help both staff and their patients to collaborate in a process of developing an agreed narrative of the patient's life experiences that would account for and provide an understanding of their presentation. This narrative can then be used as a basis for treatment planning.

A BIOPSYCHOSOCIAL MODEL
OF PERSONALITY DISORDER

This model has been developed in a clinical setting to meet the needs of a multi-disciplinary team with diverse therapeutic backgrounds. It has been designed to obtain core psychosocial information that can be used in treatment planning, whatever the theoretical orientation of the professional delivering the intervention. The model is divided into three sections.

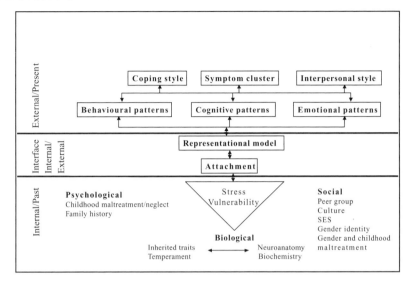

Figure 3.1 A biopsychosocial model of personality disorder

- *Internal/Past.* This represents the impact of our past experiences (from childhood to the recent past) and biological predispositions upon our thoughts, feelings and behaviour. These influence what we remember and how we remember it. For example, John was a competitive individual (biological factor) who experienced an abusive childhood (psychological factor). This led John to feel angry and rejected, to think that others might hurt or reject him and thus hurt/reject them before they could harm him.

- *Interface Internal/External.* This represents the way in which we make sense of our experiences and develop expectations of others. For example, John was raised in an emotionally neglectful environment where his needs were not met and he experienced multiple hurts and rejection. As a consequence, John developed the expectation that no one would provide him with emotional support and comfort. His assumption was that other people would also be neglectful and/or harmful, which resulted in a distrustful and wary approach to people in general, and a hypersensitivity to being rejected or let down.

- *External/Present.* This represents how we express our beliefs/emotions about others and ourselves and is the part of our personality that can be observed by others. For example, John assumed others were potentially harmful and because of this was waiting for people to let him down or harm him. His belief that he would be harmed/let down at some point raised his anxiety, which in turn led him to act in such a manner as to provoke the hurt/let down, in order to confirm his belief and thereby reduce his anxiety.

These concepts overlap and the interface between internal and external experience reflects the reality that events are constantly being assessed and processed by the mind and become part of our internal/past. However, the distinctions between the concepts in the model offer a useful framework for staff and patients to discuss the problems being encountered.

INTERNAL/PAST

BIOLOGICAL FACTORS

Inheritance and Temperament

Research suggests that inheritance and environment each account for approximately 50 per cent of the difference in personality traits between patients (Jang & Vernon, 2001). The environmental effect seems to result from the 'unique environment', which is the particular way in which patients are treated differently within their social environment, for example parental favouritism, being singled out for bullying or abuse etc. The evidence base developed from inheritance studies has resulted in the suggestion that there are three inherited causal mechanisms in the development of personality disorder (Paris, 1996), consistent with the three clusters of personality disorder outlined in the categorical model described in Chapter 2. First, it has been found that antisocial personality, borderline personality and substance abuse frequently occur together in family studies, resulting in the hypothesis that they form a group of impulsive spectrum disorders associated with a common temperament that would reflect the Dramatic/ Erratic cluster, Cluster B. Second, patients with schizoid, paranoid and schizotypal personality disorder tend to have relatives with schizophrenia or schizophrenia spectrum disorders that would reflect the Odd/Eccentric cluster, Cluster A. Third, patients with avoidant, dependent and compulsive personality disorder tend to have relatives with anxiety disorders that would reflect the Anxious/Avoidant cluster, Cluster C.

'Temperament' can be defined as biological variability in emotional responsiveness, fixed by genetic factors. From this original base it has been observed that children affect the quality of the environment they receive by shaping the responses of carers to conform to their temperament (Scarr and McCartney, 1983). For example, children with 'difficult' temperaments have an increased risk of developing conflict with their parents (Rothbart and Ahadi, 1994). These temperamental difficulties can increase vulnerability to develop personality disorder in two ways. First, the child finds it more difficult to develop warm and supportive relationships with friends and family (Rutter and Quinton, 1984). Second, the child may be sensitive to distress and respond more extremely to negative events (Paris, 1996).

Neuroanatomical and Biochemical Factors

Research in neuroanatomy has shown associations between the development or stimulation of particular areas of the brain and particular emotional difficulties. The emotional difficulties identified are a propensity to violent and impulsive behaviour and deficits in emotional processing (Hoptman, 2003). Therefore, there seem to be some aspects of personality disorder that have developed because of problems with the structure of the brain. However, it is unclear whether the brain has been like this since birth or has been affected by life experiences. Research into brain biochemistry has shown we inherit 'chemical templates' that produce and regulate proteins involved in the structure of the nervous system (Zuckerman, 1995). Therefore, we are not born 'impulsive sensation seekers' or 'antisocial personalities' but have differing levels of reactivity to stimulation of brain structures, guided by an individual 'chemical template'.

PSYCHOLOGICAL FACTORS

Childhood Maltreatment/Neglect

A history of childhood abuse or neglect appears to be associated with a diagnosis of personality disorder. Those infants raised in environments lacking in individual attention, cognitive stimulation, emotional affection or other enrichment have also consistently shown lower intelligence and a greater tendency to display autistic spectrum disorders (Perry, 2002). It is apparent that childhood neglect leads to physiological changes in children, with a lack of sensory input in infancy being associated with a range of problems with brain development. These findings suggest a global set of abnormalities matched by functional abnormalities in cognitive, emotional, behavioural and social functioning.

Research suggests that personality disordered patients frequently report having had problems in bonding with their parents and report difficulties concerned with a lack of affection (neglect), lack of discipline/boundaries (under-control) or lack of autonomy (over-control) (Paris, 1996). However, difficulties with parental bonding are not specific to personality disorder and have been reported for patients with various psychiatric diagnoses (Parker, 1983).

Post-traumatic stress disorder occurs when an individual has been overwhelmed by terror and helplessness. It is manifest in the reliving of traumatic events, avoidance of remembering the trauma and heightened arousal linked to perceived threat. Many people abused in childhood have been placed in terrifying situations where they have felt helpless. Therefore, it is not surprising that in clinical settings many patients with personality disorder, particularly borderline personality disorder, are observed to suffer from post-traumatic stress disorder (Herman, 1992).

Furthermore, it has been observed that neurophysiological changes take place in patients with post-traumatic stress disorder. These changes would indicate a decrease in the ability to speak and an increase in the ability to visualise (Rauch et al., 1996). This could explain the tendency towards flashbacks and the difficulty with speech noted when patients with personality disorder attempt to recall traumatic material (de Zulueta, 1999). However, trauma alone is neither a necessary nor sufficient cause in the diagnosis of personality disorder, and other factors including temperamental vulnerability and multiple distressing life experiences are also necessary in the aetiology of a personality disorder (Paris, 1996).

Family History

There is evidence of a high degree of psychological and social dysfunction in the families of patients who develop personality disorder and in particular the presence of depression, alcoholism and personality disorder amongst parents (Paris, 1996). There would also appear to be a high instance of poverty, unemployment, family breakdown, periods of time in local authority care and witnessing of domestic violence amongst patients who are subsequently diagnosed as personality disordered (Paris, 1996). With respect to antisocial personality disorder, one study (Robins, 1966) showed that, in families with children who later developed antisocial behaviour, the highest risk factor for the development of psychopathy and antisocial behaviours was antisocial behaviour in the father, although there was also a high frequency of antisocial behaviour in the mother and more parental alcoholism. It was hypothesised that patients with antisocial personalities develop within a family structure where there is a chronic failure to discipline or supervise children (West and Farrington, 1973).

SOCIAL FACTORS

Culture

Cross-cultural studies have shown that the same personality traits occur in the majority of human societies but could not determine whether the differences indicated biological differences between cultures or the cultural shaping of personality traits by social expectation (Paris, 1996).

Peer Groups

One influential theory (Harris, 1995) has suggested that patients move during childhood from forming major relationships with their families to their peer groups. As a consequence, the functioning of these peer groups has a significant influence upon the development of their behaviour and attitudes, which can influence their personality functioning. One study assessing this theory found some support for peer influence in shaping personality (Loehlin, 1997). In addition, American research has indicated that those belonging to delinquent peer groups are more likely to misuse substances, behave antisocially and become members of urban gangs (Patterson, 1986).

Socio-Economic Disadvantage

Little systematic research has been carried out in this area, but there is an indication that poverty, unemployment and poor scholastic achievement are correlated with raised levels of antisocial activity and the diagnosis of personality disorder in particular patients. The majority of studies of the community prevalence of antisocial personality disorder indicate a clear link with low socio-economic status (Kohn, Dohrenwend & Mirotznik, 1998).

Gender and Childhood Maltreatment

Girls are at a higher risk of intra-familial sexual abuse, whereas boys are more likely to be sexually molested by strangers or to be physically abused (Rogers and Terry, 1984). Community survey estimates of unwanted sexual contact with adults for boys and girls before the age of 18 vary from 38 per cent (Russell, 1986) to 59 per cent (Wyatt, 1985). Another indication of childhood sexual victimisation comes from lifetime prevalence studies of rape using the retrospective accounts of female adult victims. One study found that 21.6 per cent of first rapes occurred when the victim was less than 12 years of age and 32.4 per cent when the victim was 12–17 years (Tjaden and Thoennes, 1998). The gender ratio of victims of sexual assault in childhood has been estimated to be between 1.5 and 3 females to every one male (Katz and Watkins, 1998). Therefore, there are gender differences in the probability of different types of childhood maltreatment. This is likely to predispose men and women to different kinds of personality dysfunction, in the context of male and female identities developing differentially in society as a whole.

STRESS VULNERABILITY

It is difficult to determine whether biological, psychological or social causes are predominant in any individual case, or to discriminate between these factors. Social rules determine which behaviours society considers disordered. These rules are important during the identification of certain behaviours, thoughts and emotional responses as unacceptable and serve to shape the responses of patients to meet the needs of their society. This would indicate that there is a link between cultural norms and the threshold for diagnosing personality disorder. Therefore, the diagnosis of personality disorder is influenced by a combination of biopsychosocial factors, gender-linked role expectations and childhood social injury, psychological manifestations of which are often present in childhood and early adolescence (Rutter, Giller, Hagell and West, 1999). This triple combination is also at work in increasing the chances of people having other problems, such as substance misuse and chronic depression or anxiety, which overlap with, and sometimes contribute to, the diagnosis of personality disorder. Personality disorder may, therefore, be conceptualised within a stress-vulnerability model. This model suggests that each individual has a different level of vulnerability to the development of psychopathological experiences. Patients vary in their biological and psychological resilience to stress, and to become vulnerable to stress they must have experienced environmental stressors. If an individual's vulnerability is great, low levels of environmental stress might be enough to cause problems. If the individual is more resilient, problems will develop only when high levels of environmental stress are experienced.

The stress-vulnerability model can explain why some patients develop personality disorder where others do not, but does not fully account for variations in vulnerability to personality disorder. There is evidence to suggest that 25 per cent of patients traumatised during childhood later develop significant psychopathology as adults (Werner and Smith, 1992). As the majority do not, this would indicate that some patients are more resilient to the development of psychological distress. It may be that adaptive personality traits protect certain patients against psychopathology. This resilience to distress may be based upon an ability to develop active coping styles in seeking social support (Runtz and Schallow, 1997). Social mechanisms may explain the relative lack of vulnerability of some children. These children would appear to recognise early on in their lives that their parent's behaviour is pathological and look elsewhere for attachment and behavioural models (Werner and Smith, 1992).

INTERFACE INTERNAL/EXTERNAL

Consideration of the Internal/Past aims to identify what events/experiences have shaped a patient's development and how these events/experiences have been influenced by biological factors. The Interface Internal/External helps to identify how these events/experiences have developed into an identifiable 'sense of self' and way of relating to others. These two concepts relate to, and are influenced by, each other. A personal identity, or sense of self, is a reflection of how we see ourselves and is affected by our interpretation of how others treat us. Our ability to relate to others develops through early social experiences in our relationships with our major carers, often referred to as attachment relationships, and is affected by subsequent experiences/events. Therefore, how we present ourselves to others is a reflection of how we feel about ourselves and how we perceive that others see us.

The majority of people have experienced a childhood environment that was predictable, supportive, protective and nurturing. This allows them to develop a sense of self and others that is accurate enough to be useful in predicting how they will react to events and how others will react to them. This, in turn, allows them to develop co-operative socially adaptive relationships with their peers that are able to adapt to meet changing circumstances.

Unfortunately, core problems that patients with personality disorder experience are difficulties with a sense of self, and the ability to relate to others. A sense of self develops during the first four to six years of a child's life and is affected by the emotional environment in which the child lives. For example, an emotionally neglected child would have greater difficulty developing a coherent sense of self as they lack the experience of social contact in which to develop this sense of self, and they can become socially isolated and display autistic features. The sense of self develops to become a way in which we see ourselves within our social context – what is termed a 'representational model'. It informs our attitudes towards and expectations of others and shapes our impression of the behaviour of others. For instance, a person who has experienced multiple losses of carers would be more likely to expect other carers or intimate partners to leave them at some point, thus potentially leading them to withhold their emotional commitment to others and to show a reluctance to rely on or to trust in the ongoing support of others. Emotional bonds with others are significantly influenced and shaped by our early relationships, or 'attachments', with our major caregivers, usually our parents. A representational model can be seen as an internalised view of how we will relate to others and how we interpret the way they behave to us. An attachment to a major caregiver can be seen as the emotional matrix within which a child develops. Some understanding of these concepts is important in making sense of the experience of patients with personality disorder.

ATTACHMENT

Attachment theory developed as an attempt to explain and understand the role of close intimate relationships in human development. Over time, methods of measuring attachment in humans have been developed and the central role of attachment in emotional development has become clear (Bowlby, 1988). Young children develop an attachment to their caregivers by the age of 12 months; this attachment remains stable over time and is predictive of adolescent behaviour. Four attachment styles have been identified:

Secure	A child able to effectively express their needs in an environment where they receive predictable, consistent and emotionally warm nurturing focussed upon providing safety, stability and security for the child.
Anxious	A child is unsure that a caregiver will provide a consistent and/or predictable and/or emotionally warm environment. The child becomes anxious that some or all of his or her emotional/physical needs will not be met and reacts by displaying this anxiety in their behaviour. Children in this situation are often observed to be clingy and/or demanding and/or appeasing.
Ambivalent	A child concerned that a parent may emotionally reject her or him. The child experiences a caregiver who is not able to provide consistent, predictable or emotionally warm responses and at times ignores or rejects the child

	when the child needs an emotional response from the caregiver. Children in this situation are often observed to be unsure whether they will receive a positive response to appeals for care and can show emotional withdrawal from the caregiver.
Disorganised	A child who does not receive any effective emotional nurturing. This attachment style is often linked to child abuse by the caregiver, but can also be associated with the caregiver being unable to emotionally engage with the child for other reasons e.g. severe depression. Children in this situation are observed to be wary and can appear 'frozen' and unable to make a decision whether to approach or withdraw from the caregiver.

A secure attachment relationship provides a secure base from which a child can explore their environment, in the knowledge that a caring and concerned adult will ensure their safety and protect them from danger. Attachment is perceived to have a biological base and is a necessary component of all human functioning (Bowlby, 1988). We all need to maintain close intimate bonds with our peers and the major expression of this attachment need can be seen in our tendency to form intimate bonds with our sexual partners. Therefore, our attachment style continues to have relevance to our psychosocial functioning throughout our lives. The three variations of insecure attachment (anxious, ambivalent and disorganised) are associated with increased vulnerability to psychopathology in adulthood. The expression of this pathology can be conceptualised as three different types of disorder (Goldberg, 2000):

Internalising Disorders	Associated with anxious attachment, a child experiences an inconsistent caregiver and becomes preoccupied with maintaining the attention and emotional focus of the caregiver. The child limits his or her focus to the attachment relationship and does not feel safe enough to explore the wider environment. The children become fearful of new situations/challenges, become enmeshed in family issues and are otherwise isolated and withdrawn.
Externalising Disorders	Associated with ambivalent attachment, children experience a caregiver who does not

respond to their needs and learn to ignore their own feelings of distress. The child becomes distrusting of people and may believe people are uncaring. This can lead to aggression and a disregard for the rights of others.

Disorganisation Disorder   Associated with disorganised attachment, which is associated with psychological disturbance and its predisposing risk factors. This disorder is associated with expressions of dissociative phenomena (stilling, freezing, stereotyped movements). The severity of these symptoms is likely to reflect the length and severity of the disorganised environment the child experienced. Children who experience a short-term understandable breakdown in their attachment environment, for example a caregiver experiencing the loss of a significant attachment figure, are likely to experience short-term disorganisation but can remain securely attached. Children who experience long-term disorganisation, for example inappropriate care by a disturbed or abusive caregiver, are likely to experience an insecure/non-existent attachment. This can lead to significant problems with emotional attachment to others throughout their lives.

INTERNAL REPRESENTATIONAL MODEL

The earliest sense of self, from birth to eight months, is concerned with the here and now, experiencing events with no awareness of past or future. Children then begin to develop a sense of themselves as existing within a context that has a past and a future. At this stage children begin to reflect upon their lives, and as their ability to do so develops they begin to reflect on the past or future with positive and negative expectations, which can shape their responses to events and expectations of others. This sense of self is focussed upon what has happened or will happen to the child. By the age of three, children begin to be able to consider events that may happen somewhere to someone – that is, they remove themselves from the centre of their thinking. This process increases in sophistication until the child, by the age of six to seven, is able to consider abstract concepts and their relationship to each other. These different perceptions of self continue to exist alongside each other throughout our lives. We may get 'lost in the moment' when involved in particular activities, for example listening to music, we may continue to reflect upon particular circumstances or situations, thinking what if?/if only!, or we may observe our general tendency to behave in certain ways, and reflect upon this tendency considering the emotional and/or intellectual effect it has upon us. Each of these perceptions of self is involved in our development of our representational model. Therefore, a representational model can be conceptualised as the expression of our sense of self. Our memory of events and experiences and their emotional impact is filtered through our perception of self and results in an emotional, cognitive and/or behavioural response.

To function as a well rounded individual who has a clear and consistent sense of her or his own identity requires an individual to be able to stand back and reflect upon her- or himself and her or his life, with an ability to consider her or his views and beliefs as constructs that are open to interpretation. People with a personality disorder have usually failed to develop such a coherent and reflective sense of their identity. Therefore, the representational models of those with personality disorder are likely to lack depth, focussing more upon responses to particular events and/or unable to consider alternative explanations for the motives of the behaviour of themselves or others, rather than reflecting upon a general tendency for themselves or others to behave in particular ways. For example, a couple separate after a long marriage; one partner has a coherent sense of self and the other does not. The partner with a coherent sense of self would be likely to grieve appropriately for the loss of the relationship and reflect upon the events leading to the deterioration in the relationship and incorporate insights from this process into his or her sense of self. The partner with a poorly formed sense of self would be more likely to ruminate over particular events, become angry/distressed at the loss of the partner, be unable to tolerate or reflect upon this loss and may fail to grieve the loss appropriately and/or experience some mental health problems.

The concept of an internalised model of how other people will perceive us is common to most psychological therapies. Cognitive behavioural therapists refer to schema or schemata, the deeply held beliefs about others and ourselves – for example, 'I am worthless', 'other people hate me'. Psychodynamic therapists refer to introjects or object relations, the internalising of the values and beliefs of our major attachment figures – for example, 'I must work hard' could be an expression of a family work ethic connected to praise for achievement from an attachment figure. Other therapies refer to life scripts as expressions of expectations linked to outcomes. For example, if a person believes he or she will have conflict in relationships he or she is likely to act in a manner that would create the very conflict they expect. Therefore, the internal representational model represents a common theme within psychological therapies that we hold in our heads a template of social expectations which influences and shapes our responses to events. This is evident in the information we concentrate upon in situations and the feelings engendered by these situations. For instance, if a person who is afraid of dogs sees a dog with no apparent owner in sight she or he would be likely to focus on the danger of the situation, feel fearful and expect the dog to attack her or him. Another individual who has an affinity with dogs may observe the dog to be lost, uncertain and in need of human companionship.

EXTERNAL/PRESENT

The Interface Internal/External identifies how the individual experiences of patients can be shaped into a coherent set of beliefs, attitudes and expectations. The External/Present identifies how these beliefs, attitudes and expectations are communicated to others. This section is concerned with the outward expression of personality disorder through the major modes of human expression, our thoughts, feelings and actions. I do not propose to develop this section in great detail as much of the relevant information will be covered in other chapters on assessment, therapy and working with those with personality disorder. However, there are three general points I consider to be of relevance to the maintaining factors for personality disorder.

(a) A personality disorder represents the individual's best attempt to cope. The manifestation of distress evident in patients with personality disorder usually becomes apparent at a point in their lives when their chosen way of coping has broken down because of problems in their interpersonal world. For example John, in the example used at the start of this chapter, entered services after being refused access to his child. Prior to this, John had used inappropriate expressions of anger to attempt to control his environment but the use of this coping strategy with his child had merely exacerbated the problem and overwhelmed John's ability to cope. In working with patients with personality disorder it is important to bear in mind that however aberrant a person's coping strategy appears to be it is the best he or she has been able to develop, given his or her biological predisposition and psychosocial experiences.

(b) The ability to develop and maintain a constructive alliance with patients with personality disorder is hampered by their difficulties with a sense of self and poor understanding of interpersonal relationships. In order to be able to accurately and effectively interpret the behaviour of an individual with a personality disorder, a good understanding of her or his representational model is required. This is only possible if a thorough assessment, including objective measures of personality disorder and a comprehensive clinical interview, is carried out. Having completed an assessment, the complex nature of the interpersonal dynamics between professional and patient evident with personality disorder will require regular clinical supervision. The supervision process needs to concentrate upon enabling professionals to review, reflect upon and understand the underlying emotional themes (dependency, avoidance, aggression etc.) in the therapeutic relationship, which can in turn strengthen and develop the therapeutic alliance or enable professionals to recognise when and why they should consider changing/ending their input.

(c) Working with patients with a personality disorder is an emotionally challenging and at times frustrating experience. Trying to engage in an interpersonal relationship with an individual who has a limited ability to understand his or her emotional response to events and has difficulty relating to others is not the easiest of things to attempt. Patients with personality disorder tend to expect professionals to conform to their expectations of other people. The dependent patient expects the professional to look after and take care of him or her, thus when asked to take responsibility and assume autonomy he or she can become distressed. The borderline patient expects professionals to have a close and involved relationship but cannot believe this is possible. The professional may initially be seen as insightful, empathic and caring (idealised) but when some minor difficulty occurs in the therapeutic relationship, it can be perceived as uncaring and insensitive (denigrated). To maximise the chances of success there needs to be a conscious focus upon the purpose, limits and structure of the relationship, more commonly referred to as 'boundaries'. The ability of the professional to model and shape good interactions in relationships can help to lessen the possibility of misperceptions and inappropriate demands occurring. This requires the professional to form an effective attachment focus for the individual with personality disorder. This places an emphasis upon the professional to provide a consistent, predictable and emotionally warm stance. In practice, this means being able to be open and honest whilst maintaining an empathic understanding of the patient.

CONCLUSION

This chapter started with a description of a man at the end of his tether who could not understand his distress and the effect it had upon his ability to function. John had experienced events that had prevented him from developing a coherent sense of self. He had difficulty understanding his own motivations and, consequently, had extreme difficulty understanding and predicting the behaviour of others. His experience of rejection and harm led him to assume others might be harmful to him, and his fear that others might harm him resulted in acts of violence to others. It is the combination of difficulties with personal identity and an inability to accurately interpret the behaviour of others that is at the heart of problems associated with personality disorder. Patients with a personality disorder have experienced life events that prevent them from developing well rounded personalities with the ability to respond flexibly and adaptively to a wide range of interpersonal situations. Instead these patients develop fixed and rigid beliefs regarding the behaviour of others and/or maladaptive coping strategies to cope with distress.

For example, an individual who assumes relationships are all good or all bad is regularly faced with the reality that friends/partners show both good and bad features but she or he cannot tolerate this and becomes distressed by the apparent contradiction. Patients with personality disorder need help to develop and maintain a coherent sense of self and to increase their ability to be able to interact constructively with others. Understanding what has had such an adverse impact upon their functioning increases the likelihood that their distress will be understood. For many years, patients with personality disorder have been dismissed as 'attention seeking', 'manipulative' and 'deviant'. I hope this chapter has helped to redress the balance a little, and has given some indication why patients with personality disorder present as they do.

REFERENCES

Bowlby, J. (1988). *A secure base: Clinical applications of attachment theory.* London: Routledge.
de Zulueta, F. (1999). Borderline personality disorder as seen from an attachment perspective: A review. *Criminal Behaviour and Mental Health, 9,* 237–253.

Goldberg, S. (2000). *Attachment and development*. London: Arnold

Harris, J. R. (1995). Where is the child's environment? A group socialization theory of development. *Psychological Review, 102,* 458–489.

Herman, J. (1992). *Trauma and Recovery: The aftermath of violence from domestic abuse to political terror.* New York: Basic.

Hoptman, M. J. (2003). Neuroimaging studies of violence and antisocial behaviour. *Journal of Psychiatric Practice, 9,* 265–278.

Jang, K. L. & Vernon, P. A. (2001). Genetics. In W. J. Livesley (Ed.), *Handbook of personality disorder: Theory, research, and treatment* (pp. 177–195). New York: Guilford.

Katz, R. C. & Watkins, J. (1998). Adult victims of child abuse. In A. S. Bellack and M. Hersen (Eds), *Comprehensive Clinical Psychology* (Vol. 9). New York: Pergamon.

Kohn, R., Dohrenwend, B. P. & Mirotznik, J. (1998). Epidemiological findings on selected psychiatric disorders in the general population. In B. P. Dohrenwend (Ed.), *Adversity stress and psychopathology* (pp. 235–284). London: Oxford University Press.

Loehlin, J. C. (1997). A test of J. R. Harris's theory of peer influences on personality. *Journal of Personality and Social Psychology, 72,* 1197–1201.

Paris, J. (1996). *Social factors in personality disorder: A biopsychosocial approach to etiology and treatment.* Cambridge: Cambridge University Press.

Parker, G. (1983). *Parental overprotection: A risk factor in psychosocial development.* New York: Grune and Stratton.

Patterson, G. R. (1986). Performance models for antisocial boys. *American Psychologist, 41,* 432–444.

Perry, B. D. (2002). Childhood experience and the expression of genetic potential: What childhood neglect tells us about nature and nurture. *Brain and Mind, 3,* 79–100.

Rauch, S. L., van der Kolk, B. A., Fisler, R. E., Alpert, N. M., Orr, S. P., Savage, C. R., Fischman, A. J., Jenike, M. A. & Pitman, R. K. (1996). A symptom provocation study of posttraumatic stress disorder using positron emission tomography and script driven imagery. *Archives of General Psychiatry, 53,* 380–387.

Robins, L. N. (1966). *Deviant children grown up.* Baltimore, OH: Williams and Wilkins.

Rogers, C. M. & Terry, T. (1984). Clinical interventions with boy victims of sexual abuse. In J. Stuart & J. Greer (Eds), *Victims of sexual aggression. Treatment of children, women, and men* (pp. 91–104). New York: Van Nostrand.

Rothbart, M. K. & Ahadi, S. A. (1994). Temperament and the development of personality. *Journal of Abnormal Psychology, 103,* 55–66.

Runtz, M. G. & Schallow, J. R. (1997). Social support and coping strategies as mediators of adult adjustment following childhood maltreatment. *Child Abuse and Neglect, 21,* 211–226.

Russell, D. (1986). *The secret trauma: Incest in the lives of girls and women.* New York: Basic.

Rutter, M., Giller, H., Hagell, A. & West, D. (1999). Antisocial behaviour by young people. *Journal of Forensic Psychiatry, 10,* 472–475.

Rutter, M. & Quinton, D. (1984). Long-term follow-up of women institutionalized in childhood. *British Journal of Developmental Psychology, 18,* 225–234.

Scarr, S. & McCartney, K. (1983). How people make their own environments: A theory of genotype–environment effects. *Child Development, 54,* 424–435.

Tjaden, P. & Thoennes, R. (1998) *The national violence against women survey.* Washington: US Department of Justice.

Werner, E. E. & Smith, R. S. (1992). *Overcoming the odds: High risk children from birth to adulthood.* New York: Cornell University Press.

West, D. J. & Farrington, D. P. (1973). *Who becomes delinquent?* London: Heinemann.

Wyatt, G. E. (1985). The sexual abuse of Afro-American and White-American women in childhood. *Child Abuse and Neglect*, *9*, 507–519.

Zuckerman, M. (1995). Good and bad humors: Biochemical bases of personality and its disorders. *Psychological Science*, *6*, 325–332.

4

Psychological Theories Regarding the Development of Personality Disorder

JIM MOOREY

KATE DAVIDSON

MARK EVANS

JANET FEIGENBAUM

This chapter considers the development and maintenance of personality disorders from a psychological perspective. Although our emphasis is on the *psychological* aspects it is important to note the *multifactorial* nature of personality disorders, and hence this chapter can be seen as a complement to Chapter 3. The four theoretical accounts outlined here will provide an introduction to the understanding that informs the four models of therapy described in Chapter 5: Psychodynamic–interpersonal therapy, cognitive therapy, cognitive analytic therapy and dialectical behaviour therapy. These models of therapy – and hence the theory to which they relate – have been selected for two reasons: first, they are in common use, both in mental health services and research trials; second, they allow the illustration of a range of key psychological principles. They have *not* been selected in order to give the impression that any particular approach(es) is (are) being endorsed. Furthermore, the order in which they are presented holds no significance. It is acknowledged that there exist many other psychological theories and

Personality Disorder and Community Mental Health Teams: A Practitioner's Guide. Edited by M. J. Sampson, R. A. McCubbin and P. Tyrer. © 2006 John Wiley & Sons, Ltd.

therapies that address personality functioning, and indeed that many services adopt an 'integrated' approach, in which several different approaches are combined. However, it is hoped that by focusing on these approaches the reader will gain a clear introduction to the central theoretical foundations of some of the major psychological therapies.

Of necessity, important areas have been mentioned only briefly. It is recognised that some of the ideas can, on first reading, appear highly complex. Readers are encouraged to go over this chapter more than once, and to follow up some of the key references, in order to develop their understanding of the theoretical aspects of these models.

A PSYCHODYNAMIC MODEL

JIM MOOREY

We may conceptualise 'personality disorders' in terms of *disturbances in a person's experience of self* (Kernberg, 1967; Kohut, 1971; Winnicott, 1960). A distinction may be made between secondary disturbances 'within' the self (very roughly, typical of Axis I disorders), and primary disturbances 'of' the self (very roughly, typical of Axis II disorders). Various types of primary disturbance in the experience of self can be distinguished, these distinctions capturing different aspects of the phenomenology of 'personality disorders'. However, there is no straightforward correlation between these distinctions, based on psychodynamics and phenomenology, and psychiatric classifications (Brooke, 1994; Kohut & Wolf, 1978: Wolf, 1994). In this section I will present a general account of the development and disruption of the sense of self that will be relevant to most if not all personality disorders.

THE DEFINITION OF 'SELF'

It is extremely difficult to arrive at an adequate definition of the term 'self'. There is no generally agreed definition, and the term has been used in various ways. The following points may help to clarify how I will be using the term in this section. The self can be regarded as a process that organises and structures experience in a particular way. There are many forms of self experience that we could differentiate, but for our purposes we may emphasise a fundamental distinction between two aspects of the self, which we may term *self as subject* and *self as object*. The subjective sense of self refers to the observing, knowing, introspecting and self-reflecting aspects of self. We may think of this subjective sense of self as an inner perspective, or viewpoint, an inner metaphorical 'eye'. The objective sense of self refers to those features of self that can be observed and known, and can be objects of introspection or be reflected upon. This dual aspect account of self can be elaborated and extended in many ways, but the basic distinction will suffice for our purposes.

THE DEVELOPMENT OF SELF

The experience of self develops through the maturation of fundamental psychological functions that make possible an increasingly complex organising and structuring of the experience of self and others. Daniel Stern has described the early stages of this process in terms of the development of four 'senses of self', in which 'sense' means 'simple (non-self-reflexive) awareness' (Stern, 1985, p. 7). Stern describes two embryonic senses of self, and the form of relatedness associated with each, that emerge in the first six months of life. The sense of an *emergent self*, along with the domain of *emergent relatedness* – the sense of self in relation to objects – is present from birth, and is detectable during the first 2 months of life. The sense of *core self* emerges, along with the domain of *core relatedness*, during months 2–6. This involves a sense of self as a separate, bounded, physical entity, with a sense of agency, affectivity and temporal continuity. The sense of *subjective self* emerges between 6 and 18 months, along with the domain of *intersubjective relatedness*. The key development in the experience of self during this period is the sense that the contents of the infant's mind can be shared with another, and that others have minds. The fourth sense of self described by Stern is the sense of verbal or *objective self*, which emerges from about 18 months, along with the domain of *verbal relatedness*. At about this time symbolic functioning becomes apparent in the emergence of symbolic play and the use of language. The subsequent increasing sophistication of symbolic activity is associated with an increasing organisation and differentiation of the objective sense of self.

Stern has repeatedly emphasised the *interpersonal* context of the development of the various senses of self – that is, the central importance of the relationship between infant and care-givers. Early attachments are crucial because they impact upon key mental processes that generate the representational systems that underpin the sense of self and other (Bowlby, 1988; Fonagy, 2001). Care-givers' '*responsiveness* to infant affect is a key determinant' of the security of attachment (Holmes, 1997, p. 234). In a classic paper Winncott describes the process of *mirroring* through which the infant sees, or discovers, himself or herself reflected in the mother's face: 'the mother is looking at the baby and *what she looks like is related to what she sees there*' (Winnicott, 1967, p. 112). It is the care-giver's *attunement* to the infant that is crucial: 'How well the caretaker apprehends the state of the infant, the *specificity* of his/her *recognition* will, among other factors, determine the nature and degree of the infant's experience' (Stern et al., 1998, p. 907). These metaphors of mirroring and attunement attempt to describe the capacity of care-givers to understand the infant's mental state, to see the world from the infant's point of view.

Some of the details of this process have been well described by Gergely and Watson (1996) in relation to the development of emotional self-awareness and self-regulation. Through 'affect-mirroring' care-givers enable infants to identify and differentiate their emotional experiences, and to manage or regulate them. To put this crudely: how the care-giver responds to the infant's emotional states shapes the way those emotions are processed and experienced by the infant. This ability to empathise with the infant's experience and respond appropriately impacts on the development of the representational capacities that underpin the experience of self. *An interpersonal process becomes internalised as an intrapsychic one.* We may say that the responses of the primary attachment figures are eventually experienced as the infant's 'self'. In this sense, what we come to experience as our private sense of self is an interpersonal, relational product, *self is always self-in-relation-to-other.*

THE DISRUPTION OF SELF

There are various ways in which the experience of self may be disrupted or disturbed. Stern describes four 'crucial invariants' (1985, p. 76) that must become reliable features of experience, in order for the increasing organisation and differentiation associated with the development of the different senses of self to occur. Each of these crucial invariants is vulnerable to disruption:

  Continuity refers to the experience of being the same self, the same person, existing through changes in time and place; the sense of 'going on being' (Winnicott, 1958) – being a self with a personal history, stable attributes and a stable identity.
  Coherence refers to the structural clarity and stability of the sense of the self. Self is experienced as an embodied and bounded entity, differentiated from others, with a personal inner world, inner space and inner

life, in which thoughts, feelings, fantasies and memories are experienced as private and containable.

Agency refers to the sense of responsibility, ownership and control, of thought, feeling and action. The self is experienced as autonomous and independent, with the power of will, and the capacity to initiate or inhibit impulses and intentions.

Affectivity refers to the emotional tone, affective colouring or sense of value of the experience of self. Self is experienced as essentially good, worthwhile, capable and secure. Fluctuations in these feelings, even when negative, are experienced as temporary, circumscribed and manageable.

When the continuity, coherence, agency and affectivity of the sense of self has not been reliably established in experience, we may describe the resulting difficulties as *disruptions* in the sense of self. These disruptions range from mild to very severe, and are likely to be conspicuous features of most if not all personality disorders.

Both the development and the disruption of the sense of self are crucially dependent on the quality of the care-giving environment. In particular, they depend on the *empathic responsiveness* of the primary attachment figures. Experiences of abuse, neglect, traumatic separation or loss, inconsistent or unreliable care and the less obvious but nonetheless important forms of care-giving *misattunement*, may contribute to the disruption of the development of self. More specifically, deficiencies in the care-giving environment impact on key psychological and biological processes that underpin the development of the senses of self. I will briefly describe two key psychological functions, intimately connected with the development of experience of self, that appear to be particularly sensitive to the impact of the early care-giving environment: mentalisation and memory.

Mentalisation

Mentalisation is an 'intersubjectively acquired abstract reflexive implicit awareness of mental states' (Fonagy, 2001, p. 168). When fully developed, mentalisation is an explicit symbolic function involving the secondary, or higher order, representation of primary mental representations. It is the capacity to reflect on one's own mental states (thoughts, feelings, beliefs, desires etc.), and to attribute mental states to others, as an explanation of their behaviour. Mentalisation is the central psychological function facilitating the emergence of the objective sense of self. Developmental research suggests the earliest indications of this capacity emerge towards the end of the first year of life, and continue to develop in sophistication through to age five or six (Fonagy, 1991; Stern et al., 1998).

Mentalisation involves being able to recognise, tolerate and respond to one's own, and others', mental states. However, 'Understanding the nature of the mental world cannot be done alone, it requires seeing the self in the eye of the other' (Fonagy, 1995, p. 43). Mentalisation is dependent on whether primary attachment figures recognise, tolerate and respond empathically to the infant. Deficits in care will impact on how an infant represents their own mental states, and also how they represent the thoughts, feelings, wishes and motives of an abusive, neglectful or poorly attuned primary attachment figure. Mentalisation makes possible the defensive distortion of mental representations to disguise or disown unmanageable experiences of self and other. However, traumatic experience may lead to the processes involved in generating second order representations of mental states being defensively inhibited (Fonagy, 1991). Trauma may result in the formation of multiple primary representations of self and other that are poorly integrated (giving rise to multiple shifting and contradictory experiences of self and others), poorly differentiated (giving rise to unclear boundaries between self and others) and one dimensional (self and others are experienced in polarised ways, as all good or all bad). Self-reflection – being able to think about one's own mental states and those of others – appears to be crucial to the development of affect regulation, impulse control, self-monitoring, the experience of self-agency and interpersonal relatedness (Fonagy, 2001; Fonagy & Target, 1996; Hobson, 1993, 2002).

Memory

The experience of a continuous and coherent sense of self is crucially dependent on the development of *memory*. Of fundamental importance is the differentiation of various types of independent memory system. At the first level of approximation we may distinguish two types of memory: implicit (procedural) and explicit (declarative).

We can further distinguish two implicit systems: *procedural* and *perceptual*. The former refers to learnt behaviours, such as skills, and the latter to perceptual recognition. These implicit memory systems become evident during the first six months of life, and are based on non-symbolic representations (Fonagy, 1999; Schacter, 1992). We may also distinguish two explicit (declarative) memory systems: the *semantic* and the *episodic*. Declarative memory depends on the capacity to symbolise, that is, for second order representation. Semantic memory refers to memory of facts and begins in the second half of the first year, becoming declarative during the second half of the second year, when words are first used. Episodic memory may be divided into recent and remote. Recent episodic memory refers to unremarkable events or experiences of the previous week or so, and emerges early in the third year of life. Remote episodic memory has also been termed 'autobiographical memory', and refers to events or experiences associated with the self. Autobiographical memory emerges in the fifth year of life (Meares, 1995; Nelson, 1992).

Stern et al. (1998) note that from the first year of life interpersonal experience is represented in implicit procedural systems as *implicit relational knowing*, which integrates affect, cognition and behavioural/interactive dimensions. Such 'knowing' represents 'a-way-of-being-with-the-other' (Stern, 1994, p. 36), or more precisely 'a-way-of-experiencing-the-other' (Fonagy, 1999, p. 218). Meares (1999; Meares, Stevenson & Gordon, 1999; Meares, 2000) has emphasised that mental functions that are the slowest to develop are the most fragile, and hence most vulnerable to disruption through the impact of trauma. In particular, he notes that traumatic experience will be represented hierarchically. Even after the capacity for autobiographical memory emerges, traumatic experience may still be represented semantically or procedurally because of the disruptive effects of trauma. This means the memory cannot be 'recovered' as it has not been represented in a symbolic form that would make it accessible to consciousness. Meares describes how the relatively sequestered non-episodic traumatic memory can be activated, leading to a rapid shift in sense of self, or state of consciousness, characterised by reduction or loss of self-reflective capacity (the objective sense of self), dissociation and acting out of a procedural representation of responses to trauma.

To summarise:

- Generally, 'personality disorders' may be conceptualised as manifestations of a primary disturbance in a person's experience of self, involving disruptions in the continuity, coherence, agency and affectivity of the self.
- The development of various 'senses of self' is dependent on the maturation of key psychological functions (such as mentalisation and memory), that enable increasingly complex organising, differentiating and structuring of experience of self and other.
- The maturation of these psychological functions, in particular second order (symbolic) representational capacities, is primarily dependent on the responsiveness of attachment figures to the infant's emotional experience.

COGNITIVE THEORY OF PERSONALITY DISORDER

KATE DAVIDSON

THE INTERACTION BETWEEN GENETICALLY DETERMINED BEHAVIOURAL STRATEGIES AND THE ENVIRONMENT

Innate Behavioural Strategies

Beck and colleagues (Beck, Freeman & Associates, 1990; Beck, Freeman, Davis & Associates, 2004) suggest that personality patterns are derived from genetically determined personality traits (described as 'strategies') that facilitate survival and reproduction. A strategy is seen as a genetically programmed behaviour that has evolved to meet biological goals (e.g. survival, food, reproduction). The process of natural selection is thought to have brought about a fit between genetically programmed behaviour and the environment. The problems of those with personality disorder arise as a result of a mismatch between the demands of the environment and genetically programmed behavioural strategies.

Patterns of programmed behaviour that may have had survival value in more primitive settings, such as exhibitionism or competitiveness, may interfere with goal-directed behaviour in our present culture and may also conflict with the dominant social norms of the culture. For example, behaviours that increase the likelihood of being able to attract a mate when there is a shortage of suitable partners, or of being able to obtain scarce resources such as food by behaving competitively, may well have survival and reproductive value in a more primitive culture. However, in our culture, where it is less likely that there are shortages of mates and food, such personality traits may be regarded negatively by others and may be less than optimal for group cohesion and bonding, where these are valued by the dominant group. Strategies such as extremes of competitiveness would be regarded as being maladaptive in the latter circumstances. It is not that these behavioural strategies or personality traits are in themselves maladaptive, it is when these are used inflexibly and not in accordance with societal values that they are problematic. In personality disorder, the problem lies in these strategies being evident in almost all situations, regardless of the context. When behavioural strategies are inflexible and hypervalent, they cannot be regarded as adaptive as specific circumstances are not taken into account.

Behavioural Strategies and Environmental Influences

In cognitive theory, the individual's innate behavioural strategies are seen as being additionally influenced by the specific environment in which the person lives. Environmental consequences to these programmed strategies can increase or dampen their expression (Cottraux & Blackburn, 2001). This can lead to some traits being overdeveloped while others are underdeveloped (Beck et al., 1990). For example, a family environment where success and winning is consistently rewarded while failure is punished would enhance competitiveness traits (overdeveloped strategy). This environment would not enhance the person's underdeveloped behaviour strategies of giving and sharing. Problems arise when a person does not have a wide enough repertoire of strategies to deal with the demands of modern society.

SCHEMA AND BELIEFS

An interaction between a person's innate behavioural strategies and specific environment consequences will influence how they organise and make sense of the world (their schema development). For instance, in the example above a person's competitive strategy may be enhanced by specific environmental consequences and this could lead them to develop rigid beliefs and conditional assumptions around ability and general worth. In cognitive theory, beliefs are a subset of a more global structure labelled 'schema'.

Schema are the central component of any cognitive model of personality disorders (Cottraux & Blackburn, 2001). The concept of a schema evolved from Kelly's personal construct theory (Kelly, 1955). Kelly proposed that people seek consistency and predictability. In cognitive theory a schema is a cognitive structure that 'arises naturally from the intuition that regularities among similar events leads to their being connected in memory to form a memory structure, or schema, for that class of events' (Williams, Watts, MacLeod & Mathews, 1997, p. 210). Essentially, a schema helps us make sense of something new, as we can refer back to similar events and make use of 'a consistent internal structure, used as a template to organise new information' (Williams et al., 1997, p. 211). Schema are important in cognitive theories of personality disorders as they serve to select and synthesise new incoming information, activate the affective and motivational arousal systems and are ultimately involved in the selection and implementation of a response strategy. They are in effect the 'generals' of the information processing system and govern all other systems. In cognitive theory of personality, schema are the fundament units of personality (Beck et al., 1990). Personality disorder occurs when a person's schema are 'maladaptive' for the environment within which the person is living.

Cognitive theory proposes that there are particular subsets of schema that are important in personality disorder. These are conditional and unconditional beliefs, early maladaptive schemas and schema modes.

Conditional and Unconditional Beliefs

Cognitive theory proposes that core beliefs and conditional assumptions are important in the maintenance of personality disorders. Core beliefs are unconditional in their statements about self and others, e.g. 'I am bad', while dysfunctional conditional beliefs or assumptions are recognisable because they are expressed in terms of 'conditional' phrases such as 'If I do X, then Y will happen'. An example from a depressed patient might be a belief that 'If my children behave badly, then I am a bad mother'.

In disorders such as depression, dysfunctional beliefs are activated during an episode of depression and appear to become dormant on recovery, whereas in personality disorder it is thought that the core beliefs and conditional assumptions are more stable and rigid, and therefore less open to change. Consequently, the person is trapped in very rigid ways of seeing the world and coping and their behaviour only serves to reinforce their maladaptive schema, thus keeping them in a pattern of a 'self-fulfilling prophecy'.

Certain core beliefs and overt behavioural strategies are associated with specific personality disorders. Table 4.1 illustrates the typical beliefs and behavioural strategies associated with some types of personality disorder. For example, an individual with a dependent personality disorder will be likely to hold a belief that he or she is helpless and cannot do things without the help of others. It would make sense that an individual who holds this belief would develop behavioural strategies that involve attachment to others who will protect, help or even 'rescue' them. This behavioural strategy develops and strengthens (becomes overdeveloped) at the expense of a behavioural strategy that would increase independence and autonomy (which is underdeveloped). In personality disorder, beliefs take an unconditional form, usually stated as 'I am ... ' or 'others are ....' and 'the world is ...'. A patient with antisocial personality disorder might hold an

Table 4.1 The relationship between core beliefs and behavioural strategies in personality disorder

Personality disorder type	Core beliefs	Behavioural strategy
Avoidant	I will get hurt	avoidance
Dependent	I am helpless	attachment
Antisocial	I can do what I want to others	exploitation
Paranoid	Other people are a threat to me	vigilance
Borderline	I am bad	self-degradation & punishment

unconditional core belief such as 'other people are there for me to use for my own ends' or 'I am able to do what I want at all times'. In personality disorder the content of the unconditional beliefs concerns mainly self and others and the world, rather than the future.

Davidson (2000) has suggested that individuals with borderline personality disorder hold core beliefs related to low self-esteem, that might be expressed as 'I am bad' or 'I am worthless'. These beliefs facilitate and are reinforced by overdeveloped behavioural strategies of self-degradation and self-punishment. The underdeveloped behavioural strategies are likely to be the reciprocal of these and concerned with difficulties in self-nurturance. Although the cognitive model does predict that specific beliefs will be associated with specific disorders, in reality individuals with personality disorder often have more than one type of personality disorder and are likely to hold more than one dominant core belief. For example, an individual with dependent personality disorder may also suffer from a co-existing avoidant personality disorder, and as a result is likely to share the beliefs that are also associated with avoidant personality disorder. These two disorders are two out of three disorders in the same cluster of personality disorders, known as the fearful and anxious or Cluster C (DSM-IV: APA, 1994), indicating that disorders in the same cluster may share similar attributes.

Early Maladaptive Schemas

Young (1990) proposes the existence of a specific subset of a person's schemas which are important in personality disorder. He termed these 'early maladaptive schemas'. Although Young (1990) made no specific connection between the various early maladaptive schema and personality disorder diagnostic categories, his ideas have become increasingly influential in attempts to understand personality disorder.

Early maladaptive schema (EMSs) are 'the deepest level of cognition and affect' (Young & Behary, 1998, p. 345) and according to Young, Klosko and Wieshaar (2003) incorporate elements of Beck's (1996) ideas of core belief and schema modes (see next section). Early maladaptive schemas (as with the concept of schema described previously) are thought to develop from the cumulative effects of an interplay between *early* life dysfunctional experiences with others and the child's innate temperament (Young & Behary, 1998).

Early maladaptive schemas develop in childhood, are elaborated throughout one's lifetime and are seen to be self-defeating cognitive patterns that are separate from an individual's maladaptive behaviours. A person's behavioural patterns develop as a *response* to early maladaptive schemas. Early maladaptive schemas, like other schema, are *unconditional* and *highly pervasive*, activated by a large variety of situations and therefore difficult to shift. Negative affect is associated with the activation of schemas. Young et al. (2003) suggest that although early maladaptive schemas may no longer be reality-based, at one point the schema would have been a realistic appraisal of a person's situation. For example, if a child experiences sexual abuse, the child is likely to develop schemas concerned with being harmed and vulnerable, and being mistrusting of others. These schemas are realistic given the child's circumstances, but may not be realistic or adaptive in other situations and may not reflect the nature of new relationships formed at a later stage of life. In adulthood, however, a patient with such beliefs will continue to mistrust others, expecting that he or she will be abused, hurt or humiliated. These early maladaptive schemas are egosyntonic and described as feeling 'right' to the individual and are therefore not questioned, even though there may be evidence suggesting that they are not accurate and that the beliefs themselves are causing more problems and distress to the patient.

Eighteen schemas have been proposed by Young, grouped into five broad categories of unmet emotional needs called 'schema domains' (Young et al., 2003). The domains are concerned with (1) disconnection and rejection, (2) impaired autonomy and performance, (3) impaired limits, (4) other directedness and (5) overvigilance and inhibition. Many of the problems patients with personality disorders present can be conceptualised using these schema. Young goes on to propose that schemas are reinforced through three different behavioural coping styles: schema maintenance, schema avoidance and schema compensation.

Schema maintenance is the process by which information or evidence that would disconfirm the schema is resisted, through cognitive distortions and through self-defeating behavioural patterns. The patient cannot take into account new information that would disconfirm what she believes to be true of herself or other people. Information that would appear to be evidence directly disconfirming a schema is dismissed or discounted and may even appear to be totally ignored. One patient, Julie, believed that she was defective and was unable to recognise when other people were being kind to her such as by offering her compliments. She would assume that other people would not want to befriend someone as 'defective' as her. She would either simply fail to respond to friendly overtures, dismiss others as being insincere, or react in an unfriendly manner by removing herself from the situation as quickly as possible, believing that the person would find out that she was defective if she stayed in the situation for longer. These strategies maintained her 'defectiveness' schema.

Schema avoidance occurs when a combination of schema activation and intense emotions are so unpleasant that individuals automatically attempt to suppress or avoid triggering the schema or the unpleasant affect associated with the schema. Avoidance can operate at a cognitive, affective or behavioural level. One patient with mistrust and abuse schema found trusting people extremely difficult and this included avoiding opening up in sessions through a fear of making herself 'vulnerable'. Many patients also demonstrate overt behavioural avoidance, whereby situations or events are avoided to prevent a re-awakening of a schema or set of schemas. One patient avoided contact with a member of his family who had abused him as a child, thus decreasing the likelihood of re-experiencing distress associated with that individual and the associated memories.

Schema compensation involves overcompensating for a negative schema by acting in the direction opposite to the schema's content. This process can often appear adaptive, as it is a partially successful attempt to challenge early dysfunctional schemas. However, the strategies themselves may create new problems by simply masking the underlying schema, making them difficult to identify and modify. A clinical example comes to mind of a young man in his 30s who presented himself as 'one of the cleverest and most moral of people around', yet he had no hard evidence to demonstrate this might be true, barring a degree in science. Underlying his presentation of grandiosity and criticism of others, and understood only through a careful formulation of his problems, it became apparent that as a child he had been afraid of being regarded as being slower at school than his clever sisters and brothers. He had failed his first attempt at an academic entrance examination to a private school, had been kept back a class year when he did get a place at the school and so on. His early maladaptive schema was around defectiveness and shame. Around the age of 12, he had deliberately developed an interpersonal style of being confident and denigrating people who worked hard or who excelled at school. He may have even bullied other children at school. He began to 'believe' that he was very clever and that others who worked hard at school and who got good marks were 'stupid'.

Schema Modes

Both Beck (1996) and Young et al. (2003) see another aspect of schema as important in personality disorder, and introduce the concept of 'schema modes'. However, Beck and Young vary slightly in their conceptualisation of what a schema mode is. Young et al. (2003) note that Beck (1996) sees a mode as the 'active process' of schema, in terms of the activation of particular programmed behavioural strategies, which involve the affective, motivational and behavioural components. Essentially, Beck's schema mode is very similar to the idea of early maladaptive schemas.

Young et al. (2003, p. 49), by contrast, use the concept of modes to differentiate between 'schemas and coping styles as traits (consistent patterns) and schemas and coping styles as states (shifting patterns of activation)'. A mode represents 'a group of schemata or processes that are currently active for an individual' (Young & Behary, 1998, p. 350).

In this view, a schema mode is the main 'state' we are in at any given moment in time. Young et al. (2003) use the term 'flip' to describe the switching of modes and note that all of us 'flip' from time to time. A mild form of a schema mode expression would be flipping from a lonely to scared mood. Young et al. (2003) identified 10 main modes separated into four main mode categories: 'child', 'dysfunctional coping', 'dysfunctional parent' and 'healthy adult' modes. The concept of schema modes can explain the rapid shifts (likened to dissociation) that many patients with borderline personality disorder present with, when they can rapidly flip into different states. For instance, a patient with borderline personality disorder may rapidly flip between appearing submissive, disconnected and cut off (detached protector mode) one minute to being angry and/or attacking (angry and impulsive child mode) the next.

SUMMARY

Cognitive theories of personality disorder propose that people have innate programmed strategies designed to help people meet their biological goals. Genetic variability means that people vary in the nature of their behavioural strategies. Environmental influences can enhance and dampen these strategies. These innate strategies and environmental influences determine the nature of a person's schema, schema being the 'key' component of personality and personality disorders. People with personality disorders are seen to have maladaptive schema and a limited repertoire of behavioural strategies. This prevents them from obtaining their goals and causes conflict with the social group. Cognitive theory proposes that there are several subsets of schema that can be important in personality disorder: conditional and unconditional beliefs, early maladaptive schema and schema modes.

THE COGNITIVE ANALYTIC MODEL

MARK EVANS

Cognitive analytic therapy (CAT) is a brief, focused therapy devised by Dr Tony Ryle that is now widely used in Britain's National Health Service to treat a variety of psychological problems. Arising from Ryle's original attempts at theoretical integration (Ryle, 1978), CAT pragmatically combines cognitive ideas from personal construct theory (Kelly, 1955) and psychoanalytic concepts (from object relation theory). This integration of theory allows a blending of attention to the detail of both intra-psychic as well as inter-personal mechanisms.

In this section we will briefly explore the development of CAT theoretical concepts which can be divided into: (a) the *procedural sequence model (PSM)* – a proposed explanation for all aim-directed action; (b) the *procedural sequence object relation model (PSORM)* – a theory that embraces personality structure, intrapsychic mechanisms and interpersonal communication; (c) the *multiple self states model (MSSM)* – an explanation for the specific difficulties encountered with people who have severe personality disorder.

Essentially the procedural sequence model was a model of one-person psychology that became subsumed within the procedural sequence object relations model, which describes two roles in relation to each other. The multiple self states model takes these principles further and accounts for the particular problems of personality disorder. To finish, there will be a brief acknowledgement of the influence of a strand of Russian psychology on the CAT conceptualisation of the social formation of the mind.

PROCEDURAL SEQUENCE MODEL (PSM)

The first real landmark in the development of CAT theory was the description of the procedural sequence model (Ryle, 1982). Drawing heavily from information-processing models and personal construct theory, the PSM works on the assumption that people actively 'construct' their realities and relate to the world through 'procedures'. These are sequences of wishes, thoughts, actions, emotions and appraisals, which are deployed in order to achieve an aim. Every human activity can thus be construed in terms of 'procedures', which are seen to be the building blocks of all aim-directed action (see Figure 4.1). Their basic structure is as follows (after Ryle, 1995).

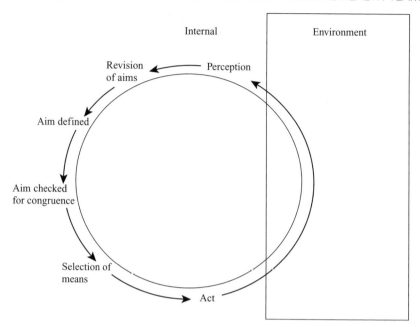

Figure 4.1 Procedural sequence model

- An aim is defined (either in response to an internal or external event).
- The aim is checked for congruence with other aims and values, i.e. for personal meaning.
- An evaluation of the situation is made, including a prediction of one's capacity to affect it, the likely consequences of achieving the aim and a consideration of the range of available means.
- The person acts.
- Consequences of the enactment are evaluated.
- There is confirmation or revision of the aim and the means.

According to the PSM, we construct our perception of reality through the lenses of our procedures, which tend to be self-perpetuating and resistant to change. Problems arise for the individual when they continue to engage in procedures that are self-limiting, ineffective or harmful.

Ryle described three categories of neurotic or faulty procedures. *Traps* arise from negative assumptions that generate acts producing consequences that reinforce the assumptions; the person acting within a *dilemma* does so as though available action or possible roles were limited to polarised alternatives or false dichotomies, usually without being aware that this is the case; *snags* (subtle negative aspects of gains) occur when appropriate goals or roles are abandoned on the assumption that others would oppose them or as if they were forbidden or dangerous. The individual may be more or less aware that he acts in this way and may not relate this to feelings such as guilt.

PROCEDURAL SEQUENCE OBJECT RELATIONS MODEL (PSORM)

In his 1985 paper 'Cognitive theory, object relations and the self', Ryle introduced a distinctly interpersonal dimension to procedures culminating in the procedural sequence object relations model (Ryle, 1985). Here, the concept of reciprocal roles (RR) was introduced, whereby the prediction of one's actions was emphasised in terms of the response of others. Reciprocal roles are seen to develop more on the basis of actual lived experience of early relationships rather than arising from innate instinctual drives, setting CAT theoretically close to Fairbairn (1952) and an interpretation of his work by Thomas Ogden (1983) and apart from Klein (1935). Historically, an infant learns to enact both parental and child roles, to others and to the self. Hence each relationship teaches two reciprocal roles. A child who is nurtured and cared for not only learns the reciprocal role of being nurtured and cared for but also the role of being nurturing and caring, as may be demonstrated with others and in play.

Figure 4.2 shows a schematic representation of how two people's procedures impact on each other. Memories and expectations of and attitudes towards the other will influence each stage of the procedural sequence, including the likely response, so that one person occupying a particular role tends to elicit a reciprocal role in the other. In this way, the concept of procedures can be broadened to describe reciprocal role procedures. For example, a man who sees the world as a dangerous place and full of potential persecutors may act in a way that elicits actual persecution from others, which confirms and reinforces his sense of the world as being a dangerous place.

The practice of describing the core of someone's personality in terms of a set of reciprocal roles has been adopted in CAT as a heuristic device in order to link and explain a range of behaviours. In therapy, the map of reciprocal roles may be acknowledged as not representing the whole of the person (including the healthier aspects), but rather is seen as a (hopefully) accurate description of problematic reciprocal role procedures. Figure 4.3 depicts an example of the predominant reciprocal roles found in a person who is well enough functioning and does not have significant personality difficulties. Notice the variety of reciprocal roles and their relatively benign nature.

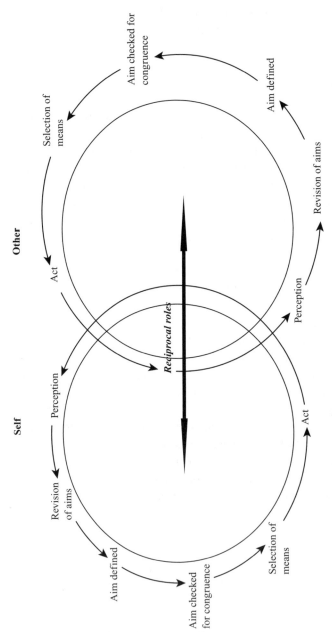

Figure 4.2 Procedural sequence object relations model showing formation of reciprocal roles

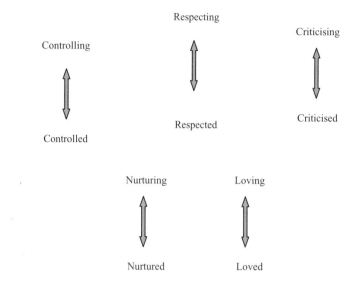

Figure 4.3 Reciprocal role repertoire: healthily functioning/neurotic person

When constructing the core reciprocal roles, the therapist draws on a range of data including the patient's history, current patterns of self-management and of relating to others and the emerging transference and counter-transference responses. Sometimes this involves hypothesising about what roles might have been replaced by avoidant, defensive or symptomatic procedures. Once established, the stability of such procedures is explained by the confirming reciprocations of the enacted role that are usually elicited from others, leaving the core repertoire unchanged. This explanation offers a more general understanding of the stability of personality. In this way it is suggested that one's repertoire of reciprocal roles is the basis of relating to others (one role being played, the other elicited) and also of self-management. If I have strong criticising/criticised reciprocal roles as part of my personality make-up, then I will not only enact (or have the potential to enact) a criticising role towards others but also towards myself.

THE MULTIPLE SELF STATES MODEL (MSSM)

Ryle's experience over many years of working with more seriously disturbed patients revealed real difficulties in understanding and reformulating when there was rapid or confusing movement between reciprocal roles. As a result he formulated a new theory of borderline personality, which has been named the *multiple self states model*. Horowitz's (1979) notion of 'states of mind' was acknowledged, whilst the concept of 'states' was broadened to incorporate not only mood but also the dominant object relations and defensive structures employed by the subject. Ryle suggested that 'states of mind' should really be termed 'states of being' and should in addition encompass behaviour. Also crucially, 'states of mind' only refer to one pole of a reciprocal role pairing. By diagrammatically depicting 'states' with their corresponding reciprocal roles in place, it becomes possible to work interpersonally with more potential for therapeutic change. An example of this would be with a patient who is easily in touch with the victim (child-derived) reciprocal role but who needs help in recognising his/her own actual or potential enactment of (parent-derived) persecuting or abusing roles.

Under normal circumstances, individuals appear to move between their reciprocal role pairings in response to changes in their current activity, relationships and social context. Here reciprocal role patterns consist of mutually compatible procedures and transitions between them are smooth and appropriate. When changes between reciprocal roles are experienced as being more abrupt, confusing and uncomfortable for the patient and those present, especially when they appear unprovoked, it is more helpful to think of movement between dissociated 'self states'. Rather than representing random variations or the deliberate sowing of confusion, these movements characteristic of borderline patients can be seen as the alternate dominance of a limited range of contrasting role patterns, each having stable and recognisable characteristics.

In CAT theory, a 'self state' is akin to a dissociated reciprocal role pairing whilst a 'state' represents one pole of that reciprocal role. In borderline patients the range of procedures from each self state tends to be limited and narrow and can often be described in terms of a single reciprocal role pattern. Once the different self states have been identified and transitions between them monitored, a self states sequential diagram (SSSD) can be constructed. This will depict how procedures are generated from different self states and how some procedures may lead to 'state shifts' (an abrupt movement between self states).

Whilst the multiple self states model has been used to explain the specific symptomatology of borderline personality disorder (Ryle, 1997), the descriptions of developmental arrest could as well apply to other types of personality disorder. It is also worth remembering that different types of personality disorder often co-exist. The model is based on the proposition that borderline pathology can be understood in terms of damage (from both trauma and deprivation) affecting three levels of development.

Level 1. The restriction or distortion of the reciprocal role repertoire. The reciprocal roles acquired through such experience are typically those of neglecting, abandoning and abusing to emotionally deprived, ashamed and either rebellious or crushed. These patterns are frequently re-enacted with others together with procedures resulting from repressed impulses, e.g. perfectionist, passive, submissive, placatory or avoidant behaviours.

Level 2. The incomplete development or disruption of higher order procedures responsible for mobilising, connecting and sequencing level 1 procedures. The function of these meta-procedures is connection: they serve to mobilise and link the reciprocal role repertoire of level 1, therefore constituting an important aspect of the basic structure of the self. Disruption can occur at this level by incoherent, neglectful and contradictory experiences or by trauma-induced dissociation (often secondary to physical or sexual abuse).

Level 3. The incomplete development or disruption of self-reflection. This function is inhibited by a narrowed capacity for attention and deficient vocabulary for emotional language, as well as the discontinuity of experience and memory consequent upon level 2 dissociations.

Figure 4.4 depicts a typical RR diagram for a person with borderline personality disorder. Notice both the intensity of the reciprocal roles and

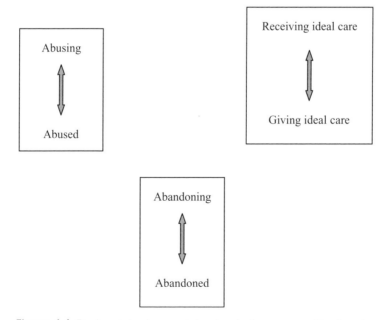

Figure 4.4 Reciprocal role repertoire: borderline personality disorder

also the lack of variety of the repertoire. Boxes have been placed around the RR pairings to indicate the degree of dissociation involved as the patient can feel a confusing disruption in continuity of experience when moving between them. This confusion is also felt by others present. The seeking/ giving special care reciprocal roles represent a compensatory reaction to neglect or trauma and may be powerfully craved in fantasy or enacted with others, usually in a way that cannot be sustained.

THEORETICAL INFLUENCE OF VYGOTSKY AND BAKHTIN

In the early 1990s a discourse developed between Mikael Leiman and Ryle in which the ideas of the Russian psychologist Vygotsky and his student, Bakhtin, were introduced to elaborate a more social and culturally based understanding of the development of personality (Leiman, 1997; Ryle, 1997). Ryle and Leiman have argued for the central importance of signs such as words and gestures in human relating developed via 'joint sign-mediated activity' between care-giver and infant (Leiman, 1992, 1994, 1995; Ryle, 1991, 1995). There is only space to acknowledge this development here but the interested reader is referred to Ryle and Kerr (2002) or Hepple and Sutton (2004) for a useful overview.

THE DIALECTICAL BEHAVIOURAL MODEL

JANET FEIGENBAUM

Dialectical behavioural therapy (DBT) was originally developed for the treatment of women diagnosed with borderline personality disorder (BPD) in the community (Linehan, 1993a, 1993b; Linehan, Armstrong, Suarez, Allmon & Heard, 1991). Since then, DBT has been further modified and evaluated for use with patients with co-morbid substance abuse (Linehan et al., 1999), for an eating disorder population (Telch, Agras & Linehan, 2001), and for use in in-patient settings (Bohus et al., 2000). However, it remains primarily a body of theory relating specifically to the treatment of BPD.

DBT shares many of the fundamental features of cognitive behavioural therapy (Beck et al., 1990; Davidson, 2000). Unique to DBT, however, is the focus on 'dialectics' (see below), an emphasis on the role of validation (and invalidation) and a comprehensive structure to the therapy that supports both patients and therapists (as described in Chapter 5). Like classical behaviour therapy, DBT places an emphasis on the importance of learning theory for understanding the transactional relationship between individuals and their environment in the development and maintenance of the problematic behaviours associated with BPD.

DBT conceives BPD as caused by a combination of specific deficits of psychological function and distorted motivations. DBT aims to offer a range of change-enhancing strategies (contingency management, exposure-based procedures, problem-solving, skills training and cognitive restructuring) combined with an array of motivation-focused interventions (validation, mindfulness, a focus on distress tolerance). The comprehensive quality of the intervention is rooted in the assumption of a pervasive skills deficit. Skills deficits include (1) the capacity to regulate emotions, (2) the ability to tolerate emotional distress, (3) ineffectiveness in managing interpersonal conflicts and (4) lack of adequate capacity to control attention in order to 'skilfully participate in the moment'. The enhancement of skills is not viewed as sufficient, as learning experiences are assumed to have interfered with the patients' motivation to change. A further part of the model is the assumption that skill generalisation will only occur if the skill deficits are addressed in the context of the patient's natural environment.

BPD AS A DISORDER OF EMOTIONAL DYSREGULATION

During childhood and adolescence, we are expected to learn how to manage our emotional experiences. The DBT model suggests that individuals with BPD have learnt dysfunctional means of managing or coping with their intense emotional experiences. Many patients with BPD use deliberate self-harm or suicide attempts as a means of regulating their emotional experiences; others have developed means of avoiding their intense emotional responses such as through substance abuse or dissociation. Thus the primary focus of DBT is on reducing these dysfunctional behaviours and increasing functional means of modulating emotional responses.

When in a state of emotional arousal, our cognitive processing systems cease to function effectively. This leads to difficulties with effective problem-solving, poor access to our memories for previous coping strategies and limited capacity to consider the consequences of our actions. This cognitive confusion during emotional arousal can then lead to behavioural dysregulation, in which the individual acts impulsively to reduce the emotional intensity of the moment. However, in the longer term the individual may experience further emotional arousal as a result of the impulsive act. For example, the use of sexual encounters to reduce loneliness or self-disgust may be followed by feelings of shame or increased self-loathing. The combination of lowered cognitive problem-solving capacity and impulsivity often underlies suicide attempts and acts of self-harm. Interpersonal dysregulation is characterised in BPD by extreme efforts to avoid abandonment or rejection, and unstable relationships. When feelings of rejection are aroused, the individual may respond with anger, which in turn may lead to further rejection by others. Once again, emotional and interpersonal dysregulation comes to generate a vicious cycle.

INVALIDATING ENVIRONMENTS

DBT gives a crucial developmental role to the invalidating childhood environment in which erratic and inappropriate responses are given by insensitive and thoughtless caregivers – a child who expresses anger may be dismissed; one who says she did her best is told that she did not. Persistent divergence between inner experience and outer responses, the invalidating environment, not only leads to emotional dysregulation but also results in an uncertainty in later life about the validity of inner experience and the accuracy of one's interpretation of events.

One of the fundamental tasks of parenting is to assist children with developing an understanding of their emotional experiences, a means of communicating these experiences and the means to manage or modify these experiences. Invalidating families fail to provide the child with these key skills. The ability to correctly identify our emotions allows us to select the appropriate cognitive or behaviour skill to modify the experience. There is considerable evidence linking the experience of early neglect to later BPD (Zanarini et al., 2000).

The most obvious example of an invalidating environment is childhood abuse. In sexual abuse the child is treated as an object for the gratification of others, without attention to the child's emotional or physical needs. Often the perpetrator will deliberately further undermine the child's sense of reality in order to ensure that the family secret is not revealed. Sexual abuse may also be accompanied by emotional neglect or physical abuse, which further invalidates the child's emotional experiences. Abuse is present in the histories of about 66–75 per cent of patients with BPD (Johnson, Cohen, Brown, Smailes & Bernstein, 1999).

Individuals with BPD are sensitive to abandonment and rejection. Feelings of impending abandonment, and disillusionment, among individuals with BPD (Gunderson, 1996) are likely to have arisen from the impact of early childhood experiences of abuse or neglect on the individual's sense of self-worth, as well as their experience of emotional abandonment by the primary caregivers. In many cases this may include physical abandonment through the death of a parent, parental separation or removal into care. The individual with BPD is assumed to become vigilant of rejection, looking for signals of abandonment. One of the problematic consequences of an expectation of abandonment is the testing of boundaries and relationships. The individual who expects to be rejected may seek to find the limits of acceptable behaviour in order to identify 'when they will be rejected'.

Invalidating environments often lead to self-invalidation of one's own emotional experiences (i.e. 'I shouldn't feel this way' or 'It is shameful to feel this way') or the avoidance of emotional experiences (i.e. dissociation; substance misuse). Self-invalidation reduces the individual's capacity to identify and modulate their emotional experiences.

DIALECTICS

'Dialectics' are a concept grounded in philosophy and science. In the context of DBT dialectics imply that analysis of small components, or individual parts, of a system is of limited value and the part needs to be viewed in relation to the whole. In this way DBT differs from standard behavioural treatment, which focuses on breaking down the whole into components. There are three main tenets of dialectics: the inter-connectedness of the world; that truth can be found as a synthesis of differing views; that change is inevitable and constant. DBT uses these principles to guide understanding of the experiences and behaviours of patients with BPD and to structure the therapy.

The concept of *inter-connectedness* allows us to understand more fully the importance of taking a 'whole system' approach to identifying and managing change. When an individual makes changes in their behaviour, the responses from the social network may support or impede progress. The DBT therapist using dialectic understanding may tackle a specific problem from a skills-based perspective but relate it to areas of the patient's life; he may take the attitude that learning new skills may on its own not be enough; he may recognise that well used skills may need to be lost as others are learned. The actions and reactions of patients will affect the therapist, who will in turn affect the patient. When we address a painful issue with our patients, many respond with anger (storming out, complaints) or silence, both of which may result in the therapist moving to a different issue, thus colluding with the patient in avoiding painful discussions. From the learning theory perspective, the patient punishes the therapist for addressing a painful topic, and the therapist rewards the patient for this punishing behaviour by moving away from the painful subject.

The second principle is that individual reality is comprised of opposing forces, a thesis and antithesis, which are not static. Reality is viewed as being in a state of continuous flux. The borderline patient is stuck within polarities without synthesis, the most fundamental of which is accepting herself as she is and recognising a need for change. The resolution of these tensions is found in *synthesis*, which in itself may create further dialectical tensions. Linehan (1993a) identifies a number of dialectics experienced by patients with BPD. The process of therapy itself is a dialectic, which inevitably leads to a focus in DBT on the relationship between the patient and therapist. Throughout therapy patients often experience a desire to remain 'the same' as this is recognisable and 'safe', yet therapy itself is about change. The patient may oscillate between these two poles. At the 'safe' end, the patient will resist suggestions for change; at the 'change' end the patient may become overwhelmed and exhausted. The synthesis will lie in recognising the dialectical tension and managing change in steps.

The third principle of dialectics is that of *constant change*. Therapy is a process of change, and therefore the therapy and the therapist must continually adapt to the changes occurring. For example, in the early stages of therapy, the emphasis may be on acceptance and understanding, 'the patient is doing the best they can, given their experiences and skills'. However, as therapy progresses the balance may shift to an emphasis on change as new skills are acquired. For the patient, getting what is desired may be as problematic as being denied it; learning new skills that lead to improvement may invalidate their previous understanding and expectations of self and others.

LEARNING THEORY

The principles of learning theory state that a behaviour will continue or increase when reinforced (positively through associated reward or negatively through reduction or cessation of contingent adverse experience), will reduce or cease when punished and will slowly extinguish when previous reinforcement is removed. The DBT model emphasises the identification of stimuli that trigger dysfunctional behaviours through previously learned associations and the contingencies that shape the frequency and continuation of a behaviour. These contingencies may be internal to the individual (i.e. feelings of relief, reduction in anxiety) or external (i.e. increased attention, praise). Contingencies present in the environment may be complex. For example, admission to hospital after a threat of self-harm may be both positively reinforcing (feeling cared for and nurtured) or negatively reinforcing (less lonely, less stressed, less anxious about personal safety) as well as punishing (loss of privacy or freedom). The function of behaviours will depend upon the range and relative strengths of these contingencies. Thus, the DBT model emphasises the interaction between the actions of the individual and the response of the social environment in the development and maintenance of dysfunctional behaviours.

LINEHAN'S BIOPSYCHOSOCIAL MODEL OF BPD

Linehan's (1993a) biopsychosocial model provides an integration of the influences considered above. It suggests that BPD is primarily a dysfunction of the emotional regulation system, which is part of an inter-dependent set of systems involving cognition, behaviour, inter-personal communication and self-identity. Arousal in any one or more of these systems will result in dysregulation in the others. The relationship between the individual and the environment can modify levels of dysregulation, both increasing and decreasing.

Developmentally, when the environment is invalidating of a child a number of problems arise. The child fails to learn how to label emotional states, thus making managing them difficult. For example, maltreated toddlers have difficulty in learning to use internal state words (Beeghly and Cicchetti, 1994) or organise emotional reactions against a background of inter-personal conflict (Toth, Maughan, Manly, Spagnola and Cicchetti, 2002). In failing to acknowledge the emotional distress of children, the parents may undermine the acquisition of the key skills in regulating emotion or tolerating distress. Invalidating environments can lead the individual to distrust their own emotional reactions to events, resulting in self-invalidation. The individual is left with a complex and intense emotional internal world in which they have no skills to understand or manage their experiences. Yet they are able to observe that other people appear to be able to cope with their emotional experiences and to manage their lives. The child comes to believe that other people are able to solve life's problems relatively easily and that s/he is alone in feeling incapable of solving life's problems. In adulthood this may present as issues of poor self-efficacy, dependency or excessive help-seeking behaviour. Finally, invalidating environments may lead to fears of abandonment and rejection, which influence the individual's ability to sustain positive, trusting relationships.

CONCLUSION

In this chapter we have provided a brief overview of four ways of thinking about some of the key psychological aspects of personality disorders. These four perspectives inform distinct ways of working with patients, as we shall see in Chapter 5. In concluding this chapter, we would like to emphasise that the theoretical ideas presented here should not be viewed as competing, or as mutually exclusive. Although there are certainly differences in the models presented, it will be apparent that there is also considerable agreement. Much of what at first sight appears to be differences may be seen on examination to be differences in language and emphasis. We would suggest that these accounts are far more complementary than contradictory. It is important to remember that people who may attract a diagnosis of 'person-ality disorder' are *persons* – individuals with complex cognitive, affective, interpersonal and behavioural characteristics that no single account can hope to understand fully. In a field where little is known for certain, and where providing a responsive and effective service to patients with complex needs is often difficult, there is much we can learn from each of these accounts, and each can be appreciated as offering something of value.

REFERENCES

American Psychiatric Association (APA). (1994). *Diagnostic and statistical manual of mental disorders* (4th ed.). Washington, DC: Author.

Beck, A. T. (1996). Beyond belief: A theory of modes, personality, and psychopathology. In P. Salkovskis (Ed.), *Frontiers of cognitive therapy* (pp. 1–25). New York: Guildford.

Beck, A. T., Freeman, A. & Associates. (1990). *Cognitive therapy of personality disorders.* New York: Guilford.

Beck, A. T., Freeman, A., Davis, D. D. & Associates. (2004). *Cognitive therapy of personality disorders* (2nd ed.). New York: Guilford.

Beeghly, M. & Cicchetti, D. (1994). Child maltreatment, attachment, and the self system: Emergence of an internal state lexicon in toddlers at high social risk. *Development and Psychopathology, 6*, 5–30.

Bohus, M., Haaf, B., Stiglmayr, C., Pohl, U., Boehme, R. & Linehan, M. (2000). Evaluation of inpatient dialectical–behavioral therapy for borderline personality disorder – A prospective study. *Behaviour Research and Therapy, 38*, 875–887.

Bowlby, J. (1988). *A secure base: clinical applications of attachment theory.* London: Tavistock/Routledge.

Brooke, R. (1994). Assessment for psychotherapy: Clinical indicators of self cohesion. *British Journal of Psychotherapy, 10*, 317–330.

Cottraux, J. C. & Blackburn, I. M. (2001). Cognitive therapy. In J. Livesley (Ed.), *Handbook of personality disorders: Theory, research and treatment* (pp. 377–399). London: Guildford.

Davidson, K. M. (2000). *Cognitive therapy for personality disorders: A guide for clinicians.* London: Arnold (Hodder).

Fairbairn, B. D. (1952). *Psychoanalytic studies of the personality.* London: Tavistock.

Fonagy, P. (1991). Thinking about thinking: Some clinical and theoretical considerations in the treatment of a borderline patient. *International Journal of Psychoanalysis, 72*, 639–656.

Fonagy, P. (1995). Playing with reality: The development of psychic reality and its malfunction in borderline patients. *International Journal of Psychoanalysis, 76*, 39–44.

Fonagy, P. (1999). Memory and therapeutic action. *International Journal of Psychoanalysis*, *80*, 215–223.

Fonagy, P. (2001). *Attachment Theory and Psychoanalysis*. New York: Other.

Fonagy, P. & Target, M. (1996). Playing with reality II: Theory of mind and the normal development of psychic reality. *International Journal of Psychoanalysis*, *77*, 217–233.

Gergely, G. & Watson, J. (1996). The social biofeedback theory of parental affect-mirroring: The development of emotional self-awareness and self-control in infancy. *International Journal of Psychoanalysis*, *77*, 1181–1212.

Gunderson, J. G. (1996). The borderline patient's intolerance of aloneness: Insecure attachments and therapist availability. *American Journal of Psychiatry*, *153*, 752–758.

Hepple, J. & Sutton, L. (Eds). (2004). *Cognitive analytic therapy and later life. A new perspective on old age*. Hove: Brunner-Routledge.

Hobson, P. R. (1993). *Autism and the development of mind*. Hove: Erlbaum.

Hobson, P. R. (2002). *The cradle of thought*. London: MacMillan.

Holmes, J. (1997). Attachment, autonomy, intimacy: Some clinical implications of attachment theory. *British Journal of Medical Psychology*, *70*, 231–248.

Horowitz, M. J. (1979). *States of mind*. New York: Plenum.

Johnson, J. G., Cohen, P., Brown, J., Smailes, E. & Bernstein, D. P. (1999). Childhood maltreatment increases risk for personality disorders during early adulthood. *Archives of General Psychiatry*, *56*, 600–605.

Kelly, G. A. (1955). *The psychology of personal constructs*. New York: Norton.

Kernberg, O. (1967). Borderline personality organisation. *Journal of the American Psychoanalytic Association*, *15*, 641–685.

Klein, M. (1935). A contribution to the psychogenesis of manic-depressive states. In *Contributions to psychoanalysis* (pp. 282–310). New York: McGraw-Hill.

Kohut, H. (1971). *The analysis of the self*. New York: International Universities Press.

Kohut, H. & Wolf, E. S. (1978). The disorders of the self and their treatment. *International Journal of Psychoanalysis*, *59*, 413–425.

Leiman, M. (1992). The concept of sign in the work of Vygotsky, Winnicott and Bakhtin: Further integration of object relations theory and activity theory. *British Journal of Medical Psychology*, *65*, 209–221.

Leiman, M. (1994). Projective identification as early joint action sequences: A Vygotskian addendum to the procedural sequence object relations model. *British Journal of Medical Psychology*, *67*, 97–106.

Leiman, M. (1995). Early development. In A. Ryle (Ed.), *Cognitive analytic therapy: Developments in theory and practice* (pp. 103–121). Chichester: Wiley.

Leiman, M. (1997). Procedures as dialogical sequences: A revised version of the fundamental concept in cognitive analytic therapy. *British Journal of Medical Psychology*, *70*, 193–207.

Linehan, M. M. (1993a). *Cognitive–behavioral treatment of borderline personality*. New York: Guilford.

Linehan, M. M. (1993b). *Skills training manual for treating borderline personality disorder*. New York: Guildford.

Linehan, M. M, Armstrong, H. E., Suarez, A., Allmon, D. & Heard H. L. (1991). Cognitive behavioral treatment of chronically parasuicidal borderline patients. *Archives of General Psychiatry*, *48*, 1060–1064.

Linehan, M. M., Schmidt, H., Dimeff, L. A., Craft, J. C., Kanter, J. & Comtois, K. A. (1999). Dialectical behavioral therapy for patients with borderline personality disorder and drug-dependence. *American Journal of Addiction*. *8*, 279–292.

Meares, R. (1995). Episodic memory, trauma and the narrative of self. *Contemporary Psychoanalysis. 31*, 541–555.

Meares, R. (1999). The 'adualistic' representation of trauma: On malignant internalization. *American Journal of Psychotherapy, 53*, 392–402.

Meares, R. (2000). *Intimacy and alienation*. London: Routledge.

Meares, R., Stevenson, J. & Gordon, E. (1999). A Jacksonian and biopsychosocial hypothesis concerning borderline and related phenomena. *Australian and New Zealand Journal of Psychiatry, 33*, 831–840.

Nelson, K. (1992). Emergence of autobiographical memory at four. *Human Development, 35*, 172–177.

Ogden, T, H. (1983). The concept of internal object relations. *International Journal of Psychoanalysis, 64*, 227–241.

Ryle, A. (1978). A common language for the psychotherapies. *British Journal of Psychiatry, 132*, 585–594.

Ryle, A. (1982). *Psychotherapy: A cognitive integration of theory and practice*. London: Academic.

Ryle, A. (1985). Cognitive theory, object relations and the self. *British Journal of Medical Psychology, 58*, 1–7.

Ryle, A. (1991). Object relations and activity theory: A proposed link by way of the procedural sequence model. *British Journal of Medical Psychology, 64*, 307–316.

Ryle, A. (Ed.). (1995). *Cognitive analytic therapy: developments in theory and practice*. Chichester: Wiley.

Ryle, A. (1997). *Cognitive analytic therapy and borderline personality disorder: The model and the method*. Chichester: Wiley.

Ryle, A. & Kerr, I. (2002). *Introducing cognitive analytic therapy*. Chichester: Wiley.

Schacter, D. (1992). Understanding implicit memory. *American Psychologist, 47*, 559–569.

Stern, D. N. (1985). *The interpersonal world of the infant: A view from psychoanalysis and developmental psychology*. New York: Basic.

Stern, D. N. (1994). One way to build a clinically relevant baby. *Infant Mental Health Journal, 15*, 36–54.

Stern, D. N., Sander, L. W., Nahum, J. P., Harrison, A. M., Lyons-Ruth, K., Morgan, A. C., Bruschweiler-Stern, N. & Tronick, E. Z. (1998). Non-interpretive mechanisms in psycho-analytic therapy. *International Journal of Psychoanalysis, 79*, 903–921.

Telch, C. F., Agras, W. S. & Linehan, M. M. (2001). Dialectical behavioral therapy for binge eating disorder. *Journal of Consulting and Clinical Psychology, 69*, 1061–1065.

Toth, S. L., Maughan, A., Manly, J. T., Spagnola, M. & Cicchetti, D. (2002). The relative efficacy of two interventions in altering maltreated preschool children's representational models: Implications for attachment theory. *Developmental Psychopathology, 14*, 877–908.

Williams, J. M. G., Watts, F. N., MacLeod, C. & Mathews, A. (1997). *Cognitive psychology and emotional disorders* (2nd ed.). Chichester: Wiley.

Winnicott, D. (1958/1965). The capacity to be alone. In *The maturational processes and the facilitating environment*. New York: International Universities Press.

Winnicott, D. (1960/1965). Ego distinction in terms of true and false self. In *The maturational processes and the facilitating environment*. New York: International Universities Press.

Winnicott, D. (1967/1971). Mirror-role of mother in child development. In *Playing and reality*. London: Tavistock.

Wolf, E. S. (1994). Varieties of disorders of the self. *British Journal of Psychotherapy, 11*, 198–208.

Young, J. E. (1990). *Cognitive therapy for personality disorders: A schemas-focused approach*. Florida: Professional Resource Exchange.

Young, J. E. & Behary, W. T. (1998). Schema-focused therapy for personality disorders. In N. Tarrier, A. Wells & G. Haddock (Eds), *Treating complex cases: The cognitive behavioural therapy approach*. Chichester: Wiley.

Young, J. E., Klosko, J. S., Weishaar, M. E. (2003). *Schema therapy: a practitioner's guide*. New York: Guilford.

Zanarini, M. C., Frankenburg, F. R., Reich, D. B., Marino, M. F., Lewis, R. E., Williams, A. A. & Khera, G. S. (2000). Biparental failure in the childhood experiences of borderline patients. *Journal of Personality Disorder, 14*, 264–273.

5

Psychological Therapies for Personality Disorder

JIM MOOREY

KATE DAVIDSON

MARK EVANS

JANET FEIGENBAUM

In the previous chapter we presented an outline of the psychological theories behind four approaches to therapy for patients with personality disorders. In this chapter we will consider the implications of these ideas for clinical practice. The four models of therapy presented here have developed specific ways of working, that are based on rationales derived from the theoretical perspectives outlined in Chapter 4. Taken together, the two chapters provide an introduction to the theory and practice of four of the most widely employed models of psychotherapy for patients with personality disorders currently available in the United Kingdom.

PSYCHODYNAMIC–INTERPERSONAL THERAPY

JIM MOOREY

In the previous chapter we reviewed personality disorders within a developmental framework, in particular the development of the sense of self. From this perspective we can regard many aspects of the presentation of

Personality Disorder and Community Mental Health Teams: A Practitioner's Guide. Edited by
M. J. Sampson, R. A. McCubbin and P. Tyrer. © 2006 John Wiley & Sons, Ltd.

personality disorders as manifestations of disturbances in the continuity, coherence, agency and affectivity of the sense of self. In this section we will consider an approach to therapy based on this perspective.

THE CONVERSATIONAL MODEL: BACKGROUND

The approach to therapy presented here was termed the conversational model by Robert Hobson (Hobson, 1985). The model was developed by Hobson in association with his colleague Russell Meares as 'a way of understanding and treating the problem of disrupted personality development.' (Meares, 2000, p. XI). The model integrates a range of influences from psychodynamic, interpersonal and existential–humanistic traditions. The heart of the approach emphasises that *persons are not things*, and that the essential focus of therapy is *interpersonal experience*. Psychotherapy is seen as primarily a human encounter, rather than a technical procedure (Margison, 2002; Moorey & Guthrie, 2003; Meares, 2004).

From the earliest publications (e.g. Hobson, 1971) there has been a strong commitment to empirical investigation of the process and outcome of the model. Within a research context, the alternative name *psychodynamic interpersonal therapy* (PIT) has been adopted since 1994. Evidence for the effectiveness of the model with different patient populations include somatisation (Creed et al., 2003; Guthrie, Creed, Dawson & Tomenson, 1991; Hamilton et al., 2000), depression (Barkham et al., 1996; Shapiro et al., 1994), treatment resistant psychiatric out patients (Guthrie et al., 1999), self-harm (Guthrie et al., 2001), and patients presenting with borderline personality disorder (Meares, Stevenson & Comerford, 1999; Stevenson & Meares, 1992, 1999). In comparison with cognitive–behaviour therapy (CBT), outcome has been found to be broadly equivalent (Barkham et al., 1996; Shapiro & Firth, 1987; Shapiro et al., 1994). Currently, a randomised controlled trial is underway comparing PIT with supportive therapy for patients with concurrent Cluster B personality disorders and Axis I disorders, presenting at two psychotherapy centres. The treatment durations in these studies range from four sessions (treatment for self-harm) to twice weekly for one year (borderline personality). From the beginning there has been a commitment to developing and evaluating methods of training in the model (Guthrie et al., 2004; Mackay, West, Moorey, Guthrie & Margison, 2001; Margison, 2002).

The basic elements of the practice of the conversational model include:

- use of statements rather than questions
- use of language of mutuality: 'I' and 'we'

- a negotiating style
- basing comments on cues presented by the patient
- focusing on feelings
- focusing on immediate experience: the 'here and now' of the therapeutic relationship
- use of *understanding hypotheses* (an expression of empathy, a statement about what the patient may be experiencing at the present moment), *linking hypotheses* (statements noting patterns, parallels or connections between aspects of therapy at different times and between aspects of therapy and the patient's past and present), *explanatory hypotheses* (what is understood traditionally as a psychodynamic interpretation: a statement that introduces possible reasons for, or causes of, disturbances in experience and relationships, typically in terms of unconscious processes)
- use of metaphor.

Early in therapy the conversational model emphasises the importance of establishing a secure treatment frame, and developing a therapeutic alliance (as described in Chapter 12 of this volume). In terms of the general style of therapy, the conversational model has been strongly influenced by what may be regarded as the 'maternal' orientation of Winnicott and Kohut, hence emphasises the adaptive and developmental needs of patients. Given this 'maternal' emphasis, therapists working within the model are trained to be alert to the kinds of difficulty noted by Kernberg and colleagues (Kernberg, Selzer, Koenigsberg, Carr & Applebaum, 1989) – in particular, the counter-transference pull towards enacting the role of a 'good mother' that can lead to the avoidance of necessary limit setting and confrontation.

In a brief review such as this we can only consider general principles of the approach. Specific details of the technique can be found in a range of publications, in particular those by Hobson (1985) and Meares (2000).

THE CONVERSATIONAL MODEL: THE RESTORATION OF SELF

'The self arises and remains between people' (Hobson 1971, p. 97).
'I can only find myself in and between me and my fellows in conversation' (Hobson, 1985, p. 135).

Personality disorders may be conceptualised in terms of disruption to the sense of self. One important factor contributing to such disruption appears to be deficits in care that we may describe generally as forms of *devaluing misattunement*. As noted, deficits in the care-giving environment impact upon key psychological functions that underpin the sense of self, in particular mentalisation and memory. Prominent features of the presentation of most personality disorders may be understood as manifestations of the loss of, or reduction of, mentalising capacity, and the activation and intrusion of a traumatic memory system.

Hobson (1985) has emphasised that psychotherapy involves a process of 'symbolic transformation' in which *conversation* becomes both the reflection of, and vehicle for, change. As Meares notes, 'The aim of therapy is to restore, generate, and potentiate that particular kind of consciousness that we are calling self. . . Particular states of consciousness cannot be conceived in isolation. They arise in the context of particular forms of relatedness, which are necessarily mediated by conversation' (Meares, 2004, p. 51). Hence, the aim of this approach is to potentiate a particular experience of self, to restore a sense of self that has been lost or compromised by traumatic experience, by means of a particular form of conversation.

This process of restoring the sense of self, that is, the process of psychotherapeutic change, has two main aspects:

1. *Facilitating mentalisation, or self-reflection.* The restoration of the experience of self as object necessarily involves facilitating self-reflective activity, that is, encouraging mentalising capacities. As Fonagy notes, 'The symbolic representation of mental states may be seen as a pre-requisite for a sense of identity, they form the core of a sense of psychological self' (Fonagy and Target, 2005, p. 194). The conversational model emphasizes that it is the facilitation of a particular form of self-reflective activity that is crucial. Psychotherapy aims to facilitate a form of conversation that is associative, non-linear, feeling-based and meta-phorical; a conversation, involving 'a language of the heart', that is 'intimate' rather than 'alienated' (Hobson, 1985, pp. 17–29; Meares, 2000, pp. 121–138).

2. *Facilitating integration of the traumatic memory system.* While the first aspect may be thought of as the facilitation of a *process* – mentalisation, this second aspect may be seen as a transformation of the *content* of the primary and secondary representations of self and other. The traumatic memory system, which may be triggered by cues that in some way resemble the original trauma, includes cognitive, affective, physiological and behavioural aspects: '. . .unthinkable thoughts and feelings that cannot be felt intrude into consciousness as unaccountable and often unnameable states of fear, despair, loneliness, dread and the like and intrude into the body as psychosomatic disorders' (Thomas Ogden, foreword to Meares, 2000, p. x). The integration into the objective sense of self of the sequestered traumatic memory system does not

involve the recovery of memories, as these are likely to be represented in non-declarative memory systems. However, the consequences of their activation can be symbolically represented if they can be reflected upon. Further, the content of primary representations – implicit procedural knowledge of relationships – can change as a consequence of the quality of the therapeutic relationship, particularly as manifested in 'moments of meeting' (Hobson, 1985; Stern et al., 1998).

We may see the work of therapy as developing sufficient self-reflective capacity to assimilate the traumatic memory system through the process of mentalisation. The goal of therapy is therefore to *mentalise the traumatic memory system.* It is important to note that facilitating mentalisation and the integration of the traumatic memory system is unlikely to be accomplished by giving instructions or advice. Where the capacity for self-reflection has been defensively or developmentally inhibited, the restoration or reinstatement of this capacity may be facilitated by a process analogous to the attunement of a care-giver.

Thinking of psychotherapy in this way owes a great debt to Donald Winnicott, who wrote 'This glimpse of the baby's and child's seeing the self in the mother's face and afterwards in the mirror, gives a way of looking at analysis and the psychotherapeutic task. Psychotherapy is not making clever and apt interpretations; by and large it is a long-term giving back what the patient brings. *It is a complex derivative of the face that reflects what is there to be seen.* I like to think of my work this way, and to think that if I do this well enough the patient will find his or her own self, and will be able to exist and to feel real' (emphasis added, Winnicott, 1967, p. 117).

This process has also been well described by Kenneth Wright: 'That which has distorted the self is... the symbolic reflection of the Other. That which can undo this distortion is likewise a symbolic reflection. But in order for a new formation of the self to take place there has to be a new subjective holding – an allowing of that in the subject which previously was not allowed – to be, and in a sense, to be born again' (Wright, 1991, p. 300).

THE CONVERSATIONAL MODEL: A (DISGUISED) CASE ILLUSTRATION

Sally was a 27 year old unemployed single woman who was referred for psychotherapy assessment by her GP, who asked for 'some help in managing this difficult woman'. Sally described a long-standing history of depression and panic attacks, a range of medically unexplained gastro-intestinal symptoms, and two serious suicide attempts, one after a boyfriend ended their relationship, and another following a severe sexual assault that occurred in her late teens. Sally also described a history of drug and alcohol abuse from her early teens. In her early years she suffered neglect and physical and sexual abuse, from her elder brother and her mother. Both her mother and father had serious drug and alcohol problems. Sally's father died from a drug overdose when she was five. Sally described a history of unstable and frequently violent relationships, with Sally being both victim of violence, and at times the perpetrator. It was clear that Sally had had considerable contact with health service provision in a range of settings, most of which had been unsatisfactory. However, Sally had been able to stop drinking and using illegal drugs for over a year, and seemed motivated to work in therapy. Despite reservations Sally was offered a year of once weekly therapy. (For an account of assessment for psychotherapy based on an understanding of 'self pathology' see Brooke, 1994.) After being on a waiting list for six months Sally was seen by a male therapist.

Sally's therapy did not begin well. At her first appointment she was 20 minutes late and very angry:

Sally: (Angry) Before we start I want to know why I've had to wait so long. I've been waiting for ages and it's made my stomach worse, I feel sick every time I eat... last week I was close to drinking again, that's what happens when you just leave people waiting, not knowing what's happening. Like my GP, you wait for ages then just get fobbed off, they don't want to know. They give you tablets just to shut you up... it makes no difference... people don't understand what it's like being passed around all the time, you get used to one person then they piss off. I expected to see 'Dr Smith' (the psychotherapy assessor). Why do I have to see you, I got used to seeing 'Dr Smith'.

Therapist: (Rejecting) If you would prefer to go back on the waiting list I will see if you can be seen by 'Dr Smith'.

Sally: (Anxious) Oh... No... I mean... I'm just sounding off again... its not your fault... I'm just fucked up....

These first few minutes of Sally's first session illustrate several characteristic features of psychotherapy with patients presenting with personality disorders, in particular 'borderline states'. First we may note what Meares calls the presentation of a *'chronicle'*. This is often an account of symptoms, or of current events involving conflict with others. The 'chronicle' is usually highly stereotyped, concrete and disconnected from the internal world, that is, it lacks self-reflection: 'The chronicle, which reflects a state of disconnection from inner experience, is told in a relationship of disconnection' (Meares, 2000, p. 123). The patient's disrupted sense of self manifests in a lack of mentalisation, in which it is as if the patient is caught in the distress of symptoms and interpersonal conflict, in a condition Meares calls 'stimulus entrapment' (Meares, 1997).

We may also note the sudden shift that seems to occur in the patient's experience of themselves and the therapist. The unconscious processes whereby patients attempt to recreate within the therapy specific patterns of interaction that reflect early relationships can put therapists under considerable pressure to enact a particular role in response to the patient's presentation. Joseph Sandler (1976) has described the therapist's 'role responsiveness' and emphasised the importance of therapists *understanding* rather than *enacting* the roles they are being pressured to adopt. As Moeller (1977) noted, therapists need to 'grasp *both sides* of the role relationship, subject *and* object; grasp, that is, the whole relationship intrapsychically before he can be in any position to understand the situation of the patient' (quoted by Sandler, Dare & Holder, 1992, p. 91).

Further, the roles can switch, in what Meares calls 'reversals', a term derived from Freud: 'The representation of self fused with the alien other produces oscillations in selfstate, in which, at times, the individual appears as the frightened and helpless victim and at others, perhaps a few seconds later, as the traumatising other' (Meares, 2000, p. 87). In the above example the therapist initially felt victimised in response to the patient's attacking and rejecting presentation; the therapist then adopts a rejecting role in retaliation, thereby activating a reversal. An important aspect of the work of therapy is to *understand and reflect on these patterns rather than to simply enact them*, as unfortunately happened in this example. We may understand these shifts and reversals in terms of the activation of the traumatic memory system (Meares, 1993, 1999).

An important aspect of early formulation is to anticipate, on the basis of the patient's reported past and current relationships, as well as interaction with the assessor and therapist, what interpersonal patterns are likely to be activated in the therapy. Although pressures towards role enactments and reversals are challenges for therapy, they also offer important opportunities for facilitating patients' self-reflective capacities. It is precisely when the traumatic memory system has been activated that self-reflective capacities are most compromised – hence it is at that moment, as it happens within the therapy relationship, that the therapist works to facilitate self-reflection rather than re-enactment.

'The therapeutic conversation begins in the language of alienation. A principal therapeutic task is to transform this kind of conversation into another' (Meares, 2000, p. 121). The goal of therapy is to move from an alienated, non-self-reflective conversation towards a conversation that is personal, self-reflective and intimate, that is, a conversation that potentiates mentalising capacities, and a consequent increase in the continuity, coherence and affective valuing of the sense of self. This movement is described by Meares as 'transforming the chronicle'. It can be facilitated by a process of 'empathic resonance'. Here is an example from four months after the start of therapy:

Sally: I tried to talk to Steve about my stomach pains... and depression and things... he didn't... or couldn't understand, or even listen, I couldn't get through to him, he said... you know... 'look on the bright side', that type of shit... I think it's pointless... talking to people...

Therapist: You sound angry with Steve... but also it's upsetting... painful... to try, and yet, not be heard... (silence)... I wonder, I'm not sure... if, perhaps, you are feeling something similar here with me... Er... can you get through to me... will I be able, or want to listen, to understand... will I turn away from the darkness... not see your pain... will it be pointless talking to me...

(Sally makes eye contact with therapist, nods agreement and becomes tearful, then starts to express her fears about engaging in therapy, the risk of becoming dependent on the therapist and then being abandoned.)

This response from the therapist illustrates a number of features of the conversational model: the use of statements rather than questions, a negotiating style and use of personal pronouns, picking up cues and using the patient's language, use of understanding and linking hypotheses, focusing on feelings and working in the here and now. We also note a fundamental aspect of the model, the use of metaphor: 'a means of visualising the inner world' (Meares, 2000, p. 125). For example, note the use of metaphors involving looking, and light and darkness. The various aspects of the model contribute to creating an empathic resonance to the patient, in which the patient feels understood and valued, in order to facilitate the emergence of a form of conversation marked by self-reflection and intimacy.

Therapists working in the conversational model aim for an optimal level of attunement through empathic resonance, involving verbal and non-verbal aspects, with the aim of facilitating a safe containing relationship, in which inhibited or disrupted self-reflective capacities can be facilitated. Assimilation, or integration, of the traumatic memory system can then be facilitated, most importantly through understanding and working with selfstate oscillations and reversals, as they occur within the therapeutic relationship. In this way, restoration of the continuity, coherence, agency and affectivity of the experience of self can be potentiated.

COGNITIVE THERAPY

KATE DAVIDSON

Cognitive therapies for personality disorders (Axis II) and clinical disorders (Axis I) share many features. Both adhere to the *core principles* of cognitive therapy, which involve the setting of an appropriate agenda so the therapy is focused; using the therapeutic relationship appropriately; helping the patients to make connections between how they think, feel and behave; using questioning to help increase the patients' understanding of their difficulties; utilising change methods to help modify maladaptive thinking (these can be either cognitive or behavioural, and include verbal reattribution strategies and behavioural experiments) and emphasising the need for the patients to work on the problems between sessions.

Essentially, cognitive therapy for both Axis I and Axis II disorders aims to address maladaptive patterns of thinking and behaviour. Both emphasise the collaborative and open nature of the therapeutic relationship, educate the patient about the model of therapy and utilise a formulation in guiding the specific strategies used in treatment. However, there are also some important differences. These differences are summarised in Table 5.1 and discussed below.

The developments in cognitive therapy for the treatment of personality disorder are guided by cognitive theory relating to personality disorder, discussed in Chapter 4. Essentially, cognitive therapy for personality disorders puts more emphasis on 'higher order' cognitive processes (schema) than cognitive therapy for Axis I clinical disorders. The following sections provide an overview of the main elements of cognitive therapy for personality disorders.

FORMULATION

Formulation of problems within the cognitive model is the starting point for all cognitive therapies. In cognitive therapy for personality disorders, the therapist has to have substantial knowledge of the cognitive model for personality disorder in order to integrate the information elicited from the patient into a comprehensive and pragmatic understanding of the patient's problem. A case formulation is essential to provide the necessary idiosyncratic understanding of the individual patient and their clinical problems. The case formulation allows the therapist to gain an understanding of the individual and the problems experienced, and from this understanding the therapist is able to design a specific treatment, targeting the patient's

Table 5.1 Differences between cognitive therapy for Axis I and personality disorders (adapted from Davidson (2000). *Cognitive therapy for personality disorders: A guide for clinicians.* London: Arnold (Hodder)).

	Axis I	Personality disorder
Treatment duration	Short term (up to 16 sessions)	Long term (up to 30 sessions)
Therapeutic relationship	Collaborative Open	Collaborative Clear boundaries between patient and therapist
Problem time line	Here and now	Here and now Lifetime
Cognitive level	Negative automatic thoughts Dysfunctional assumptions	Core beliefs/early maladaptive schema
Behavioural level	Shorter-term behaviours associated with onset of illness or maintained by illness	Long-standing behaviours associated with personality disorder
Overall aim of therapy	Return to 'normal' or 'usual' functioning	Learning new ways of behaving and thinking

idiosyncratic beliefs and behavioural patterns that maintain the patient's difficulties. In the treatment of personality disorder, patients with the same type of personality disorder will be more similar to each other than to those who have a different type of disorder, but each individual patient will have an individualised treatment programme that will be shaped by their specific problems, beliefs and behavioural patterns.

Figure 5.1 illustrates a brief diagrammatic cognitive formulation of a patient, John, with antisocial personality disorder, who entered treatment at the age of 38 when his girlfriend became pregnant. John's relationship with his girlfriend was problematic, partly due to his inability to understand that she had rights, needs and desires that might conflict with his own. He wanted to be a 'good father' to this unborn child and was becoming distressed because his girlfriend was not sure that their relationship should continue. There was a real risk that John might harm his girlfriend and the unborn child.

The formulation is central to cognitive therapy for patients such as John, as it provides the therapist and patient with an understanding of the patient's problems, with the emphasis on key cognitive factors such as schema/core beliefs. It can also be used to foresee difficulties that may arise in therapy. For example, in John's case his schema compensation behaviours, of *putting*

Critical experiences

- in childhood:

Mother (single parent) died of overdose when John was six years old.

Repeated rejection from caregivers due to 'acting out' behaviour.

No stable home life in childhood and lived on street from age 16 until 18.

- in adulthood:

Brief spells in prison for theft, possession of drugs.

Repeated breakdowns in relationships with men and women.

Early maladaptive schema

Abandonment/Mistrust and Abuse/Defectiveness

Core beliefs

I'm bad/I'm unlovable

I can cope with anything

I can do what I want

Other people will let me down

Cognitive and behavioural consequences

Schema Compensation ⟺ Schema Avoidance ⟺ Schema Maintenance

Puts own needs first   Keeps people at a distance   Rejects others who show him affection

Behavioural strategies

Over-developed ⟺ **Under-developed**

Autonomy   Reciprocity

Exploitation

Figure 5.1 Cognitive formulation: example of a patient (John) with antisocial personality disorder

his own needs first (pushing boundaries) and under-developed *reciprocity*, will make it difficult for John to develop a relationship with his therapist that is adaptive.

THE THERAPEUTIC RELATIONSHIP

Working with individuals with personality disorder requires the therapist to be more aware of the relationship he or she has with the patient. Usually in cognitive therapy for Axis I disorders the therapeutic relationship is relatively straightforward. The therapist behaves in a straightforward, professional manner and is warm, open and genuine towards the patient. In cognitive therapy for personality disorder, the patient's difficulties with other people are likely to come into play within the therapeutic relationship. In John's case it may be extremely difficult for the cognitive therapist to use guided discovery (questions) to help John see the impact that he has on others, given his over-developed behavioural strategy that leads him to act in a manner that exploits and uses other people. He also believes that other people will let him down, as they have done in the past. As a consequence, he may have difficulty trusting the therapist sufficiently and he could appear to be resistant to change. As John's case formulation anticipates these problems, it is possible for the therapist to try to circumvent these difficulties arising in therapy. For example, it would be counter-productive to be overly *directive*, as this would leave John feeling attacked and cause him to withdraw from therapy (utilise his over-developed strategy of autonomy).

The therapist in John's case must also avoid being drawn into adopting a 'placatory style' to *avoid* confrontation. This would be equally unhelpful as it may lead John to become more exploitative (over-developed strategy). In John's case, the therapist needs to remain consistent with the focus and nature of therapy and not be drawn into an interaction that does not follow the core principles of cognitive therapy. John needs to understand how his current problems have arisen through the use of a shared formulation and how these problems (beliefs and over-developed behavioural strategies) are now working against his aim to improve his quality of life and his ability to develop more stable and fulfilling relationships. Clear boundaries, in not only the timing but also the process of the therapy, would be important in this case. The problems associated with a patient's personality disorder can make it *more difficult* for therapists to adhere to the core principles of cognitive therapy.

The therapeutic relationship in cognitive therapy for personality disorders may also be used as a *therapeutic tool* to identify and modify early maladaptive schema or core beliefs associated with relationships. For example, John may behave in a way that 'tests out' whether the therapist would let him down. By identifying the belief 'other people will let him down' and addressing where this came from, the therapist and John can then look at how this could impact on therapy. They can explore the advantages and disadvantages of holding this belief, and devise behavioural experiments to test out his predictions or train John to observe the deleterious impact this belief has on relationships.

In cognitive therapy, the way the therapeutic relationship is used can vary. Young, Klosko and Weishaar (2003) highlight the therapeutic relationship as an explicit agent for change through 're-parenting', whereby the patient is given a corrective *emotional* experience through this relationship. Davidson (2000), on the other hand, regards the therapeutic relationship as playing an important role in changing beliefs and behaviours and views it as a 'laboratory' for arriving at hypotheses and testing out assumptions that patients may hold about others. Both agree that therapists need to be aware of their own assumptions and behaviours and how these impact on the patient in therapy and, in particular, how the patient's feelings, thoughts and behaviours may activate a dysfunctional response in the therapist.

BELIEF MODIFICATION – HELPING THE PATIENT TO FIND NEW WAYS OF THINKING AND BEHAVING

As stated in Chapter 4, beliefs associated with personality disorder are thought to be unconditional, and often formed by childhood experiences. These beliefs are rigid, pervasive and activated by many situations. Information that does not fit with the beliefs or early maladaptive schema is processed in such a way that it has no impact on the overall form of the schema. It is either ignored, distorted to fit with the existing schema, or simply avoided – by processing information in this manner, the schema and/or belief remains intact. Cognitive therapy must somehow change this process so that contradictory information becomes assimilated and integrated into a new belief. How this is done depends on the exact model.

Davidson (2000) has suggested that it may be more effective to explicitly replace the old belief with a new more adaptive belief once the patient has recognised the old belief, considered its origins and understood the impact that it has on contemporary social and emotional functioning, including interpersonal relationships. Finding a new, more appropriate and adaptive belief takes time and effort and has to appeal to the patient's heart as well as head. The patient is then trained to recognise information that fits with a new, more adaptive belief and with new behaviours that would be associated with a new belief. The new more adaptive belief is not simply the 'opposite' of the old belief. It is likely to be more subtle and tentative. For example, John may learn that 'thinking of others and considering their needs is better for me', or a borderline patient who was sexually abused in childhood and who held a belief that 'all people will use me' might consider a new more adaptive belief such as 'other people can have my interests at heart some of the time'. The therapist and patient have to work on how to make these judgments of others and how trust in others can be developed and assessed in practice.

In essence, Davidson (2000) advocates an approach that is *consistent with* the core features of cognitive therapy. By contrast, Young and his colleagues (Young et al., 2003) place additional emphasis on 'experiential' techniques such as using 'imagery dialogues', revisiting childhood interactions or emotional catharsis (emotional expression or ventilating), and suggest that these techniques help the patient get in touch with strong affect and cognitions. As noted, they also put greater emphasis on the therapeutic relationship and draw on ideas from other theoretical models, for example object relations theory. They believe that generating strong affect and cognitions related to this will more readily facilitate change and allow a focus on the 'deeper' schema level of early maladaptive schema.

MORE SESSIONS OVER A LONGER PERIOD OF TIME

Cognitive therapy for Axis I disorders is brisk and brief, and in practice often requires fewer than ten sessions. In comparison, cognitive therapy for personality disorders is likely to take place over at least one year and 30 sessions of therapy would not be uncommon. This is understandable as individuals with personality disorder have to learn new ways of behaving and new ways of thinking about themselves and others.

EVIDENCE OF EFFECTIVENESS

Research evidence from methodologically adequate trials of cognitive therapy for personality disorder is in its infancy. Such trials are taking place and the evidence for the effectiveness of cognitive therapy will hopefully be forthcoming. Patients with personality disorders are likely to require expert therapists to help them to overcome their longstanding problems and to acquire new more adaptive strategies. Establishing evidence-based practice for this group of patients will be a key issue in the future.

COGNITIVE ANALYTIC THERAPY

MARK EVANS

Cognitive analytic therapy (CAT) is a form of brief therapy that usually lasts between 16 and 24 sessions. For patients with personality disorder, the longer version is usually given together with three or four follow-up appointments. CAT was originally conceived as a result of Ryle's research (Ryle, 1975) with repertory grids (Kelly, 1955) and there have since been several published controlled trials of its efficacy (Brockman, Poynton, Ryle & Watson, 1987; Cluley, Smeeton, Cochrane & Cordon, personal communication; Fosbury, Bosley, Ryle, Sonksen & Judd, 1997; Treasure et al., 1995). Also, three larger scale randomised controlled trials of CAT are currently underway with their results not yet available. For further information about published CAT research the reader is directed to Appendix One of Ryle and Kerr (2002).

CAT is most distinguishable from other psychodynamic therapies by its collaborative use of tools and techniques. Whilst attempts are made to understand the inner world and the types of relationship pattern entered into, the therapist will be checking out with the patient their perception of the process and meaning of the encounter. This makes CAT a particularly accessible form of therapy for highly sensitive and troubled patients.

The skilled CAT therapist should *be* interested, engaged, reflective and aware of the potential for collusion in reciprocal role procedures (see previous chapter for explanation of terms). The therapist will be working within the general framework of (a) *reformulation* of personal problems and symptoms, in terms of reciprocal role procedures, (b) *recognition* of when these are occurring and (c) *revision* of such procedures. In CAT this is referred to as taking 'exits'.

During the first three or four sessions of therapy, the CAT therapist takes a relatively active stance in enquiring about the patient's family and early life experience as well as current concerns and problems. The aims here are to gain a clearer interpersonal perspective on the patient's presenting problems, to build a therapeutic alliance and to remoralise. As with other brief therapies, a focus is sought which in CAT is derived from a reframing of the presenting problem into an understanding of self states and reciprocal role procedures.

Pen and paper tasks are often employed during the early sessions, both as a means of fostering this active enquiry and in order to deliver useful information to aid both patient and therapist in deciding which problematic procedures to address. Usually a *psychotherapy file* is given out after the first session. This questionnaire asks the patient to identify which of the examples of dilemmas, traps, snags and states apply and enquires about the patient's propensity for dissociation. As with the use of all the CAT 'tools', collaboration and the changing of wording is actively encouraged. Other between-session self-monitoring techniques such as the keeping of mood or symptom diaries or the creation of 'lifelines' are often informative.

By session four or five, the intention is to arrive at an explicit written formulation which is shared with the patient, called the *reformulation letter*. For this, information is harvested not only from what the patient shares in sessions but also from 'homework' tasks as well as the therapists' in-session counter-transference feelings. The reformulation letter attempts to make sense of troublesome patterns of relating (reciprocal role procedures) in terms of their origins and how they continue to narrow personal choice and freedom. In the letter, a therapeutic focus is agreed upon together with the predominant maladaptive procedures, which are named. The letter is always presented to the patient in a draft form for which comment and collaboration are invited.

Although tentative procedural understandings will already have been worked out during the early sessions, hearing the letter read out is usually a powerful and moving experience for the patient. The style is one which validates attempts to deal with personal problems and their inherent aims, whilst pointing out how these may fail and even worsen the situation. Crucially, by reformulating the patient's predominant self states, predictions can be made about potential problems for the therapeutic relationship, which may avert future alliance ruptures or render them more amenable to reflection and hence repair.

Once the reformulation has been agreed upon, subsequent sessions are used to focus on the target problem(s) and identified problematic procedures. This can be achieved through in-session monitoring of the week's events, aided perhaps by the use of a diary. Patients are encouraged to reflect on their ability to recognise and modify maladaptive procedures, which may be rated using a visual analogue scale.

Another potent source of material for the monitoring of reciprocal role procedures is the therapeutic relationship itself. Reciprocal roles that occur in the patient's everyday life will probably be enacted during the therapy sessions and it is the therapist's job to spot when this is happening. This is particularly important for more extreme and therapy-threatening enactments, which commonly occur when working with patients with severe personality disorders. Examples of such enactments would be a patient walking out of a session in an agitated state or a patient who increases self-harming as a result of starting therapy. The CAT therapist's task here is to recognise when they are being invited to collude in a reciprocal role enactment, and then to point this out in a non-threatening way, which allows the patient to re-engage with the work of therapy and to be less self-destructive.

The CAT diagram is another reformulatory tool that can greatly assist in this process of recognising and containing in-session enactments.

Essentially a flow diagram, it presents a summary depiction of the procedures that have already been described in the reformulation letter. The diagram is usually constructed after the reformulation letter and in most cases then takes the place of the letter for monitoring of procedures. In the case of patients who require early containment and who demonstrate either aggressive, self-destructive or therapy-threatening behaviours, an initial draft diagram can be usefully employed to help mend the alliance. The diagram can be seen as a jointly constructed third position that allows an easing of the pressure within the therapy dyad. Transference and counter-transference feelings (reciprocal role enactments) can become more manageable and less personalised if they can be understood and contained within an external diagram. A later aim for the therapist may be for the feelings to become fully owned between the therapy couple, but the CAT tools can be used at different times to modulate the encounter and to keep it within bearable limits. In CAT this is described as working within the patient's 'zone of proximal development' (ZPD), a term derived from Vygotsky (1978), which essentially refers to the amount of emotional support versus distance that needs to be maintained between the therapist and patient in order to optimise the therapeutic gains.

Many techniques that are not specific to CAT may be flexibly employed to promote change. These range from behavioural techniques such as graded exposure to gestalt-informed interventions such as the empty chair technique. The choice will depend on the therapist's particular skills as well as the predominant pattern of defence that the patient employs. The aim at this point in the therapy is to facilitate the patient's own creativity in devising exits from problematic procedures that are increasingly and more rapidly being recognised.

Being a time-limited therapy, there is a focus on ending even from the outset. This is important because all people have interpersonal procedures for dealing with separation and loss, and for some an abandoning–abandoned reciprocal role is prominent. Consequently, feelings about ending are sensitively explored with the patient, especially during the latter half of therapy.

CAT has a distinctive tool, the *goodbye letter*, for paying appropriate attention to the termination of therapy. This document, given to the patient at the penultimate session, summarises the work done together, highlighting what has been achieved as well as difficulties encountered. Predictions may be made about future stressors and how the patient might attempt to manage these. The patient is also invited to write a goodbye letter giving his/her view. This is another useful opportunity for both parties to reflect and collaborate. As well as helping to reduce the inevitable perceived power imbalance, it allows the therapist to gain further insight into the patient's experience of therapy. In the final session, further thoughts and feelings about the goodbye letter and ending can be explored. Follow-up sessions are arranged, which serve as useful anchor points for patients, in which they can explore with the therapist how they have coped without the more intensive weekly therapeutic relationship.

CYNTHIA: A CASE ILLUSTRATION

Cynthia is a 40 year old woman who recently resigned her post as a manager working with elderly people in the health service. She gave permission for the use of this case material although her real name as well as details in her history have been changed in order to protect confidentiality.

Having been an energetic and committed employee who stopped work after becoming increasingly depressed and suicidal, Cynthia had previously experienced several discrete episodes of not being able to cope in her life. When unwell, she would be referred by her general practitioner to a psychiatrist or to the community mental health team. There was often a great sense of urgency with these referrals, with concerns that she might kill herself as she would sporadically cut herself with a knife and occasionally took large amounts of paracetamol without informing others.

Cynthia described a difficult childhood in which she never remembers meeting her real father before he died. Her mother was a strict and difficult woman, who was often ill in bed, and who would be controlling and contemptuous despite Cynthia's desperate and persistent attempts to look after her and to please. Cynthia described a warm relationship with her stepfather during her early life until her age of ten, when her mother left him for Jack. Jack repeatedly sexually abused Cynthia with her mother's collusion until she left home. Cynthia had also suffered significant physical illnesses during her childhood. At the age of seven she recovered from a life threatening illness, which left her with a minor weakness in her left leg, and in her teenage years she was severely injured in a road traffic accident.

She reported past experience of mental healthcare as being mixed but predominantly negative. Whilst conceding that she did not really know what she wanted from professionals, Cynthia was clear that she felt 'passed from pillar to post' and was angry with the psychiatrist who had called her 'raving mad'. At times she had requested admission into hospital but this was never granted as she was told that there was a lack of beds. At psychotherapy assessment it was recommended that she have cognitive analytic therapy as a structured approach to make sense of and gain control over her confusing and changeable mood states.

Cynthia agreed that this would be a useful objective of therapy and she attended regularly for sessions. Her presenting symptoms were of feeling overwhelmed and depressed with disabling panic attacks. She also experienced troublesome flashbacks, and significant and unpredictable mood swings. Cynthia found it difficult to cooperate with filling in the psychotherapy file, from which we identified a fear of being harshly judged or exposed in therapy. The therapist's counter-transference feelings were of being overwhelmed and fearing criticism, which was used as a way of trying to understand Cynthia's internal state. An emerging diagram helped in this process by depicting a judgmental, controlling to anxiously striving reciprocal role and a self-persecuting procedure, which left Cynthia feeling desperate and scared (see Figure 5.2).

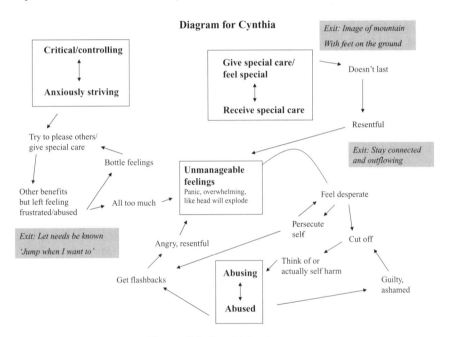

Figure 5.2 Cynthia's diagram

It proved impossible to read out the reformulation letter at session five. Cynthia had presented in an out of control and distressed state, to the extent that the therapist felt it would have been too overwhelming for her to do so (outside her zone of proximal development). The letter was therefore given to her and she read it just before attending for the next session. Cynthia had expected to 'rubbish' the letter in her own mind but was surprised that she did not do so, instead feeling generally heard and understood. However, there were some factual errors in the letter, which she was able to correct, and the therapist was aware that much from Cynthia's history had not been verbalised but only hinted at.

After session six there was a break in therapy and she returned feeling very distressed, overwhelmed and in immense physical pain. She described hearing internal voices telling her to self-harm and during the session her daughter rang Cynthia's mobile phone twice to check up on her. She described this mental state as 'just existing'.

Over the following sessions Cynthia complained of either feeling distressed and at her wits' end, or somehow superhuman and special that she had survived a trauma that others would not have done. Other health professionals expressing amazement at how she had been so strong for so long reinforced this latter state. The therapist attempted to stay with and explore the feelings of the 'just existing' state when they were around and also to acknowledge the often rapid and subtle switches to the other special state. Slowly, Cynthia began to recognise a persecutory reciprocal role procedure, whereby she would have a catastrophic and self-punishing reaction when in touch with unmanageable feelings, which made her feel increasingly hopeless and suicidal (leading to the 'just existing' state).

By sessions 10 and 11 Cynthia was beginning to feel more contained and was able to tell her children that she wanted more space. The therapist's wondering as to whether she had ever really told her story before seemed to hit home and Cynthia was able to say more of her experiences of deprivation and abuse as a child. She realised that she had used an 'abused' label as a way of avoiding talking about the real experiences of what it has been like for her. Together we were able to make the link between this self-labelling with the accompanying high expectations she had of herself and the special state, where it is as if she does not have the usual needs and vulnerabilities of others. The exit that we later discovered involved keeping her feet on the ground and staying in touch with her vulnerability.

Slowly, her bodily reaction of feeling physically sick when looking at the CAT diagram changed into one where she could acknowledge that it was a useful 'piece of paper'. Her thought now was that she would not have got so far and so fast without it. She also identified the importance of her doing the work of therapy in the presence of a reflective other person rather than on her own. Following another break, Cynthia returned looking relaxed and well. She said that she was feeling calm for the first time in her life and was increasingly able to identify how she had continually strived to please others but at the expense of her own feelings, which could leave her feeling frustrated or even abused.

During the second half of therapy, the ending was alluded to regularly by both parties. Cynthia spoke of her stepfather's death and the fact that she had never really been able to let go of him. It felt to her as if by acknowledging his death all goodness within her would be taken away, never to return. She also became increasingly aware of her mother's persistent lack of empathy for Cynthia. Cynthia had always felt that she had to keep her mother happy, yet still felt blamed for all her mother's problems. She experienced more flashbacks of how her mother had treated her over the years and began to question the fantasy that she was holding on to, that her mother would one day approve of her (which would result in her difficulties being resolved).

In a closing session, Cynthia brought a dream, which seemed to bring to life the reciprocal role procedures on the diagram. In the dream she was striving to perform superhuman feats in order to keep a woman happy. This was at the expense of her own physical health and her own internal desires, which became evident in the latter part of the dream in which she jumped across both tracks to join a train in the service of the other woman. In the dream she had the thought that she could 'jump when I want to' (and not at others' demanding), which was adopted as an 'exit', allowing a more active and assertive response. Cynthia started to feel overwhelmed again at the penultimate session and linked this with the fact that all the good figures in her life had always left her (Cynthia's feelings of grief for a lost good object were worked with and reflected upon during follow-up sessions, to a degree whereby she was able to not feel paralysed by the feelings and was also able to mobilise her own resources). However, the therapist was able to read out the goodbye letter and Cynthia reciprocated by bringing her own letter the following week. In this she could acknowledge the improvements in her life, which she maintained at follow-up: a calmness of mind, increased confidence, lack of further self-harming as well as her successfully having completing early modules of a computing course (despite considerable anxieties) and a decision to restart driving lessons after many years.

Comment

Cynthia had previously struggled with other therapies, whose lack of structure and transparency had ultimately proven to be too provocative. Also, a therapy that did not have a specific theoretical understanding of two-person relationships would likely have involved Cynthia in eliciting powerful caring or rejecting enactments from others, which, if not understood, would not have helped her change her internal world. CAT provided a framework within which the therapist could provide containment through clarity and structure as well as to understand and work with intense and confusingly changeable reciprocal role relationships. It is proposed that in the presence of a reflective therapist, who was able enough to resist a re-enactment of abandoning, judgmental or overly admiring reciprocal roles, the patient managed to identify and rehearse her own exits to ingrained problematic procedures, as well as to internalise a more 'caring to', 'cared for' reciprocal role.

DIALECTICAL BEHAVIOURAL THERAPY

JANET FEIGENBAUM

Dialectical behavioural therapy (DBT) developed from the cognitive behavioural model of treatment, and thus shares many of the key components. However, in order to address issues specific to patents with borderline personality disorder (BPD) Linehan (1993a, 1993b) added a number of components considered necessary to increase commitment to treatment, to promote engagement and to initiate a process of therapeutic change. These additions include consideration of the principles of dialectics, an enhanced emphasis on learning theory and a focus on validation (acceptance).

Alongside the emphasis on developing new skills (or capabilities), DBT places equal weight on the need to address issues of motivation within the patient and the therapist. Poor motivation in either the patient or the therapist can lead to drop-outs from therapy or failure to progress in treatment. Poor motivation may arise from characteristics within the individual such as fear, inhibition, frustration or depression, or factors associated with the external environment or social network. These factors apply across both the patient and the therapist.

This chapter describes four different aspects of DBT: its functions, the different 'modes' of therapy, the stages of therapy and the strategies used. Finally, brief mention will be made of the relation between DBT and mindfulness.

THE FUNCTIONS OF A DBT PROGRAMME

DBT has been designed as a programme of treatment. There are five main functions that must be addressed.

- To enhance the capabilities of the patient, through the teaching of new skills or the activation of existing skills not used effectively.
- To improve motivation to use these new skills in a range of settings. Learning a new skill is difficult and requires extensive practice. When individuals are emotionally aroused, newly learnt, or rarely used, skills

may be forgotten, while dysfunctional, often over-learnt, patterns of behaviour are employed.

- To ensure that the new skills are able to be employed in a range of settings and experiences. During therapy, skills are most often taught and learnt through discussion, modelling, role play and rehearsal with a therapist or in a group. The skills are learnt in a particular setting when emotional arousal is likely to be controlled and the use of the skill feels 'safe' to the patient. During learning of the new skill, the therapist or group provides useful and supportive feedback on the use of the skill. However, the individual must be able to use the skill when highly emotionally aroused, when faced with a social context that may be resistant to the use of the skill, or in which a creative variation of the skill must be employed to be effective.

- To provide a structure to the environment that supports both the patient and the therapist in the development and use of new skills or capabilities.

- To provide a means of enhancing the therapist's own skills and motivation to continue to work with the patient. Patients with BPD present a range of difficulties that require the therapist to continue to develop their own skills, to monitor stress and burn-out and to ensure that they are not responding to efforts of the patients to shape or modify the therapist's behaviour.

DBT MODES

Traditional DBT has a number of modes for ensuring that these five functions are addressed. When these standard modes are not feasible, the expectation is on the DBT team to identify creative and valid solutions to ensure that the five functions are provided effectively (Swales, Heard & Williams, 2000). For example, in some settings the provision of skill training groups may be difficult due to problems with numbers or distance. In other settings, the provision of telephone consultation may be problematic for practical and financial reasons relating to the restrictions of the health care system or staff. The modes are as follows.

Developing New Capabilities: Skills Training Group

The skill training group is designed to enhance the capabilities of the patient. The group functions as a psychoeducational group and is structured specifically for the learning and rehearsal of new skills. The skills training group is divided into four modules: mindfulness, emotional regulation, interpersonal effectiveness and distress tolerance. The group meets weekly for 2–2½ hours. The group sessions begin with a review of the homework from the previous week. Group members are asked to describe their use of the skill discussed in the previous week, obstacles to using the skill and concerns or queries about using the skill. A new skill is then introduced. The skill is discussed including commitment to trying out the new skill and completing the homework (including planning opportunities for using the skill or identifying obstacles to using the skill). Patients typically remain in the skills training group for a year, thus participating in each module twice during this time.

Skill Use and Motivation: Individual Therapy Sessions

All patients in DBT receive an hour a week of individual therapy with their primary therapist. The function of individual therapy is to relate the skills learnt to the specific goals and targets of the patient. During the first phase of DBT, individual sessions have a clear structure and focus. The patient is asked to present his or her diary card for the previous week and this is used to set the agenda for the session. Behavioural chain analyses relating to the targets of the session are conducted, and a solution analysis identified. Relevant skills identified in the solution analysis are discussed and rehearsed in the session. During the individual session, the therapist and patient will identify and address commitment to therapy and motivation to change as problems are identified.

Generalisation: Telephone Consultation

Generalisation of skills can be achieved through a range of methods. In the original DBT structure, telephone consultation was used as an immediate and powerful means of generalization. The patient is given a contact phone number (i.e. mobile phone number) for their individual therapist and offered the opportunity to phone for help in identifying and using their newly learnt skills when away from the treatment centre. The purpose of these brief telephone consultations is to assist the patient in identifying an appropriate skill to employ and to overcome obstacles to using the skill effectively. In order to provide this telephone consultation, therapists need to be assisted by their team in observing their own limits with respect to hours during which the telephone is available and length of telephone contacts. There are a number of other means of generalization to the environment that can be employed. These include flashcards, handouts, audio or video tapes of the skills, teaching the skills to family members or friends of the patient, planned phone calls during the working day and training in-patient or out-of-hours staff to provide skill generalisation, to list a few.

Structuring the Environment: Case Management

Structuring the environment can be provided through the care programme approach meetings, through meetings with family members or through *in vivo* coaching of the patient in a range of settings. The main aim in structuring the environment is to ensure that the patient is given opportunities to use new skills and that the environment, or social network, recognizes, facilitates and reinforces the effective use of new skills.

Therapist Skills and Motivation: The Consultation Meeting

The therapist's own skills and motivation for treatment are addressed in a weekly DBT team consultation meeting. This two-hour meeting is an essential feature of DBT. During the consultation meeting, therapists bring case material from specific patients to discuss, with the emphasis on improving their delivery of DBT. This provides an opportunity for the team to ensure that a dialectical stance is taken with respect to the issues presented by the patient, that the therapist is adhering to the main strategies and techniques of DBT and that issues of therapist motivation are noted and addressed. The second half of the consultation meeting is devoted to learning and practising therapeutic skills relevant to delivering the DBT programme effectively.

STAGES AND TARGETS OF THERAPY

DBT is organised into five stages of therapy. The targets of therapy are specific to each stage. Prior to therapy proper, the patient is said to be in the 'pre-commitment' stage.

Pre-Commitment

The pre-commitment stage usually requires three to six weeks. During this phase the therapist explains the treatment model, shares with the patient an understanding of their difficulties as derived from the assessment and the biosocial model, and orients the patient to the expectations of therapy. The patient must commit to reducing self-harming behaviours, to work on interpersonal difficulties which may interfere with the process of therapy and to work on building new skills. The DBT model acknowledges that the therapist will become a primary reinforcer to facilitate change; therefore, during this phase there is an emphasis on building the therapeutic relationship.

In the pre-commitment stage, the target is to obtain a commitment from the patient to work on developing new skills to reduce life-threatening behaviours and therapy-interfering behaviours. The therapist adopts a 'dialectical' stance, highlighting both the need for change and the difficulties with change. This approach increases commitment and allows both the therapist and the patient to identify possible obstacles to treatment, which may need to be addressed. If at any stage in therapy commitment to the targets, or to therapy, becomes problematic, the therapist will return to the commitment strategies.

Stage One

The focus of the first stage of therapy is on the development of new behavioural skills for reducing life-threatening behaviours, reducing therapy-interfering behaviours and reducing quality-of-life-threatening behaviours (see below for further discussion of targeting). Thus the focus is on immediate risk and difficulties that interfere with the patient's ability to attend therapy.

The stage one target hierarchy addresses issues according to level of risk to the patient and to the therapy: (1) suicidal or self-harm behaviours, (2) therapy-interfering behaviours and (3) quality-of-life-interfering behaviours. These targets may not be mutually exclusive, and often quality of life behaviours are relevant to self-harming behaviours. For example, if the patient regularly self-harms when drinking alcohol, substance misuse may become a highly relevant target. It is through the development of new skills (obtained in group and individual sessions) that the patient gains the means of reducing risk behaviours and remaining in therapy.

Stage Two

The goal of stage two is to reduce post-traumatic stress. This will include exposure to traumatic memories and emotional processing of past experiences. The rationale is that the patient will need the emotional and behavioural skills learnt in stage one in order to manage the intensity of stage two and resolve the trauma effectively and safely. The most common approach in stage two is the use of exposure-based models for post-traumatic stress. During stage two there may be a re-emergence of stage one targets, such as suicidal/self-harming behaviour or avoidance of sessions, at which time the therapist and patient will return to addressing stage one targets.

Stages Three and Four

In her original development of the therapy, Linehan (1993a) described the focus of stage three as 'increasing self-respect and achieving individual goals'. During this stage the patient increases her or his ability to trust her- or himself, to self-validate and to maintain this trust and self-reliance independent of the therapist. Swales et al. (2000) identify a further stage four, which 'focuses on transcending the problems of daily life and, instead, resolving existential issues of life'. Stages three and four may be achieved outside the DBT programme.

STRATEGIES IN DBT

As described in Chapter 4, one of the key dialectics in therapy is the tension between acceptance and change. If the emphasis in therapy is primarily on change, a patient may feel invalidated (i.e. ashamed, threatened, frustrated or defeated) and potentially unable to collaborate with treatment. However, if the emphasis is on acceptance the patient may become entrenched in the view that he or she *cannot* change, leading to hopelessness. Thus the therapist must balance problem solving (change) with validation (acceptance).

Problem-Solving Strategies – Behavioural Chain Analysis

The main problem-solving strategy used in DBT is the behavioural chain analysis. The patient and therapist use the diary card to identify the target of the chain analysis. They then identify, in detail, the affective, cognitive, behavioural, interpersonal and environmental triggers that led up to the target event and the consequences of the event. From the behavioural chain analysis, a solution analysis will be generated, drawing upon existing functional skills of the patient and suggesting new skills. In the solution analysis, the therapist will help the patient to identify alternatives, or exit points, from the links in the chain. The therapist must ensure that behavioural rehearsal of relevant skills be undertaken in session. Any obstacles to using the solutions identified will be resolved with further problem solving.

CASE ILLUSTRATION

Target – Joanna took 12 paracetamol early Sunday morning.
   Chain analysis: Saturday evening Joanna waited for her boyfriend to arrive. When he failed to arrive, she rang his mobile phone. He answered from the pub saying he had met some friends and was staying for a drink.

Joanna felt angry and lonely. She thinks 'he prefers to be with his mates. He thinks I am boring and messed up. He is going to leave me'. She begins to feel restless and begins pacing the flat. As she paces, she notices the shirts she ironed for her boyfriend. She thinks 'he just uses me, he doesn't love me'. She begins to feel more angry. Her stomach and shoulders begin to hurt. She rings him again, but his phone is switched off. She thinks 'he doesn't want to be with me'. She becomes further overwhelmed with thoughts of being rejected and her head begins to hurt. She goes to find some paracetamol. When holding the packet she thinks 'I can't stand feeling this way any longer', and takes the whole packet. When she awakes the next day she finds that her boyfriend has rung several times, worried about her and apologising for not seeing her.

Solution analysis: Joanne identified a number of points in the chain in which she could have used skills to prevent the outcome.

(1) assertiveness skills to tackle concerns with boyfriend on the phone
(2) anger management skills to notice and reduce anger
(3) relaxation techniques to manage stomach, shoulder and head pain
(4) cognitive restructuring of 'jumping to conclusions' ('he's leaving me')
(5) resisting 'action urge' to take pills.

Validation Strategies

Acceptance is provided mainly through the use of validation. Validation strategies are used in therapy to balance change strategies, to help the patient to learn to validate themselves, to strengthen the therapeutic relationship and as a form of feedback (Linehan, 1993a). There are six levels of validation.

(1) *Listening and observing.* The therapist is attentive and interested in the patient. Examples include good eye contact, nodding appropriately, and resisting any urges to look at the clock.
(2) *Accurate reflection.* The therapist provides accurate summaries of the patient's expressed experiences.
(3) *Articulating the unverbalised.* At this level of validation the therapist will use skills and knowledge to communicate what the patient may be thinking or feeling, but which has not been stated. Through this the therapist shows that she or he has not only been listening, but has observed changes in emotion or made links to previous information, indicating to the patient that the therapist is actively involved in the patient's experiences.

(4) *Validating in terms of past events*. This involves helping the patient to make sense of his or her actions, or reactions, in terms of past experiences and biological predisposition. This type of validation does not suggest that the problem behaviours cannot be changed in the future, but may reduce self-invalidation and shame, both of which may interfere with therapeutic progress.

(5) *Validation in terms of current circumstances*. Essentially the therapist acknowledges that at 'that moment in time', the response of the patient was understandable given their history, their existing skills and the environmental situation. The therapist must exercise caution not to validate the dysfunctional. For example, the patient avoids coming to a session after cutting her wrists because she is feeling shame and is afraid that the therapist will be angry. One can validate the desire to hide when feeling shame. However, avoiding the session and feeling afraid of the therapist's reactions are dysfunctional as they prevent the learning of new skills.

(6) *Radical genuineness*. This is the opposite to treating the patient as fragile; instead the therapist must treat the patient as capable, effective and reasonable. For example, Steve reports that every weekend when his son comes to visit they have loud arguments in which he says things he regrets afterwards. The therapist believes that this may be due to difficulties that Steve has with acknowledging that his son is becoming an adolescent. The therapist offers the hypothesis (as a hypothesis) to Steve that perhaps he is not allowing his son to 'grow up' and not giving him the same freedoms available to other children his age. However, the therapist would highlight the dialectical tensions: that Steve has normal parental concerns about allowing his son more freedom, that Steve has limited time with his son, that his son needs time to be with his friends and that it is normal for teenagers to spend time away from home.

Dialectical Strategies

There are a number of dialectical strategies that may be employed in DBT. In addition to identifying dialectical tensions as they arise, and facilitating a synthesis to these tensions, the DBT therapist will use dialectical strategies to promote a shared view and to facilitate change. This requires creating a balance between acceptance and change, nurturance and challenge, flexibility and stability, amongst many. Linehan suggests that in order to utilise dialectical strategies effectively one must remain alert, and provide fluidity within the session, moving swiftly but confidently between positions. A range of dialectical strategies are provided in the DBT manual (Linehan,

1993a). The most commonly known include devil's advocate, 'making lemonade out of lemons' (best of a bad job) and use of metaphor.

Mindfulness

Derived from Zen spiritual practices, mindfulness is regarded as a core skill of DBT (and is increasingly used in a range of psychological treatments; see, e.g., Kabat-Zinn, 2003; Segal, Williams & Teasdale, 2002). Mindfulness can be divided into the 'what' skills (observing, describing, participating) and 'how' skills (taking a non-judgemental stance, focusing on one thing in the moment and being effective). These skills are used to balance states of mind within the individual, of which there are three: 'reasonable mind' 'emotional mind' and 'wise mind'. In a 'reasonable mind' state an individual is able to think rationally and logically, whilst in an 'emotional mind' state the individual's mind is dominated by a current feeling, where reason and logic are problematic. The 'wise' mind, an integration of reasonable and emotional mind, allows the individual to find a synthesis between emotional experience and logical thought.

CONCLUSIONS

The four approaches to therapy presented in this chapter provide different ways of understanding and working with patients with personality disorders. Each model of therapy has certain distinct features, or specific factors, unique to the particular approach. However, as noted in the previous chapter, given the current state of knowledge, it is reasonable to adopt a *pluralist* view of therapy, recognising that the evidence, such as it is, suggests that no single model can claim to be the only 'true' or 'right' approach. As far as we can judge at present, outcome data suggests each of these models can be effective. Each model has a particular emphasis, and way of working, that may be helpful to some therapists and some patients, while other therapists and other patients may work more effectively with an alternative model. This would suggest that psychotherapy services for patients with personality disorders may be made responsive to patients' needs by offering a range of approaches, such as those outlined in this chapter. Further, it is important to be aware of the significance of *common factors*, that is, those features of psychotherapy shared by all effective therapies. A good case can be made for the claim that effective therapies share important common elements, that contribute more significantly to outcome than the specific techniques by means of which therapies may be differentiated. One central common factor that each of the four approaches described here gives considerable attention to is the quality of the therapeutic relationship, or what we may term the treatment alliance. A more detailed consideration of the treatment alliance, and the importance of common factors, is provided in Chapter 12.

REFERENCES

Barkham, M., Rees, A., Shapiro, D. A., Stiles, W. B., Agnew, R. M., Halstead, J., Culverwell, A. & Harrington, V. M. G. (1996). Outcome of time-limited psychotherapy in applied settings: Replicating the Second Sheffield Psychotherapy Project. *Journal of Consulting and Clinical Psychotherapy*, *64*, 1079–1085.

Brockman, B., Poynton, A., Ryle A. & Watson, J. P. (1987). Effectiveness of time limited therapy carried out by trainees; a comparison of methods. *British Journal of Psychiatry*, *151*, 602–609.

Brooke, R. (1994). Assessment for psychotherapy: Clinical indicators of self cohesion and self pathology. *British Journal of Psychotherapy*, *10*, 317–330.

Creed, F. H., Fernandes, L., Guthrie, E., Palmer, S., Ratcliffe, J., Read, N., Rigby, C., Thompson, D. & Tomenson, B. (2003). The cost-effectiveness of psychotherapy and paroxetine for severe irritable bowel syndrome. *Gastroenterology*, *124*, 303–317.

Davidson, K. M. (2000). *Cognitive therapy for personality disorders: A guide for clinicians.* London: Arnold (Hodder).

Fonagy, P. & Target, M. (2005) Some reflections on the therapeutic action of psychoanalytic therapy. In J. S. Auerbach, K. N. Levy & C.E. Schaffer (Eds), *Relatedness, self-definition and mental representation.* London: Routledge, 191–212.

Fosbury, J. A., Bosley, C. M., Ryle, A., Sonksen, P. H. & Judd, S. L. (1997). A trial of cognitive analytic therapy in poorly controlled type 1 patients. *Diabetes Care*, *20*, 959–964.

Guthrie, E., Creed, F., Dawson, D. & Tomenson, B. (1991). A controlled trial of psychological treatment for the irritable bowel syndrome. *Gastroenterology*, *100*, 450–457.

Guthrie, E., Kapur, N., Mackway-Jones, K., Chew-Graham, C., Moorey, J., Mendel, E., Marion-Francis, F., Sanderson, S., Turpin, C., Boddy, G. & Tomenson, B. (2001). Randomized controlled trial of brief psychological intervention after deliberate self poisoning. *British Medical Journal*, *323*, 135–138.

Guthrie, E., Margison, F., Mackay, H., Chew-Graham, C., Moorey, J. & Sibbald, B. (2004). Effectiveness of psychodynamic interpersonal therapy training for primary care counselors. *Psychotherapy Research*, *14*, 161–175.

Guthrie, E., Moorey, J., Margison, F., Barker, H., Palmer, S., McGrath, G., Tomenson, B. & Creed, F. (1999). Cost-effectiveness of brief psychodynamic–interpersonal therapy in high utilizers of psychiatric services. *Archives of General Psychiatry*, *56*, 519–526.

Hamilton, J., Guthrie, E., Creed, F., Thompson, D., Tomenson, B., Bennett, R., Moriarty, K., Stephens, W. & Liston, R. (2000). A randomized controlled trial of psychotherapy in patients with chronic functional dyspepsia. *Gastroenterology*, *119*, 661–669.

Hobson, R. F. (1971). Imagination and amplification in psychotherapy. *Journal of Analytical Psychology*, *16*, 79–105.

Hobson, R. F. (1985). *Forms of feeling.* London: Tavistock.

Kabat-Zinn, J. (2003). Mindfulness-based interventions in context: Past, present, and future. *Clinical Psychology Science and Practice*, *10*, 144–156.

Kelly, G. A. (1955). *The psychology of personal constructs*. New York: Norton.

Kernberg, O., Selzer, M., Koenigsberg, H., Carr, A. & Applebaum, A. (1989). *Psychodynamic psychotherapy of borderline patients*. New York: Basic.

Linehan, M. M. (1993a). *Cognitive–behavioral treatment of borderline personality*. New York: Guildford.

Linehan, M. M. (1993b). *Skills training manual for treating borderline personality disorder*. New York: Guildford.

Mackay, H. C., West, W., Moorey, J., Guthrie, E. & Margison, F. (2001). Counsellors' experiences of changing their practice: Learning the psychodynamic-interpersonal model of therapy. *Counselling and Psychotherapy Research*, *1*(1), 29–39.

Margison, F. (2002). Psychodynamic interpersonal therapy. In J. Holmes & A. Bateman (Eds), *Integration in psychotherapy: Models and methods*. London: Routledge, 107–124.

Meares, R. (1993). Reversals: on certain pathologies of identification. In A. Goldberg (Ed.), *Progress in self psychology* (Vol. 9). Hillsdale, NJ: Analytic.

Meares, R. (1997). Stimulus entrapment. *Psychoanalytic Inquiry*, *17*, 223–234.

Meares, R. (1999). The 'adualistic' representation of trauma: on malignant internalization. *American Journal of Psychotherapy*, *53*, 392–402.

Meares, R. (2000). *Intimacy and alienation*. London: Routledge.

Meares, R. (2004). An outline of the conversational model. *American Journal of Psychotherapy*, *1*, 51–57.

Meares, R., Stevenson, J., & Comerford, A. (1999). Psychotherapy with borderline patients, part I: A comparison between treated and untreated cohorts. *Australian and New Zealand Journal of Psychiatry*, *33*, 467–472.

Moorey, J., & Guthrie, E. (2003). Persons and experience: Essential aspects of psychodynamic interpersonal therapy. *Psychodynamic Practice*, *9*, 547–564.

Ryle, A. (1975). *Frames and cages*. London: Chatto and Windus.

Ryle, A. & Kerr, I. (2002). *Introducing cognitive analytic therapy*. Chichester: Wiley.

Sandler, J. (1976). Countertransference and role-responsiveness. *International Review of Psychoanalysis*, *3*, 43–47.

Sandler, J., Dare, C. & Holder, A. (1992). *The patient and the analyst*. London: Karnac.

Seagal, Z. V., Williams, J. G. W. & Teasdale, J. D. (2002). *Mindfulness-based cognitive therapy for depression: A new approach for preventing relapse*. New York: Guildford.

Shapiro, D. A., Barkham, M., Rees, A., Hardy, G. E., Reynolds, S. & Startup, M. (1994). Effects of treatment duration and severity of depression on the effectiveness of cognitive–behavioural and psychodynamic–interpersonal psychotherapy. *Journal of Consulting and Clinical Psychology*, *62*, 522–534.

Shapiro, D. A. & Firth, J. (1987) Prescriptive vs exploratory psychotherapy: Outcomes of the Sheffield Psychotherapy Project. *British Journal of Psychiatry*, *151*, 790–799.

Stern, D. N., Sander, L. W., Nahum, J. P., Harrison, A. M., Lyons-Ruth, K, Morgan, A. C., Bruschweiler-Stern, N. & Tronick, E. Z. (1998). Non-interpretive mechanisms in psychoanalytic therapy. *International Journal of Psycho-Analysis*, *79*, 903–921.

Stevenson, J. & Meares, R. (1992). An outcome study of psychotherapy in borderline personality disorder. *American Journal of Psychiatry*, *149*, 358–362.

Stevenson, J. & Meares, R. (1999). Psychotherapy with borderline patients, part 11: A preliminary cost–benefit analysis. *Australian and New Zealand Journal of Psychiatry*, *33*, 473–477.

Swales, M., Heard, H. L. & Williams, J. G. M. (2000). Linehan's dialectical behaviour therapy (DBT) for borderline personality disorder: Overview and adaptation. *Journal of Mental Health*, *9*, 7–23.

Treasure, J., Todd, G., Brolley, M., Tiller, J., Nehmad, A. & Denman, F. (1995). A pilot study of a randomised trial of cognitive analytic therapy for adult anorexia nervosa. *Behaviour Research and Therapy*, *33*, 363–367.

Vygotsky, L. S. (1978). *Mind in society*. Cambridge, MA: Harvard University Press.

Winnicott, D. W. (1967/1971). Mirror-role of mother and family in child development. In *Playing and reality*. London: Routledge, 111–118.

Wright, K. (1991) *Vision and separation*. London: Free Association.

Young, J., Klosko, J. & Weishaar, M. (2003). *Schema therapy. A practitioner's guide*. New York: Guildford.

6

Therapeutic Communities and Day Services for People with Personality Disorders

KATE HELLIN

The difficulties experienced by people with personality disorders are likely to have originated early in their lives and to have become a fundamental part of them, expressed over time and in many situations. Difficulty in making and sustaining good relationships is a central aspect of personality disorder. This can be understood in terms of an early absence of secure relationships with sufficiently reliable and consistent parental figures. A secure attachment allows the person to develop a sense of themselves as separate from others, with clear interpersonal boundaries. Without this, people tend to feel fragmented. They experience extremes of emotions and similarly see those around them in extremes too, e.g. as being near perfect or utterly contemptible. Difficulty in achieving a more moderate and integrated sense of themselves lies at the heart of the difficulties in coping with both intimacy and separation. People with borderline personality disorders (the group that CMHTs are most likely to meet) find it hard to tolerate both closeness and being alone.

It is ironic that services for this group also tend to offer extremes, and so reinforce the very difficulties that they aim to alleviate. Services provide what they can. This might, rarely, be formal weekly psychotherapy, or *ad hoc* occasional input. Both leave expanses of time within which people can feel very alone. When the individual cannot cope in relative isolation, the situation is likely to escalate into crisis. The nature of people's distress

Personality Disorder and Community Mental Health Teams: A Practitioner's Guide. Edited by
M. J. Sampson, R. A. McCubbin and P. Tyrer. © 2006 John Wiley & Sons, Ltd.

will often manifest in severe self-harming and suicidal behaviour. They may be admitted for in-patient psychiatric treatment, usually on an acute ward, full of others' proximity, and suffer loss of privacy and of control of everyday aspects of their lives. Their distress increases.

The experience of in-patient stays in general psychiatric in-patient units is often aversive for the individual, family and friends, as well as for staff. In-patient facilities are geared towards those with severe mental illness. There is limited opportunity for staff to formulate an understanding of the person with personality disorder, to consider the emotional impact of being with them and to work with them therapeutically. They often feel they have little to offer. Whilst in-patient admission to acute psychiatric wards may be necessary in the short term and during crisis, the potential for fundamental change for someone with personality disorder, in a psychiatric ward, is limited.

If out-patient treatment is not enough and in-patient treatment too much or the wrong kind, where is the middle ground? The answer might lie in day services (known in American literature as partial hospitalisation) and those therapeutic communities that provide a specialist service for people with personality disorder, in the form of both residential and day services.

This chapter will begin by considering common elements of day services and the specific features of therapeutic communities. It will focus on the therapeutic ingredients of these modalities. For ease of reference, I shall refer to the recipients of the service as *participants* or *members* to distinguish them from *staff*, although staff are participants and members too, of course. The emphasis here will be on services for people with borderline personality disorder as this is the group who are present in greatest numbers in community mental health services.

CHARACTERISTICS OF DAY SERVICES AND THERAPEUTIC COMMUNITIES

Day services and therapeutic communities, as discussed here, are those with an emphasis on an intensive experience, with the aim of bringing about therapeutic change and rehabilitation for their members. These contrast with day hospitals or day care, which are concerned more with the long-term support/maintenance of people with severe mental health problems and managing crises with those who might otherwise be in-patients.

A day service for people with personality disorders and a day hospital for people with psychoses may have a number of features in common, e.g. a similar range of meetings and activities. However, the cultures of the services are likely to be very different. The former are likely to be emotionally expressive and intensive. In the latter, change will be slow and facilitated gently so as to avoid the possibility of relapse caused by high levels of emotion.

Day services for people with personality disorders may draw from a range of theoretical perspectives or they may be focused around a particular orientation such as a psychoanalytically informed day programme (see, e.g., Bateman & Fonagy, 1999, 2001). A general principle is that in an intensive environment, the person's inner world is played out between the person and others, i.e. externalised so that the intrapsychic becomes interpersonal and can be observed and addressed.

An example may clarify this. Typically, different aspects of individuals resonate with different people in the staff team. Some people think Annie is callous, manipulative and not motivated to change, while others, with equal fervour, find her sensitive, vulnerable and deserving. Who is right? Maybe both groups are. Different aspects of people also affect different sub-groups of the staff team in different ways. The team can become divided and conflicts can develop about how to work with Annie, whether the team should be working with her at all and so on. Differences between staff members can be thought of as valuable information about aspects of the individual, or about psychological processes in the service as a whole.

The day service or therapeutic community has the explicit purpose of being able to take a whole community or whole staff team approach, see the differences and find ways of integrating them. Coherent staff teams are then better able to work consistently with the fragmented service members, enabling them to recognise and integrate the different aspects of themselves, and their perceptions of others. Principles of group psychotherapy, systems and milieu therapy are key here and even services with a different theoretical grounding are likely to be informed by them.

Both day services and therapeutic communities offer an intensive, structured clinical approach within a therapeutic milieu. The programmes will vary in length from seven days a week, residential, to once-weekly day programmes, comprising a number of elements/components. Membership may be time limited, extending from a few weeks to months or even years, or be of an indefinite duration. Regular attendance is normally seen as crucial. Lateness and intermittent attendance is likely to be challenged as part of the therapy.

Most of the work takes place in groups although people may, in some services, also have individual therapy as part of the programme. Typically, participants will attend small groups with an interpersonal and psychodynamic focus, creative therapies such as art, psychodrama and music, and

Time	Monday	Tuesday	Wednesday	Thursday	Friday	Saturday	Sunday
9.00 – 9.30			Staff Handover				Staff Handover
9.30 – 10.45			Community Meeting				
10.45 – 11.15	Aftergroup	Aftergroup	Aftergroup	Aftergroup	Aftergroup	Aftergroup	
11.15 – 12.30	Small Group New Residents Group	Deep Clean	11.15 - 12.15 1st Wed - Elections 2nd Wed - Reviews or New Resident Groups 3rd Wed - Staff Study Day 4th & 5th Wed - Reviews or New Resident Groups	11.15 - 12.15 Housekeeping Group Visitors Group Research Group Focus Groups	Small Group New Residents Group		
12.45 – 1.00	Cleaning	Cleaning	Cleaning	Cleaning	Cleaning		
	health clinic	health clinic	health clinic	health clinic	health clinic		
	Lunch	Lunch	Lunch	Lunch	Lunch		
2.45 (3.15 Tues) – 4.30	Art / Psychodrama	New Residents 1.00pm Selection 1.00pm Sports & Games 3.15 - 4.30 Network 3.15 - 4.30	Art / Psychodrama	Work Group or Leavers' Group/Transition Group	Welfare or Workgroup		
4.30 – 5.00	Aftergroup	Community Tea	Aftergroup		Community Tea		
5.00			Handover				Handover
7.00			Dinner				Dinner
9.00 – 9.45			Elected residents meet with staff				Elected residents meet with staff
10.00 – 10.30			Registration and informal meeting				Registration and informal meeting
10.45			Closing and securing the building				Closing and securing the building

Figure 6.1 Example of a therapeutic community programme

skill-based groups, which may utilise cognitive and behavioural methods. Dependent on participants' needs, family and couple therapy may also be offered along with other groups, to address specific tasks. There will usually be a regular meeting of the whole service in a large group, often called the community meeting. A typical therapeutic community programme is shown in Figure 6.1.

These day services and therapeutic communities offer an intense and comprehensive approach. A lot can happen in the time available. There is the opportunity for integration of learning across different parts of the programme. Experiences and information from one event will be shared and processed in other parts. Material uncovered in a psychotherapy group is available to be addressed more practically in a skill-development group. Participants work with different staff and peers. They benefit from the range of therapeutic approaches, role-models and breadth of interpersonal experience and from the feedback on offer. Peer feedback is a crucial therapeutic element.

The time-limited nature of many day programmes can intensify the work, although it is not clear what the appropriate time limit is for different people. Increasingly, the literature shows that extended follow-up through out-patient groups and individual support is important in maintaining changes (e.g. Chiesa & Fonagy, 2002).

Although, for economic and political reasons, there is an increasing emphasis on day rather than in-patient services, for some people a residential service may be still be the best option. Day or out-patient settings may not be containing enough where the person is especially distressed and unable to manage their feelings safely, or where an abuser lives nearby. Emotions can feel insurmountable in the night and there may be a greater risk of self-harm and suicide attempts. The 24-hour support in a residential setting can help and there is the chance to learn from others about how to cope with sleeping difficulties. It is harder to drop out when things feel tough if you live there and may be far from home. For many, the service is a place of safety and security where they can focus on their own needs rather than getting caught up in other demands. There is more opportunity to engage in the daily living tasks (e.g. cooking, cleaning) and more unstructured time, both of which can be powerful agents of change. Indeed, a residential setting will intensify all the therapeutic aspects of the approach.

On the other hand, a residential setting may be particularly prone to insularity. People may find the adjustment of leaving and re-integrating into their home environments more difficult from a residential than a day service. Learning across environments is likely to be easier when someone is going home each day or for parts of the week.

SPECIFIC FEATURES OF THERAPEUTIC COMMUNITIES

The term 'therapeutic community' was originally used in the 1940s to indicate a shift from psychiatric treatment involving incarceration and substantial loss of dignity to a more humane approach. A decade later, the expression was simultaneously coined on either side of the Atlantic to describe quite different approaches.

In the UK, therapeutic communities developed as places where the hierarchical differences between staff and patients were eroded. They shared power to make decisions about the running of the service and treatment of the community members. These therapeutic communities are sometimes known as 'democratic therapeutic communities', and will be described in more detail in this chapter.

In the USA, the term became used for organisations treating ex-alcohol or drug users in an authoritarian, hierarchical regime. These are often run without professionals: staff are drawn from ex-residents. These are sometimes known as 'concept' houses (Kennard, 1998).

There are also a number of 'therapeutic communities' that attend to spiritual, social, religious and philosophical dimensions of distress and human experience, and sometimes share the same term. These often exist as part of the anti-psychiatry movement and would not consider themselves as forms of treatment.

Although people with personality disorders may join any of the types of therapeutic community, it is the democratic therapeutic communities that aim to address the specific difficulties associated with personality disorders. It is this type of therapeutic community that this chapter will focus on.

In the UK, there are 28 therapeutic communities that offer services to people with personality disorders. Of these, two are in prisons and 17 are voluntary agencies. Only nine are National Health Service resources (Association of Therapeutic Communities, 2005).

In a therapeutic community, the *therapeutic environment* itself is the primary agent of change. Control by staff and by external forces is minimised. Authority is invested in the structure and ground rules of each service, rather than in the staff. Participants take over staff functions to a significant degree. Members of the community take as great a role as possible in the day-to-day running and decision-making of the community, supported by staff where necessary. In many cases, therapeutic community members will be responsible for making decisions about admitting people to the community. They will also sometimes vote to discharge those who repeatedly break the community rules and do not take responsibility for themselves and their actions. The importance of such decisions encourages members to participate and to take personal responsibility. They are considered to be experts in their own and each other's conditions.

For people who have tended to be at the receiving end of badly used or abusive power, this may be the first time their views and thoughts have been taken seriously. Participants have real power in the running of the service and they experience the consequences of both their actions and their inactions. This occurs in a setting in which the consequences of one's decisions and actions are clear and open to examination, feedback and response by the community as a whole. This stands in contrast to the unwitting paternalism of mental health services in general, where people can often feel little or no control over their treatment.

The difference between day services and therapeutic communities is a blurred one. There will always be limits to the degree of authority and responsibility the therapeutic community members have. Services may use therapeutic community principles to varying degrees, depending on the philosophical approach, service setting and client group. These will be determined by the context of the therapeutic community. For example, in a risk-averse political climate, a therapeutic community will be more restricted. A service that can select people who can take full responsibility for themselves and who are freely choosing to attend, can expect and demand more of its members and apply therapeutic community principles more completely. The limitations will be greater, for example, in a prison unit, and the therapeutic community principles more modified. Here, members' practical responsibilities may be limited to certain tasks such as serving food. The emphasis is on optimising the scope for individual responsibility within such severe constraints.

BOUNDARIES

The idea of the day service as a middle ground between residential and out-patient services has been touched on earlier. A day programme must establish and maintain a therapeutic culture in which participants' powerful feelings can be contained without them feeling intruded upon and overwhelmed. Clear structures and day service rules are enforced compassionately but firmly. To work within the boundaries, participants must agree to take responsibility for themselves (or try to).

The ethos of individual responsibility for one's own behaviour and own safety is central to the maintenance of safety in the day service. There are rules concerning the use of drugs and alcohol, violence towards self, others and property, disclosure of dangerous behaviour, confidentiality and attendance, and a clear process by which breaches of these are dealt with. An individual must actively decide to join the programme and thereby to respect the rules. The purpose of the rules must be to create a therapeutic culture in which people can feel safe enough to be themselves and open up.

People with personality disorders tend to challenge the rules, which they experience as coming from staff/malign authority figures. In a healthy and therapeutic day service culture, the rules will be understood by its participants as necessary for safety and owned by the whole community, rather than seen as being imposed by staff. Peer pressure, coupled with the emphasis on individual responsibility, rather than staff intervention, becomes the means by which rules are maintained.

STRUCTURED PROGRAMMES

Day services and therapeutic communities have a highly structured programme with an expectation that people will attend everything and will adhere to strict time boundaries.

The structured programme and rules provide the framework for the involvement of participants and the means of achieving the tasks that are part of the service. People with personality disorders often lead chaotic and disorganised lives. The structure offers a very different experience. It takes some getting used to, and initially people feel restricted and infantilised. It is perceived as an external authority being imposed upon them. Issues with authority are activated. As new people settle in, they usually begin to appreciate that the structure provides a predictable, stable context for the intense and frightening feelings. This is akin to the secure base, or consistent parental figure, which was often lacking at crucial formative times in childhood. Gradually, most participants internalise the structure and become more able to organise themselves, although challenges to the structure (lateness, missing groups) are often an ongoing part of the therapeutic process for some people as this internalisation takes place.

ENGAGEMENT

People with personality disorders often have unsatisfactory experiences of 'helping' services. This results in fraught and unsatisfactory encounters between staff and the individual, with both parties attacking and/or withdrawing from the other, often without much awareness of this. Because of this, there needs to be an active focus, beyond that of traditional services, on engaging people and addressing the rifts that can easily develop.

In some day services and therapeutic communities, individual therapy is the primary means of engaging people into the programme. A regular one-to-one therapy creates a special and intimate relationship, and a different therapeutic experience. It intensifies transference feelings, which can be explored in the individual therapy and beyond. The person will be encouraged to share what is spoken of in individual therapy in other parts of the service so that others can respond to it, and the individual can learn more about him- or herself. However, for some, the extreme feelings of anger, love, hatred, disappointment and envy stirred up by such intimacy makes the contact untenable.

One danger is that a person may resist sharing her or his special relationship and will value the individual therapy and denigrate the rest. This can be hard to challenge by staff and participants alike. The person can feel that the only good thing she or he has is being attacked and cling on even more tenaciously to her or his position.

The group setting of day services and therapeutic communities offers an alternative means of engaging people. In groups, the transference feelings tend to be more dilute and people form attachments with the service as a whole, and the individuals within it in a less intense and polarised way. They are more likely to form alliances with their peers, who have 'been there too'.

In therapeutic communities, the aim is for people to feel part of the community by taking up real roles and becoming a necessary part of the community functioning. This develops their sense of belonging and of engagement, without entering the emotional extremes of attachment to an individual.

GROUP THERAPY

Groups can be a powerful agent of change. Peers learn to use an emotional language and model the appropriate expression of feelings. Through the experience of others' and their own feelings, people become more able to differentiate their own feelings, talk about them and express them appropriately. Peer and staff feedback play a vital role in helping people to recognise their patterns of relating to others. Group members hear about others' experiences and increase their capacity to understand and empathise with others. People learn better ways of coping from others. They can address issues with authority through exploration of feelings about authority figures in the group. There is the opportunity for people to take on a variety of social roles and try out different ways of functioning. A large enough and sufficiently well functioning group will contain members who can provide a counter-view and create a balance of views. It also helps to ensure that a core value is maintained, i.e. that 'truth' is relative.

Creative therapies (art therapy, music therapy, drama therapy and psychodrama) offer an opportunity to find symbols for feelings, which some find easier than words alone. Others' witness to someone's images helps them to understand and reflect on themselves.

Many programmes have additional groups with specific tasks depending on the philosophy of the programme and the needs of the participants. These might include cognitive behaviour therapy groups (for anxiety, depression, anger management, eating problems), problem-solving groups, relationship and family groups, groups for relaxation, skills development and budgeting, and practical groups, with support for dealing with housing, social services, other agencies etc.

THE DAY-TO-DAY RUNNING OF THE SERVICE AND UNSTRUCTURED TIME

Unlike a day service, participants in a therapeutic community will be involved in activities that are genuinely necessary for the service to function. In other words, community members may be totally responsible for buying and cooking food, cleaning, laundry, administration, managing finances of the service and so on.

Undertaking these jobs gives therapeutic community members a real means of joining the community and developing a valued and necessary role. One of the usual questions at a selection group is 'can you cook?', with collective delight when the applicant turns out to be a chef. Where people lack daily living skills, they will be supported, in small work groups, to learn these and typically become very accomplished.

The day-to-day running of the service gives people experiences of particular kinds of interaction that are revealing of interpersonal issues and are sources of learning. For example, someone's tendency to take over from others and dominate may be more visible in a group that is designing the new brick barbeque than in a psychotherapy group, where they control that tendency. Similarly, an individual's avoidance of and attachment to particular jobs provides material for examination in the community.

The structure of groups, and rotas for cooking, cleaning etc., creates a series of boundaried spaces within which people's feelings and interactions become evident, and can then be explored. The therapeutic aspects of unstructured time may be equally important and significant. In unstructured times, people can choose what they do, whether they spend time alone or with others, how they negotiate which television channel to watch, whether to put their own wishes and needs before those of someone else. In this time, real events take place between people, which, as with everything else, is material on which the whole community can reflect. People in one therapeutic community saw the unstructured time as a safe space in which to make and explore real relationships, where destructive patterns could become evident and therefore available to work on and change. Some people report this as being the most useful aspect of time in a day service or therapeutic community.

COMMUNITY MEETINGS OR LARGE GROUP MEETINGS

Most in-patient treatments and day services have at least one large group meeting a week that involves everyone in the programme: staff and participants. It provides a framework to support the change-orientated activity of the rest of the programme. The community meeting is a place in which systemic issues can be addressed, i.e. those things that relate to the programme as a whole. Such a meeting can be seen as a 'milieu biopsy' or a window onto the programme, and the ideal place to address the differences between different people in the service.

Its form depends on the theoretical philosophy of the programme. In the therapeutic community, the community meeting is central and has specific purposes. The coming together of all members, both staff and participants, creates the opportunity for sharing information, which can then be discussed, debated and decided upon collectively. This creates cohesion and a sense of wholeness. It allows differences to be expressed and explored publicly and limits the tendency for people to feel that things are said behind closed doors. This can be particularly important for people who have grown up in an atmosphere of unhealthy 'secrets', and those whose contributions have never been validated or valued.

Business issues relating to the running of the community are addressed: elections for jobs, decisions about task allocation, boundary issues between groups or in the community as a whole.

The community meeting is also the place in which breaches of the community rules will be addressed. There is full scope for feedback to someone behaving in a disturbing or dangerous way from both those who are sympathetic and those who are not. This is also the place to enact sanctions, the therapeutic community's consequences for breaches of the rules. In a therapeutic community where consensus cannot be reached, decisions will often be made by democratic vote.

THE ROLE OF STAFF

Staff have a range of roles in day services and therapeutic communities. They must maintain the boundaries of the service, which will be attacked a great deal by its participants, sometimes by staff themselves and sometimes by external demands. When a service is working well, the boundary maintenance is carried out by the service participants as much as by staff, but the healthy functioning of any service is always in flux depending upon its membership, recent events or traumas, staff and member changes and so on. At times of greatest disruption, the staff may need to be more active in keeping the boundaries in place.

Staff need to watch out for destructive group processes such as scapegoating, idealisation and splitting. These are ways in which people with personality disorder often cope with their feelings and the intensity of the day service and therapeutic community setting can exacerbate these tendencies. It is common for individuals, the service or sub-groups within it to be idealised, while those outside are seen in unduly negative ways. This can severely damage the therapeutic potential of the service. Loyalty to the idealised service or group becomes paramount and suppresses the freedom to question, criticise and explore. The opportunity to learn is lost. The culture can become indoctrinating, cultlike and at the extreme highly destructive.

Services in which these dynamics are prevalent lose healthy relationships with 'the outside world'. As well as questioning, understanding, interpreting and exploring such destructive dynamics in the service, staff need to maintain their relationships with their professional networks and organisations/bodies beyond the immediate service. This enables them to keep their wider perspectives and to recognise the destructive dynamics for what they are.

Typically, people with personality disorders have been subject to more *doing to* than *being with*. Contact between mental health staff and people with personality disorders is often borne out of crisis. The mental health system demands action to manage the crisis. Staff become active and controlling, which may be felt as abusive: a repeat of early abusive experiences. On the other hand, clear decisive action may be the best way of containing someone's extreme feelings. The skill comes in judging when to act and when not to.

This kind of judgement occurs in many situations other than crisis. In therapeutic communities, running the service day to day provides people with powerful and direct learning experiences. Staff have to make personal judgements about whether they should intervene or stand back and let someone get things wrong. The achievement of the particular task is secondary to the process, i.e. the opportunity for people to try things out and learn from the experience of getting it right or wrong.

Such judgements can be extremely difficult when the decisions are about issues of safety and risk. On joining a therapeutic community, staff often undergo huge adjustments as they reconcile their notions of professionalism (in which they are the healthy party, the patients 'sick') with the principle of sharing responsibility and authority, equally more often than not, with service participants. Working out these issues is an ongoing process and can be confusing and stressful.

Being with people with personality disorder elicits very powerful feelings. Individual staff need to look after themselves emotionally: attend to work and home boundaries and be aware of the tendency to become over-involved and burnt out.

Staff teams also need to look after themselves. Staff relationships are seen as a major source of information and understanding and as an agent of change. Too often, the splits and conflicts that develop in those working with this client group occur between professional groups, between services. They become entwined with pre-existing rivalries and animosities and there is little chance of really resolving these.

Just as the community meeting offers the opportunity for a whole group view for the participants of the service, staff group supervision can provide the opportunity for staff to think together clearly, rationally, reliably and non-judgementally about the programme members and wider dynamic currents. This helps the team to act thoughtfully and consistently and to reach balanced judgements as far as possible.

In most services, there is also a special staff meeting. The aim of this is to address the working relationships between staff as the means of understanding the different experiences that different staff members and staff subgroups may have of individual participants in the service. Here staff talk and think about their feelings, reactions, relationships and conflicts *with each other*, and try to process their emotions. Staff need to be confident that feelings are not dangerous and that they are survivable. In these ways, staff can make sense of participants' and their own feelings and manage these in ways that are helpful. Good, integrated functioning of the staff team provides an experience of good early parenting and containment: an experience that has often been absent for those who develop personality difficulties. A divided staff team runs the risk of perpetuating the fragmentation that many people with personality disorder suffer.

SAFETY

People with personality disorders very often cannot experience their feelings simply and directly, and cannot express or process these appropriately. This difficulty lies at the heart of self-harm, drug and substance misuse, and results in troubled, chaotic and damaging interpersonal relationships. It may cause people, consciously or unconsciously, to precipitate crises. Crises give the person the chance to feel and express feelings, and to test out the staff, other participants and the programme boundaries. Helping people to express and tolerate their feelings better is often seen as a primary task in a day programme or therapeutic community.

There is sometimes anxiety about addressing strong feelings in a day service setting, for fear of escalating the emotional temperature and overwhelming participants' coping strategies. These dilemmas often occur just before the end of the day and can be understood as an example of boundary-testing, which needs to be addressed in itself. Not addressing feelings within the boundary of the day programme increases the chances of emotion being inappropriately and perhaps dangerously expressed outside the relative safety of the programme.

Structured techniques can help with this. For example, empty chair work and role-playing encourage feelings, but have a discrete ending, which can help people wind down. Some programmes have an explicit arrangement for situations where more time is needed to support someone to recover sufficiently from strong feelings to be safe. This may be in the form of additional time with designated people, but should have its own limits, which are understood clearly by all, including the distressed or angry participant.

The safety of the service depends on service participants agreeing to the structure and rules. The decision about whether to offer someone a place in the service will partly be determined by an assessment of someone's capacity to use the structure, rules and therapy in order to remain safe. In most day services this judgement will be a professional one, made by staff on the basis of an assessment. In therapeutic communities, the decision will also be based on discussion between the applicant, other service members, staff and often carers. Service participants are often particularly attuned to the accounts of applicants and can draw upon their direct experience and a sense of identification to judge an individual's capacity to use the approach within acceptable limits of safety. In many therapeutic communities the decision about admission is made in a meeting with a majority membership of participants and a minority of staff, on a democratic vote.

Similarly, when working in the therapeutic community with people who are tending to express their distress through acts of violence (breaching the rules), the community as a whole, including the individual and staff, will come together to consider how to support the person. Their task is to decide whether the person can or will be able to use the support and structures available and whether the risks they present to themselves and others are acceptable or manageable. In a therapeutic community, this decision will ultimately be made by the majority membership of service participants, not by staff alone.

In a therapeutic community, both staff and participants should be clear that the statutory responsibilities of staff must be upheld throughout the process. Safety is maintained through the collaborative relationship between staff, participants, carers and outside agencies. Service operation cannot be maintained if that collaboration breaks down, and in these circumstances crisis meetings are held to address the issue. Failure to reach an adequate resolution would mean the democratic therapeutic community approach had become untenable and staff would become solely responsible for managing risk.

This is not likely to happen, however, because service participants bear individual and collective responsibility for safety and for maintaining it. This ensures that they invest in the system. If the system fails, the service will not be viable. These high stakes mean that service participants are motivated to take responsibility for keeping their service safe and functioning.

EVIDENCE OF EFFECTIVENESS

The published literature about the effectiveness of day services and therapeutic communities for people with personality disorder comes largely from Canada, Norway and Britain, and shows evidence for the effectiveness of both. A full review of the evidence base for these approaches is beyond the scope of this chapter and what follows will be selective. On the whole, those attending the Canadian and Norwegian services have symptoms of less severity than those in the British services. For this reason, the focus here will be on the British literature and, in particular, on the randomised control trials that have been published.

A randomised controlled trial has examined the effect of up to 18 months of a psycho-analytically orientated day programme (group and individual work) for people with borderline personality disorder, compared with general psychiatric care. Frequency of suicide attempts and self-harm, number and duration of in-patient admissions, use of psychotropic medication and self-reported anxiety, depression, general symptom distress, interpersonal functioning and social adjustment all improved in the group of people who attended the day programme, in comparison with those who received general psychiatric care (Bateman & Fonagy, 1999). These gains were maintained and, on most measures, continued to improve over an 18-month follow-up. This was in contrast to those who received routine psychiatric care, who made little change over the same period (Bateman & Fonagy, 2001). This suggests that the day programme stimulated longer-term changes, which continued after the treatment.

The case for the effectiveness of therapeutic community treatment in general has probably been best made through a meta-analysis. This reviewed the literature worldwide and identified over 8000 relevant papers, including ten randomised controlled trials, ten studies that compared different institutions and 32 with some kind of control. Only 29 of these met rigorous methodological standards. The meta-analysis of these gave 'very strong support to the effectiveness of therapeutic community treatment' (Lees, Manning & Rawlings, 1999).

There are some difficulties in drawing specific conclusions from this work. The definition of therapeutic community employed by the studies was quite variable and it is impossible to know what may have been the therapeutic ingredients of any of the treatment programmes. Numbers were often low and attrition rates high. There is great difficulty in truly randomising the allocation of participants to the treatment programmes in a therapeutic community and so the randomised controlled trials are, at best, partial.

There are a number of studies that have been carried out in a residential therapeutic community population. For example, Dolan, Warren and Norton (1997), at one-year follow-up, found a significant reduction in borderline symptoms in 42.9 per cent of people treated in a residential therapeutic community, compared with a reduction of 17.9 per cent in a comparison group who were not admitted.

While there is some reasonable evidence for the effectiveness of day services and therapeutic communities for people with personality disorder, there is little that systematically examines what works for whom and what are the crucial ingredients for people with varying needs.

HOW DOES THIS APPLY TO CMHTs?

In Britain, there are relatively few National Health Service therapeutic communities for people with personality disorders. Likewise, day services of the intensive, therapeutic nature described here are not available evenly across the country. For many CMHT staff who have neither resource available locally, this chapter may seem academic if its purpose is to better inform them to make appropriate referrals.

In fact, some of the principles used in therapeutic communities and day services may be useful in CMHTs. However dispersed and un-unified a CMHT may feel to its members, it is a naturally occurring group within which the interpersonal patterns that its clients (and staff) bring will be expressed. By considering the CMHT as a whole, it may be possible to think about the impact of particular clients and how the service responds in more or less therapeutic ways. The CMHT environment will be affected by whether there is commonality of philosophy and purpose amongst its members. It will depend upon the degree of respect for others and the recognition of skills, abilities and functional aspects of each other and of service participants and appreciation of the importance of relationships. This includes understanding the potential splits between caregivers, and the need for staff to have support. There may be scope for CMHTs to find ways of harnessing the healthy aspects of their clients' functioning: for example, making the client central in his or her own risk assessment.

Perhaps, CMHTs can take from therapeutic communities and day services the notion that their functioning as a team will affect how they are able to do their work. Team reflective practice, akin to the special staff meetings described earlier, may be a means of addressing this. Here, CMHT members consider their styles, stances and working practices and inter-relationships and how these support or conflict with their task. Such a meta-view can help to put things into perspective and be a big support in the difficult work with people with personality disorders.

ACKNOWLEDGEMENTS

The chapter reads infinitely better for the critical but kind comments from Joyce Davies, Kate Edynbry, Phil Hartley, Matthew Haslam, Matthew Kemsley, Michael Göpfert and Tori Otero. Michael Stoker helped me get up to date with the research literature and Jenny Davenport word processed the programme, which is adapted from the Webb House Therapeutic Community programme. Ilia Maltezou and Matt Nicoll helped me to understand the importance of unstructured time.

REFERENCES

Association of Therapeutic Communities. (2005). http://therapeuticcommunities.org
Bateman, A. & Fonagy, P. (1999). Effectiveness of partial hospitalization in the treatment of borderline personality disorder: A randomised controlled trial. *American Journal of Psychiatry 156*(10), 1563–1569.
Bateman, A. & Fonagy, P. (2001). Treatment of borderline personality disorder with psycho-analytically orientated partial hospitalization: An 18-month follow-up. *American Journal of Psychiatry 158*(1), 36–42.

Chiesa, M. & Fonagy, P. (2002). From the therapeutic community to the community: A preliminary evaluation of a psychosocial outpatient service for severe personality disorders. *Therapeutic Communities 23*(4), 247–259.

Dolan, B. M., Warren, F. & Norton, K. (1997). Changes in borderline symptoms one year after therapeutic community treatment for personality disorder. *British Journal of Psychiatry, 171*, 274–279.

Kennard, D. (1998). *An introduction to therapeutic communities.* London: Kingsley.

Lees, J., Manning, N. & Rawlings, B. (1999). *Therapeutic community effectiveness: A systematic international review of therapeutic community treatment for people with personality disorders and mentally disordered offenders* (NHS Centre for Reviews and Dissemination Report 17). York: University of York.

7

Pharmacotherapy and Personality Disorders

GILES NEWTON-HOWES

INTRODUCTION

Patients who live in the community and have personality disorders regularly experience episodes of suffering and distress for which they may seek relief through their support networks. When approaching their community teams, patients are often looking for immediate relief, a 'magic pill' that will treat their ills. Their distress is often felt acutely by their community workers and this regularly leads to medical review and subsequent prescription of medication. For this reason, patients with personality disorders, particularly those who are seeking treatment, are invariably taking prescribed drugs and have generally taken a variety of medicines in the past. Often a new drug is added to an existing regime, leading to ever increasing levels of polypharmacy. Some studies show almost one-half of borderline patients take between three and eight prescribed medications. But is there any rationale behind the prescription of medication to this group of patients? This chapter will first look at the issues surrounding the prescription of drugs to patients with personality disorder in general, followed by an overview of the evidence for prescribing. Finally, some special issues, which a mental health practitioner needs to consider, will be touched on.

From a pharmacological perspective, patients with personality disorders fall into two groups, those who seek treatment and those who do not (Tyrer, Mitchard, Methuen & Ranger, 2003). The types of symptom suffered by patients with personality disorder do not inevitably lead to their presentation

Personality Disorder and Community Mental Health Teams: A Practitioner's Guide. Edited by M. J. Sampson, R. A. McCubbin and P. Tyrer. © 2006 John Wiley & Sons, Ltd.

to a community mental health team (CMHT), despite significant social and psychological morbidity. It is the former of these two groups, those seeking treatment, who usually present to community teams, and it is a sub-category of these patients, those with borderline personality, on whom most of the evidence for prescribing is based. Due to the dearth of evidence for patients with other personality pathologies, this chapter will focus on the evidence for patients with borderline personality disorder. As will become apparent, however, this group of people has a broad clinical picture, which has been sub-categorised along dimensional lines (see below). Within each dimensional sub-category, pharmacological evidence for treatment is considered and can to some extent be transferred to patients with other categorical personality disorders but similar dimensional presentations, considering the overlap that exists within the categorical diagnoses as they currently exist.

OVERVIEW OF PRESCRIBING IN THE COMMUNITY FOR PERSONALITY DISORDERS

When prescribing for personality pathology it is important to have a clear outline of what will be done, how it will be assessed, when treatment will be reviewed or stopped (see Table 7.1) and how this will be agreed upon with the patient. This is important, to prevent the unnecessary (and potentially dangerous) combination of multiple medicines and to prevent long term prescribing of medication if it offers little or no benefit for the patient. It also clarifies what the patients may expect of the medication and empowers them to be active decision-makers in the process of prescribing and review. As community patients see medical personnel less frequently than those in hospital, it is important for the patients' care co-ordinators to be involved in

Table 7.1 General principles in prescribing for personality disorder
(adapted from Soloff, 1998)

1. Clarify symptoms or symptom cluster to be targeted.
2. Choose appropriate medication to trial.
3. Agree an initial treatment plan with the patient.
4. Discuss the risks and benefits of treatment.
5. Ensure a minimum trial period is agreed within which no other medication will be trialled.
6. Review the patient regularly to assess medication effectiveness.
7. After symptom relief, agree with the patient an appropriate withdrawal strategy, bearing in mind the potential meaning of this action to the patient.

the process of prescribing and review, as they are usually in the best position to monitor progress.

The first step in the prescribing process is to clarify what is being treated. In general terms, pharmacotherapy is aimed both at acute mental state crises in the personality disordered patient and occasionally at longer term trait problems. Expert opinion encourages a dimensional and symptomatic approach to this, even when traits are targeted as opposed to mental state problems (American Psychiatric Association, 2001).

Following this clarification, the second step is to agree a plan for treatment with the patient. The expectation of immediate relief needs to be moderated by the realisation that most drugs take two to four weeks to work and a patient must be prepared to persevere for this length of time if medication is to be trialled with a realistic hope of success. Similarly, the conceptualisation of a pill designed to remedy a person's character is doomed from the outset. Personality disorder is not an 'illness' with a 'cure' and no drug (prescription or otherwise) can change a person's personality *per se*. Rather, particular symptom clusters may be positively altered by the prescription of medication (see below), although the evidence for longer term benefits of pharmacotherapy remains weak. Ideally, an agreement not to prescribe another medication within the initial four-week window should be sought, to prevent repeated drug-seeking behaviour. There is some evidence to suggest that antipsychotic medication, unlike most other psychotropics, may be more rapidly acting than this, but become less effective over time. Nevertheless, a clear approach to prescribing (that takes account of the treatment frame, see Chapter 12) offers the patient a degree of containment and clarifies expectations.

After the introduction of medication, regular monitoring for effectiveness is the third step. Whilst doing this it is important to bear in mind that the acute crisis of the personality disordered is usually self-limited and most of the evidence in the literature does not follow up patients extensively. One study by Cornelius, Soloff, Perel and Ulrich followed up patients with borderline personality disorder for 16 weeks (not long considering personality disorders are pervasive and lifelong) and found only 'irritability' was improved compared with placebo when patients used haloperidol or phenalzine (Cornelius, Soloff, Perel & Ulrich, 1993). As the evidence for long term treatment is sparse at best, it is important to review the treatment's effectiveness for each individual and reconsider prescribing when symptom relief is achieved. The decision to continue, alter dosage or stop medication needs to be a joint decision based on clinical judgement. Caution is needed when stopping medication as personality disordered patients may be more susceptible to withdrawal phenomena and patients may interpret the withdrawal of medication as abandonment, leading to a worsening of symptoms. Ultimately a 'patient based evidence' approach, combining information from research with what is known about a patient and their personal history, may prove more effective than using an 'evidence based medicine' model relying solely on the literature.

MENTAL STATE VERSUS PERSONALITY TRAIT PRESCRIBING

There has been some debate about the internal logic of prescribing at all for personality disorders. As is clear from Chapter 2, personality pathology is not a disease that fits the classical medical model and some argue that trying to pharmacologically alter the fundamental nature of a person, their personality, makes little medical sense. Despite this argument, these patients continue to suffer intra-personal and interpersonal distress and are likely to continue to seek help for their problems. Both the patient's need for help and prevailing social policy indicate that exploring all avenues to treat people is sensible. There is also beginning to accumulate in the psychiatric literature some evidence that pharmacological interventions can be of some benefit to these patients.

Others suggest that the differentiation between mental state and personality trait is somewhat arbitrary and prescribing in personality disorders is actually treating a symptom cluster more akin to major mental illness (Axis I disorder) as opposed to personality (Axis II disorder). The evidence for this is growing, and on that basis, for example, the diagnosis of schizotypal disorder in the ICD-10 is now listed alongside schizophrenia and other major psychotic illnesses. This argument is, however, primarily one of classification as opposed to treatment. With our current level of understanding, and the evidence to date, some limited guidance can be provided for the rational prescribing in personality as it is currently conceptualised.

METHODOLOGICAL CONSIDERATIONS

When reviewing the evidence regarding the prescribing for personality disorder, it is important to bear in mind the strength of the papers published and the particular problems in using a rigid scientific approach to study this group of patients. There is a generally recognised hierarchy of evidence on which clinical practice is based. The strongest evidence comes from the double blind, placebo controlled, randomised controlled trial (RCT) and the weakest from expert opinion. In general, the best studies have large numbers of patients and good follow-up and are run over an extended period of time. Unfortunately much of the research into pharmacotherapy in personality disorders has not used the RCT method and many that have are either small in number, have short follow-up times or both. This means caution is needed when considering the conclusions from published papers. We can, however, draw some tentative conclusions from the literature to date.

It is also worth bearing in mind the particular problems of the patient population studied. Although all personality disorders are enduring and include dysfunctional inner experiences, the actual presentation of the different personality pathologies varies considerably. Even within one categorical diagnosis, for example borderline personality disorder, the presentation may be one of affect dysregulation, self-harming and aggression or sexual ambivalence, chronic feelings of emptiness and a need for, but difficulty with, close relationships. For this reason there is a growing trend towards considering personality pathology as a dimensional construct, as discussed in Chapter 2. Similarly, the most consistent and robust findings for drug treatments revolve around three types of symptom cluster: cognitive/perceptual disturbance, affect dysregulation and impulsive–behavioural dyscontrol (see Table 7.2). It is within the context of these three personality dimensions that specific prescribing practices are best considered.

Table 7.2 Symptom clusters in personality disorder (adapted)
(reproduced with kind permission: *Advances in Psychiatric Treatment*; Tyrer & Bateman, 2004)

---

1. Cognitive/perceptual disturbance – this includes suspiciousness, paranoia, confused thinking, occasional reality distortion, ideas of reference, derealisation and depersonalisation illusions and occasional hallucinations.
2. Affect dysregulation – this includes lability of mood, rejection sensitivity, intense anger, feelings of emptiness, loneliness, anhedonia, dysphoria and anxiety.
3. Impulse dyscontrol – this includes sensation seeking, reckless behaviour, low frustration tolerance, assaults, impulsive binges, recurrent suicidal threats and behaviour and self-mutilation.

WHAT DRUGS FOR WHOM?

COGNITIVE/PERCEPTUAL PERSONALITY PATHOLOGY

A common sense approach to prescribing in personality disorder suggests that drugs that are effective in Axis I diagnoses may also be effective for symptom clusters in personality disorder that mirror them. We could therefore expect patients who are suspicious, odd, display magical thinking and so on (see Table 7.2) to possibly respond to antipsychotic medication. Surprisingly, the earliest case reports with these patients examined the use of psychogenics, such as lysergic acid (LSD). In current practice, however, both typical and atypical antipsychotics have a place in the treatment of schizotypal, schizoid and some borderline patients. These drugs appear to be effective when cognitive/perceptual disturbance is at the fore. Seven RCTs have to date been conducted using typical and atypical (risperidone and olanzapine) drugs and these studies show some initial improvement. The longer term studies, however, do not suggest these effects are sustained. With this evidence in mind, a trial of an antipsychotic may be warranted in this group of patients but continued prescribing should be on the basis of ongoing review with the patient and their acceptance of treatment.

Case illustration – Mr N. T., a person with schizoid personality disorder

Mr N. T., a 43 year old man, came into contact with psychiatric services after his family raised concerns that he had few friends, no job and rarely left the house. They were also concerned about Mr N. T.'s level of alcohol consumption, which reached 100 units a week (about three bottles of vodka). Although Mr N. T. did not feel he had any problem apart from his drinking he agreed to a psychological assessment and a diagnosis of schizoid personality disorder was made using the Personality Assessment Scale (PAS) (Tyrer & Alexander, 1979). Mr N. T. found the diagnosis unhelpful and was reluctant to accept any form of psychosocial or psychological management for this, but did agree to an inpatient detoxification and to see his psychiatrist for follow-up. Unsurprisingly, he refused any form of group follow-up. Whilst an inpatient he agreed to a trial of flupenthixol, which was prescribed at 3 mg BD. He continued to take this after discharge and although he felt it made no difference, he did agree there was less conflict at home and from time to time he felt happier. His family reported significantly less irritability, more interaction and less introspection. Furthermore, he went on to get a job as a projectionist.

Mr N. T. is an excellent example of how a trial of treatment aimed at a particular cluster of symptoms, in this case cognitive/perceptual disturbance and its behavioural consequences, may improve the functionality of a patient and his ability to exist in society. A clear temporal relationship existed between initiation of treatment and both a subjective and objective improvement. This was measured clinically using both patient and family reports, with close monitoring by the patient's psychiatrist. Mr N. T. is also an excellent example of realistic aims in a prescribing protocol; he was not 'cured' and neither the treating physician nor patient sought this. Rather, both the patient (albeit reluctantly) and his family noticed improvements in his ability to function within society and some improvement in his interpersonal relationships.

AFFECT DYSREGULATION PERSONALITY PATHOLOGY

This group of patients presents the mental health practitioner with some of the most difficult and challenging problems in everyday clinical life. Their mood is labile; they often become angry and interpret innocent behaviours as personal attacks. Furthermore they often feel empty, lonely and anxious around others. They are a group of patients who obviously need help and support but with whom it can be difficult to maintain any rapport. The very problems they have with their own internal emotional state and their difficulties with others are both their presenting pathology and the major stumbling block in accessing any type of management. These patients often project their desperation onto their mental health practitioners and the practitioner's desire to help means that a pharmacological approach is often tried. Although there is some evidence that this group of patients benefit from drug treatment, it is important with this group of patients not only to follow the community prescribing guidelines but also to be aware of the reasons each worker may have for considering medication. It may be that a brief period of increased community supervision, programmes aimed at an acute cause of a crisis or simply the containment of a patient's anxiety and anger by the care co-ordinator themselves may be sufficient to manage any crisis. If, however, these approaches are clearly not sufficient and the patient is prepared to work with the team, a trial of treatment is warranted. This should be given particular attention if the patient has previously shown a good response to a trial of medication.

The early studies in this group of patients were not encouraging. Soloff and colleagues looked at the effect of amitriptyline in borderline personality disorder and found it was not helpful (Soloff et al., 1986). In fact, there was some concern relating to an increase in suicidal behaviours in a small group of patients. This led to a rapid decline in the use of principally noradrenergic antidepressants in personality pathology. No other RCT has been published using this type of drug specifically for affective dysregulation in personality disorder. Long term data is not so discouraging. In a two-year follow-up of patients treated for depression and anxiety disorders with dothiepin (a tricyclic antidepressant), personality status did not affect outcome (Tyrer, Seivewright, Ferguson, Murphy & Johnson, 1993). This does not support the notion of a worse outcome for this group with tricyclic antidepressants over time – however, caution is clearly needed.

The American Psychiatric Association (2001) recommends the use of a selective serotonin reuptake inhibitor (SSRI) as a first line treatment for affective dysregulation. There are a number of studies suggesting SSRIs improve impulsivity, aggression and anger in patients, and in clinical situations where these symptoms appear to be the behavioural manifestation of affect dysregulation this approach is clearly sensible. Not only do these drugs have a measurable clinical response in such patients, but there are biological theories that support the notion of up-regulation in the serotonergic system improving such symptoms.

Further supporting this theory is the evidence that monoamine oxidase inhibitors (MAOIs) are also a powerful group of drugs to consider with affective dyscontrol. Clear improvements in both depressive and borderline psychopathology have been found with phenelzine, an MAOI. Caution, however, is needed when prescribing MAOIs to this group of patients. It is important that the patient understands the purpose of the prescription and has realistic expectations. It is also important to monitor progress closely in the community. As these antidepressants do not have an immediate clinical effect, serious deterioration may in fact require a brief period of hospitalisation. Such deterioration may also lead to self-harming behaviours, including overdose. This very real and potentially fatal risk plays a major part in influencing prescribing practice. Of the two most strongly evidenced antidepressants, MAOIs are rarely prescribed because of their potentially unsafe nature (they can cause severe hypertensive crises, the so-called 'cheese-reaction'). The relatively benign effects of overdose with SSRIs, coupled with some evidence of their efficacy, makes them the first choice for symptoms of affective dysregulation. However, even SSRIs are not without controversy. There are some case reports of increasing suicidality in patients started on this class of drug and this necessitates close monitoring during its initiation.

Case illustration – Mr J. L., a person with borderline personality disorder

Mr J. L., a 37 year old man, had regular contact with psychiatric services, primarily via Accident and Emergency, where he would present in crisis. The normal pattern was that an interpersonal interaction had gone badly, leading to an increasing feeling of worthlessness accompanied by intense anger. These problems were compounded by binges on alcohol that Mr J. L. used in an attempt to 'self-medicate'. Follow-up in the community was difficult as Mr J. L. only presented in crisis and would avoid any contact when relatively settled. When in crisis he was very difficult to communicate with and brief admissions generally ensued. During one admission Mr J. L. was started on a trial of fluoxetine (an SSRI) to assist with his feelings of emptiness and low mood. There were no side-effects reported by Mr J. L. and he was discharged on 40 mg a day. Although his contact with services remained sporadic, his visits to Accident and Emergency dropped dramatically and he was more prepared to accept increased community support when stressed. Most noticeably, on medical review, Mr J. L. himself noted the fluoxetine made him calmer, despite continuing to have mood dips as before. He also noted it appeared to be more effective than another SSRI, which he had trialled before.

The case of Mr J. L. highlights a number of issues. First, the failure of one SSRI should not lead to therapeutic nihilism. For up to 50 per cent of patients a switch to a second SSRI may be effective. Second, the medication provided a backdrop against which the patient allowed for an effective community package to be implemented, and finally, the patient again was aware of an improvement within himself, becoming an active and important part of the review process. Without such input from both the patient and his community team the added support provided by the SSRI would have led to little functional and behavioural improvement in the patient. In this case it is most productive to see the prescription as an adjunctive treatment to the community package rather than the primary treatment modality.

In some cases, the most prominent symptoms of affective instability may include social shyness, anxiety and avoidance, leading to loneliness and withdrawal. In these situations the evidence for using SSRIs or other antidepressants is less robust. It may be that in this group of patients a trial of benzodiazepines is of some value. Patients with socially phobic traits have been shown to improve with alprazolam and single case reports also suggest some benefit. Expert opinion also recommends a trial of a benzodiazepine in this situation. Caution is needed if this is to be tried as this class of drugs is addictive and there are some reports of serious deterioration in affect dyscontrol (Gardner & Cowdry, 1985). As the trial of a benzodiazepine may prove particularly unhelpful, careful consent, monitoring and community support is required.

IMPULSIVE/BEHAVIOURAL PERSONALITY PATHOLOGY

This cluster of symptoms overlaps somewhat in its behavioural manifestations with the affect dysregulation group and it is therefore unsurprising that the prescribing for the two groups follows broadly similar pathways. Again, SSRI antidepressants are the most robustly studied group of medications to show a response when impulsive sensation-seeking behaviour and aggression are the prominent features of the personality disorder. Fluoxetine is the most studied of all the SSRIs and it is therefore the most sensible option if the patient's history does not suggest a different antidepressant would be more appropriate. Two recent American studies support the use of SSRIs (both use fluoxitine) for this group (Coccaro & Kavoussi, 1997; Salzman et al., 1995). Both papers showed reductions in aggression, up to 12 weeks after the initiation of treatment, this being a common indicator of impulsive dyscontrol.

There is unfortunately no evidence to suggest such improvements will persist over years and the treatment does not have an immediate effect. For this reason the addition of an antipsychotic drug during periods of crisis may be helpful. The antipsychotic drugs have a calming effect and their onset of action is more rapid than any of their counterparts, making them potentially invaluable at a point of crisis (Cornelius et al., 1993; Soloff et al., 1986). Although there is no direct evidence for the use of both an SSRI and antipsychotic in combination (indeed there is no evidence for the use of any two psychotropic drugs in combination in personality disorder), their prescriptions have different aims. The antipsychotic is given to offer immediate relief and a wealth of information is available recommending the use of typical antipsychotics in situations similarly requiring rapid tranquillisation. By contrast, the SSRI is aimed at longer control of impulsivity and aggression. Added to this is the long clinical experience with these two drugs in combination, supporting their safe co-administration.

Case illustration – Ms S. B., a person with borderline personality disorder

Ms S. B. was a 29 year old woman with a long history of emotionally unstable personality disorder, impulsive type (also fulfilling the criteria for borderline personality disorder). This was most obviously manifest in her capricious mood, dangerous behaviours and aggressive outbursts directed at her partner, particularly when he attempted to intervene with Ms S. B.'s occasionally reckless plans. Although usually managed well in the community by her team, Ms S. B's partner found her threats of suicide and parasuicidal behaviour occasionally too emotionally difficult to handle, leading to a breakdown in their home environment. Ms S. B. saw her GP following such a dispute and was prescribed paroxetine. Her partner noted a quelling in Ms S. B.'s mood swings within three months and although her psychiatric input remained at the same level, her team noted fewer contacts with threats to kill herself. When her psychiatrist reviewed her, Ms. S. B. put the improvement in her relationship down to her buying a dog, although she had owned the dog for six months prior to her GP visit. Despite some sexual side-effects and denying the paroxetine had any obvious beneficial effect, Ms S. B. stated she was compliant with the prescription and happy to continue it.

This case displays the improvement in impulsivity that is reported with SSRIs. Although the original reason for the prescription was not clear, her community team was able to engage the patient in the monitoring of the medication and documentation of its beneficial and adverse effects. The patient played an active role in weighing up the pros and cons of the SSRI and decided to continue to take it in this case.

The mood stabilisers lithium, sodium valproate and carbamazepine are also logical choices considering the capriciousness of this group. The older research into this group of patients is almost entirely in patients with a presumptive diagnosis of personality disorder, with only the later studies focusing on the borderline group. As early as 1976, Sheard and colleagues showed lithium reduced major aggression in a secure setting and, although personality pathology was not formally assessed, this suggests benefits in patients with aggression as a common presenting feature (Sheard, Martin, Bridges & Wagner, 1976). This finding has been replicated in a variety of settings, adding strength to the generalisability of this finding. As lithium is a drug with a relatively small therapeutic window (a small dose range between ineffective and toxic), careful monitoring of both the prescribing and signs of lithium toxicity are necessary in the community. The relative dangerousness of this drug in overdose may also limit its practical use. More recently, both carbamazepine and sodium valproate (as the semi-sodium) have been the subject of small RCTs looking for effects in borderline personality disorder. While the evidence for carbamezipine is very weak, treatment with valproate reduces the impulsive aggression associated with this group in much the same fashion as lithium does. The advantage of valproate over lithium is its less fatal profile in overdose. Although the evidence for lithium is probably stronger than that for valproate, the latter is probably the current drug of choice for safety reasons if a mood stabiliser is to be tried.

EVIDENCE FOR THE USE OF OTHER DRUGS IN PERSONALITY DISORDER

As we can see, there is a reasonable, albeit small, evidence base for the prescription of the SSRI and MAOI categories of antidepressant in patients with predominantly borderline personality disorder. There is also evidence to suggest that a trial of a mood stabiliser or an antipsychotic, particularly during a time of crisis, may be of benefit. Beyond this, the evidence for other prescribing is very weak. One study conducted in England found that flupenthixol was effective in reducing the number of episodes of self-harm in patients who recurrently presented with this problem (Montgomery & Montgomery, 1982). By extension from the trials of older antipsychotics, there is an heuristic logic to recommend the use of newer atypical antipsychotic to patients with personality disorder who are acutely distressed. Apart from one trial with olanzapine and one with risperidone, however, there is no other evidence for the prescription of the newer antipsychotics. Both of these trials reported positive benefits when the active drug was compared with a placebo, although the numbers in both trials were small. This dearth of evidence for the newer antipsychotics needs to be borne in mind as most clinicians will preferentially prescribe these drugs for Axis I disorders and it may be more appropriate to prescribe an older typical antipsychotic for personality pathology.

A number of studies have explored the use of a variety of benzodiazepines in personality and there may be a place for their use in acute anxiety (see above). Alprazolam has been shown to reduce avoidance and increase sociability, two behavioural problems associated with Cluster C personality disorders (Reich, Noyes & Yates, 1989). The issue of dependence, however, and its suitability for long term treatment, do not support its prescription. Furthermore, there is some argument about whether mental state, as opposed to personality trait, is being treated, although this question is, perhaps, of more esoteric than practical interest. Single small trials, and theory, have potentially recommended a variety of other drugs. Expert opinion has compared the core symptoms of adult attention deficit/hyperactivity disorder (inattention, impulsivity and hyperactivity) to those of personality disorder as well as the social morbidity that exists with both conditions (Newton-Howes, 2004). This has led to the presumption that psychostimulants, proven effective in adult ADHD, may also be useful in personality disorder, particularly with impulse dyscontrol. Any evidence in personality, however, remains anecdotal and this should not be a first line drug to consider. Other pharmacological possibilities considered in the literature include venlafaxine, naltrexone and buspirone; however, they should not be considered as more than options that require further investigation at the current time.

SPECIAL CONSIDERATIONS FOR PRESCRIBING IN THE COMMUNITY TO PERSONALITY DISORDERED PATIENTS

When prescribing for a patient with personality problems in the community, there are a number of special issues to consider. First, it is important to ensure informed consent is obtained from the patient. This requires a frank discussion about the possible benefits expected from any prescribing and any side-effects that may accompany it. Information pertaining to the prognosis with pre-scription of a drug for Axis I mental illnesses will not hold true if the same drug is being prescribed for a different reason. For example, the use of an SSRI for major depression has a different evidence base and different outcomes than the prescription of the same SSRI for impulse dyscontrol. In general, the evidence of improvement is weaker in personality disorder and there is some suggestion of more susceptibility to side-effects, making all clinical treatment a 'trial' for each patient. It is important the patient is aware of this, to minimise the chance of catastrophising if a pharmacological intervention proves fruitless. It is also important that the patient is an active participant in the prescribing process rather than passively accepting a pill.

Second, a diagnosis of personality disorder does not prevent the prescribing of medication to treat co-morbid Axis I conditions. Schizophrenia, depression and anxiety disorders should all be considered and managed pharmacologi-cally if this is warranted. The presence of personality pathology may worsen the outcome of an Axis I disorder (Newton-Howes, Tyrer & Johnson, 2005), but it should not lead to therapeutic nihilism as, conversely, more vigorous management may be necessary. Occasionally, the phenomenology found may be difficult to classify as being part of either an Axis I disorder or personality pathology. A community team is in a unique position to monitor the difference between trait and state markers and, subsequently, provide information to help guide prescribing, should this be problematic.

Third, there is a large overlap between personality disorder and alcohol and drug disorder. Over half of all patients in alcohol services and over a third in drug dependence services have a diagnosable personality disorder (Bowden-Jones et al., 2004). This can pose particular problems in the comm-unity due to the prevalence of alcohol and its disinhibiting and depressant effects in this population. Not only can alcohol severely worsen an acute crisis, but it makes engagement considerably more difficult. Usually patients with personality disorder see alcohol and other drugs as their 'magic cure', despite all the evidence to the contrary. Unfortunately, they tend to minimise the role of alcohol and its associated problems during general psychiatric review. The evidence suggests personality disorder and co-morbid alcohol or drug disorder leads to worsening psychopathology and social morbidity. A community team needs to be aware of the possibility of binge drinking and drug taking behaviour and its hazardous use, in order to intervene and arrange review before a drug or alcohol problem becomes unmanageable. Consumption of illicit drugs may also alter the safety profile of a prescribed medication and therefore good liaison between medical staff and other community workers is essential to minimise prescribing risk.

Finally, the risk of deliberate self-harm, particularly by overdose, needs to be considered. As most psychotropic drugs do not have an instant effect, individual crises will not be immediately resolved by the prescription of a drug. Furthermore, a potentially suicidal patient will receive a number of tablets if a prescription is given. In this situation liaison between the psychiatrist, GP, community practitioner and carers is essential to ensure safe prescribing. The number of tablets a patient has at home, the supervision of dispensing and the risk of overdose should all affect the number of tablets patients have in their possession at any one time. These issues should not necessarily preclude a trial of medication. In particularly vulnerable patients, short prescriptions with initially intensive input maximise the likelihood of success and minimise the chance of overdose. It is also important to consider the patient's history and take this into account. Patients with significant histories of overdosing need to have special precautions in place to ensure their safety.

CONCLUSION

The evidence for prescribing in personality disorders is steadily accumulating in the literature. Although the evidence is not strong enough for definitive guidelines to yet be drawn up, a number of strategies can now be reasonably trialled, particularly in patients with borderline personality disorder (American Psychiatric Association, 2001). Pharmacological approaches can be trialled alongside other forms of therapy or as the primary approach, although its use as the sole treatment modality is not widely accepted as the norm. When prescribing for patients with personality disorder in the community, it is important to consider what is being treated, why medication is being selected for this and to weigh up with the patient the risks and benefits of a pharmacological approach. It is also important that patients are adequately reviewed and monitored by their community teams to ensure the treatment is effective and to prevent polypharmacy, which is entirely without an evidence base. Ultimately, the notion of patient-based evidence, the successful synthesis of the patients' current mental state, their history and the information available in the literature, is most likely to lead to selecting the best drug to trial and maximising its chances of being effective. A combined agreement between prescriber, community practitioner and the patient is necessary to ensure both rational and successful prescribing.

REFERENCES

American Psychiatric Association. (2001). Practice guidelines for the treatment of patients with borderline personality disorder. *American Journal of Psychiatry, 158* (Suppl.), 1–52.

Bowden-Jones, O., Iqbal, M. Z., Tyrer, P., Seivewright, N., Cooper, C., Judd, A. & Weaver, T. (2004). Prevalence of personality disorder in alcohol and drug services and associated comorbidity. *Addiction, 99*, 1306–1314.

Coccaro E. F. & Kavoussi R. J. (1997). Fluoxetine and impulsive aggressive behaviour in personality-disordered subjects. *Archives of General Psychiatry, 54*, 1081–1088.

Cornelius, J. R., Soloff, P. H., Perel, J. M. & Ulrich, R. F. (1993). Continuation pharmacotherapy of borderline personality disorder with holoperidol and phenelzine. *American Journal of Psychiatry, 150*, 1843–1848.

Gardner, D. L. & Cowdry, R. W. (1985). Alprazolam-induced dyscontrol in borderline personality disorder. *American Journal of Psychiatry, 142*, 98–100.

Montgomery, S. A. & Montgomery, D. (1982). Pharmacological prevention of suicidal behaviour. *Journal of Affective Disorders, 4*, 291–298.

Newton-Howes, G. (2004). What happens to children with attention deficit/hyperactivity disorder when they grow up? *Journal of the Royal Society of Medicine, 97*, 531–535.

Newton-Howes, G., Tyrer, P. & Johnson T. (2005). Personality disorder and the outcome of depression: A meta-analysis of published studies. *British Journal of Psychiatry*, in press.

Reich, J., Noyes, R. & Yates, W. (1989). Alprazolam treatment of avoidant personality traits in socially phobic patients. *Journal of Clinical Psychiatry, 50*, 91–95.

Salzman, C., Woolfson, A. N., Schatzburg, A., Looper, J., Henke, R., Albanese, M., Schwartz, J. & Miyawaki, E. (1995). Effect of fluoxetine on anger in symptomatic volunteers with borderline personality disorder. *Journal of Clinical Psychopharmacology, 15*, 23–29.

Sheard, M. H., Martin, J. L., Bridges, C. I. & Wagner, E. (1976). The effect of lithium on unipolar aggressive behaviour in man. *American Journal of Psychiatry, 133*, 1409–1413.

Soloff, P. H. (1998). Algorithms for pharmacological treatment of personality dimensions: Symptom specific treatments for cognitive–perceptual, affective, and impulsive–behavioural dysregulation. *Bulletin of the Menninger Clinic, 62*, 195–214.

Soloff, P. H., George, A., Nathan, R. S., Shulz, P. M., Ulrich, R. F. & Perel, J. M. (1986). Progress in pharmacotherapy of borderline disorders: A double blind study of amitriptyline, haloperidol and placebo. *Archives of General Psychiatry, 43*, 691–697.

Tyrer, P. & Alexander, J. (1979). Classification of personality disorder. *British Journal of Psychiatry, 135*, 163–167.

Tyrer, P. & Bateman A. (2004). Drug treatments for personality disorders. *Advances in Psychiatric Treatment, 10*, 391.

Tyrer, P., Seivewright, N., Ferguson, B., Murphy, S. & Johnson, A. L. (1993). The Nottingham Study of neurotic disorder: Effect of personality status on response to drug treatment, cognitive therapy and self-help over two years. *British Journal of Psychiatry, 162*, 219–226.

Tyrer, P., Mitchard, S., Methuen, C. & Ranger, M. (2003). Treatment-rejecting and treatment seeking personality disorders: Type R and S. *Journal of Personality Disorder, 17*, 265–270.

SECTION TWO

Treatment and Management in Community Mental Health Teams

8

People's Experiences of Having a Diagnosis of Personality Disorder

REX HAIGH

The words didn't really sink in. Having been a patient of a psychiatric clinic for over a year – I had 'depression' – I was being told by my psychiatrist that the diagnosis had changed; I was no longer depressed but had 'Borderline Personality Disorder'. It didn't register, until he went on to say that this wasn't treatable so he was stopping my day care, my therapy. He was referring me on to someone else so I could be their problem – he didn't deal with 'Borderlines'.

I was no longer ill – I was Borderline, this demon who could not be treated, who did not belong in this clinic. Too bad to be helped. No point in treatment – this was for life. Outcast, set apart from the other patients who I had made friends with. 'Not good enough' for my psychiatrist to go on treating – had to be dumped elsewhere. A non-person, no rights, no voice, no dignity. No future.

The ambulance pulled up in the dark, in front of the magnificent Victorian building – the old lunatic asylum. Tired, doped and dirty I was guided through a bleak door into a cold corridor with chairs. All my possessions were taken away – I didn't care. Became aware of other patients, conversation around me 'it's dangerous here', 'I've been here 14 months', 'they inject you here' and more. Shouting, crying, futility of knowing this was where I was meant to be safe – but feeling nothing but danger.

Personality Disorder and Community Mental Health Teams: A Practitioner's Guide. Edited by M. J. Sampson, R. A. McCubbin and P. Tyrer. © 2006 John Wiley & Sons, Ltd.

It was late – I had sleeping pills thrust down me, then shown a bed in a dormitory with pink flimsy curtains to surround me. Didn't keep out the stench of shit from some of the other beds. Didn't give safety, privacy, dignity. But I obviously didn't deserve that – my 'illness', my personality disorder made me nothing but an animal. No sleep in these conditions. But stayed dressed, crouched on top of the bed for the night-time hours too scared to go to the toilet, to get a drink – too scared to be alive.

Vanessa

SERVICE USER CONSULTATION AND THE NATIONAL PERSONALITY DISORDER DEVELOPMENT PROGRAMME

In late 2001, a group of appropriately experienced clinicians, researchers and other experts was invited by civil servants at the Department of Health in London to help formulate a strategy for personality disorder, the fruits of which became the Policy Implementation Guide *No Longer A Diagnosis of Exclusion* (National Institute for Mental Health for England, NIMHE, 2003). For the task, the expert advisors were divided into three working groups: forensic, general services and education.[1] For the first four months of the work, there was no service user representation, and the committee of experts deliberated on details of epidemiology, research evidence and theoretical service models. Although it was acknowledged that the absence of service users' voices needed to be put right, it was felt that this committee of powerful, articulate and eminent professionals was not somewhere a lone service user, or pair of service users, would find a useful role. It could well result in unhelpful isolation, marginalisation or polarisation.

---

[1] The major share of funding was known to be in the forensic field, as it was a high profile government intention to tackle the 'DSPD' problem – dangerous people with severe personality disorder. The allocation of funding to non-forensic services was initially described as the 'DSPD Community Programme' with the task of establishing 'step-down' facilities from the high security units. Between then and 2005, this evolved into the 'National Personality Disorder Development Programme' which, at the time of writing, aims to integrate pathway planning, commissioning and development between what had previously been seen as four 'silos':

- the continuing DSPD programme
- the non-forensic developments: 11 pilot sites and PCT local growth money
- the workforce development funding ('Capabilities Framework')
- the handover from national to local commissioning of Henderson Hospital and its replicates.

It was therefore decided to set up a parallel reference group of service users, to meet monthly in London over the spring and summer of 2002, with one clinician (RH), one administrator (A-MA) and the Department of Health Senior Policy Advisor (AH), being present at both the service users' and professionals' groups to ensure thorough communication between them. The service users' group was selected by asking all clinicians on the expert advisory group to recommend between two and four of their patients or ex-patients, who would be able to travel to London, approximately monthly, over the summer and autumn. Three other clinicians were also invited to co-facilitate (KH, FM and GW).[2] Other consultative activities were also incorporated, including discussions with representatives of relevant service user bodies, a meeting in Newcastle for those from the North who were interested in contributing, and a widespread email cascade for other opinions. Sixteen people were thus recruited for the London focus groups. In the first session, they were briefed about the work and received a short research presentation from the leader of a service user group who had just completed some detailed service user research into the experience of being diagnosed with personality disorder (Castillo, 2003). The subsequent function of this focus group was to be in constructive dialogue with the expert advisory group. The members would be given specific suggested tasks by the expert group, and give detailed feedback on work done by the expert advisory group. In effect, it became a symmetrical process, with the focus group meeting between each of the expert groups and vice versa. The specific tasks included detailed discussion of helpful and unhelpful aspects of services, preparation of vignettes for each personality disorder cluster and unpacking complex concepts such as 'respect' and 'care'.

The group immediately established a cohesion around its central task: members soon mentioned the value of being listened to and taken seriously – which was an uncommon experience for several of them. Discussion was often animated and emotional; the two hour group was kept strictly to time, with refreshments available before and afterwards, and a break in the middle. In many respects, it was working like a well functioning business or community meeting in a therapeutic community. It is impossible to judge the impact the group had on the overall task, but there was a perception that the topic 'came to life' for the civil servants who were to draft the policy guidance. What had previously been a somewhat dry and technical discussion, related to gathering and giving due weight to different experts' opinions, had become rather less straightforward, and more authentic. The objective 'PD problem' had come to life as real individuals who met each month, with uncomfortable

---

[2] Names given in 'acknowledgements'.

stories to tell about how their treatment in the mental health services had been less than satisfactory. It was clearly a new, and rather energising, experience for many of them to be listened to, generally believed and treated with respect and dignity. Service user involvement had clearly moved beyond a token consultation with an advocacy organisation or membership of a committee: those who were needing services were relating to policy makers on a similar footing to professional experts.

The group ran its planned length, partings and endings were made and consent for contact details to be kept for further work was obtained. Some of the participants are still (in 2005) involved in Department of Health work in personality disorder, and the original ethos of it being a continuing process rather than a single consultation exercise has been maintained.

THE STICKY LABEL AND STIGMA

In 1996 my children were taken away from me. A social worker arrived on my doorstep saying she had received a phone call from a 'friend' stating she was concerned that I'd harm the children. Since then my son has remained in the custody of his father, who has a history of violence, and whose parenting abilities have never been assessed by the Local Authority. I did not need 'help' from Social Services on that day. It was forced on me. Previously, when I had asked for assistance, they had placed the children twice at my request. The point being that when I felt I needed help I had always asked for it. I love my children, I would never harm them, and have never self-harmed when they have been in the house. I saw a TV programme about Munchausen's Syndrome by Proxy. It seems it is considered to be a way in which Personality Disordered mothers respond to their children. I wonder if this explains why Social Services were so ready to take away my children.

Anon.

Mental disorders all carry stigma, and personality disorder more than most – in the field of mental health, it has parallels to the public and professional perception of cancer in general health services half a century ago. There is widespread public misunderstanding that it equates to frightening violent criminals with sinister and irrational motives, as portrayed with some gusto in horror films and tabloid newspapers. Alternatively, as in the example above, that personality disorder makes people unsuitable parents and not to be trusted looking after children. There is very little understanding of the high incidence of personality disorders, and the variety of forms they take:

'dangerous and severe personality disorder' (DSPD), a severe form of antisocial personality disorder with a high assessment of risk, concerns the government because of the priority given to public safety, and the public because it is the only one given mainstream media attention. Any others that gain public attention are also seen in terms of risk and danger to others, and not vulnerability or environmental failure. One service user with a forensic history described the DSPD parts of the proposed mental health legislation as like the 'Dangerous Dogs Act'.

Amongst professionals, the strongly held perception is that people with personality disorder are not easy to help, and that the condition is almost or completely untreatable. Those with personality disorder have been described as 'the patients psychiatrists dislike', and many reported being called time-wasters, difficult, manipulative, bed-wasters or attention seeking. Service users felt blamed for their condition while simply seeking basic acceptance and someone to listen to them. Being excluded from various services was common, in health and other sectors. When the usual response in mental health services was to be told 'you're not mentally ill', despite suffering profound and often longstanding distress, the understandable reaction was to feel rejected and various other strong emotions: frequently alienation, anger, hopelessness and worthlessness.

Some people diagnosable with personality disorder acknowledge that accurate diagnosis can be a useful process, but that it needs to be undertaken with support and sensitivity, and backed up with the provision of reliable information. There is a wide spectrum of service users' views about the label 'personality disorder' itself. At one end, there is the view that it is a diagnosis that is an appalling, degrading and dehumanising way of describing some-body that should never be used ('it just says I'm a bad person and nothing can be done about it'). Alternatively, for some it brings understanding to long-standing distress and alienation, and opens doors to a path towards recovery ('at last, I'm not alone, it's not my fault').

Some service users express a preference for different forms of words, such as dropping the 'disorder' term (thus, for example, being known as somebody with 'borderline personality' or 'emotional instability', rather than 'border-line personality *disorder*' or 'emotionally unstable *personality disorder*') or use less specific descriptions such as 'longstanding emotional distress'. Other suggestions include those that are based on theory or aetiology, which give understanding and legitimacy to one's experience and difficulties; examples are 'attachment disorder' (or 'attachment *disturbance*', and 'attachment seeking' rather than 'attention seeking') or 'complex post-traumatic stress disorder'. However, it is often pointed out that any new label is soon likely to accumulate negative connotations, so there is nothing to be gained for long by changing the wording of the diagnosis itself. The alternative view is that the exact juxtaposition of the two words 'personality' and 'disorder' is *prima facie* evidence that someone's very personhood is judged to be wanting, and that they are not a good enough person (Hadden & Haigh, 2002). Some people preferred terms such as 'emotional distress' or felt that a more appropriate description would be 'attachment seeking'.

STAFF AND SENSITIVITY

There isn't much I remember about the details of that first interview. There seemed to be more interest in self-harm and symptoms rather than me. The only positive thing I remember was regarding the medication. 'Right, we'll put you on something we know works' he said, but it didn't. It seemed to be a lifetime before the next appointment came: it matched the first in its failure to connect with me, or even attempt to engage with me. Again it was symptoms – and a prescription for an increased dose of medication. This medication did have an effect that I noticed. The effect was akin to being drunk without the pleasure of getting there – or my usual decisions to stop before I reached that particular feeling of the senses being felt through cotton wool. The high felt artificial, and uncomfortable: I soon realised that I could slash my wrists and feel good about it.

Luckily, this didn't fit with the reasons I self-harmed, nor a deeper driving force for survival which I believe I have. A few weeks after leaving the hospital I came off the medication, and started to use alcohol to avoid dealing with my anger. However, the purchase of a games console saw alcohol consumption tail off dramatically. My next appointment had been put much further away. As the doctor seemed uninterested in me, I didn't make an appointment. Even now I can justify the hospital's part by saying that I was just one of so many, and probably not as needy as most. Much of this is hazy, and I think I was offered subsequent appointments but didn't make contact or turn up.

After the death of my mother, a change of location, and about a year's drinking I found myself perking up when another psychiatrist's appointment came through. Compared with my previous experience of a hospital setting, this was much more welcoming and friendly, with its carpeted flooring in the waiting room and soft chairs, with bright and cheerful walls. However, there the positive experience ended. Although I did succeed in my fight to stay off medication, the psychiatrist failed to connect, nor from memory, did he even challenge me to engage. Eventually it was suggested that I conform to the rest of the world in my appearance, despite my suggestion that I'd feel false. I left that meeting feeling less than satisfied, and on reflection I think that is where I disconnected from the process. At the next meeting I had 'conformed', as the psychiatrist had put it, but inside the wall was up, and I was saying just what he wanted to hear to get me out of the place. When I left, better on the outside and fooling myself on the inside, I was assured that I would be kept on the books just in case there was a relapse. About a year later I did experience a relapse but when I phoned up for an appointment, I was told that I'd been taken off the books and I would have to be referred again. My response internally was 'well if you can't be bothered neither can I'.

Eddie

After reading my notes, he declared that I had a possibly anti-social personality that only I, not he, could do anything about (I didn't understand that one, doctors gave you pills and made you better, didn't they?) but that I was depressed, which he could (and did!) help me with.

Gordon

Therapeutic pessimism is perceived by service users, and many service users can describe how a negative experience on initial referral, often to a psychiatrist, makes engagement less likely. If somebody is told that they are suffering from an untreatable condition, or something for which there are no effective or proven therapies, it feels tantamount to saying 'you are a no-hoper'. The psychological cancer analogy is again useful: it would not be acceptable to make such a statement for physical illness, without at least offering care and palliation, or referral to a suitable specialist.

Users were perceptive in having sophisticated ideas about staff who were and were not suitably skilled to handle therapeutic relationships. For example, they were well aware how unsafe it felt to be with staff who were somewhat fearful of them, and how alienated and unheard they felt when therapists acted in rigid and defensive ways. The underlying theoretical basis, which could be well understood by all service users, was attachment, which was particularly felt when handled badly – such as no notice being given of endings or changes. A particularly sharply felt transgression of this is removal of services once people show any improvement; this creates perverse incentives to remain unwell, or worse: 'There is a link between hurting yourself and getting support and treatment. It is hard to resist self-harming behaviour when, you know if you do it, you will get treatment'.

The whole range of issues that come to prominence in people with a history of environmental failure – such as deprivation, abuse, trauma or loss – need to be handled with particular sensitivity, and service users are generally astute at identifying staff with such sensitivity. Feelings of exclusion relating to membership of minority groups were also highlighted as needing genuine empathic attention, rather than straightforward protocol-based care – and service users are very quick to spot the real thing.

Staff with their own vulnerabilities were perceived as having much more insight into the difficulties of patients, although it was recognised that in clinical settings problems arise when staff begin to share their own problems with patients and boundaries break down. However, it was felt to be therapeutically important for there to be at least some acknowledged shared experience between patient and professional, and for professionals to be in touch with the patient's distress although not overwhelmed by it.

You don't realise how ill you are at the time. It seemed quite reasonable to me to lie in bed all day thinking that I could be perfectly content if people would just go away and leave me alone. Luckily they didn't, and I obediently plodded off to whoever my GP thought might help me. The more I told them I was shy and didn't like groups, the more they put me into groups and the longer I was ill the more intensive the groups got. It was all a bit daunting and I wasn't sure if it was really worth the bother.

After I had been ill for several years, someone new joined the group I was attending. We'd been in the same group a couple of years before and she told me that she could see I had changed and seemed much more lively than I had been. It was so encouraging to have that independent feedback. Maybe all this therapy was helping after all.

Katherine

UNCARING SYSTEMS

Hospitals certainly have their places (I honestly believe my admission saved my life) but they are not good places to go for a rest. I declined sleeping pills my first night and what an eye-opener (literally) it was. People on hypnotics snore like drunks and a wardfull snore so forcefully that the nurses had to force towels into the cracks around the windows and doors to stop the ageing building from shaking itself apart.

Next morning, un-rested, I found myself standing next to a very agitated patient in line for breakfast. I particularly remember his hair looked like a cross between a scarecrow and Don King. 'What are you in for?' he asked. 'Depression and anxiety' I replied. 'Me too' he said 'Just don't let them give you ECT' he said. Just then he got to the front of the queue and tried to help himself to breakfast only to be stopped by a nurse with a clip-board saying 'You know you can't eat before ECT'. I'd gone in for a rest, was now on a 72 hour observation, what had I let myself in for?

Gordon

There is widespread agreement that there are not enough services available for people with personality disorder. More services specifically for people diagnosable with personality disorder were strongly advocated by all service users; those who had experienced them were aware of a difference in approach and ethos, which they saw as useful. This was even the case for people who had not been ready for definitive treatment, or had dropped out of it before completing a course or programme of therapy.

In the main, service users' experiences of general adult mental health services were negative. Unhelpful attitudes from staff were encountered, who would see 'just the label', and were often prejudiced about the condition, and belittling or patronising in manner. Staff in acute settings were also seen as usually unavailable, needing to be too much in control, unable to contain difficult feelings and too prone to jump to conclusions before understanding a person's situation.

A clear need was identified for 'time out', which was not often met. For example, when somebody was going through a stressful time and starting to think about harming themselves, the only options were generally seen to be saying nothing (and then getting better or falling into a full-blown crisis), or to ask for help, and either be refused through being too well or simply by dint of the personality disorder diagnosis, or be admitted to an acute unit as a high suicide risk, often involuntarily with enforced medication. In the latter case, it would frequently lead to strong emotions – possibly related to previous abuse of power – and an escalation of unmanageable behaviour. At such times, service users would value some low-key 'crisis bed' provision to prevent a situation becoming unmanageable, perhaps for up to three days, but not in an environment such as many acute wards, which often make the situation worse.

Although the benefits of care planning and case management were acknowledged, the experience was that procedures were often not followed or not found helpful. In particular, there was a sense that the process reduced individuals' autonomy and resulted in people being 'processed' for the sake of an administrative need, without any intention of trying to achieve therapeutic understanding or change. Service users noted that staff themselves often had similar negative feelings about the anti-therapeutic nature of the systems within which they were expected to work.

LACK OF INFORMATION AND AWARENESS

Unlike other conditions, there is little easily available printed information for patients. More is available on the internet, and some websites are thought to be particularly helpful, such as the one run by Borderline UK (BUK, 2005), who also produce information leaflets and a regular newsletter. Borderline UK, which is a voluntary organisation, also run a peer support and information service by telephone and internet. Widespread distribution of leaflets and posters, such as in GP surgeries and other health settings, would help to raise awareness. This could help turn the diagnosis of personality disorder into something that could be openly discussed between users and professionals, which is rarely the case at the moment.

One of the most effective ways of explaining the experience of personality disorder to mental health staff, and others who come into professional contact with personality disorder, is for those with the diagnosis to organise and put on teaching events themselves. As well as giving vivid and often moving accounts of the distress and difficulties, it also fosters a sense of empowerment and effectiveness to be able to teach professionals, and promote wider understanding of the condition. It was also thought of as the best way of changing the 'manipulative and difficult patient' prejudice.

Service users would also like to see TV soap operas, discussions and documentaries being used as effective ways of communicating information to large audiences, who are often ill-informed by media portrayal of mental health matters. It was acknowledged that it is difficult to control how mental health is portrayed, and it would need to be done carefully to prevent 'putting ideas into people's heads' in relation to self-harm, eating disorders or personality disorder – which they themselves recognised as a potential danger. However, if such initiatives managed to raise awareness enough to 'stop it being a dirty secret', and not show it as an unexplainable, irrational, frightening or sinister madness, many would benefit from feeling less ashamed and alienated.

PREVENTATIVE POSSIBILITIES

Had I been helped when younger I would not have got this bad.

Anon.

I started needing help at the age of seven. However, social services and the school could not identify with me and on home visits I had to behave the way my parents – well, my mother – said. While at school between the ages of nine and fifteen I secretly sought out several counselling services but found they were not the help I desperately needed. After my fifth suicide attempt at the age of twenty-one I found myself fifteen miles away from home in the countryside, in hospital. As an Asian girl I felt extremely alone – I felt it was us against the staff. At one point I was on so much medication that I thought I saw flying saucers so I woke the whole ward up. The night staff were not amused. After six weeks I was released and given a CPN, but didn't get to see her until after six months. I found her very helpful in providing me with day centres to go to, and a women's centre and to get me back into the community – but she was unable to get me the help I really needed. After another three years I finally got onto the waiting list for a specialist service which I must say was the only place that's really helped me.

Satty

Being able to look back, I can now see how ill I was, and how oblivious everyone around me was to what was actually going on in my mind. Through old parental messages of 'suffer in silence', and 'don't create a fuss', I'd suffered for years without realising, reaching a point of disconnection with both the outside world and myself where I could survive without notice. At work I managed to train my abilities of avoidance and being invisible, neither doing too much nor too little to warrant attention, quite happy for people to get to know the surface me without seeing the real me – that was someone even I didn't know, or wasn't aware of. The flip side of that was that I couldn't see I was tearing myself apart from the inside out.

Eddie

As long as I can remember I have always known something was wrong. I didn't know what, I just knew. I was adopted as a baby and my parents were always open about it. For many years, this seemed to explain 'why' I was different but did little to alleviate the pain or confusion, nor did it help me understand how other people coped or fitted in. I can remember as a child always feeling lonely and disconnected in relationships both familial and otherwise. I fantasised about my 'real' family whilst remaining detached from my real one. I was obsessive and jealous in my childhood friendships, never seeing them as genuine. I began to develop a very skewed view of them, believing that you constantly needed to impress people to win friendship or love. Many children go through a stealing phase but I got stuck using my ill-gotten gains to try to impress or buy love.

As a teenager, I was obsessed with getting a girl-friend (something that never happened) and as embarrassing as it is to recall would have to describe my behaviour as obsessive and 'stalkeresque'. I developed a veneer of sociability, however, and most people outside of my family were unaware of my escalating criminality and instability.

Gordon

Early intervention was often highlighted as being crucial to the prevention of major deterioration in personality disorder. Where it did not happen, a career as a 'professional patient' or lifelong mental health service user was often felt to be the best of the bad options available – others being criminality, vagrancy or death.

Self-harm, particularly cutting, is becoming a significant problem at secondary schools, and the national curriculum could be an important opportunity for introducing a non-stigmatising way of learning about mental health, as part of 'personal, social and health education' or 'citizenship'. Service users could be very effectively engaged in teaching by discussing their own histories, and encouraging open discussion about suitable ways of dealing with difficult feelings. This could have a preventative function by educating adolescents about vulnerability, helping to dispel common myths about the value of being 'hard', and showing how and when to seek help.

The need for specific facilities covering an age range of about 15–25 was suggested and supported by service users, as the developmental attitude of adolescent services towards intervention and treatability was widely appreciated. However, these sorts of resource are currently only available to a small proportion of adolescents who could benefit from it, and there are several more years when helpful preventative work could be done.

The impact on parenting was also mentioned, particularly by service users who were parents themselves; they felt that after suitable therapy they were able to be better parents to their children and give things that they had never received themselves. This would hopefully make for better balanced children and less disturbance in the following generations.

AS BAD AS IT GETS: UNHELPFUL FEATURES FOR PERSONALITY DISORDER SERVICES

The following quotes are compiled from numerous conversations with service users about their experiences of general and specialist services.

My GP, who wanted to give me more pills and get me out as soon as possible, looked on his computer and found that there's a service in the main town about half an hour away by bus, but isn't available here because it's a different Trust area and they don't have a contract.

They only see new patients between 10 am and 3 pm, and there's a two year waiting list for a first appointment. Then you have to wait again to see a therapist regularly, if they agree that you're the right sort of patient for them. If you want to pay, they can give you a list of private therapists who might be able to help.

The local team is a bit short of staff at the moment, so they are running with agency nurses and junior doctors – who try their best. But it's unlikely you'd see the same person for more than a couple of months, and they're not really specialists in this sort of work.

What you get depends on the diagnosis mainly. If you're seriously mentally ill, or a serious risk to other people, they'll prioritise you. If you haven't got any history of being in mental health services, it doesn't matter if you've been miserable all your life. They say most people are like that – they don't expect anybody to get better.

They try very hard, and promise to arrange the sort of treatment people need. But when it comes to your turn – usually months later – the service has been changed, somebody has left and they can't give it to you any more. So you need to start all over again.

Don't go telling them you're in crisis – they'll just give you the number for the crisis team. And they're not meant to accept anybody with 'PD'. And don't tell them what you want, or they'll take against you straight away.

If you do something like cut yourself, they'll give you some time – but mostly negative time telling you not to do it again – they never try and understand *why* you needed to cut yourself. They're not interested in that sort of thing.

If you're up to it, it's good – but you need to be feeling strong. The therapists hardly say anything, they're really mysterious and just give sort of feedback comments that can sometimes be really helpful. But sometimes it's like you think 'what planet are they on?' – and they've got no idea of what you're actually going through.

They told Social Services about me as soon as they heard about my husband coming out of prison – they didn't listen to me after that, and they just gave me some talk about it being their 'legal obligation'. I didn't trust any of them after that, and I don't think I will ever again.

If you go in there, you go in for real – as soon as I got on the ward they had a nurse sitting with me all the time at the bottom of my bed. I remember one who was bored stiff, just sat there chewing gum, and reading comics – and never said a word to me. The only excitement was when the meds trolley came round and I didn't want to take it. Sometimes they called in the heavy mob when I got upset. I wanted to go, and they wanted me to go, but it just didn't happen. I was there for nearly a year.

HELPFUL FEATURES FOR PERSONALITY DISORDER SERVICES

What do I want from a mental health service?

Honesty, support and safety. Risk is such a negative word and safety should be for everyone, without exception, including staff.

Otherwise, it depends on where I am on my journey from ignorance of illness to getting better.

At the start I want someone to be there, letting me hide in the safety of my ignorance, and holding me through the scary times until I want to move forward.

Then I want to be heard, and to be felt to be heard, and not have to resort to drastic measures before I am heard.

When I decide to move forward I want someone to be there and support me while I face potentially life-threatening issues (whether in fact or in mind, as to me they are equally real).

When I start seeing a future, I want support and encouragement, and not to have to fall to pieces before I get it.

Eddie

AN IDEAL SERVICE

These quotes are distilled from many conversations, and a specific piece of work at the Department of Health with representatives from different service user and carer organisations. Needless to say, a single service with all these features does not yet exist!

> Is part of the real community, in a college, or church hall or leisure centre, and somewhere that you can just go before you get to crisis point – and ask for advice or just talk to people.

> But most importantly it's a place that feels safe, where people can feel they belong, and just rub along together.

> Everybody signs a membership agreement about acceptable behaviour. There's rarely any trouble, though you're out for a year if you break the big rules. If you go for therapy you need to agree to tell your GP (and psychiatrist if you've got one) – then you get booked into the system.

> They do some therapy groups there as part of the programme, but you get the chance to choose different things once you've had a chance to talk about what you need.

They do run open groups for everybody who comes, like drop-ins – some are creative, like art (a lot of the members do art and sell paintings at the annual show), others are practical like computer and office skills, and the 'choices' group is about 'access to therapy', where you get the chance to talk to therapists and people who have been through it all themselves, to decide if and when it's right for you.

There's an internet café on the premises, and a chat room for people to get in touch if they want support out of hours. Some people hardly ever come along – they just talk on the net. But it's members-only, so people are all part of the network of relationships you have there.

It's run by a mixture of professional staff and people who've been through it themselves, who are also paid hourly as part of them getting on their feet.

They expect everybody to do well – there's a lot of subtle pressure to not just waste your time. But there's no place to hide once you're in the therapy. It's tough love.

You know what to expect there. They have leaflets about just what happens, and nobody is secretive about how it works. There's a link to a project for people who don't speak English, but everybody's welcome as part of the general hurly-burly.

When people finish therapy, they usually arrange themselves into self-help groups, while they get back on their feet. Several of the therapy groups themselves have ex-service users, 'experts by experience' or 'XBXs' they're called, helping to run them.

It's a good atmosphere there, and nicely fitted out. People respect it, and look after it. They accept you for what you are, and don't judge. It's hard for most people to be able to trust others after what's often happened to them – but it seems safe there. People talk, and open up.

CONCLUSION

My personal view of PD is that it's like an old car or house, however grand the restoration, day to day maintenance is necessary to preserve it. Living with PD can be a roller-coaster but it's probably possible, in fact it's certainly possible, to have a meaningful life.

Gordon

It is worth noting that service users' main preoccupation is with the general way in which they are treated, or perhaps 'processed', than the specific need for treatment or details of therapy. The message that comes over loudest is that they are asking for acceptance and validation, rather than therapy focussed on change.

This could be seen as a potential source of conflict between service users and professionals, with service users effectively saying 'all we're asking for is that you treat us with respect', and clinicians responding 'but that's *not* all you need – you'll have to do the hard work of change if you want to get a more normal life'.

In fact, this can be clarified by distinguishing between the contributions of those who had received specific treatment (and felt at least some benefit from it), and those who had not. The latter were in the majority, and did not know what was possible and had little idea of what definitive therapeutic interventions were like – they just knew that they had not received any treatment that had made a noticeable difference. Most of those who had received formal therapy – of any type – were appreciative of that, and thought that it should be more widely available. This was not uncritical appreciation, as they were often sharply and perceptively critical of details of it – most commonly that it had not been enough, or that it had finished precipitately. A very small proportion of the discussions supported the view that 'therapy was useless' or 'it made me worse'.

The call for more non-specific acceptance seeking than definitive therapy also has a simple theoretical basis. If personality disorders are accepted as relational disturbances – bringing mechanisms of disturbed primary attachment to play – then the preverbal characteristics of need, such as asking for recognition, acceptance and validation simply as a human being, are likely to be predominant, hence the acceptance-seeking or attachment-seeking presentation. The main task in personality disorder work is often leading people from that undifferentiated state of neediness into a formal frame for verbal-based therapy. It is easy enough to offer empathic and genuine acceptance to people so needy, and it is also uncomplicated to offer formal therapy to those who accept the need for rigour required in change-orientated work. Good services, taking a 'whole system' or 'pathway-based' approach, need to do a great deal of work to manage the path between the two.

ACKNOWLEDGEMENTS

The material for this chapter all comes from numerous service users with whom I have sat in therapy, seminar, discussion, activity and focus groups, and had many interesting, moving and often funny conversations. I would particularly thank those who participated in the London focus groups for the Department of Health, and the Support, Training And Recovery System of the

Thames Valley Initiative: Lesley Allen, Mary-Ann Ambrose, Dale Ashman, Heather Castillo, Kath Clouston, Vicky Cox, Kevin Emrys, Eddie Griffin, Gordon Gunnarsen, Yolandé Hadden, Kevin Healy, Cameron Jordan, Fiona McGruer, Liz Main, Satvinder Mann, Sheena Money, Anna Mills, Peter Oates, Paul Priami, Sarah Mulholland, Hannah Stein, Jayne Treby, Kati Turner, Nicky Tysoe, Gary Winship and others who did not want to be named. Little of this would have been possible without the initial willingness of Alison Hooper, and the considerable practical problem-solving abilities of Anne-Marie Archard, Manisha Gohil, Joanne Andrews and Sue Robinson.

REFERENCES

Borderline UK (BUK). (2005). *Information on BPD and related issues.* Retrieved September 7, 2005, from www.borderlineuk.co.uk
Castillo, H. (2003). *Personality disorder: Temperament or trauma?* London: Kingsley.
Hadden, Y., & Haigh, R. (2002). Personality Disorder: How much more stigmatising could a label be? *Dialogue* No. 9, 1–2.
National Institute for Mental Health for England (NIMHE). (2003). *Personality disorder: No longer a diagnosis of exclusion.* London: Author.

9

An Introduction to Community Mental Health Teams (CMHTs): How Do They Relate to Patients with Personality Disorders?

TOM BURNS

THE ORIGINS OF CMHTs

Some form of multidisciplinary mental health team forms the basis of specialist care for individuals with mental illnesses in most of the developed world. While their configuration (and theoretical underpinnings) may differ in different health care cultures, they are often remarkably similar. This should not surprise us. Unlike the current vogue for 'top-down' imposition of service structures (Department of Health, 1999; Stein & Santos, 1998), the basic model of CMHTs has evolved slowly over several decades. This evolution has been led by mental health professionals faced with the challenges of providing adequate and effective care for individuals who would previously have received it in hospitals for long periods. For all their failings these hospitals were able to offer easy, co-ordinated access to the range of whatever care they had on offer. As the move from the large institutions gathered pace in the late 1950s, the rather basic out-patient services had to expand and refine the care they offered. It rapidly becomes clear to anyone working with severe mental illnesses that no one individual or profession could comprehensively cover the range of their needs (Campell, Hotchkiss, Bradshaw & Porteous, 1998).

Personality Disorder and Community Mental Health Teams: A Practitioner's Guide.   Edited by M. J. Sampson, R. A. McCubbin and P. Tyrer. © 2006 John Wiley & Sons, Ltd.

SECTORISED CARE

CMHTs developed early in the UK and in France (Kovess, Boisguerin, Antoine & Reynauld, 1995) because of a move to sectorised care. 'Sectors' were much smaller than the 'catchment areas' which were served by individual mental hospitals and were usually subdivisions of them (i.e., a single hospital catchment area comprised several sector services). Both the UK and French developments emphasised the importance of decentralised services, with care available as near to the patient's normal residence as possible. The French 'secteur' system drew heavily on sociological thinking and has not been quite as durable. The UK move to highly sectorised care was much more pragmatic and driven, in considerable measure, by the Percy Report (Percy, 1957) and the 1959 Mental Health Act that followed it (Department of Health, 1959). This extraordinarily prescient Act required hospitals that admitted involuntary patients to provide them with out-patient follow-up after discharge. It also required collaboration with local authority social services in that follow-up care and even authorised local authority spending on support of the mentally ill in the community. These two requirements (of providing follow-up and liaising with social services) made subdivision of catchment areas essential if it was to be workable. Neither task can be effectively carried out for populations of a million plus.

THERAPEUTIC COMMUNITIES

The rapid development of CMHTs in the 1960s coincided with the high point of the therapeutic community movement started by Maxwell Jones and Tom Main just after the Second World War (Jones, 1952). While ostensibly separate developments, both reflected and absorbed the liberal ethos of the 1960s (Burns, 2000), with an emphasis on role-blurring and democratisation. This stressed common humanity and empathy equally with specialised skills in the care and support of patients. Consequently, it eroded much of professional demarcation that characterised other services. This sharing of tasks and ideology plus the recognition of the corrosive impact of the chronically low social status of the mentally ill (Goffman, 1960) generated a culture of egalitarianism (and mild anti-authoritarianism) that has characterised CMHTs to this day. Leadership remains a live issue in most CMHTs, particularly the role of senior doctors.

THE CURRENT STATE: SECTORISED VERSUS 'FUNCTIONALISED' TEAMS

By the 1990s over 80 per cent of the UK was served by generic 'sectorised' CMHTs (Johnson & Thornicroft, 1993), as was much of Italy (Fioritti, Lo &

Melega, 1997) and Northern Europe. There were (and are) important differences in how these sectorised teams work – in much of Europe in-patient and out-patient services are rigorously separated. In Italy the divide is even less than in the UK, with nursing staff working across both areas. The greatest changes, however, have come from the influence of US and Australian developments.

In the US, generic community mental health services followed a different path – the Community Mental Health Centres launched in Kennedy's 'New Deal'. Overly ambitious and unattractive to staff, their failure was rapidly obvious (Talbott, Clark, Sharfstein & Klein, 1987) and their remit and influence have contracted. Public outrage at the neglect of the severely mentally ill in the US resulted in a range of innovations and demonstration services. Most of these built upon the concept of case management (Intagliata, 1982) and involved partial teams. Of these developments the most influential has been the assertive community treatment (ACT) team introduced after a landmark study in Wisconsin (Stein & Test, 1980).

The ACT team is a 'functionalised' team in that it targets a specific patient group (those with chronic and often rapidly relapsing psychosis) and has a sharply defined service model and structure. The ACT approach has been replicated widely (Marshall & Lockwood, 1998) and is the basis for the assertive outreach teams prescribed in the UK's NHS plan (Department of Health, 2000). Hoult's replication in Sydney (Hoult, Rosen & Reynolds, 1984) shifted the emphasis to crisis management and has formed the basis of another NHS plan prescribed team, the 'crisis resolution/home treatment' team. Likewise, an Australian approach to first episode psychosis has generated an 'early intervention service' prescription. It was thought that these teams would replace sector teams following a model pioneered in North Birmingham (Sainsbury Centre for Mental Health, 1998).

Despite this, the demise of sectorised services has not occurred and eventually even this approach has been subject to the same detailed descriptive approach, published as a *Mental Health Policy Implementation Guide* (MHPIG; Department of Health, 2002). Functionalised teams are increasingly seen more as an 'add-on' than a 'replacement' for sector CMHTs, and their availability dependent on resourcing (Thornicroft & Tansella, 2004). Following the same thinking, there is now a drive in the UK to develop specific, targeted personality disorder services and a number of pilot projects have been established (National Institute for Mental Health in England, 2003). However, these are few and far between and in their infancy.

It has been estimated that between 10 and 13 per cent of the adult population suffer from some diagnosable personality problem (Coid, 2003), with somewhere between one-third and two-thirds of psychiatric in-patients with a significant personality disorder (Moran, 2002). For the foreseeable future some form of generic, locality based CMHT is likely to remain the main provider of secondary mental health care, especially for those with complex needs (which inevitably will mean most of those with personality disorders).

What are these teams like and how do they work?

THE TASKS OF THE CMHT

ASSESSMENT AND ADVICE

CMHTs are specialist mental health teams and operate as secondary services. Patterns of access vary internationally but most require a referral from another health (or social care) professional. In the UK the vast majority of referrals are from primary care physicians with a smaller number from social services and accident and emergency departments. The expectation has traditionally been that the CMHT would assess all these referrals and, depending on that assessment, either take them on for treatment or advise the referrer on management. There are differing opinions on whether referrals should be 'triaged' as recommended in the MHPIG. While this can be a way of keeping workload down to reasonable levels, some consider that having a high threshold for consideration deprives the referrers (and CMHT trainees) of essential learning about 'caseness'.

Originally, assessments were conducted entirely by doctors, with patients referred on to other team members for specific inputs. Increasingly this has been replaced with initial assessments being conducted by any trained mental health professional on the team. In many teams there is a process of matching for assessments at an allocation meeting with, for example, anxiety disorders being routed to the clinical psychologist, psychotic disorders to the community psychiatric nurse (CPN) and depression in individuals in particular socially adverse situations being seen by the social worker. In some teams the practice has evolved of 'joint assessments', usually by a medical and non-medical member (Burns, Beadsmoore, Bhat, Oliver & Mathers, 1993), and this has been recommended as preferred practice in the MHPIG.

Assessment may result in advice to the referrer or the team in taking on the patient for treatment. Advice can be about further management where the primary care team may, with guidance, contain the appropriate skills (e.g. prescribing, counselling). Sometimes the advice is to reassure the referrer that the problem is not so serious and nothing further needs to be done. The importance of this 'second opinion' role is one that CMHTs often overlook but is highly valued by most referrers.

TREATMENT AND THE CARE PROGRAMME APPROACH (CPA)

Where patients have significant disorders needing more input than the primary care team can provide (severe depression, psychosis, complex anxiety disorders etc.), they are taken on by the CMHT for treatment. This care is shared with the referring GP, who still retains responsibility for overall medical care. Although over half of the caseload of CMHTs comprises severe and long term disorders such as psychoses, most of the referrals are for less severe and time-limited problems (Greenwood, Chisholm, Burns & Harvey, 2000). For these more short term disorders treatment is generally by one professional and most often in an out-patient setting, usually involves just half a dozen contacts over a few months (Burns, Raftery, Beadsmoore, McGuigan & Dickson, 1993) or a limited structured treatment. At the completion of the treatment the patient is referred back to the care of the GP.

The core of the CMHT's work is, however, the care of patients with disorders whose care requires longer, more comprehensive input, usually involving several members of the team. Over the last decade there has been a concerted effort to establish this focus embodied in the procedures of CPA (Department of Health, 1990). Essentially, this requires teams to make a clearer distinction between moderate, time limited disorders and the more severe long term ones by allocating them to two 'tiers' of CPA. The simpler cases are 'standard CPA' and dealt with through assessment and discharge letters and professional notes.

'Enhanced CPA' requires specific paperwork and procedures to ensure and co-ordinate effective review and multidisciplinary work. In short, each patient on enhanced CPA must have a named key worker (called a 'care co-ordinator'), who maintains an up-to-date record of their clinical and social needs, with an indication of who is responsible for meeting them and a clearly identified date for their review. These reviews are expected to be multidisciplinary and involve the patient (to whom the conclusions should be copied) and other involved carers where possible. The CPA process aims to provide a wider understanding of the patient's needs than the purely medical. It usually involves a thorough assessment of risk when appropriate and contingency plans for emergency and out-of-hours presentations.

The range of treatments proposed in the MHPIG for generic CMHTs is extensive and shown in Table 9.1. Clearly not all teams can offer all of these treatments, but most can make a credible effort with the majority.

Table 9.1 CMHT interventions: adapted from MHPIG (Department of Health. (2002). *Community mental health teams (Mental Health Policy Implementation Guide, MHPIG)*. London: Author).

Primarily, but not exclusively, for those with short term needs

Psychological therapies	Routinely assessed as an option. Driven by (1) patient needs (2) staff training and expertise (3) resource availability	Type A: psychological treatment as an integral component of mental health care; includes social skills training, anxiety management and family therapy, but not stand alone treatments
	Most CMHTs should be able to provide types A & B and refer for type C	Type B: eclectic psychological therapy and counselling: a series of sessions following a formulation of the problem; can be informed by more than one theoretical framework
		Type C: formal psychotherapy, i.e. psychotherapy practised within a particular theoretical model; CMHTs should be able to facilitate access when required

Primarily, but not exclusively, for those with severe and enduring illness

Physical health care	Every patient registered with GP	Actively encourage
	Encourage and support contact	Help in keeping appointments
	Identify and discuss physical health problems with GPs	Raised mortality and morbidity mean it remains a priority
Continuity of care	Care co-ordinator takes responsibility for continuity	Clear written instructions available
	Contact frequency varies by need and procedures for out of hours and cover clarified	Capacity for increased frequency ensured
	Contact maintained during admissions and good liaison with primary care	'Inreach' standards formulated

Table 9.1 (*Continued*)

Medication	Team responsible for prescribing, administering and monitoring medication	Depots administered in patient's home or agreed location; periods of direct observed meds possible
	Close links with primary care	
	Structured side-effect monitoring and concordance enhancement	Includes dosette boxes, explanations, negotiations etc.
Basics of daily living	Identification of vulnerabilities and direct help and support	Assertive advocacy with agencies (e.g. landlord etc.)
	Involvement of support workers as well as MH professionals	Assess when to 'do for' or 'do with'
Vocation and education	Encourage to seek occupation where possible	
	Keep a resource file: provide practical help with applications etc.	
Support	Time to provide emotional support to user and carer	Living with SMI is demanding and demoralising
Family and carer support and help	Carer's needs assessment at least once a year	Independent of patient's wishes
	Involve families in CPA	Respect decision not to
	Attention to dependent children	Recognition of impact on children – not detailed parenting assessment
	Education about illness and treatment	
	Behavioural family management available	
Treatment of substance abuse	All team members should assess substance abuse	Possible individual with special interest
	Offer advice on alternative treatment if not available within the team and provide basis harm reduction input	Establish links with local substance misuse services; Obtain training; ensure CPA clarity; joint care preferable for psychotic individuals
Relapse prevention	Individualised relapse prevention plans agreed	Some patients have highly specific 'relapse signatures'
	Identify and reduce stressors	

STAFFING OF THE CMHT

In the NHS, secondary care services are technically 'consultant based'. This means that all patients cared for in them have a named consultant. This is particularly important in the use of the Mental Health Act (Department of Health, 1983) where detained patients must have a 'responsible medical officer' (RMO). As a consequence, CMHTs always contain a consultant psychiatrist. The degree to which that consultant operates as a member of the team or the leader of the team varies enormously, as does practice with respect as to whether teams are configured around a single consultant or several. The MHPIG, for ease of description, outlines the staffing of an ideal team based on a single consultant and serving the needs of a population of about 40 000 (it gives a range of 10 000–60 000). The team is larger than is the average, though not excessively so. The staffing is outlined in Table 9.2.

Table 9.2 CMHT staffing: adapted from MHPIG (Department of Health. (2002). *Community mental health teams (Mental Health Policy Implementation Guide, MHPIG)*. London: Author).

8 care co-ordinators each with a maximum caseload of 35 (increasingly this is targeted at 30)	In addition to key working need key skills:
Team manager with 30–50% caseload to be drawn from one of these	communicate clearly maintain multidisciplinary notes cross cover between disciplines within limits of their skills broad understanding of team's patients
Of the 8 care co-ordinators:	
3–4 community psychiatric nurses (CPNs)	within and outside the CMHT SWs need to maintain strong links with social services
2–3 social workers (SWs)	
1–1.5 occupational therapists (OTs)	CP and OT services may be on a sessional basis; skill sharing may be needed
1–1.5 clinical psychologists (CPs)	For seasonal staff there needs to be clarity about their commitment and CPA responsibility
1 full time consultant psychiatrist	fully integrated in the team and 'care co-ordinator' for some standard CPA patients
1–1.5 non-consultant medical staff (e.g. trainee or staff grade)	
1–3 mental health support workers	individuals with health or social care experience; should reflect local population and need
1–1.5 administration staff	adequate to support CPA documentation and administration

While this represents the current ideal, there are clearly absolute essentials for running a CMHT. Teams cannot function without medical, nursing or social worker members. Medical and social work staff are legal requirements in the UK, to provide care for patients under the Mental Health Act, and without nursing staff direct care (in particular medication) cannot be delivered. Clearly, such a team is impoverished if it is without the professional perspectives brought by clinical psychology and occupational therapy, but in practice CMHTs often have to operate either permanently or temporarily without such inputs.

CASELOADS AND PROCEDURES

An important benefit of the CPA approach is that it has forced teams to recognise that they have to draw boundaries concerning what they can and cannot do. The proposal in the MHPIG that a team caseload should not exceed 350 (and those on enhanced CPA should be on individual care co-ordinators' caseloads of not more than 35) has ensured that they actively manage their caseloads. For each new addition, someone must be assessed as ready for discharge back to the GP.

CMHTs have regular team meetings when ongoing care is reviewed (and care programmes updated and rewritten). It is at these meetings that assessment pressures are addressed, work distributed effectively and difficult decisions made about adjusting individual caseloads. Teams vary considerably in how they approach CPA reviews. One team may emphasise maximising multidisciplinary input and ensuring regularity with frequent, brief focused reviews by the whole team (Burns & Leibowitz, 1997). This approach usually involves the patient and family negotiating with the care co-ordinator prior to the team meeting. Another team may have longer individualised CPA reviews with just the care co-ordinator and perhaps the consultant and team leader and the patient and family. It may be appropriate to vary the format according to patient need. Discharge and transfer decisions and planning (particularly for patients who have had difficult or stormy illnesses) may also involve multidisciplinary meetings.

INPATIENT CARE

In the UK CMHTs generally continue to care for their patients during hospital admissions and the consultant retains medical responsibility. It is usual for the whole CMHT to attend the in-patient ward rounds (or at least all those who care co-ordinate current in-patients) and most retain contact with their in-patients (so-called 'inreach work'). CMHTs are best placed to make admission and discharge decisions, as they know both the patient's usual level of functioning and the level of support and input they can offer.

LIAISON

Attempts to define rigorously who should be cared for in primary care and who in secondary care have proved elusive, and attempts to develop structured filters and thresholds have been generally unsuccessful (Slade et al. 2001). Diagnosis is a poor indicator of the need for secondary care. Most depression is treated by GPs, but severity or a whole range of complicating factors (isolation, co-occurring substance abuse, suicidal risk) may necessitate secondary care. Even in psychoses the picture is complex – between a fifth and a third of patients with schizophrenia are cared for solely by their GP (Kendrick, Burns, Freeling & Sibbald, 1994)). The result is that to remain efficient and effective CMHTs have to maintain regular liaison with those who refer to them to manage the threshold.

Various approaches to managing this boundary have been tried and the most enduring seems to be a regular face-to-face liaison meeting (Burns & Bale, 1997). Liaison is time consuming but most teams that have established it well with local referrers consider it time well spent. CMHTs also have to arrange effective liaison with a range of agencies – housing, social services, police and voluntary providers of accommodation and day care. How extensive these need to be and their precise format will differ from setting to setting. The act of showing willing and acknowledging the relevance of the other agencies may be almost as important as the information exchange that takes place.

CMHTs AND THE CARE OF INDIVIDUALS WITH PERSONALITY DISORDERS

As pointed out at the beginning of this chapter, individuals with personality disorders comprise a significant proportion of the clinical load of CMHTs. This should come as no surprise.

First, individual/s with personality disorders have higher rates of mental illness than the general population. Struggling with difficulties of personality and all the attendant complications of personal relationships that this brings, raises vulnerability to a range of mental health problems – depression and anxiety because of rejection and criticism, substance abuse as a consequence of a maladaptive search for an accepting peer group or as self-medication for the disappointments of an unsuccessful and unrewarding life. The individual with personality problems not only experiences increased stress and vulnerability because of poor interpersonal relationships, but is often deprived of the emotional protection that close family and friends provide against adversity (Albert, Becker, McCrone & Thornicroft, 1998).

Second, individuals with personality disorder with such problems are simply more difficult to help. Virtually all treatments for mental health problems are grounded in relationships. Trusting relationships may be very difficult to sustain between the individual with personality disorder and their GP or other potential carer. The very complexity of the relationship may make otherwise fairly simple treatments (e.g. treating a moderate depression with antidepressants and supportive counselling) impossible in primary care. As a consequence, they may be referred to secondary care not because they require a complex or sophisticated treatment, but because helping them accept a simple treatment is, in itself, so complex. Managing the relationship is the problem rather than the treatment. The GP, rightly, will expect CMHT staff to be more skilled and more prepared to negotiate this challenge.

WHY ARE PERSONALITY DISORDERS TREATED DIFFERENTLY BY CMHTs?

Any observer of psychiatric practice 30 years ago would have found CMHT staff quite unfazed about the issue of individuals with personality disorder. Sure, they could be more 'tricky' than others (the treatments did not go to plan so easily etc.), but that was just part of the job in the same way that GPs accepted their group of 'heartsink' patients (O'Dowd, 1988). However, in recent decades individuals with personality disorder have increasingly been discriminated against by CMHTs. The UK government's recent policy document, *Personality Disorder: No Longer a Diagnosis of Exclusion* (National Institute for Mental Health in England, 2003) and the move to establish specific personality disorder teams across the country is in recognition of this. There are two powerful forces that have driven this change – the increasing importance of evidence-based practice and increasing professional accountability. Many would argue that this emphasis on accountability has gone beyond a healthy audit and become a pernicious blame culture. Whichever is the case, CMHT professionals are much more circumspect about what they do and what the implications are for the whole service and for the patient in the longer term.

THE 'TREATABILITY' OF PERSONALITY DISORDERS

Psychopathic personality disorder is unique among mental disorders in the 1959 and 1983 Mental Health Acts (Department of Health, 1983) in that there is a specific requirement that it must be judged 'treatable' to justify involuntary detention. Although the provisions in the Act are restricted to psychopathic personality disorder, given the poor specificity of personality disorder diagnosis, this special provision has influenced thinking about all individuals with personality disorder – particularly those with Cluster B presentations (American Psychiatric Association, 1994). Not all patients with other mental disorders such as depression or schizophrenia respond to treatment, so why is there this special requirement for personality disorder?

At the time of the 1959 MHA, the consensus was that there were no effective treatments for personality disorder in its own right. Indeed there was considerable doubt that personality disorder was sensibly considered in the same category as mental illness at all. It did not demonstrate the discrete onset or phasic character of most of the mental illnesses with periods of qualitatively distinct recovery. The balance of opinion was against including personality disorder, and for restricting the remit of the Mental Health Act (MHA) to mental illness and mental handicap (as it was then called). However, there was intense interest in the UK in the early 1950s in the role of therapeutic communities in the rehabilitation of war neuroses and more widely of soldiers with significant problems in readapting to civilian life (Jones, 1952). Maxwell Jones argued persuasively for the need to include this group in the MHA, so that research could continue into their treatment. A necessary concession to achieve this from his sceptical colleagues was the 'treatability' clause. As with other diagnostic categories accepted into schema against professional doubts 'to allow for research' to either validate or reject them (Frances, 1980), no such process ensued and the diagnosis was simply accepted.

Personality disorders are seen by most CMHT professionals as inherently not treatable (though this is changing, stimulated by new treatments dealt with elsewhere in this volume). In an era of evidence based practice it is increasingly difficult to defend time devoted to caring for individuals without clear evidence of an effective treatment – even less so when that attempt at treatment is often stressful and where the professional may believe (very rightly in many cases) that they cannot modify risks for which they will be held accountable. It is much easier to try and exclude such individuals from 'a hard-pressed service'.

THE CARE PROGRAMME APPROACH (CPA) AND THE FOCUS
ON THE SEVERELY MENTALLY ILL (SMI)

Recognised failings in the care of a severely mentally ill man who went on to kill a total stranger (Ritchie, 1994) led to the introduction of a more systematic and reliable approach to the care and monitoring of individuals with the most severe illnesses. The CPA required teams to focus on the care of this group and, through a system of regular review, clear accountability and structured paperwork, to provide continuity of comprehensive care (Department of Health, 1990). Whatever the criticisms of some of the clumsy terminology and bureaucracy of the CPA, it has sharpened up CMHT practice and introduced reflective thought into who should, and should not, be maintained on caseloads. Most teams now devote over half of their time to individuals with psychotic illnesses, who receive a significantly better deal than they used to. An inevitable consequence of this is that those individuals whose problems are less enduring and less severe inevitably get less attention, and some get none. For many teams this has meant a raising of the threshold for what CMHTs take on from primary care, and for many individuals with personality disorder refusal to get involved at all. For this latter group, their low priority for the CMHT is bolstered by the lack of evidence of specific therapeutic interventions available to them.

THE SPECIFIC OBLIGATIONS OF CMHTs TO INDIVIDUALS WITH PERSONALITY DISORDERS: WHAT CAN CMHT STAFF DO TO HELP?

Individuals with personality disorder have undoubtedly been hard done by recently in CMHT services. It can be enormously difficult to distinguish the degree to which an individual's problems are entirely an expression of his or her personality or, as is so often the case, the expression of a perfectly treatable disorder modified by that personality. Perhaps the most common example is self-damaging and disorganised behaviour in some individuals when they are depressed, which responds to antidepressant treatment, as opposed to pure 'borderline' behaviour, which is unlikely to be helped by such treatments. Clearly, the threshold has been set too high and the current response of establishing personality disorder services reflects an awareness of this.

The new personality disorder services will provide much needed specia-list care for a small number of very disabled individuals. Hopefully, they will also develop trainable skills and strategies that can be disseminated. It is unlikely, however, that they will significantly reduce the need for CMHTs to work with individuals with personality disorder in the near future. What can CMHT staff do to help these individuals and, perhaps more importantly, to avoid making things worse?

ACCURATE ASSESSMENT AND HONEST FEEDBACK

It is a common belief that telling a patient that they suffer from a personality disorder (not the treatable depression or anxiety state for which they were referred) will always be unwelcome. This is not so. Patients often have a more realistic understanding of their problems than we assume and comply with referrals more in hope than out of any strong conviction. Helping to outline the limits of options for change can be a positive experience. I can think of several patients who have welcomed a frank discussion of the difficulties they face and the fact that antidepressants, or indeed psychotherapy (both of which they may have tried several times) will not make a big difference. We should try and explore ways for them of coping and living with their own unique personal style. At the very least, they feel understood and accepted for what they are, not 'palmed off' with an ill-fitting diagnosis and ineffective treatment. At the other extreme it can be an enormous relief to be told this is how it is, the task is to adapt to it, not wait for it to go away. Patients may already have come to the conclusion that the fruitless round of referrals and consultations is doing nothing for them but have felt obliged to go along with them.

Sensitive wording is essential. It helps to stress that all of us are different and that the world would be a very dull place without strong and varied personalities. Seeking socially and personally acceptable strategies that are *consonant* with their personality rather than trying to balance or neutralise it seems to work better. It is of little value to tell a timid, obsessional librarian to 'get out more' and join an amateur dramatics club (while this may be just right for a histrionic individual vainly trying to 'be more ordinary' and a dutiful spouse). Where impulsivity is complicated by alcohol abuse an honest discussion of the risks for them of drinking (and the inability of psychiatrists to shield them from the consequences) can help reframe a failing personal strategy for dealing with persisting chaos. Just as in discussing the risks of cannabis use with a schizophrenia patient, much of the focus, inevitably, will be acknowledging that while it may be okay for others, it simply is not for them. The dangers lie in the *interaction* of the drug with them as an individual, not in the drug itself.

Managing expectations to reasonable levels is often a central component of work with individuals with personality disorder. They suffer from disappointments, intense dysphoric emotions and depressive illnesses like everyone else. What makes coping with these so difficult for them is the addition of low self-esteem, isolation and a limited repertoire of interpersonal skills. Honesty about what is, and is not, achievable is essential.

Equally detailed and honest feedback can be just as important to the referring GP or social worker. Letting the GP know that this is an individual who is likely to complain of sadness and disappointment on and off, because of unfulfilled relationships and perhaps unattainable expectations, means that temporary support and sympathy are needed – not another course of antidepressants or a referral to the CMHT. An honest opinion needs to be an accurate and informed opinion if it is to do any good. Individuals with personality disorder are due a careful and detailed assessment of their problems to support our opinions and advice. Simply stating 'there is no evidence of mental illness' is not an adequate response.

Again careful and positive wording is essential. Individuals with personality disorder feel they have been stigmatised and that many of the terms used about them are pejorative (National Institute for Mental Health in England, 2003). The recent practice of requiring CMHTs to copy their letters to patients is particularly helpful here. The wording of these letters should emphasise the positive while recognising the difficulties. CMHT staff all have extensive experience in approaching difficult issues with patients. One of the skills we acquire in this is the choice of wording to explore them without demeaning or insulting our patients. We need to bring this skill to our letter writing so that it can serve as a guide to the GP as to how to phrase such issues, but also be a letter that patients can perhaps read and reread at times of reflection.

AVOIDING IATROGENIC DAMAGE

It is possible for health care staff to make things worse, rather than better, for individuals with personality disorder – probably more so than in other disorders. The most dramatic example of this is when self-damaging individuals are admitted to hospitals for prolonged periods during which their self-damaging escalates, marked by the imposition of restrictions and coercion. The more they do it the harder it is to discharge them, despite it often being obvious that they are now considerably worse than before they came in. The cutting (which increasingly is the behaviour associated in young women with such admissions) expresses a degree of self-loathing and a need for affection and sympathy (Linehan, Armstrong, Suarez & Allmon,

1991). The often ill concealed resentment in the staff simply exaggerates the self-loathing and need and the circumstances escalate. In extreme cases patients become trapped in hospital for years and acquire such reputations that effective rehabilitation becomes impossible. Even without a specialist personality disorder service, CMHTs can do much to avoid these tragedies (for tragedies they are – four or five years trapped in such a cycle can destroy families and blight a life permanently).

Simply refusing admission is not enough in itself (though often vital). An alternative has to be offered. A simple behavioural approach of 'not rewarding' pathological behaviour is doomed. The patient will simply 'up the ante' until he or she (usually she) cannot be ignored. Experience suggests that a relatively easy admission, for a very short time which is acknowledged at the start, can defuse potential disasters. This needs to be complemented by follow-up that is not contingent on further self-harm. For instance, seeing the patient every week for the first couple of months and offering to see them between sessions if they request it but *not* if they self-harm. If that happens it can be picked up at the next session. Many teams find 'contracts' helpful in these situations. Such contracts emphasise partnership and encourage more responsible behaviour and mutual recognition. However, if their wording is too mechanical or punitive they can backfire. They need to enshrine some optimism.

These approaches are not easy. Enormous pressure is brought to bear on staff, from both the patient and those around them. Sometimes it is not possible to resist and admission may defuse the situation. Remaining in a general in-patient ward for long periods is rarely helpful, however. Sometimes the MHA is used but, again, is only useful in containing a brief life-threatening situation, almost never a useful long-term strategy.

Mental health staff can also do their patient less obvious, but equally destructive, harm by locking them into long term dependent relationships that hold out an unrealistic hope of dramatic changes. This is not to criticise dependent relationships – a healthy dependency may be the only route forward to mature independence. The long term support recommended above involves a degree of dependency, but it does not imply 'special powers' in the staff member. The skill is to be able to help the patients try and understand and cope with what they bring to you, not to 'make them different'. Unskilful or poorly handled long term out-patient relationships can allow patients to believe that there is some process that we bring to it that will eventually remove or cure their personality disorder. This is misleading and potentially damaging. If patients come to believe their salvation lies in the sessions they have with you then they are distracted from investigating other ways of changing and coping. This is (given there is absolutely no evidence to believe that psychiatric out-patient sessions do effect a cure) damaging. Similarly, sending patients off for non-specific psychotherapy or embarking on repeated complex courses of antidepressants can deprive them of a rounded understanding of themselves and a chance to come to terms with this.

CLARITY ABOUT RESPONSIBILITIES

Much of what has been written here about managing personality disorders within a CMHT has focused on the need for a frank acknowledgement of the limitations of such services. This is not to engender therapeutic nihilism but to recognise the realistic arena for our joint work and to avoid distracting the patient into wishful thinking. Its aim has been to help and protect the patient. However, such frankness is equally important to protect CMHT staff. We now live and work in an increasingly risk-averse and accountable culture. Mental health professionals have regularly been directly criticised for acts committed by their patients, often when there is clearly no way they could have influenced these acts. The UK is possibly outstanding in this respect, with a risk preoccupation that astounds our foreign visitors.

Ever since the Ritchie report (1994), all homicides by people who have had recent contact with mental health services (and this includes those with personality disorders and substance abuse but no demonstrable mental illness) have been subject to thorough internal and external reviews. These inquiries have had major impacts on careers and services, and have regularly criticised 'poor communication between agencies'. Individuals with personality disorder are characteristically involved with a wide range of agencies – hospitals, primary care, social services, police, substance abuse teams etc. The potential for confusion is limitless. With few other disorders is it more important to be clear who is doing what and who is taking responsibility for what.

Where information is regularly passing between these agencies, we need to ensure that the patient knows this if we are not to lose their trust altogether. Where health care is undertaking something that may impact dramatically on housing or perhaps child care we need to make sure that social services are kept informed. Perhaps even more importantly, we need to be clear about when we are not involved and where we have nothing to add. This is particularly critical around issues of personal and criminal responsibility.

Despite protestations to the contrary, it remains all too common for police to drop charges against individuals once they know they are under the care of a CMHT, even when it is clear to all involved that the crime in question had nothing to do with mental illness (e.g. a patient with schizophrenia who steals to support his cannabis habit). This can be frustrating because we know that the patients, despite their psychosis, knew what they were doing and could learn from punishment. The offending behaviour here is not central to the clinical problem. Indeed, increased offending behaviour may indicate remission in some psychotic patients! With some individuals with personality disorder, however, it may go directly to the core issues. Our work to try and help the individuals recognise the medium to long term disadvantages of their impulsive behaviour or intoxication are hopelessly undermined if the police do not take action. Even more worrying is if we believe the patient is genuinely dangerous and the behaviour is discounted by the police.

Social services, GPs and the police will often ask CMHTs to keep someone on their books and monitor them because it is believed they pose a risk. This is a very tricky issue for CMHTs. Some consider that the more agencies involved, the greater the likelihood that deterioration in mental state or escalating risk will be spotted and addressed. Some teams believe they *cannot* discharge someone who poses a risk (and the proposed new mental health law in England seems to imply this). There is a contrary view on this. If the CMHT does not consider it has an intervention that will significantly reduce that risk (or a treatment to improve the well-being of the patient) then it is better to be crystal clear about it and discharge the patient. This is certainly the author's view. If there is nothing we can do, it is not neutral but potentially damaging to remain involved. It gives a spurious sense of security where none exists and may detract from those who really are in a position to do something to prevent them for 'doing it'. In this way it is bad for the patient. It is also bad for the professionals because remaining involved implies that we believe we have some potential to alter events and therefore will, quite correctly, be asked to account for why we did not.

CONCLUSIONS

An honest and careful acknowledgement of what CMHTs can and cannot do to help (when we have established a detailed understanding of the individuals and, hopefully, transmitted to them that we do understand their situation), is probably our most powerful tool. The temptation to reject these individuals out of hand must be resisted. Similarly, we must resist taking the easy option of shoe-horning them into diagnoses which (although they carry more optimistic treatments) are simply not accurate. There is a delicate balance to be found, between taking enough responsibility to foster collaborative work without implying the authority and abilities that we do not possess. We have no option but to try and seek out that balance for each individual with personality disorder we confront.

REFERENCES

Albert, M., Becker, T., McCrone, P. & Thornicroft, G. (1998). Social networks and mental health service utilisation – a literature review. *International Journal of Social Psychiatry*, *44*, 248–266.

American Psychiatric Association. (1994). *Diagnostic and statistical manual of mental disorders* (4th ed.). Washington, DC: Author.

Burns, T. (2000). Maxwell Jones Lecture: The legacy of therapeutic community practice in modern community mental health services. *Therapeutic Communities*, *21*, 165–174.

Burns, T. & Bale, R. (1997). Establishing a mental health liaison attachment with primary care. *Advances in Psychiatric Treatment*, *3*, 219–224.

Burns, T., Beadsmoore, A., Bhat, A. V., Oliver, A. & Mathers, C. (1993). A controlled trial of home-based acute psychiatric services. I: Clinical and social outcome. *British Journal of Psychiatry*, *163*, 49–54.

Burns, T. & Leibowitz, J. (1997). The Care Programme Approach: Time for frank talking. *Psychiatric Bulletin*, *21*, 426–429.

Burns, T., Raftery, J., Beadsmoore, A., McGuigan, S. & Dickson, M. (1993). A controlled trial of home-based acute psychiatric services. II: Treatment patterns and costs. *British Journal of Psychiatry*, *163*, 55–61.

Campbell, H., Hotchkiss, R., Bradshaw, M. & Porteous, M (1998). Critical care pathways. *British Medical Journal*, *316*, 133–137.

Coid, J. (2003). Epidemiology, public health and the problem of personality disorder. *Britian Journal of Psychiatry Supplement*, *44*, 3–10.

Department of Health. (1959). *The Mental Health Act: England and Wales*. London: Author.

Department of Health. (1983). *The Mental Health Act: England and Wales*. London: Author.

Department of Health. (1990). *The Care Programme Approach for people with a mental illness referred to the special psychiatric services*. London: Author.

Department of Health. (1999). *Modern standards and service models: National service framework for mental health*. London: Author.

Department of Health. (2000). *The NHS plan – A plan for investment, a plan for reform*. London: Author.

Department of Health. (2002). *Community mental health teams (Mental Health Policy Implementation Guide, MHPIG)*. London: Author.

Fioritti, A., Lo, R. L. & Melega, V. (1997). Reform said or done? The case of Emilia-Romagna within the Italian psychiatric context. *American Journal of Psychiatry*, *154*, 94–98.

Frances, A. (1980). The DSM-III personality disorders section: A commentary. *American Journal Psychiatry*, *137*, 1050–1054.

Goffman, I. (1960). *Asylums: Essays on the social situation of mental patients and other inmates*. Harmondsworth, UK: Penguin.

Greenwood, N., Chisholm, B., Burns, T. & Harvey, K. (2000). Community mental health team caseloads and diagnostic case mix. *Psychiatric Bulletin*, *24*, 290–293.

Hoult, J., Rosen, A. & Reynolds, I. (1984). Community orientated treatment compared to psychiatric hospital orientated treatment. *Social Science and Medicine*, *18*, 1005–1010.

Intagliata, J. (1982). Improving the quality of community care for the chronically mentally disabled: The role of case management. *Schizophrenia Bulletin*, *8*, 655–674.

Johnson, S. & Thornicroft, G. (1993). The sectorisation of psychiatric services in England and Wales. *Social Psychiatry and Psychiatric Epidemiology*, *28*, 45–47.

Jones, M. (1952). *Social psychiatry: A study of therapeutic communities*. London: Tavistock.

Kendrick, T., Burns, T., Freeling, P. & Sibbald, B.l. (1994). Provision of care to general practice patients with disabling long-term mental illness: A survey in 16 practices. *British Journal of General Practice*, *44*, 301–305.

Kovess, V., Boisguerin, B., Antoine, D. & Reynauld, M. (1995). Has the sectorization of psychiatric services in France really been effective? *Social Psychiatry and Psychiatric Epidemiology*, *30*, 132–138.

Linehan, M. M., Armstrong, H. E., Suarez, A. & Allmon, D. (1991). Cognitive–behavioral treatment of chronically parasuicidal borderline patients. *Archives of General Psychiatry*, *48*, 1060–1064.

Marshall, M. & Lockwood, A. (1998). *Assertive Community Treatment for people with severe mental disorders* (Cochrane Review).

Moran, P. (2002). The epidemiology of personality disorders. *Psychiatry*, *1*, 8–11.

National Institute for Mental Health in England. (2003). *Personality disorder: No longer a diagnosis of exclusion*. London: Department of Health.

O'Dowd, T. C. (1988). Five years of 'heartsink' patients in general practice. *British Medical Journal*, *ii*, 528–530.

Percy, L. (1957). *Report of the Royal Commission on the law relating to mental illness and mental deficiency. 1954–1957*. Chairperson: Lord Percy. Cmnd 169. HMSO.

Ritchie, J. H. (1994). *The report of the enquiry into the care and treatment of Christopher Clunis presented to the Chairman of the North East Thames and South East Thames Regional Health Authorities*. London: HMSO.

Sainsbury Centre for Mental Health. (1998). *Keys to engagement: A review of care for people with serious mental illness who are hard to engage with services*. London: Sainsbury Centre for Mental Health.

Slade, M., Cahill, S., Kelsey, W., Powell, R., Strathdee, G. et al. (2001). Threshold 3: The feasibility of the Threshold Assessment Grid (TAG) for routine assessment of the severity of mental health problems. *Social Psychiatry and Psychiatric Epidemiology*, *36*, 516–521.

Stein, L. I. & Santos, A. B. (1998). *Assertive community treatment of persons with severe mental illness*. New York: Norton.

Stein, L. I. & Test, M. A. (1980). Alternative to mental hospital treatment. I. Conceptual model, treatment program, and clinical evaluation. *Archives of General Psychiatry*, *37*, 392–397.

Talbott, J. A., Clark, G. H. J., Sharfstein, S. S. & Klein, J. (1987). Issues in developing standards governing psychiatric practice in community mental health centers. *Hospital and Community Psychiatry*, *38*, 1198–1202.

Thornicroft, G. & Tansella, M. (2004). Components of a modern mental health service: A pragmatic balance of community and hospital care: Overview of systematic evidence. *British Journal of Psychiatry*, *185*, 283–290.

10

When Can Contact with the Community Mental Health Team (CMHT) be Considered 'Treatment'?

REMY McCUBBIN

In Section One of this book, ideas relating to the concept of 'personality disorder' and its treatment were presented. The chapters in that section can be seen as the individual 'components' of treatment, which must be understood by anyone attempting to help those experiencing the kinds of difficulty subsumed under the diagnosis. In Section Two, it is intended to provide a more detailed examination of the particular role of *community mental health teams* (CMHTs) in relation to this group of patients. This requires a consideration of the way that the different components of treatment can be *combined*, in order to provide coherent and effective interventions.

When considering the responsibilities of CMHTs in relation to personality disorder, a number of important themes emerge – some of these are consistent with the work of teams in relation to other patient groups; some are unique. This chapter is an attempt to consider the involvement of services at the level of the CMHT, in order to clarify when 'contact' (between teams and patients) can be considered 'treatment', and how this can be optimised. The chapter begins with a consideration of the concept of 'treatment' in general terms, before describing in detail the key features of CMHT interventions that allow for effective support of people with personality disorders.

Personality Disorder and Community Mental Health Teams: A Practitioner's Guide.   Edited by
M. J. Sampson, R. A. McCubbin and P. Tyrer. © 2006 John Wiley & Sons, Ltd.

Throughout this chapter, key points will be illustrated with reference to a particular (fictitious) case illustration – the case of 'Susan' (see below). The use of this approach is not intended to suggest that the particular details of this patient's presentation are uniquely informative. Rather, the aim is to clarify a number of points, which can be generalised to other patients with very different presentations.

CASE ILLUSTRATION – SUSAN

Susan is a 29 year old woman, referred to the CMHT by her GP after she presented to the Accident and Emergency Department three times in a period of a month. On each occasion, she has been taken there by her mother following an overdose of paracetamol. She has no history of contact with secondary care psychiatric services, but has in the past been referred to a counsellor at her GP's practice. She has, however, failed to attend for two appointments made for her, and has been discharged from that service.

In the course of assessment it emerges that Susan lives with her mother, who controls the running of the household and all parenting decisions regarding Susan's two year old daughter – her mother is of the view that Susan is not a responsible parent. Aside from this, the two women spend little time together, with Susan spending much of the day in her bedroom. Susan has throughout her life been extremely timid and shy, and rarely leaves the house alone. She worked briefly, between the ages of 19 and 21, but has never lived away from home. No friends have called to the house for her since her schooldays. The father of her child is a man who lived next door for a short while, but who moved away when Susan became pregnant and has not been seen since. Susan's own father died when she was four, and her mother has since had a series of short-term relationships, but none of these men have ever shared the family home. Susan has one brother, who is two years younger than her.

Susan describes herself as extremely depressed, and feeling resentful of her mother, who she sees as over-controlling. When her mother is present, however, she gives no indication of this resentment, other than to stop talking. She says she has no ideas about how the CMHT might be able to help her, and her mother says this is typical of her – that she 'just expects everyone else to do everything for her'. Susan reports smoking cannabis about four times a week, supplied to her by her younger brother. She also reports a range of symptoms sufficient to meet the diagnostic criteria for major depressive disorder.

In terms of the risk of further acts of self-harm, she reports having taken overdoses infrequently since the age of 18, and that she regularly cuts herself at times when she and her mother have argued. The wounds have never required medical attention, and she has always concealed them from her mother. Lately, however, her mother has found out about Susan's overdoses, which have greatly increased in frequency and in terms of the number of tablets she takes. Susan is unable to give any guarantee that she will be able to resist the urge to self-harm in the future. Indeed, she seems to be seeking admission to the acute in-patient ward, saying it is only this that will keep her safe. Her mother assures staff that the two year old girl is being well cared for, and is settled in terms of her behaviour.

WHAT CONSTITUTES 'TREATMENT'? (AND WHAT DOES NOT)

CMHTs potentially offer a great variety of interventions to help support patients such as Susan. They may provide a framework for understanding the problems being encountered, offer medication or talking therapies for psychological symptoms and monitor the effects of these, organise a place of safety in times of crisis and support people with financial and housing needs. Deciding on the best course of action in trying to help a particular patient, however, is no easy matter.

IDENTIFYING PATIENTS' NEEDS

In order to plan their interventions, CMHTs require a hierarchy of intended goals for each patient. They need to be able to separate out, and agree on, the different areas of difficulty being addressed, and the order in which this is to be done. Broadly, the aim of all interventions is to reduce the distress experienced by patients and those they have contact with, as well as to increase patients' functioning and reduce the risk of anyone coming to harm. Within this, it is essential to be clear about the different *areas of need*, in which more specific goals can be identified. For personality-disordered patients, these can be summarised as follows.

- Needs arising out of physical health problems and social circumstances (e.g. housing, finance, child care).
- Axis I symptom management (e.g. anxiety, depression, substance use).
- Areas of psychological functioning distinct from Axis I or Axis II diagnoses (e.g. self-esteem or assertiveness).
- Influencing the inter-personal environment, so as to minimise the impact of Axis II difficulties. This can include the idea of the CMHT itself being part

of the patient's inter-personal environment, and having some sort of 'supportive' or 'containing' role.

- Helping patients to *personally overcome* their Axis II difficulties.
- Influencing the amount/nature of contact between patients and other services (GPs, primary care services, housing authorities, police etc.), with a view to achieving gains in any of the first five areas. This might include the provision of a 'consultation' service to such agencies.
- Minimising the risk of harm to the patient and those around them.

The dilemmas facing CMHTs often relate to questions of which areas of need take priority over the others. Clearly, a high priority will always be given to managing any areas of risk appropriately. The patient, their family, the CMHT staff and members of the public must be kept safe before any other interventions can be implemented. While it is not expected or even desirable to *eliminate* risk entirely (as is clear from other chapters, many forms of treatment require clients to encounter and manage risky situations in the short term), the degree of risk associated with a particular, planned approach must be judged to be acceptable by everyone in the CMHT.

While the importance of attending to risk is generally agreed on, CMHTs can encounter significant problems in deciding which of the other areas of need should be addressed first, in order to achieve this. In the case of Susan, risk might be identified in terms of her self-harming behaviour and, potentially, emotional neglect experienced by her daughter. Managing these risks, while considering possible interventions addressing the other areas of need, is one of the most complicated issues facing the team.

Even when there is no identifiable risk, there can be disagreement within the CMHT as to which difficulties should be addressed. In addition to symptoms of anxiety and depression, Susan has difficulties associated with substance abuse, her relationship with her mother and, it might be inferred, her self-esteem. CMHT staff will be familiar with such constellations of difficulties, some of which may be thought of in terms of formal diagnoses, some of which exist outside such categories. In 'personality' terms, Susan might be thought of as exhibiting features of avoidant, dependent or border-line personality disorders. Again, such co-morbidity is common. How is the team to decide which of these areas of need are to be addressed?

THE NEED TO PRIORITISE PERSONALITY FUNCTIONING

For an intervention to be considered 'treatment for the personality disorder', the *primary* goal must surely be to reduce or ameliorate the effects of the patient's personality difficulties. While needs in the first three areas listed above cannot be overlooked, it is when addressing needs relating specifically to personality functioning that CMHTs can be said to be offering 'personality disorder' treatment.

This can be illustrated with regard to the question of when to address Axis I difficulties. When both Axis I and Axis II difficulties are present, there is the option of providing a discrete, 'standard' Axis I intervention, *as well as* an intervention aimed at improving personality functioning. For some CMHT practitioners, the availability of proven, effective treatments for the Axis I difficulties suggests an obligation to offer these to the patient in all cases. However, to do so would run the risk of ignoring or even reinforcing the patient's personality difficulties. For example: were a CMHT to address one of Susan's Axis I difficulties (e.g. depression) without taking *any* account of her Axis II problems, it would have to be acknowledged that no personality disorder 'treatment' was being provided. Alternatively, were they to address her depression in such a way that reinforced her sense of being dependent on others, they might actually intensify the severity of her personality problems.

For reasons such as these, there is a requirement to prioritise the patient's personality difficulties when planning 'personality disorder' treatment. As noted, there is a distinction between treatments aimed at the patient 'overcoming' their personality difficulties (by seeking to initiate change *in the patient*, as in, for example, some forms of psychotherapy), and treatment/support that 'takes account of' their personality disorder, in order to minimise the impact of this on the patient or others they are in contact with. The latter approaches include interventions that seek to alter:

- the patient's physical environment, e.g. nidotherapy (as described by Tyrer, Sensky & Mitchard, 2003, and later in this chapter)
- their social/inter-personal environment, e.g. family interventions
- the way some other difficulty (for example, another mental health difficulty such as depression) is managed.

Each of these interventions may be considered treatment 'for' the personality disorder to some extent, although it is sensible to acknowledge when little impact on the *patient's* functioning (specifically, in terms of their *personality* functioning) is anticipated.

The first question to be considered in planning Susan's care is therefore a general one: *taking account of the observed personality features*, how can the CMHT best approach the task of supporting her, and which of her difficulties shall be addressed? The framing of this question, with its emphasis on personality factors, will usually have an impact on the way other needs are met. Should Susan be admitted? To what extent should comfort and reassurance be offered? What will be required of Susan herself in developing and implementing a treatment plan? If the team are able to strike the right 'tone' in their interactions with Susan, the potential exists to make inroads to address those features of Susan's difficulties that can be thought of in terms of 'personality disorder'.

THE IMPORTANCE OF THE THERAPEUTIC RELATIONSHIP

From the preceding discussion, it is clear that the nature of the relationships between personality-disordered patients and the CMHT practitioners trying to help them are going to be of great importance. It is central to the very concept of personality disorder that disruptions to the relationships formed by patients help to define their status as 'patient', are implicated in the development and maintenance of the patient's difficulties and are central to what might be considered a good outcome. This inevitably includes the relationships they form with members of the CMHT.

Indeed, many would go further, and argue that the relationship between patient and practitioner is itself a primary 'active ingredient' of treatment. In this view, *all* aspects of contact between staff and patients are *potentially* 'treatment' – from the way the CMHT member conducts the assessment, responds to crises and whether they suggest ways to address problems, through to how they define 'progress' and the way they end their involvement. If practitioners are able to act in such a way as to address some of the central features of the patient's view of self and others, the potential exists to influence key aspects of the patient's personality disorder.

These ideas are developed more fully in the chapter on psychological therapies, and in Chapter 12, in which the 'treatment frame' and 'treatment alliance' are described in detail. While these concepts are relevant to all of the work undertaken by the CMHT, it is with personality-disordered patients that they assume over-riding importance. Furthermore, different approaches will be required for different forms of personality disorder, rather than following any 'generic' advice/approach to forming a therapeutic relationship. For some patients, it will be necessary to be supportive and encouraging, to a degree which for others may be contra-indicated, as it would undermine their self-efficacy (the sense of being able to manage difficulties independently).

Of course, it is equally true, and must be recognised, that every interaction is also potentially *unhelpful* (having no influence on a patient's personality difficulties) or, worse, counter-therapeutic. For example, contact with staff might serve to confirm a patient's belief that other people are not concerned by or sympathetic to their circumstances. This might be a real possibility with Susan, if the consideration of ways she might 'change' is introduced too early in her contact with the team. As seen in the chapter on users' views of services, there is often a desire within patients to be understood and accepted, which initially takes priority over attempts at 'individual empowerment'. Often, patients can feel extremely helpless, and that beneficial change is impossible – this feeling must be acknowledged.

THE NEED FOR CONSISTENCY

It is emphasised throughout the literature that services are most likely to deliver *effective* interventions when the approach adopted is *consistent*, between staff and over time (see, for example, Bateman and Tyrer, 2004). It is fundamental to the nature of personality disorder that individuals can present differently to the same clinician on separate occasions, present differently to different clinicians and can divide opinion as to what difficulties should be addressed. Establishing a shared approach, implemented by every member of the team, is seen by most working in the field as central to providing an effective intervention. While it is possible for a single element or member of staff to offer a helpful approach to a patient, the likelihood of an approach being effective is lessened if it is undermined or contradicted by another part of the service. For example, an approach centred on helping a patient to tolerate and address difficulties in their relationships (as might be imagined for Susan) could be hindered by an admissions policy recommending an in-patient stay for all those threatening self-harm. The likelihood of gains being made is greatly enhanced if a similar stance is adopted by every member of the CMHT.

Indeed, if a CMHT is divided in the approach taken to the care of a personality disordered individual, it is hard to claim that the *team* is offering an intervention for the personality disorder. For example, in supporting patients with borderline personality disorder, one common goal is the integration of different elements of personality. From this, it can be seen to be clearly unhelpful for some staff to see the patient as purely 'malicious', while others attend only to their 'vulnerability'. So long as divisions like this persist, integration of the different components of the patient's personality is unlikely to be encouraged.

Achieving consistency, however, is not easy. The following sections contain ideas about the factors that influence the likelihood of it being achieved. In this chapter, these will be considered under the following headings:

- 'core principles'
- 'the detailed formulation of the individual patient's difficulties'
- 'the treatment plan'
- 'systemic factors'.

Without these, it is unlikely that CMHTs will be able to deliver consistent, coherent interventions for personality disorders, and there is a risk that contact may not constitute treatment.

CORE PRINCIPLES FOR PERSONALITY DISORDER SERVICES

While the literature relating specifically to personality disorder services is relatively modest, consensus is emerging as to what is helpful. These ideas are referred to in publications such as *Personality Disorder: No Longer a Diagnosis of Exclusion* (National Institute for Mental Health in England, NIMHE, 2003), books on personality disorder such as that by Livesley (2001) and journal articles on service organisation, such as that by Bateman and Tyrer (2004).

In such documents, reference is made not just to the way that services should be organised and managed, but also to the 'philosophy' of the services being envisaged, and the core principles that underpin these ideas. Such principles are shared by a number of specialised services already in existence in other parts of the world (for example, the service for borderline personality disorder in New Zealand, described by Krawitz and Watson, 2003), and consistent with conclusions drawn from consultation with service users (see, e.g., Haigh, 2002). These core principles can be summarised as follows:

- the patient–practitioner relationship is the foundation of effective treatment
- staff must strive to be honest, empathic and reliable at all times
- patients are seen as being responsible for their own behaviour
- staff must attempt to validate and encourage patients at all times
- staff should admit when an approach is not working/doing harm
- care plans must be developed collaboratively
- there is a commitment on the part of services to long term involvement
- medication is used only as an adjunct to psychosocial treatments
- lengthy admissions and legislated powers are avoided whenever possible
- professionally indicated risk-taking is supported.

These themes re-emerge, and are expanded on, in other chapters. For now, however, it is simply intended to highlight the considerable consensus between authors on these principles. They can be viewed as a useful checklist, against which services are assessed, and service developments planned. They also provide the context in which specific interventions can be designed.

It is worth making the point at this stage that at a very basic level the work of CMHTs with personality disordered clients can be seen by some as fundamentally different to their work with other patients. This follows from the idea of the 'illness' model, and the belief that CMHTs are charged with 'taking care' of the mentally ill. For many, this means 'doing for' their clients, or 'taking away' their problems – be it in relation to practical needs, psychological symptoms or distress. As is emphasised repeatedly throughout this book, however, such an approach may be contra-indicated when working with certain difficulties experienced by personality disordered patients. It also contravenes the 'spirit' of the principles described above. As in many psychotherapies, the CMHT can be seen as trying to emulate a 'good enough' parent – offering a secure base, but always encouraging the patient to develop their capacity to manage independently. This is not to say that the form of the relationship between staff and patient is identical in every case, any more than a parent would relate to a bullying, aggressive child in the same way as to a shy, timid one. It does, however, give a flavour of the kinds of goals imagined for patients, in the minds of the staff who support them.

THE NEED FOR A DETAILED FORMULATION OF THE PATIENT'S DIFFICULTIES

It goes without saying that CMHTs will need to understand their patients in detail if they are to offer meaningful treatment. However, there is a clear difference between having information available and being able to organise it into a form that clearly summarises the various factors involved in the development and maintenance of the full range of a patient's difficulties, including their personality characteristics.

Nevertheless, an individualised 'case summary' of this kind is exactly what is required if CMHTs are to be able to offer consistent interventions. It is simply not possible to offer interventions developed solely to address a particular 'diagnosis', or particular features of a patient's presentation, without reference to the wider aspects of the patient's circumstances and difficulties. This follows partly from observations regarding the high degree of co-morbidity between personality disorders and with Axis I disorders, and because of the range of difficulties experienced by patients that fall outside diagnostic criteria – for example, housing or legal problems. To address a particular Axis II diagnosis would be to ignore difficulties in other areas. The decision of whether and/or how to address such difficulties must be based on an understanding of the way the various difficulties *relate to each other*. This is summarised in what is termed the 'formulation'.

The formulation must refer to the full range of the patient's difficulties, in a way that makes it clear what the main areas of need are. It must also specify the patient's primary motivations in their various social interactions (including those with the team), in order to clarify what the most helpful response will be, in light of the patient's personality functioning. Such a formulation can be an invaluable aid to planning treatment. It acts as the 'anchor' or reference point, around which events are understood and responses planned, in what can be very stormy seas.

THE CASE FOR 'INTEGRATED' APPROACHES TO FORMULATION

Given the need for an individualised formulation of the patient's difficulties, the question is raised of how such a formulation can be developed, and what form it should take. As already noted, if a team is to be offering 'treatment for the personality disorder', the personality difficulties must be a priority in guiding the intervention. For this reason, they will also have a prominent place in the formulation. Just what that place is, however, depends on the particular theoretical model or models being used.

The conclusion of most experts is that as things stand, there is no clear rationale for adopting any one of the various theoretical perspectives (as described in various chapters in Section One) over any other. Personality disorders are not purely 'biological', 'psychological' or indeed 'social' difficulties – nor are they better explained or treated using any one psychological model over any other. For this reason, many people have started to consider the value of combining several, different perspectives in the form of an 'integrated' formulation.

By adopting and synthesising elements from more than one model in the formulation, the integration of *many different* factors contributing to the patient's personality difficulties is made possible. In addition to being a more satisfying and 'complete' description of the problems, this approach potentially generates a *range* of ideas about how each area of need might be addressed. Reference can be made to features which are seen as primarily biological and to a large extent 'fixed' (such as temperament), while at the same time highlighting those aspects more amenable to change (e.g. cognition, behaviour or environment).

For example, a formulation of Susan's difficulties might make reference not just to her basic 'temperament' (shy, introverted), but draw attention to the fact that, while frequently critical towards Susan, her mother has always acted in a way that has kept Susan from being out in the world – she has always *allowed* her to spend a lot of time at home and has not required her to help with running the household. The effect of this on Susan's self-image as she was growing up might then be considered.

Very quickly, a great number of possible interventions suggest themselves. There may well be needs relating to the way she thinks about herself, the extent to which she has things done for her, the frequency with which she meets other people, as well as the extent to which her mother encourages her to leave the house. Depending on who is working in the team, and what other services are available locally, interventions addressing these can be suggested to Susan, when developing the treatment plan. It may be that she is offered cognitive therapy, day hospital or some form of family intervention involving her mother and brother. The important thing to recognise is that the range of ideas follows from an *integrated* approach to formulation. There is no one 'pure' model being used to guide this view of Susan.

Of course, advocating an integrated approach is not to suggest that *every* area of difficulty, *every* theoretical concept and *every* area of need is somehow contained within a single formulation. Developing a formulation remains highly selective, but the important point is that CMHTs working in this way are not restricted to using one specific approach. Those which a particular CMHT use on a regular basis will probably reflect the beliefs, competencies and interests of the staff within the team, but this is not necessarily a problem, given the equivalence of different approaches referred to earlier.

Integrating different theoretical perspectives is, however, not always easy. There exist between certain models fundamental and probably irreconcilable differences, in terms of the claims being made for the main causal and maintaining factors. At a very basic level, the different perspectives of biological and psychosocial perspectives are not readily integrated. Between the psychotherapies, it can be equally difficult. Certain approaches, such as cognitive therapy, focus mainly on the conscious, reportable explanations given by patients, and can encounter difficulties making sense of patterns of behaviour that the patient finds it difficult to acknowledge or explain. By contrast, the integration of other ideas is more readily achieved. To take a common example, there is widespread agreement that cognitive and behavioural conceptualisations can co-exist, with each explaining a different aspect of functioning. It is for individual CMHT practitioners to decide the extent to which they are satisfied by the specific combinations of ideas proposed in specific formulations.

While an integrated approach can appear to go against much of what is written in the rest of this book, and indeed in the wider academic literature, it is important to emphasise that approaches drawn from specific models are not 'incompatible' with integration – indeed, it is the different models that *generate* the ideas which are being integrated. For example, a 'schema therapy' view of borderline personality disorder might contribute significantly to the formulation of Susan's difficulties. However, if it is judged that she also exhibits features of another personality disorder, the formulation may need to reflect this. The 'schema' view also says nothing of the potential benefits to Susan of medication. That is where integration comes in. The door is opened to an approach truly based on understanding the *patient*, rather than attempting to 'fit the patient to the model'. The formulation is also able to guide the *whole CMHT*, rather than just one individual team member with a specialised role (e.g. psychotherapist), in their efforts to support the patient.

Potentially, adopting an integrated approach reduces the likelihood of major disagreements between members of the CMHT, as it avoids disputes over whether X *or* Y is true, significant, etc. It does, however, require each practitioner to be prepared to work in this way. It is important to note that many of the 'real life' interventions for personality disorder described in the literature (for example by MacFarlane, 2004) already utilise an integrated approach. While the 'academic' literature can be dominated by investigations and discussions of relatively 'pure' approaches, integration is in fact already extremely common in the real world.

WHAT DO INTEGRATED FORMULATIONS OF PATIENTS WITH PERSONALITY DISORDER LOOK LIKE?

Livesley (2001) proposes four 'principles' for understanding personality disorders and suggests using these as a general framework for organising interventions. It can be helpful to bear these ideas in mind when attempting to develop the formulation. The principles are as follows:

- personality disorder involves multiple domains of psychopathology
- personality disorder involves general features common to all cases, and specific features seen in some cases but not others
- personality disorder is a bio-psychological condition, with a complex biological and psychosocial aetiology
- psychosocial adversity influences the contents, processes and organisation of the personality system.

Each of these principles should be reflected in the final formulation. It is necessary to think and talk about patients' problems from each of these perspectives: biological, psychological and historical, as well as the individual's current social situation (including their attitudes towards services) – and while some common features can certainly be identified within a specified group of patients (and related to theory), each individual formulation will be different.

For Susan, a formulation would need (at a minimum) to link the following.

Historical factors: father's death; mother's parenting; boyfriend's desertion.
Temperament: shy, introverted.
Long standing psychological factors (including personality characteristics): low self-esteem; view of others as likely to be critical or unreliable; view of self as reliant on others.
Current circumstances: getting older, but failing to achieve at work or socially; dominated by mother.
Presenting problems (including unhelpful coping strategies): depression; social anxiety; difficulty expressing anger; substance use; self-harm.
Adaptive coping strategies: none identified in assessment.

When viewed in this way, it is interesting to consider where the 'personality disorder' (as a set of intense feelings or relationship difficulties) can be located. Rather than a 'description' (as in a diagnosis) there is a 'context', in terms of Susan's past, and her present circumstances. The particular form the formulation will take emerges from the varying emphases that Susan puts on these key events or difficulties, as well as the explanations she gives for particular elements of the formulation – for example, whether her self-harming is to punish herself or to release feelings of anger towards her mother. It will also reflect the knowledge base of the team. If, for example, there is an interest in cognitive analytic therapy, reference might be made to particular 'reciprocal roles' Susan is involved in, for example with her mother. By having one, agreed formulation guiding the team as a whole, it is possible to agree on the different aspects that each member of the team will be addressing, and to ensure that the overall approach is consistent.

Clearly, the integrated formulation does not come from a purely 'psychotherapeutic' perspective, but takes account of other influences, in line with the biopsychosocial model outlined in Chapter 3. Of course, it does always need to contain some 'psychological' elements, but which these are do not have to be constrained to one particular approach. In this view, the CMHT does not need to use just one psychological model, across the whole caseload – or even with an individual patient. There is potentially the freedom to combine approaches within a single formulation, provided the final form it takes is coherent, consistent and reflects the principles outlined by Livesley (2001). The criticism that such formulations are not necessarily *theoretically* 'pure' is, in this view, of secondary importance to their pragmatic utility, in terms of generating ideas for interventions addressing those aspects where change is possible.

It is recommended that formulations adopt a principle of 'minimalism' if they are likely to be of benefit. That is, they should contain the minimum number of elements required to explain the key presenting features of a patient's difficulties, and to indicate how they might be addressed. It is when formulations are simple that they can be retained in the minds of patients, and the clinicians who support them.

It is also notable that the 'full' formulation being used by the CMHT will not always be shared with the patient. Very often, ideas are included in the formulation, about which further information is being gathered or about which tentative discussions are being held with the patient. It is not always helpful or useful to refer directly to such 'tentative' ideas with the patient. Rather, most practitioners will base their face-to-face discussions with the patient on a reduced 'working' formulation, which makes reference to a specific area of the full formulation. With Susan, for example, it may be some time before she is willing to discuss feelings of resentment towards her mother. This is not seen as contravening the core principles of being honest, open and collaborative with patients, but a recognition of the need for clinicians to be sensitive in the way they develop and present the formulation. It can also help to focus on a small, specific area of the full formulation, for ease of comprehension (in the minds of both patient and practitioner).

THE NEED FOR A CLEAR TREATMENT PLAN

Following initial assessment, it will hopefully be possible for members of the CMHT to agree on an initial, basic formulation. Where significant personality difficulties are identified, these will be a central feature of the formulation, perhaps adding to the understanding of how other difficulties arose, and certainly clarifying how these other difficulties are made apparent to others (including the team). As noted, it is to be expected that the formulation will identify a range of difficulties in addition to the 'personality' problem. It is at this point that the CMHT needs to agree how to proceed.

With regard to treatments aimed specifically at the 'personality' elements of a patient's difficulties, Livesley (2001) proposes four 'general' and three 'specific' strategies for effecting change. The general strategies are:

- building and maintaining a collaborative relationship
- establishing and maintaining a consistent treatment process

- validation
- building and maintaining motivation.

These are closely related to ideas about the treatment frame and treatment alliance, discussed in Chapter 12, as well as the 'core principles' outlined earlier in this chapter. The more specific strategies for effecting change that Livesley describes relate to

- managing symptoms and crises
- promoting the more adaptive expression of basic traits
- addressing the self-concept and inter-personal problems.

'Crises' are often characterised by dysphoria, impulsive acts such as self-harm and cognitive dysregulation. Livesley proposes that relief can be gained from a mixture of medication, 'containment' (through feeling understood) and structured psychosocial interventions, such as cognitive–behavioural therapy.

'Basic traits' are seen by Livesley as stable structures developing from an interaction of the patient's genetic predisposition and environment, which are unlikely to be influenced by traditional psychotherapeutic techniques. Instead, he suggests approaches based on

- acceptance and tolerance of the basic traits (e.g. to challenge the idea that such traits are 'weaknesses')
- attenuating trait expression (e.g. avoiding rumination, which can increase distress)
- substituting more adaptive trait expression (e.g. asking for help, instead of self-harming in order to elicit care).

The 'self-concept' and 'inter-personal problems' are the hallmark of personality disorders, and Livesley recommends using a variety of approaches to try and influence the cognitive and behavioural aspects of these character-istics. This is of course the remit of most psychotherapeutic approaches. Livesley notes that very often the challenge is to develop a more stable and coherent *self-system*, and a more *integrated* representation of other people. As such, interventions are not aimed simply at challenging a 'part' of such systems.

Livesley's 'general' and 'specific' strategies draw attention to a fundamental distinction between two contrasting aims of CMHT interventions. This is the contrast between treatment plans directed towards 'containing' the patient's personality difficulties, as opposed to those helping the patient to 'overcome' them. By attending to the therapy relationship and treatment process (the general strategies) *without* reacting to crises where possible, and without attempting to help the patient to change, it is intended to offer the patient a secure, validating and predictable inter-personal environment, from which they will benefit. As noted, this 'containment' function is often what patients are requesting, and is seen by many as a primary ingredient of 'treatment'.

THE SPECIFIC CONTENT OF THE TREATMENT PLAN

If treatment plans are to incorporate all of the above functions, it is clear that they will, as with formulations, need to combine a variety of approaches, i.e. they will, again, be 'integrated'. The various interventions used in community treatment can be categorised along the lines of the chapters in Section One of this book – medication, psychotherapy (individual, family or group) and day services (usually informed by ideas developed in therapeutic communities). In addition, there are various interventions aimed at influencing the patient's physical or social environment. These include ideas derived from 'nidother-apy', referred to earlier in this chapter, wherein attempts are made to take account of the patient's difficulties (which might include personality diffi-culties) in supporting their search for appropriate accommodation, or an appropriate leisure/work environment. For example, Tyrer and Bajaj (2005) describe the case of a patient with a psychotic disorder for whom proximity to late-night cafes was judged to be of great importance in maintaining social contact. While such approaches are at an early stage of development – and for this reason were not described in detail in Section One of the book – their relevance and potential for personality disorder treatment is clear. Finally, the provision of some form of 'on-call'/crisis support service to these patients is likely to be helpful, in supporting approaches developed in the course of scheduled appointments.

For each approach, however, it must be made extremely clear what the intended *function* is, in terms of the intended benefit to the patient. It is for this reason that greater emphasis has been put on Livesley's general and specific strategies than the actions of the CMHT practitioners. This reflects the requirement to place the *patient's needs* at the centre of the treatment plan.

Which of the listed interventions the CMHT becomes involved with will vary from team to team, but there is likely to be a common 'core' set of approaches, including some form of psychotherapy, medication, crisis support and attempts to influence the patient's social and physical environment. Clearly, the final treatment plan will, in most cases, need to include much more than 'psychotherapy'. However, it is generally acknowledged that where the client accepts and is able to engage with individual or group psychotherapy, every effort should be made to provide this. It is through psychotherapy that information about the patient's inner functioning is made available to the CMHT, and where the patient is able to reflect on their experience of other services provided by the team.

The treatment plan will need to specify the intended role and, more importantly, *function* of each team member likely to be involved with the patient. It will also need to be consistent with the demands of legislation governing teams, such as the care programme approach (CPA). Written care plans should make clear to the patient the level of support which it is intended to offer, the likely benefits of medication and the circumstances under which respite/in-patient admission might be considered. In-patient services are, as noted, used only in situations of extreme crisis as a way of managing high levels of risk in the short term. While Axis I difficulties are not ignored, the way in which they are addressed is modified by the higher goal of addressing the personality disorder.

DEVELOPING AND IMPLEMENTING THE TREATMENT PLAN

The treatment plan is going to be greatly influenced by what the patient is requesting, and what they are agreeable to. For example, it might be judged desirable for the patient to enter some form of psychotherapy, and this might even be readily available through the CMHT, but it cannot be 'forced' on the patient. This applies even to the basic question of whether the personality difficulties are ever explicitly referred to in the treatment plan. For some patients, there is a complete refusal to accept or acknowledge difficulties of these kinds. For example, Susan might focus exclusively on her individual difficulties in controlling the urge to self-harm, and deny any connection between this and her relationship with her mother.

An equally important influence is, of course, the judgement of the team as to what *they* are willing and able to provide. There are frequently implicit or explicit demands made by patients, for services that the CMHT will not agree to provide. For example, the team might take the view that a patient is exaggerating their physical difficulties. While the patient might wish to be seen by a support worker on a daily basis to accompany them shopping, the CMHT might judge this inappropriate as it would exacerbate the patient's feelings of dependency and collude with their avoidance of important difficulties. For Susan, it might be judged preferable for her to stay out of hospital, in terms of the likely effects on her self-esteem and the prospects for overcoming relationship difficulties with her mother.

The relationship between the formulation and the final treatment plan is therefore not always an obvious one. The form it takes depends on negotiation and collaboration between the patient and the CMHT.

In many ways, this process reflects the practice of many forms of psychotherapy. With regard to the personality difficulties, it is helpful to relate this idea of negotiation to the 'stages of change' model, originally developed for work with patients with substance abuse problems (Prochaska & DiClemente, 1992). In this view, the patient's engagement with a particular form of treatment can be understood as being at one of six stages: pre-contemplation, contemplation, preparation, action, maintenance and termination.

Most CMHT staff are familiar with the model, so it will not be described in detail, other than to note that patients do not necessarily enter treatment feeling clear as to what their main problems are, or willing to change. It should not be assumed that patients' goals are the same as those envisaged by staff, or that patients view the proposed means of achieving these goals as credible. A good deal of time may need to be spent reaching agreement on what is and what is not a realistic aim or intervention. If the judgement of practitioners in the CMHT is that it would be helpful for the patient to try and address their personality difficulties, one of the tasks may be simply to help them *acknowledge* that there is a difficulty in this area.

THE 'SYSTEMIC' FACTORS REQUIRED FOR TEAMS TO BE ABLE TO DELIVER EFFECTIVE INTERVENTIONS

If CMHTs are to be able to offer the kinds of interventions proposed in this chapter, it is necessary to acknowledge the implicit demands made of both the teams and the treating systems in which they operate. The most important of these are as follows:

- the selection of staff suited to work of this kind
- regular, ongoing training in working with personality disorder
- frequent and regular liaison/communication with other CMHT staff
- frequent and regular clinical supervision
- consistent staff – but not working alone, to minimise the risk of 'burnout'
- guidelines clarifying the roles of each team member.

Some of these points are developed further in a document produced by the National Institute for Mental Health in England (NIMHE), entitled *The Personality Disorder Capabilities Framework* (NIMHE, 2003b), which details the training needs of a wide range of staff and professional groups (not just those in CMHTs). Ways in which these features can be established in teams are also elaborated on in other chapters, later in this book. However, attention is drawn to them here, as it is extremely unlikely that CMHTs will be able to offer consistent, coherent interventions for personality disorder if these elements are not present. They represent an acknowledgement of the demand for resources dedicated to staff time away from 'face to face' contact, if serious efforts are to be made to deliver effective services.

ARE CMHTs ABLE TO DELIVER HIGH QUALITY INTERVENTIONS FOR PERSONALITY DISORDER?

In recent years, there has been a growing acceptance that the needs of personality disordered people should be met within mental health services, and extensive discussion of the ways in which this might be done. Recent government guidance, delivered through NIMHE (2003a), suggests the formation of specialist services, providing a mix of training, consultation or direct provision of services meeting all areas of need. Currently, a number of pilot services funded through NIMHE are being established and evaluated to inform the debate.

Bateman and Tyrer (2004) contrast different service models, finding in favour of either such specialist teams or a 'divided functions' team, similar to the traditional community mental health team.

Regardless of whether specialist personality disorder services are ever established on a wide scale, however, there will always be a requirement for CMHTs to be involved with this patient group. Despite recent initiatives in the UK for the establishment of a variety of specialist mental health services (e.g. for early onset psychosis, assertive outreach, eating disorders and substance abuse) the range of proposed specialist services is far from comprehensive, and there remains a need for a 'general' mental health service, to 'fill the gaps'. Primary care services are not able to manage all levels of severity of need. Moreover, in some geographical areas, there is unlikely to be the required level of demand to justify specialist services. Most importantly, the high level of co-morbidity between mental health disorders limits the extent to which specialist services will be able to retain their 'specialist' focus.

Such specialist teams will either be 'forced' to address a wide range of difficulties (and in effect work as a CMHT for a group of clients who happen to have a particular difficulty in common), or discharge these patients to a service prepared and equipped to work with co-morbidity i.e. a CMHT. It is likely that a specialist personality disorder service would operate within similar constraints. While this remains the case, it seems likely that a significant proportion of severe personality disorder will continue to be (i) identified in the CMHT and (ii) managed by the CMHT.

As the teams with the remit to deal with many areas of need for clients with co-morbid difficulties, CMHTs potentially offer the *best* support, to the most frequently encountered patients. Both CMHTs and specialist teams are interesting models for the delivery of mental health services, and both might contribute significantly to addressing the needs of this population. However, it is likely that if both are established and operate alongside each other, *both* would be managing personality disordered clients. Moreover, the specific populations being served and the service they receive would not, in all likelihood, be identical. It is too early to predict what the differences would be, but it is likely to depend on factors such as who has access to/liaison with on-call crisis services, in-patient beds and accident and emergency services.

For these reasons, it will remain necessary for the CMHT worker to feel confident in their contact with personality disordered clients (and hence the need for books such as this one). The following chapter acknowledges the difficulties in working with personality disordered patients, and considers how to overcome these difficulties, but to answer the question posed at the head of this section, ideas *are* becoming available as to how to equip CMHTs to effectively support these patients – the challenge facing CMHTs is to see whether it is possible to implement these ideas.

By now, it will be clear that it is not the intention to promote a highly prescriptive approach to working with personality difficulties, nor to espouse one particular therapeutic approach over any others. Given the lack of basic information about the kinds of personality difficulties experienced by patients seen in CMHTs, the potential to give a misleading impression must be acknowledged. A literature dominated by considerations of 'borderline personality disorder' and individual psychotherapy can lead practitioners to think solely in these terms. This is unfortunate, when the prevalence of this or any of the other disorders within CMHT caseloads has not been properly examined. It also fails to acknowledge difficulties with the diagnosis, or the high levels of co-morbidity.

It is for this reason that this chapter has proposed a more general framework for tackling such matters. Readers are encouraged to read widely, and to understand the particular challenges facing each of their patients (as summarised in their formulations) before using a *variety* of methods to implement the strategies described above. Psychotherapy is often likened to a 'dance', in which patient and therapist meet and come apart, change direction and tempo. This metaphor can be applied to each of the CMHT members, and the CMHT as a whole, in their attempts to support personality disordered patients. It is unlikely that a highly 'rigid' approach, with a clear, sequential array of treatment targets, will be established. While a treatment plan might be kept in mind as an *intended* course, the reality will in all probability be different, and this should be expected. At one time, discussion might focus on Axis I symptoms, at another a particular difficulty with a relative. The CMHT practitioner must anticipate this. Work of this kind can hopefully be seen as challenging, creative and extremely rewarding, providing every member of the team has an understanding of their role within the overall team approach.

The years ahead represent an exciting opportunity for research into personality disorder services to take a new direction. Up until now, the interventions being put forward and evaluated have typically been based on a single modality – medication, one or other form of psychotherapy. However, all the indications are that it is a *combination* of approaches, provided in a consistent and coherent manner, which is most likely to prove effective. This chapter argues for a flexible response/approach from CMHTs, which takes advantage of whatever skills the staff possess, and the breadth of knowledge contained, provided that the final service conforms to the central framework that has been outlined. Such an approach has yet to be evaluated. However, if a team could be established to work to these key principles, it would clearly be possible to conduct research looking at the effectiveness of such an approach. Potentially, an appropriately functioning team offers much more than the sum of its parts.

REFERENCES

Bateman, A. W., & Tyrer, P. (2004). Services for personality disorder: Organisation for inclusion. *Advances in Psychiatric Treatment, 10*, 425–433.

Haigh, R. (2002). Services for people with personality disorder: the thoughts of service users. Cited in NIMHE. (2003). *Personality disorder: no longer a diagnosis of exclusion* (p. 22). London: Department of Health.

Krawitz, R., & Watson, C. (2003). *Borderline Personality Disorder: a practical guide to treatment*. New York: Oxford University Press.

Livesley, W. J. (2001). A framework for an integrated approach to treatment. In W. J. Livesley (Ed.), *Handbook of personality disorders* (pp. 570–600). New York: Guilford Press.

National Institute for Mental Health in England (NIMHE). (2003a). *Personality Disorder: No longer a diagnosis of exclusion*. Policy implementation guidance for the development of services for people with personality disorder. London: Department of Health.

National Institute for Mental Health in England (NIMHE). (2003b). *Breaking the cycle of rejection: The personality disorder capabilities framework*. Policy implementation guidance for the development of services for people with personality disorder. London: Department of Health.

Prochaska, J. O., & DiClemente, C. (1992). The trans-theoretical approach. In J. C. Norcross and M.R. Goldfried (Eds), *Handbook of psychotherapy integration* (pp. 300–334). New York: Basic.

Tyrer, P. and Bajaj, P. (2005). Nidotherapy: making the environment do the therapeutic work. *Advances in Psychiatric Treatment, 11*, 232–238.

Tyrer, P., Sensky, T., & Mitchard, S. (2003). Principles of nidotherapy in the treatment of persistent mental and personality disorders. *Psychotherapy and Psychosomatics, 72*, 350–356.

11

The Challenges Community Mental Health Teams Face in Their Work with Patients with Personality Disorders

MARK J. SAMPSON

This chapter will highlight some of the 'challenges' that community mental health team (CMHT) practitioners face in trying to meet the aspirations of government initiatives described in Chapter 1 (see National Institute for Mental Health in England, NIMHE, 2003a, 2003b). The content of this chapter has been heavily influenced by the author's work in a CMHT in Manchester, UK, and in staff training initiatives in the region. The challenges identified in the course of this training are summarised in Table 11.1. They reflect practitioners' experiences of working with patients with personality disorders.

The challenges described in Table 11.1 are consistent with those reported by CMHT practitioners in other parts of the UK (see Webb, 2005). They have been grouped here into four main areas: social and clinical environment, organisational, team (CMHT) and individual (practitioner/patient interface). These areas relate closely to the framework used in the model of organisational change by Ferlie and Shortell (2001) (see Figure 11.1).

This model identifies four 'levels' that need to be addressed if there is to be effective organisational change, and can be used to consider ways of overcoming the various challenges commonly encountered in CMHTs, in

Personality Disorder and Community Mental Health Teams: A Practitioner's Guide. Edited by M. J. Sampson, R. A. McCubbin and P. Tyrer. © 2006 John Wiley & Sons, Ltd.

Table 11.1 The challenges reported by mental health practitioners to working with patients with personality disorder

Environment – Social and Clinical	*Team (community mental health team; CMHT)*
Legislation	Lack of clear policy regarding function of service
Pressures from society to do more than is possible	
Eligibility for service	Inconsistent treatment plans
Services not set up to treat personality disorders	Different professional views on causation and treatability
Responsibility	Staffing levels
Difficulties with diagnosis	
Organisational	*Individual (Practitioner/Patient Interface)*
No clear guidance	Difficult to develop therapeutic relationship
Lack of managerial support	
Lack of clear policies on patients with personality disorders	Engagement
Unclear referral pathways	Unrealistic expectations of what services can do
Lack of appropriate supervision	Dealing with patients' strong emotions
	Frustration
	Anxiety
	Burnout
	Hopelessness
	Burden
	Feeling unskilled

relation to personality disorders. For this reason, it has been used to provide a framework for this chapter.

The first section of the chapter will consider the impact that factors in each area have on the interface between the CMHT practitioner and the patient with personality disorder. The second section will discuss ways of overcoming these 'challenges', in order to provide effective services for patients with personality disorder.

THE CHALLENGES

THE SOCIAL ENVIRONMENT – LEGISLATION

Psychiatric and mental health practice is influenced as much by public opinion and mental health legislation as by advances in treatments (Burns,

Figure 11.1 Factors that affect the practitioner/patient interface

2004). The 1930 Mental Treatment Act is an example of this. This Act was heavily influenced by public opinion and allowed for voluntary admissions to psychiatric institutions. This endorsed a more medical approach to mental illness (Burns, 2004) and paved the way for medically based treatments to mental health and the foundations of the psychiatric system we have today.

The UK Government is currently (in 2005) in the process of updating the 1983 Mental Health Act (MHA; Department of Health, 1983) and a new Bill has been proposed. Although many of the proposed changes to the 1983 MHA are welcomed, there are some aspects that may pose a challenge to psychiatric services. It looks like the new 'Act' will remove the 'treatability test' and have a broader definition of 'mental disorder,' which will also include personality disorders.

The challenge that this may pose to CMHTs is in the *social* context within which these changes are proposed. Kendell (2002) suggests that one motivation for updating the MHA is a desire to provide further 'protection for society', as the new Act potentially allows for the detention of people with a diagnosable personality disorder who are deemed dangerous to self and others. This would not have been possible under the 1983 MHA.

This change could be a challenge for psychiatric services if, by including personality disorder as a 'mental disorder', it implies that *society* will expect services to take responsibility for the behaviour of all patients with all personality disorders. This could subtly change the focus of care from 'treatment' to 'protecting society'. If so, this could lead to more punitive and restrictive treatment plans and may pull services into colluding with and reinforcing dysfunctional relationship patterns, for some patients. There may also be the danger that bringing personality disorders under the umbrella of 'mental disorder' may 'medicalise' the disorder. The next section explores reasons why this may not be helpful in the treatment and care of patients with personality disorders.

THE CLINICAL ENVIRONMENT

The Influence of the 'Illness' Model

Psychiatric services in the UK have traditionally had very strong medical and biological influences on care and treatment. Services have been guided by the view that there is something wrong with the patient's neuro-physiology (e.g. a chemical imbalance) when mental illness occurs. Although the model of psychiatric treatment has changed significantly over recent years, the biological view remains dominant. The current model of care guides services to focus on 'clinical symptoms', with less emphasis placed on the importance of social, psychological or environ-mental factors, such as patients' attachment and relationship histories.

In the UK, psychiatric services have been configured with this ethos in mind and structured to look after and treat patients with 'mental illnesses'. Historically, personality disorder has not been seen as a legitimate or treatable 'illness' and consequently is often seen as outside the remit of psychiatric services (see Kendell, 2002, for further discussion). It has been acceptable for psychiatric services to exclude patients with personality disorders. When patients with personality disorders are offered help, it is often for the treatment of an associated Axis I clinical disorder such as depression or psychosis.

The NIMHE document *Personality Disorder: No Longer a Diagnosis for Exclusion* (NIMHE, 2003a) has attempted to clarify the uncertainty about whether personality disorders are a legitimate focus of services. The move to reduce the exclusion of patients with personality disorders is long overdue. However, this can present a fundamental challenge to current psychiatric services, as many personality disorders do not fit comfortably within the 'illness' model of care. Take the case of a patient[1] who is referred to the CMHT following a serious suicide attempt. A symptom-focused approach would involve services supporting her until her mental health improves and she is no longer suicidal. However, difficulties may develop if services do not assess for, or notice, her tendency to be drawn into dependent relation-ships, which maintain the belief that she 'needs' other people (and now services) to help her cope. In this case, any threat of discharge could trigger

---

[1]For clarity this chapter will refer to patients as female and practitioners as male.

unmanageable feelings of anxiety to the extent that she considers a further suicide attempt. Traditional approaches to psychiatric care suggest that the discharge be put on hold until 'she gets better'. However, there is clearly a powerful disincentive to 'getting better' for this patient.

This case example illustrates how a symptom-focused approach can lead to poor management of patients with personality disorders and, consequently, poor outcome. Unfortunately, poor outcomes can consolidate the view that personality disorders are untreatable and are not the 'legitimate business' of mental heath services.

The illness model, with its focus on symptoms and 'cure', may also be an obstacle to developing therapeutic relationships with patients with personality disorders. Chapter 8 illustrates how many people who have experience of living with a personality disorder diagnosis report that they would like more emphasis on acceptance, attachment and validation of themselves as individuals, and less on their symptoms, diagnosis and treatment. Therefore, a psychiatric service that focuses on symptoms may find it harder to relate to patients with personality disorders.

Duty of Care and Responsibility

Current psychiatric treatment models imply that the CMHT has a duty of care towards the patient as long as they are unwell. This model of working can lead services to take a certain degree of responsibility for the patient's behaviour. However, this can be problematic for patients with personality disorders, as for many the aim of treatment is to help *them* to take more responsibility for their own actions and emotions and help them learn to cope more independently. If services and practitioners take more responsibility than is helpful this will impact on the practitioner/patient interface. Practitioners will be more likely to feel frustrated, stressed and burdened. Taking excessive responsibility may also increase the chance of the practitioner being drawn into acting in ways that are unhelpful to the patient – for example, arranging unhelpful admissions or by becoming too controlling.

Diagnosis

The process of identifying and diagnosing a personality disorder can be a significant problem for psychiatric services. Taking borderline personality disorder as an example, the majority of patients who meet this diagnosis would also meet the criteria for three or more Axis I clinical disorders (Skodol et al., 2002a). For this reason, it can be difficult to recognise the presence of a personality disorder because other psychiatric conditions are more prominent

(Bateman & Tyrer, 2004). When practitioners do notice the presence of personality difficulties, making an accurate diagnosis is difficult because a patient rarely meets the criteria for one personality disorder alone.

Even if an accurate diagnosis is made there are still difficulties. For a person to meet the diagnosis of borderline personality disorder in DSM-IV, they need to meet five of the nine criteria (American Psychiatric Association, 1994). It has been noted there are at least 151 different combinations of symptom criteria that meet the diagnosis of borderline personality disorder (Skodol et al., 2002). It is possible that two patients with the same diagnosis could share only one of the diagnostic criteria (Bateman & Fonagy, 2004). Consequently, patients with the same diagnosis can vary significantly in their symptoms, and therefore a diagnosis alone does little to guide care and treatment.

Finally, there are also problems with the diagnosis *per se*, as it does little to communicate the underlying mechanisms or *why* the patient 'acts like she does'. Take the case of a patient who was repeatedly abused, rejected and abandoned during her childhood. She may meet the criteria for a number of personality disorders depending on how she presents. Describing her as having borderline or a dependent personality disorder does little to help the practitioner or CMHT understand the difficulties she faces, only the way in which she attempts to overcome her difficulties. A diagnosis of personality disorder does not help the development of an empathic explanation (formulation) of the origins and maintenance of the patient's difficulties, which is a central component in the provision of many therapies for personality disorders (Linehan, 1993; Krawitz & Watson, 2003).

The Lack of Scientific Evidence

There is an unfortunate lack of robust research evidence available to guide CMHTs in how to provide effective care to patients with personality disorders. This lack of evidence constitutes a real obstacle to the development of specific protocols to guide services. What scientific evidence there is for the effective treatment for personality disorders tends to be for specific psychological therapies, rather than overall CMHT input, and even then is dominated by a consideration of borderline personality disorder to the exclusion of other disorders.

Training

One consequence of having a mental health care system that focuses on the care and treatment of patients with 'treatable' mental illnesses is that mental health training will understandably mirror this focus. Hence, there is at present a marked lack of training in personality disorders in most mental health professions (NIMHE, 2003b).

Practitioners report the lack of training relating to personality disorders to be a major obstacle in being able to offer effective management and co-ordinated care for patients with these problems. The lack of training, and consequently the lack of an explanatory framework for understanding personality disorders, can be a significant reason why mental health practitioners feel under-confident in working with patients with these types of problems (see NIMHE, 2003b).

This lack of an adequate explanatory framework makes practitioners unsure how to best help a patient. It also influences how practitioners perceive a patient's behaviour. Markham and Trower (2003) studied mental health nurses' perceptions and causal attributions associated with the psychiatric label of borderline personality disorder. They found that staff regard patients with this disorder to be more in control of their negative behaviour than patients with other psychiatric labels. Their study also supported Weiner's (1985) model, which suggests that the more control a person perceives somebody has over their behaviour the less sympathetic they tend to be (when the behaviour is negative). This attributional style is not limited to nurses, as other mental health professionals also make negative attributions about the behaviour of patients with personality disorders (Lewis and Appleby, 1988). These attributions are going to make it more difficult for the practitioner to be empathic towards the patient.

The lack of an agreed theoretical framework for understanding personality disorder can also provide a challenge to the CMHT as each practitioner may have a different view on what is appropriate treatment. Krawitz and Watson (2003) propose that staff are frequently 'polarised' in their views on treatment plans for patients with personality disorders, generally varying between a 'nurturing' and a more 'limit-setting' approach to care. This can lead the CMHT into offering an 'enmeshed' (over-involved) package of care in one extreme to a 'withholding' (punitive, restrictive and rigid) approach in the other.

ORGANISATIONAL FACTORS – GUIDELINES AND POLICIES

The uncertainty about the legitimacy of working with patients with personality disorders contributes to a lack of clear guidance for CMHTs on the management of patients with personality disorders. Frequently, services have no clear referral pathways and no clear guidance on treatment, admission/discharge and risk management procedures for patients with personality disorders. Consequently, when they are offered 'help' it is within the remit of existing protocols and policies. For the reasons already described, these may not be suitable.

The guidelines that do exist can be vague and as such interpreted in many ways. For instance, current government policy suggests that CMHTs should work with patients with severe personality disorders if it can be shown that the patient would 'benefit by continued contact and support' (Department of Health, 2002, p. 4). It can be very difficult for a CMHT to predict with any degree of certainty whether a patient would benefit or not from team input, or decide how this support should best be delivered.

TEAM FACTORS

Factors Relating to the Structure of the Community Mental Health Team

Although there are a number of specialist CMHTs across the country that work to a specific treatment model, e.g. dialectical behaviour therapy, for most the CMHT consists of practitioners from different professions that bring different perspectives on mental illness and care (see Burns, 2004). This can be a strength, as the patient will potentially have access to a range of assessments and treatments. However, this can also increase the risk of conflict and make a cohesive and consistent team approach more difficult. Burns (2004) describes three main areas that cause conflicts in the CMHT: professional differences, personality differences and 'projection and splitting'.

Previous sections have discussed the challenge that patients with personality disorders pose to traditional psychiatric treatments. These challenges can exacerbate underlying problems in the CMHT and increase the risk of conflict. For instance, the uncertainty about whether a patient with a personality disorder can or should be treated in the team can highlight professional and personality differences. At other times, uncertainty about care plans, poor outcome and a lack of confidence in practitioners in working with patients with these types of problem can bring to the surface a lack of respect that team members feel for each other and/or their colleagues' professions.

The way a patient relates to practitioners within the CMHT can exacerbate the differences described above. 'Projection' and 'splitting' are specific examples of this (Burns, 2004). Projection and splitting are closely related. Projection is the putting of one person's own unacceptable feelings onto another, while splitting reflects the patient's tendency to see people in extremes as either 'all good' or 'all bad' (Vaillant, 1993). Projection can lead to splitting as the patient may divert all her negative feelings onto one practitioner whilst seeing another practitioner as all good. Splitting is functional (in the short term) for the patient as it relieves uncertainty, as in her mind she has at least one secure attachment. However, it can further 'polarise' practitioners' views on treatment, as a practitioner who is seen as 'all good' may be more likely to want to offer the patient a nurturing care plan, whilst the practitioner who is seen as 'all bad' may be drawn into thinking that the patient is not being helped within the team and should be excluded (becoming more withholding). This can further enhance team conflict, particularly if there are professional and personality differences, and/or the team is fragmented with each member taking a different role for the patient.

Staffing Levels

As generic CMHTs have 'no explicit template ... and no obvious product champion they have tended to be neglected in much debate around service provision' (Burns, 2004, p. 49). Consequently, staffing levels in the CMHT can be a significant barrier to providing effective care plans to patients with personality disorders. The obstacle for many generic CMHTs is that they are often expected to have more patients on their caseloads than many 'specialist' teams such as assertive outreach or early intervention services. Inadequate staffing levels will be a significant obstacle to CMHTs working effectively with patients with personality disorders.

The Availability of Appropriate Supervision

Effective supervision is essential to being able to provide effective management of patients with personality disorders (NIMHE, 2003b). The social, clinical and organisational culture will influence not only the care and management of patients but also how supervision is applied and organised. Supervision in CMHTs tends to focus on the patient's clinical symptoms and the practitioner's caseload. This type of supervision may be ineffective in helping the practitioner deal with the unique challenges that working with patients with personality disorders presents.

THE PRACTITIONER/PATIENT INTERFACE

The factors already described will all influence the interaction between a CMHT practitioner and the patient with a personality disorder (see Figure 11.1). It is perhaps unsurprising that some mental health practitioners come to associate patients with personality disorders with feelings of hopelessness, inadequacy, frustration and burden. These feelings can lead practitioners to appear defensive and resistant to patients with problems of this nature, and difficulties in the interaction between patients and practitioners persist.

However, the individual personality characteristics of both the practitioners and the patients are likely to influence the practitioner/patient interface. Practitioners who are dominant, less reflective and inflexible will find it more difficult to interact with the patient and work effectively in a team (Burns, 2004).

Clearly, the patient's personality disorder will also influence the practitioner/patient interface. To meet the diagnosis of a personality disorder the patient needs to display an 'enduring pattern of inner experience and behaviour that deviates markedly from the expectations of the individual's culture, is pervasive and inflexible...' (American Psychiatric Association, 1994, p. 629). Therefore, the patient's personality disorder can make it difficult for the patient to seek help in the first place, or if they initiate contact it can be difficult for the CMHT to implement an effective treatment plan. For instance, a patient with borderline personality disorder may present to services during crisis but disengage as soon as the crisis resolves, while a patient who meets the diagnosis of paranoid personality disorder is going to be extremely suspicious of anyone, including mental health professionals.

OVERCOMING THE CHALLENGES

The previous section explored the challenges that CMHTs and practitioners need to address if they are going to work effectively with patients with personality disorders. Interestingly, many of the challenges described are not simply due to the *patients'* personality disorder but, rather, to do with the difficulties these types of problem pose for traditional *mental health services*. Dawson (1988) suggests that many of the 'worst' behaviours that patients with personality disorders display are essentially 'iatrogenic' and caused by poor management and treatment of patients with these types of problem. At the same time, many of the 'worst' behaviours in terms of the way practitioners and services behave towards patients with personality disorders may be caused by the way services are configured and how mental health practitioners are trained to work in this system.

In a way, overcoming the challenges to working with patients with personality disorders is not dissimilar to implementing any significant change in health care systems. If CMHTs are going to work more effectively with personality disorders, then change is required at four fundamental levels: environmental, organisational, group/team and individual (Ferlie and Shortell, 2001; cited in the NHS Modernisation Agency document *Teamworking for Improvement: Planning for Spread and Sustainability*, Department of Health, 2003). The kinds of change required in each of these areas are briefly described below.

- *The social environment*. Provide clarity and credibility as to why patients with personality disorders should be treated within generic mental health services, and legislate for this.
- *The clinical environment*. Look outside traditional 'illness' models of care and treatment. More emphasis to be placed on the role of attachment, relationship and the function of symptoms. Practitioners to be provided with the skills to work effectively with personality disorder.
- *Organisational factors*. Provide appropriate guidelines, training, services and interventions for patients with personality disorders.
- *The CMHT*. Improved team functioning and consistency in treatment provision.
- *Individual factors*. The practitioner needs to be open to new ways of working and willing to work with patients with personality disorders.

The rest of this section will consider in more detail how changes in each area may help the CMHTs to provide more effective management for patients with personality disorders.

THE SOCIAL ENVIRONMENT – LEGITIMISING PERSONALITY DISORDERS

Although the NIMHE document *Personality Disorder: No Longer a Diagnosis for Exclusion* (NIMHE, 2003a) was introduced in the 'challenges' section, it is more correctly seen as part of the solution, as it clarifies the uncertainty about whether personality disorders are a legitimate focus for services. The document aims to help services work towards providing effective and consistent management of patients with personality disorders. CMHTs will be central to this, as it is envisaged that they will have closer involvement in delivering and co-ordinating services for patients with personality disorders (see Chapter 1).

The proposed changes to the current Mental Health Act (Department of Health, 2003) – in particular, the removal of the 'treatability test' and a broader definition of 'mental disorder' that includes personality disorders – will help further improve the 'legitimacy' and 'credibility' of patients with these types of problem.

For the future, it would also help improve the legitimacy of working with patients with personality disorders if specialist mental health trusts were to be evaluated on their performance in delivering care and services offered to patients with personality disorders.

THE CLINICAL ENVIRONMENT

Incorporating New Ways of Working

If CMHTs are to work more effectively with patients with personality disorders, they will need to be open to new ideas and new ways of working. This may include CMHTs putting more emphasis on attachment and ways of coping in understanding the cause and maintenance of a patient's problems, and seeing the therapeutic relationship and service input as a legitimate 'therapeutic tool' to facilitate change. This would mean modifying the focus of input from 'treating an illness' to a more 're-parenting' model of care. These ideas, for many, present a challenge to current ways of working and will require embracing new ideas about mental illness, many of which are drawn from psychological therapies. However, this does not mean that all practitioners need to train in a particular psychotherapy, but rather that they be open to using certain, key principles that could prove more effective.

Alterations to Duty of Care and Responsibility

Another important component in managing patients with personality disorders is the amount of responsibility the CMHT takes. If CMHTs are going to offer consistent treatment and manage crises appropriately, they need to give as much responsibility as possible back to the patient. As described in Chapters 5 and 12, the CMHT needs to avoid being drawn into enacting the role of an 'overly enmeshed mother', as this could lead to them avoiding necessary limit-setting and being drawn into taking unhelpful responsibility for the patient. As a general guiding principle, the practitioner is responsible for offering 'reasonable care' whilst the patient is responsible for her behaviour (excluding when there is a significant Axis I clinical disorder, e.g. depression or psychosis, or when there is the real and immediate threat of suicide or homicide). 'Reasonable care' will depend on the individual formulation of the patient's problems.

Improving on the Information Provided by the Diagnosis

There are several, alternative approaches that CMHTs could consider in order to help them overcome the obstacles presented by diagnoses. These are described elsewhere in this volume.

It will also be necessary for the assessment to provide the CMHT with an understanding of why the patient with a personality disorder behaves as she does. This is sometimes referred to as an 'individual formulation' of the patient's problems. An accurate diagnosis and formulation of the patient's problems can help services devise care plans that, at the very least, do not exacerbate the patient's problems, and may also go some way to helping the patient break out of unhelpful ways of coping, while helping the CMHT to develop a more empathic understanding of the patient's problems.

Improving Training

The proposed new Mental Health Act and the inclusion of patients with personality disorders into mainstream psychiatric services should lead pre-qualification training programmes to allocate more energy and resources to training practitioners in how to work effectively with patients with these disorders. Training programmes should help practitioners develop skills advocated in the *Breaking the Cycle of Rejection: The Personality Disorder Capabilities Framework* document (NIHME, 2003b) described in Chapter 1. Briefly, any training programme needs to achieve the following.

- Provide the practitioner with a greater understanding of the theories underpinning personality disorders, and an explanatory framework for understanding why patients with these types of problem behave as they do.
- Help the practitioner to see the need for, and begin to explore ways of developing, individual case formulations for patients with personality disorders. This can encourage the practitioner to assess for and see the person 'behind' the diagnosis and help with validation.
- Help the practitioner to feel more confident in his/her ability to carry out clinical assessments and devise care plans that are appropriate.
- Help the practitioner to feel less anxious and more willing to work with patients with personality disorders.
- Help the practitioner to feel more confident in managing risk in patients with personality disorders.
- Help the practitioner to see why it is important to maintain professional boundaries with patients with personality disorders, and have knowledge

of how to go about this, in a way that still allows the practitioner to be caring and approachable.

- Help the practitioner to have an awareness of what patients with personality disorders want from psychiatric services and the CMHT (for instance, an increased focus on validation, acceptance and attachment).
- Increase awareness of the service barriers that make it more difficult for CMHTs to work effectively with patients with personality disorders and highlight the importance of certain issues, e.g. supervision, self-awareness and attachment.

THE ORGANISATIONAL ENVIRONMENT

Developing Guidelines and Policy for Personality Disorders

If patients with personality disorders are to be offered services, it has been suggested that they should be 'fully integrated services that provide treatment at all levels with one point of entry for expert assessment' (Bateman & Tyrer, 2004, p. 426). This means that specialist mental health trusts not only need to consider developing specialist services for patients with personality disorder, but also need to develop policies and guidelines for the effective management of personality disorders throughout all parts of the service. This should include clear mapping of the types of service and intervention available to patients with personality disorders throughout the trust.

It will also be helpful if there are clear referral pathways between services. For instance, the needs of many patients with personality disorders fall between CMHTs and primary care services. Obviously, decisions about such matters will be made locally, depending on how other services are configured and resourced. However, for general guidance Bateman and Tyrer (2004) in their paper 'Services for personality disorder: Organisation for inclusion' suggest patients with *severe* personality disorders, particularly Cluster B (antisocial, borderline, histrionic and narcissistic), and many patients with Cluster A (paranoid, schizoid and schizotypal) may not be appropriately managed by sole practitioners. Patients with these types of problem may be best managed in secondary care, as these services may be in a better position to provide co-ordinated care.

It will also be necessary for the CMHT to have guidelines in place to facilitate the clinical management and treatment of patients with these types of problem. These guidelines would need to be flexible enough to allow the CMHT to implement the core strategies required for effective management described in Chapter 10 – for instance, to produce guidelines that allow a CMHT to carry out clinically indicated risk taking in the management of potentially lethal self-harming behaviour.

Finally, the organisation needs to support the CMHT and individual practitioners in what will be a period of significant change.

Working with Service Users

The *National Service Framework for Mental Health* (Department of Health, 1999) recommends that service users and their carers be involved in planning and delivery of care. This is as important for service users with a personality disorder and their carers as for other disorders. Joint initiatives between providers and users of services can be helpful as they can enable both parties to learn from each other. Good collaboration is likely to enhance the quality of services offered and enhance service users' understanding of why services and practitioners act as they do. Such initiatives should be included in all aspects of service provision, such as commissioning, planning, training and the evaluation of services. However, difficulties with diagnosis and stigma can make it difficult to find people with relevant expertise. If this is a problem, then liaison with organisations such as Borderline UK, specialist services for personality disorders or other user groups with experience of exclusion (for example, self-harm or substance misuse) can be helpful.

IMPROVING TEAM FUNCTION

Improving the Community Mental Health Team

As described earlier, patients with certain personality disorders can exaggerate disharmony within the CMHT. If the CMHT is to be more effective in working with patients with these types of problem and offer consistent treatment, then the team needs to 'work together'. Below are some suggestions for improving team working in CMHTs. Many of the ideas below have been drawn from the NHS Modernisation Agency's document on teamworking (Department of Health, 2003).

- Spend time getting to know each other's roles and how each team member works (with respect to their role, how they work, area of expertise etc.) and define roles if ambiguity exists. This can help reduce the risk of inconsistency, inappropriate referrals and conflict.

- The whole team needs to be familiar with the policies, guidelines and ethos of the CMHT with respect to working with patients with personality disorders.
- Spend time removing inconsistencies in the team – for example, where different professions within the same CMHT may be working to different referral guidelines and geographical responsibilities.
- Work to develop team meetings that encourage all team members to actively contribute and make suggestions for patient care. Patients with personality disorders can often present real dilemmas in management and therefore a *consensus* of opinion is helpful. This can help reduce the risk of interventions becoming too enmeshed or withholding. Frequently, the aim is to have an intervention that is not too extreme in this respect (see Krawitz & Watson, 2003).
- An environment of 'openness' and non-confrontational discourse should be encouraged, so that team members feel comfortable about discussing their feelings within team meetings. The CMHT environment should encourage team members to question clinical decisions that could be non-therapeutic (e.g. offering special or withholding care). The culture of the team should take a non-blaming stance to encourage openness.
- The CMHT practitioner needs to have an understanding of the processes of projection and splitting and why some team members may be seen as 'all good' or 'all bad'.
- The CMHT needs to establish an environment or code of practice that encourages members to think and talk about patients with personality disorders in an empathic way. Hostility and prejudice should not be tolerated. However, this needs to be seen as distinct from talking about negative feelings that the patient evokes (the counter-transference), as this can be a useful process.
- Allocate time in CMHT meetings to discuss formulations and management issues for patients with personality disorders. Discussion about the care and treatment of patients with these types of problem can take up a lot of time. Therefore, having a structured format to team meetings and allocating a chairperson to keep the team on task is helpful. Identifying key questions and aims can help keep the discussions focused. These strategies can prevent meetings becoming too long and overbearing.
- The CMHT has the potential to offer the patient an array of different treatments. For effective management, a good CMHT should be flexible

and able to offer a *range* of different interventions. For instance, the team might provide

Containment/holding
Expertise in meeting social care needs
Pharmacotherapy
A model of human occupation
A recognised talking therapy (e.g. psychodynamic, CBT, schema therapy, CAT or DBT).

- Effective management requires consistent, co-ordinated care. Therefore, each CMHT practitioner needs to be clear about their role and function and that of their colleagues for each patient.
- It is also helpful if the CMHT is clear as to the type of treatment that is being offered. Chapter 10 (When can contact with the CMHT be considered 'treatment'?) provides some useful advice on this. For instance, is the intervention working to address the patient's personality disorder or acknowledging it but focusing on a clinical disorder for example, depression?
- Encourage regular attendance at meetings, as a team cannot function without its members.
- It is helpful for CMHT functioning if practitioners are flexible and prepared to help each other out as 'the whole is greater than the sum of the parts'.
- The reality for many CMHTs is that not all staff will have the attributes to work with patients with personality disorders. Staff who cannot tolerate hostility, who are rigid and who have difficulties empathically maintaining interpersonal boundaries are not well suited to working with patients with personality difficulties (Bateman Fonagy, 2004). Therefore, it may be reasonable to allocate patients with personality disorders to those practitioners who are more suited to and interested in working with them. It may also be helpful to encourage and support certain practitioners to develop further specialist skills in working with patients with personality disorders (see NIMHE, 2003b).
- In a well functioning team, all members work together and information is shared (Bateman & Tyrer, 2004).
- If the CMHT is not functioning effectively, this needs to be addressed and management informed. If not, this will impact on patient care and increase the risk of malpractice.

Staffing

A CMHT can only offer effective treatment if it is appropriately staffed to meet the needs of the 'local' community. Therefore, it can be helpful if the organisation frequently audits CMHT caseloads and modifies staffing and training accordingly. Hunter et al. (2002) demonstrate how this can work effectively. In their study 'Two weeks in the life of a CMHT' the results helped inform the trust on current team caseloads. This led to a 'refocusing exercise' and highlighted training needs within the team.

Supervision

Supervision can provide a space to reflect on the practitioner/patient interface and help identify and address potential problems before they become too entrenched. Appropriate supervision is an excellent way to reduce many of the negative feelings that can be activated when working with a patient with a personality disorder. For example, finding out that you are taking too much responsibility for the patient's behaviour and being given permission by the supervisor to 'let go of some of this' will alleviate significant amounts of stress. Good supervision can also help practitioners identify and address areas that could be problematic in the patient's care – for instance, helping the practitioner to manage risk appropriately and maintain reasonable standards of care.

Being able to offer supervision that helps practitioners sustain appropriate interactions with patients with these types of problems is difficult. However, it is essential if CMHTs are to be able to offer more effective services to patients with personality disorders. Chapter 17 (Clinical supervision) discusses the need for and nature of appropriate supervision.

IMPROVING THE PRACTITIONER/PATIENT INTERFACE

The previous sections illustrate how changes in the social, clinical and organisational environments and the CMHT could lead the way to more effective services for patients with personality disorders. However, changes in all these domains will not help the practitioner/patient interface if an individual practitioner is not receptive to new ideas and willing to modify his behaviour accordingly. Only then will CMHTs offer effective management for patients with personality disorder.

CONCLUSION

This chapter has presented the challenges that working with patients with personality disorders pose to traditional psychiatric services and CMHTs.

Many of these are associated with the difficulties that personality disorder creates for traditional illness models of treatment and care. If a CMHT practitioner is to offer effective management and have appropriate interactions with patients with personality disorders they will need to be part of a well functioning CMHT, supported by the organisation, be encouraged to develop new skills to help them understand and work with patients with these disorders and have legislation that makes these changes possible. Although this will require effort from all parties, the rewards will be significant. The CMHT practitioner will develop new ways of conceptualising patients' problems that could help reduce practitioners' feelings of hopelessness, burden and distress, whilst also helping staff become more aware of and more proficient in using the crucial 'therapeutic tool' of their relationship. The outcomes of such changes will potentially lead to improvement in services not just for the treatment and care of patients with personality disorders, but for everybody who uses mental health services.

REFERENCES

American Psychiatric Association. (1994). *Diagnostic and statistical manual of mental disorders* (4th ed.). Washington, DC: Author.

Bateman, A. & Fonagy, P. (2004). *Psychotherapy for borderline personality disorder.* Oxford: Oxford University Press.

Bateman, A. & Tyrer, P. (2004). Services for personality disorder: Organisation for inclusion. *Advances in Psychiatric Treatment, 10,* 425–433.

Burns, T. (2004). *Community mental health teams. A guide to current practices.* Oxford: Oxford University Press.

Dawson, D. F. (1988). Treatment of the borderline patient: Relationship management. *Canadian Journal of Psychiatry, 33,* 370–374.

Department of Health. (1983). *The Mental Health Act: England and Wales.* London: Author.

Department of Health. (1999). *Modern Standards and Service Models: National Service Framework for Mental Health.* London: Author.

Department of Health. (2002). *Mental health policy implementation guide. Community mental health teams.* London: Author.

Department of Health. (2003). *Teamworking for improvement: Planning for spread and sustainability.* Leicester: NHS Modernisation Agency.

Ferlie, E. B. & Shortell, S. M. (2001). Improving quality of health care in the United Kindom and United States. A framework for change. *The Milbank Quarterly, 79,* 281–315.

Hunter, M., Jadresic, D., Blaine, A., Clancy, L., Leyshon, N., McDonald, E., Sanderson, I. & Spearing, G. (2002). Two weeks in the life of a community mental health team. A survey of case-mix and clinical activity in the north-west of Sheffield. *Psychiatric Bulletin, 26,* 9–11.

Kendell, R. E. (2002) The distinction between personality disorder and mental illness. *The British Journal of Psychiatry, 180,* 110–115.

Krawitz, R. & Watson, C. (2003). *Borderline personality disorder. A practical guide to treatment.* Oxford: Oxford University Press.

Lewis, G. & Appleby, L. (1988). Personality disorder: the patients psychiatrists dislike. *British Journal of Psychiatry, 153*, 44–49.

Linehan, M. M. (1993). *Cognitive–behavioural treatment of borderline personality disorder.* London: Guilford.

Markham, D. & Trower, P. E. (2003). The effects of the psychiatric label 'borderline personality disorder' on nursing staff's perceptions and causal attributions for challenging behaviours. *British Journal of Clinical Psychology, 42*, 243–256.

National Institute for Mental Health in England (NIMHE). (2003a). *Personality disorder: No longer a diagnosis for exclusion*, policy implementing guidance for the development of services for people with personality disorder. London: Department of Health.

National Institute for Mental Health in England. (NIMHE). (2003b) *Breaking the cycle of rejection: The personality disorder capabilities framework*, policy implementation guidance for the development of services for people with personality disorder. London: Department of Health.

Skodol, A. E., Gunderson, J. G., McGlashan, T. H., Dyck, I. R., Stout, R. L. et al. (2002a). Functional impairment in patients with schizotypal, borderline, avoidant, or obsessive – compulsive personality disorder. *The American Journal of Psychiatry, 159*, 276–283.

Skodol, A. E., Gunderson, J. G., Pfohl, B., Widiger, T. A., Livesley, W. J. & Siever, L. J. (2002b). The borderline diagnosis I: Psychopathology, comorbidity and personality structure. *Biological Psychiatry, 51*: 936–950.

Vaillant, G. E. (1993). *The Wisdom of the Ego.* London: Harvard University Press.

Webb, E. C. (2005). A focus group survey of CMHT staff views on the meaning of personality disorder. *Clinical Psychology, 48*, 3–7.

Weiner, B. (1985). An attributional theory of achievement motivation and emotion. *Psychological Review, 92*, 548–573.

12

The Treatment Frame and the Treatment Alliance

JIM MOOREY

INTRODUCTION

In this chapter I will outline some of the general principles of establishing and maintaining a 'treatment frame', and of forming a 'treatment alliance'. Although these principles were originally developed within psychoanalysis they are applicable to any form of 'therapy', and are arguably of particular relevance to any form of service provision that involves personal contact with patients presenting with personality disorders.

The material in this chapter will be presented in terms of psychotherapy. However, the reader is encouraged to think through the general principles and apply these to the particular setting in which he or she works. As we shall see, attending to the frame and the alliance is essentially about being clear about the parameters of the service being offered, and what is being asked of service providers and service users. The general principles covered in this chapter may be applied to any form of service provision, even where what is offered would perhaps not be regarded as a form of therapy, for example crisis support. We can attend to the frame and the alliance even in a single contact, thereby introducing a 'therapeutic' element. Community mental health team practitioners – psychiatrists, psychologists, community psychiatric nurses, occupational therapists, social workers and primary care mental health professionals – working within community mental health teams will be seeing patients in a range of settings, providing various types of help, care or treatment intervention. However, regardless of the setting, and regardless

Personality Disorder and Community Mental Health Teams: A Practitioner's Guide. Edited by
M. J. Sampson, R. A. McCubbin and P. Tyrer. © 2006 John Wiley & Sons, Ltd.

of the type of intervention offered, these two issues, the frame and the alliance, will be of fundamental importance.

THE TREATMENT FRAME

In this section we will review some general principles to help guide the establishment and maintenance of the treatment frame. For a useful review of the limited research on frame issues see Orlinsky, Ronnestad and Willutzki (2004).

WHAT IS THE TREATMENT FRAME?

I will use the term 'treatment frame' to refer to the structure and ground rules, or *boundaries*, of any therapeutic intervention. The treatment frame comprises boundaries of *time* and *place*, the *task* of therapy and the requirements and responsibilities associated with the *roles* of patient and therapist. These boundaries describe the general framework within which a particular therapy occurs. The frame does not describe the detailed process of therapy but rather its overall shape.

The *standard*, or basic, treatment frame will usually involve setting the parameters of therapy in the following areas.

1. Timing of sessions (time and day).
2. Length of sessions.
3. Length of contract (number of sessions or specified time period, arrangements for cancellations and planned absences, policy on missed sessions, etc.).
4. Location of sessions.
5. Setting of sessions (including specific room, arrangement of furniture, etc.).
6. Confidentiality (in particular its scope and limits).
7. Privacy (sessions should be private and without interruption).
8. The purpose, or goals, of therapy.
9. The essential tasks, responsibilities and interpersonal boundaries of the therapist.
10. The essential tasks, responsibilities and interpersonal boundaries of the patient.

Appropriate frame management, even of this standard or basic treatment frame, is a key therapeutic skill. However, because of the particular presentations of patients with personality disorders it may be necessary to establish certain pre-conditions for therapy in an *extended frame*. Such an extended frame may be necessary if therapy is to be viable, and it will require considerable expertise to manage this frame appropriately.

Kernberg and his colleagues (Kernberg, Selzer, Koenigsberg, Carr & Appelbaum, 1989) point out that additional structure may be required if patients present with particularly disruptive behaviour. When working with patients with personality disorders it is important that there are clear boundaries demarcating contact with therapeutic services. However, patients presenting with what Kernberg refers to as a 'borderline' presentation (which includes all Cluster B disturbances) are likely to put some pressure on the frame, and with some patients this pressure will be severe. This may take the form of self-destructive actions, such as self-injury or risk taking, or various forms of substance abuse, or destructive actions towards others, such as repeated aggression in one form or another. It may involve repeated attacks on previous therapies that have been sabotaged by, for example, not attending scheduled appointments without notice, dropping out of therapy, attending while intoxicated, persistent criticism and rejection of offers of help, etc. If therapy is to be undertaken these disruptive behaviours must be addressed by means of pre-conditions added to the standard frame. For example, continued therapy may be conditional on the patient maintaining abstinence or restriction of alcohol or drug use, or maintenance of a particular weight, or attendance at regular medication reviews, or co-operation with professionals involved in monitoring compliance in these matters. The general principle governing extended frames is that the additional conditions, or constraints, should be the minimum required to secure the frame and hence create conditions for a viable therapy.

Although the specific arrangements will vary – according to the type of intervention, the model of therapy employed, the particular setting and the constraints of the service in which the treatment is provided – it is important that key aspects of the frame should be made *explicit* before therapy begins. This will usually include the boundaries of time and place, the task of therapy, and essential aspects of the responsibilities associated with the roles of patient and therapist. Many aspects of the frame will be *implied*, but will not need to be articulated (for example, many aspects of what is and is not acceptable behaviour for patient and therapist will not be spelt out explicitly but will be implied by the therapist's actions in the course of therapy). Some implicit aspects of the frame may need to be made explicit, if required, in the course of therapy (for example, if a patient offers the therapist a gift).

The explicit aspects of the treatment frame should be *agreed* by patient and therapist before the therapy begins. Once agreed, these explicit features of the frame should be articulated in the form of a *contract*. The contract is a statement of the specific features of the frame that have been agreed by patient and therapist. Once the formal parameters of the treatment frame have been agreed and articulated in the form of a contract they should be maintained *consistently* for the duration of the therapy. *Therapy should not begin before the contract has been agreed.* Once the contract has been agreed, and therapy has begun, it is the responsibility of the therapist to maintain the various components of the treatment frame.

So far we have noted some of the general principles of standard and extended frames, and explicit and implicit aspects of the frame. A third fundamental distinction is that between *secure* and *insecure* frames. We may describe frames as *secure* when the boundaries – of time, place, tasks and roles – are clear, consistent and reliable. Treatment frames may be described as *insecure* when boundaries have either not been initially secured, or having once secured the frame the therapist fails to maintain it consistently. Clarity about boundaries is essential for the establishment and maintenance of a secure frame, and lack of clarity about boundaries is a key feature of insecure frames.

WHY IS THE TREATMENT FRAME IMPORTANT?

The treatment frame is important, first, because every therapy will *necessarily* take place within some form of treatment frame, and the process, or functioning, of the therapy will be *profoundly affected* by the condition of the frame. This is inevitable because frames or boundaries are both universal and necessary. As Robert Langs has observed, 'Throughout animate and inanimate nature, the frame or boundary conditions of an entity or system are a major determinant of the functioning and survival of that entity' (Langs, 1994, p. 59). As an example think of your own skin, in particular the consequences for the functioning of your body if your skin boundary breaks down.

A second reason for the importance of the frame is that it serves to *demarcate* a special time and place in which a special form of relationship and activity may occur. The frame serves to separate and distinguish therapy from other relationships and activities, in order to amplify expectancies, of both patient and therapist, and emphasise the creative potential of the therapeutic space. That is, the frame signals that this is a place where something new can develop.

Third, the treatment frame is important because the clarity, predictability and reliability of the frame provide a *secure base* from which the challenging work of therapy can be launched. The notion of a secure base, developed by Mary Ainsworth and John Bowlby (Bowlby, 1988), is particularly relevant to work with patients presenting with personality disorder. We may conceptualise many forms of personality disorder as being essentially disturbances of boundaries, in particular the experience of the boundaries of the self. We have noted in Chapter 4 that many patients presenting with borderline characteristics have experienced serious boundary violations in the form of neglect or abuse in childhood. As the child grows it is as if the boundary disturbances of the early environment become internalised to form the disrupted boundaries of the self. The inconsistency and unreliability of care-givers, and a pervasive sense of insecurity, are recurrent themes in the childhood of many patients with personality disorder. When the treatment frame is unclear or inconsistently maintained, the therapist is likely to be experienced as inconsistent and unreliable, and the therapeutic space as unsafe. The insecure base of therapy has recreated the insecure base of the early traumatic environment. The effect of this is likely to be increased anxiety and disturbance, a sense that the therapy is unable to contain the patient, acting out and perhaps withdrawal from the therapy. This lack of a secure base, repeating the lack of security of childhood, will make therapy extremely difficult if not impossible.

A fourth reason for the importance of the treatment frame is that it provides an invaluable *baseline* for observation. A patient's response to the various conditions of the frame provides a therapist with ongoing information about how the patient is experiencing the therapy. It is to be expected that many patients with personality disorder will put pressure on the frame, even when it has been carefully established through discussion and agreement and specific articulation in the form of a contact. Such pressure can have various meanings. It can be an expression of a general lack of boundaries that appears to be characteristic of patients with personality disorders, or it may have a more specific meaning, perhaps being an expression of resistance or ambivalence towards the therapy, or anger towards the therapist. However, in order for this to be understood and addressed in therapy there needs to be an explicit treatment frame to form the baseline agreement against which the patient is reacting. If the therapist does not keep the ground rules consistently, the baseline becomes unclear and patients' reactions to the frame much harder to identify and understand.

A fifth reason for the importance of the frame is provided by Donald Winnicott, who first used the expression 'frame management'. In an influential account of frame issues, Winnicott (1955) suggested that in some therapies frame management must become the *therapeutic priority*. Specifically, Winnicott argued that the more fragile the patient's sense of self, the more central frame management becomes relative to other aspects of therapeutic technique. When working with more severely disturbed patients maintaining the essential boundaries of the frame is likely to become the most important aspect of the therapy.

MANAGING THE TREATMENT FRAME

In the previous sections we have reviewed some basic principles regarding standard and extended frames, explicit and implicit aspects of the frame and secure and insecure frames. We have also considered some of the reasons for emphasising the importance of the frame. We now come to the contentious issue of frame management. We have noted that the specific details of the frame will vary according to patients' needs, service constraints, type of intervention, model of therapy etc., but once due allowance is made for these differences by far the majority of *disputes* about management of the frame concern questions of *consistency*. We have noted the importance of consistency in managing the treatment frame, and I would suspect that most therapists, regardless of their training and therapeutic allegiances, would agree with this in a general way. However, disagreements are sure to emerge once we ask what exactly is meant by consistency: does consistency mean that we should never, under any circumstances, modify or re-negotiate an aspect of the frame once it has been agreed? And should we regard the various features of the implicit frame as absolute?

Therapists' attitudes towards the frame form a continuum, with advocates of a strict (invariant) frame at one end, and those advocating a permissive (flexible) frame at the other, but despite disagreements some general principles can be identified that would probably be endorsed by most therapists. Perhaps the most basic principle is that a secure treatment frame requires a humane and sensitive response to the patient's needs. It is never a mere mechanical application of rules. From this basic principle we may suggest that a secure treatment frame is *firm but not rigid*. Clarity, consistency and reliability do not require an absolutely invariant treatment frame.

Consider the issue of the duration of sessions. One obvious situation in which a session may need to be extended would be if the therapist judged it necessary to do a risk assessment even though the session was close to ending. Although at some point it would be important to reflect on why these concerns emerged late in the session, an appropriate response to an elevated level of risk may require extending the session. However, it should always be explicitly noted with the patient that the scheduled end of the session has arrived, and the reason for the extension given. But what of a situation where a patient, after several months of therapy in which boundaries of time were carefully observed, becomes extremely upset close to the end of a session? How should the therapist manage the ending? What is happening between the patient and the therapist in this situation could be interpreted in a number of different ways. The therapist may judge that on this occasion it would be appropriate to offer a few minutes extension, but how might this be done? Again it is crucial to acknowledge the reality of the time boundary, and to say clearly why a few minutes extension will be offered. For example the therapist might say something like 'I am aware that we have reached the end of our session, and I am concerned that we have touched on some painful issues that we do not have time to work with today. Perhaps we could just sit quietly for a few minutes before ending'. The key point is that if we modify the frame we should do so for a clear therapeutic reason, and we should acknowledge that we have changed a boundary. Learning to identify the *rare occasions* when it is appropriate to modify or re-negotiate an aspect of the frame is a fundamental therapeutic skill.

The key distinction to make is between a situation that requires an appropriate modification or re-negotiation of a boundary that *maintains* the security of the frame, and a situation in which the security of the frame is *threatened*. Threats to the frame can come from the patient, or from the therapist. Threats to the frame from the patient can take various forms: attending late, missing appointments, pressurising the therapist to change the time or place of an appointment, demanding an extension of the agreed contract by additional sessions or additional time, contacting the therapist outside appointment times, attending intoxicated, lying to the therapist, not completing assignments, threatening the therapist in some way, attempting to change the therapeutic relationship into a social relationship, insisting the therapist provides some form of physical contact, attempting to manipulate or coerce the therapist by introducing conditions on the patient's attendance etc. As noted, what is taken to be a threat to the frame, and how seriously particular threats are regarded, varies between different therapists. However, once a threat has been identified how may therapists respond?

When a threat to the frame is recognised it should not be ignored. Threats to the frame need to be discussed openly in the therapy, and the disruptive impact on the therapy emphasised. Pressures on the frame need to be identified as threats to the therapy. The relevant aspect of the frame, relating to time, place, tasks or roles, should be stated or re-stated explicitly. In situations where threats to the frame have become severe some additional conditions – an extended frame – may need to be considered. The key point is that the frame should not be modified inappropriately. In these situations two fundamental principles need to be borne in mind: giving in to a patient's demands to inappropriately modify a boundary will not be therapeutic for the patient, while refusing to inappropriately modify a boundary will not make the patient worse. Maintaining a firm boundary in the face of pressure to introduce inappropriate modifications may lead to a patient withdrawing from therapy (for example), but this would suggest that this intervention is not appropriate for the patient. It is worth remembering the parable of the camel's nose, described in a classic paper on limit setting by Murphy and Guze (1960). The story goes that a camel herder pitched his tent in the desert and during the night a camel put his nose into the tent, saying 'It is very cold out here; if I can just put my nose into the tent I will be alright'. The camel herder said 'Alright, that's not asking too much, but just your nose'. Later in the night the camel driver woke and the camel's face was in the tent: 'I'm so cold. . . Just my face and I will be alright'. Once again the camel driver acquiesced: 'It is only his face, that will be alright'. As you will guess this process continues until the camel is in the tent under the blanket and the camel driver is out in the cold. Beware! An insecure frame tends to be a slippery slope.

The security of the frame can also be compromised by the therapist. Therapists will often experience intense reactions to patients with personality disorders, and these reactions can disrupt the therapist's capacity to maintain and manage the frame. Some pressure or even testing of boundaries in therapy is to be expected, in which case therapists need to be prepared to set clear limits in order to keep the frame intact. A variety of personal anxieties can lead a therapist to be too permissive with respect to the frame. Some therapists may find it difficult to establish reasonable limits without feeling they are depriving or even damaging the patient. Alternatively, limit setting may be anxiety provoking for a therapist who fears a negative – critical, hostile or rejecting – reaction from the patient. An inordinate desire to be liked or to avoid conflict may also lead to difficulties in managing an appropriately restrictive frame. An exaggerated sense of personal responsibility, grandiosity or potency, can lead therapists to assume too much of the responsibility for therapy and to ask too little of the patient. On the other hand a therapist may become too rigid, feeling that any flexibility or display of spontaneity is dangerous. It is also important to recognise that anxiety can lead therapists to impose an overly strict frame that is essentially a defence against doing the work of therapy, particularly as an avoidance of the emotional, intimate or conflictual aspects of the therapeutic encounter. When errors of frame management occur, it is essential that these be acknowledged openly with the patient and the secure frame re-established.

The following general principles of frame management summarise the points made above.

1. Be clear in your own mind about the general principles of secure and insecure frames.
2. Be clear in your own mind about the specific boundaries, explicit and implicit, of a particular therapeutic intervention.

3. Establish a clear agreed contract, which makes explicit key aspects of the frame, before therapy begins.
4. Continually monitor frame adherence, both your own and the patient's.
5. Be prepared to make explicit any implicit aspects of the frame as the situation requires.
6. Acknowledge errors of frame management, or unavoidable interruptions of the frame, and re-establish a secure frame as soon as possible.
7. Learn to recognise when an appropriate modification or re-negotiation of the frame would be helpful to the patient.
8. Remember! Resisting pressure to inappropriately modify the frame will not make the patient worse.
9. Remember! Giving in to pressure to inappropriately modify the frame will not be helpful to the patient.
10. Serious threats may require additional conditions – an extended frame – but these additional ground rules should be as minimal as possible, consistent with securing the frame.
11. Be prepared to recognise when threats to the frame are so serious as to require the ending of the contract.
12. Beware! The parable of the camel's nose...

So far, we have considered the issue of frame management with respect to individual therapy. It is important to be aware that this is not the only frame influencing the process of therapy. Institutions, departments, clinics, wards, teams etc. offer an *organisational setting*, or context within which work with patients is carried out. The organisational setting will comprise a range of frames or boundaries, or sub-systems within a larger system, within which individual therapists carry out their work (Roberts, 1994). The organisational setting can provide *secure* frames or *insecure* frames for carrying out the task of therapy. The former will tend to provide a containing structure that helps make the stress of the work manageable, while the latter will tend to increase the potential for anxiety, feelings of fragmentation and lack of containment, and powerful impulses to avoid the often difficult work of carrying out the primary task of therapy.

A prominent feature of work with patients with personality disorder is the patient's tendency to use 'primitive' defences such as splitting and projective identification (Kernberg et al., 1989). A patient's use of these defences means that there will be a potential for therapists not merely to hear about feelings of distress, fragmentation and lack of containment, but to actually experience aspects of this disturbance for themselves. Without an organisationally secure frame the therapist may find these feelings unmanageable, which in turn will limit their ability to carry out their role responsibilities in the primary task of therapy. If the wider organisational frames are compromised in some way, the containing function of the institution may break down, leading to anxiety and disruption of the organisation's primary task. It is important therefore for individual therapists to consider both the formal aspect of the contract established with clients in therapy and the position of this arrangement in the context of an organisational or institutional frame. Where either of these are *insecure* there is a risk of provoking disruptive levels of anxiety in both workers and their clients.

Within the context of multidisciplinary teams, and especially where several workers may have contact with a patient, frame issues need to be clear and agreed by all involved. In particular, team members need to be aware that the tendency for patients with personality disorders to deploy 'primitive' defences means that patients can experience team members in polarised ways that potentially disrupt co-ordinated service provision. It is essential that therapists understand the pressures that can be exerted on the frame when processes such as splitting and projective identification are operating. A lack of clarity around boundaries, in particular regarding the tasks and goals of any therapeutic intervention, and the individual roles and responsibilities within the team, can lead to the creation of insecure frames with patients, and leave therapists and other team members feeling unsupported and uncontained. Hence, work with patients with personality disorders requires careful frame management not only in relation to the patient, but also in relation to other professionals involved in their care, including supervisors and other team members.

In this section we have considered what is meant by the treatment frame, why frame issues are important and some general principles of frame management. We can see the treatment frame as an aspect of a broader concept, to which we now turn – that of the treatment alliance.

THE TREATMENT ALLIANCE

In addition to the central importance of managing the frame of therapy, a second key aspect of working with any patient regardless of the type of intervention is the 'treatment alliance'. There is now a very large body of research into the treatment alliance. In this section we will review what is meant by the treatment alliance, why it is important and how it can be facilitated.

WHAT IS THE TREATMENT ALLIANCE?

A variety of expressions have been used to refer to 'an alliance between patient and practitioner necessary for the successful carrying out of the therapeutic work' (Sandler, Dare & Holder, 1992, p. 23). The alliance involves a commitment to do the *work* of therapy. It is not simply liking the therapist, or enjoying conversation with the therapist. The alliance is usually conceived as a *working* alliance. However, in addition it is hardly plausible that a patient could sustain commitment to the work of therapy that is likely to be anxiety provoking, frustrating and difficult if he or she did not, at the same time, have positive views and feelings towards the therapist. In this view the treatment alliance involves both the commitment to do the necessary *work* of therapy, and a generally positive *regard* for the therapist.

Sandler and colleagues note that although Freud did not use the term 'treatment alliance' or enunciate the concept explicitly the idea appears to stem from Freud's earliest work (Freud, 1895); when he first wrote of making the patient a 'collaborator' he went on to write of the 'pact' between patient and therapist (Sandler et al., 1992, p. 24). Initially, what we would term the alliance was seen as part of the transference. That is, the 'friendly and affectionate' aspects of the positive transference were regarded as 'the vehicle of success in psychoanalysis, exactly as it is in other methods of treatment' (Freud, 1912; quoted by Sandler et al., 1992, p. 25). It should be emphasised once again that such positive feelings towards the therapist do not, in themselves, constitute a treatment alliance.

Bordin (1979) suggested that the alliance is comprised of three central components. There is the *bond* between patient and therapist and there is the agreement between patient and therapist on the *goals* of therapy and on the *tasks* of therapy. These three factors – bond, goals and tasks – contribute to the overall strength of the alliance. Gaston (1990) has adopted a similar approach, suggesting that the alliance is comprised of four relatively independent dimensions. The four dimensions are the following:

1. The patient's affective relationship to the therapist.
2. The therapist's empathic understanding and involvement.
3. The patient's capacity to work purposefully in therapy.
4. Patient–therapist agreement on the goals and tasks of therapy.

Different models of therapy may emphasise different aspects of these four factors. In particular, those therapists that emphasise the quality of the relationship between patient and therapist will stress points 1 and 2. By contrast, therapies more committed to technical procedures (and perhaps the Protestant work ethic) may emphasise points 3 and 4. This division also reflects a fundamental disagreement regarding the treatment alliance. Is it the alliance *in itself* that is therapeutic, or is the alliance *a vehicle* for therapeutic change? Factors 1 and 2 reflect the first emphasis, and factors 3 and 4 reflect the second.

WHY IS THE TREATMENT ALLIANCE IMPORTANT?

There are at least two reasons why the treatment alliance is important. The first is that 'the alliance has repeatedly been shown to be associated with outcome', whereas 'therapist interventions have rarely been found to contribute substantially to outcome' (Gaston, Piper, Debbane, Bienvenu & Garant, 1994). On the basis of an extensive body of research evidence, largely in the area of individual psychotherapy, the strength of the treatment alliance, measured early in therapy, appears to be the only process variable that reliably predicts outcome (Martin, Garske & Davis, 2000).

A second reason for the importance of the alliance is related to the highly emotive issue of the relative effectiveness of different therapies. As Gaston notes, specific techniques (or models of therapeutic procedure) have been found to be much less useful as predictors of outcome than you might expect. Although the results of efficacy (or effectiveness) studies may feel undermining to many therapists, it is worth reminding ourselves of the findings of this work.

The first, reassuring finding from outcome studies is that psychotherapy is effective: 'psychotherapy is beneficial. This consistent finding across thousands of studies and hundreds of meta-analyses is seemingly undebatable' (Lambert and Ogles, 2004, p. 148). 'In fact, it seems that psychotherapy is the best documented medical intervention in history. No other medical intervention has anywhere near the empirical scientific support that psychotherapy enjoys' (Howard, Orlinsky & Luegar, 1995, p. 4). However, a second finding is not so reassuring, at least for those committed to a particular form of therapy. In 1975 in a classic paper Luborsky, Singer and Luborsky reviewed outcome studies up till that time and pronounced the famous 'dodo bird verdict': 'All have won and all must have prizes!' (Luborsky, Singer & Luborsky, 1975). Similarly, Smith and Glass in an extensive meta-analytic review of 375 outcome studies wrote 'Despite volumes devoted to the theoretical differences among different schools of psychotherapy, the results of research demonstrate negligible differences in the effects produced by different therapy types' (Smith & Glass, 1977, p. 760). Landman and Dawes (1982) re-analysed the data from a sub-section of these studies (42 studies from the extended data base of 435 studies provided by Smith and Glass), including only those meeting strict quality criteria, and found the same result: 'Much to our surprise, our results were virtually identical to those of Smith and Glass based on their whole sample of 435' (Dawes, 1994, p. 54).

In 1986, Stiles, Shapiro and Elliot published a key paper, 'Are all psychotherapies equivalent?'. Their conclusion was that 'Differently labelled therapies have demonstrably different behavioural contents, yet appear to have equivalent outcomes'. The authors describe this as 'the equivalence paradox'. The paradox of 'no differential effectiveness despite obvious technical diversity' means that despite the very different theories and technical procedures of psychotherapists from different schools the evidence suggests that, across a wide range of presenting problems, outcome is similar. If we take this 'equivalence paradox' seriously, it implies that 'although we know that psychotherapy works, we do not clearly understand how it works', hence the paradox 'challenges some cherished beliefs of practitioners and underlines our comparative ignorance as to the mechanisms whereby psychotherapies achieve their results' (Stiles et al., 1986, pp. 165, 175).

The National Institute of Mental Health (NIMH) Treatment of Depression Collaborative Research Programme was probably the most expensive outcome study so far conducted (and is very unlikely ever to be repeated). Two hundred and fifty patients were randomly assigned to four conditions: cognitive behaviour therapy (CBT); interpersonal therapy (IPT); imipramine and clinical management, and placebo pill plus clinical management. This study, its interpretation and implications has generated a considerable literature, and considerable heat! Here we just need to note the general finding of no significant differences in outcome between CBT and IPT, and no significant differences between the two therapies and imipramine (although this comparison is rather more difficult to interpret, with for example imipramine appearing to work faster). It is also important to note that the superiority of CBT, IPT and imipramine over placebo was more marked the more severe the depression (Elkin, 1994; Elkin et al., 1989; Imber et al., 1990).

For thorough reviews of the psychotherapy research literature, the *Handbook of Psychotherapy and Behaviour Change* is an invaluable source. The most recent, fifth edition (Lambert, 2004) notes that most comparative studies, and meta-analytic reviews, report that outcomes across a range of adult presenting problems and therapy modalities are broadly equivalent. Some studies and reviews report a small advantage in outcomes for cognitive or cognitive–behavioural therapies for some problems, in particular severe phobias and severe obsessive–compulsive disorder, and some health conditions such as insomnia and tension headaches (Creer, Holroyd, Glasgow & Smith, 2004; Emmelkemp, 2004; Hollon & Beck, 2004). Because studies that report differential effectiveness are the exception rather than the rule, these studies have rightly been carefully scrutinised by researchers, and several criticisms have been made. For example, differences that have been reported are typically small, and when allowances are made for allegiance effects almost all differences in outcome disappear (Lambert & Ogles, 2004; Luborsky et al., 1999; Shoham & Rohrbaugh, 1999; Wampold, 2001). The overall picture, from several thousand outcome studies, has been summarised by David Shapiro: 'The clearest take-home message from the field remains that diverse treatments yield equivalent outcomes. Evidence for specifically efficacious techniques remains at best exceptional and at worst illusory' (Shapiro, 2000).

I have laboured this point because there is still, in some circles, enormous resistance to accepting it. We need not dwell on possible motivations for such resistance. However, we may accept that the overall picture from outcome research does suggest an equivalence paradox, but if so how can the paradox be resolved? Shapiro (1995) suggests the following four possibilities:

1. There may be significant differences in outcome that our methodology has, to date, failed to identify.
2. The research paradigm from which the paradox has arisen may be seriously flawed.
3. The apparent contradiction between process and outcome may be resolved by a higher order theory that encompasses both.
4. Technical diversity may not refer to the therapeutically potent elements; the 'active ingredients' may be non-specific.

Shapiro's paper provides an interesting discussion of each of these proposed resolutions, but the resolution that appears to be most plausible at this stage is number four. As noted recently by Lambert and Ogles in their extensive review,

> (B)ased on a review of the evidence, it appears that what can be firmly stated is that factors common across treatments are accounting for a substantial amount of improvement in psychotherapy patients. These so-called common factors may even account for most of the gains that result from psychological interventions. So, while we do not rule out the possibility that variables specific to one school or technique might be found to make an additional contribution, at this point it is important to recognise that the common factors are contributing a great deal to positive outcome... Common factors loom large as mediators of treatment outcome. The research base for this conclusion is substantial and multidimensional, and so we must attend to its import (2004, pp. 172, 174)

Interest in the importance of 'common factors' is often associated with the work of Jerome Frank (1961, 1973, 1982; Frank & Frank, 1993). Outcome research of the 1940s and 1950s was already demonstrating the equivalence paradox and Frank argued this was most likely due to the power of common factors (Frank, 1961). Frank (1982) suggested there were four broad categories of common factors:

1. A confiding *relationship* with a helping person.
2. A secure *setting*, which includes various symbols of healing and of the therapist's credibility.
3. A convincing, or at least plausible, *rationale* or conceptual scheme that explains the cause of the patient's symptoms.
4. Linked to the rationale is a prescribed *procedure* that requires active participation of both patient and therapist and that is believed by both to be the means to the restoration of the patient's health.

Further, Frank suggests all rationales and procedures in psychotherapy share six therapeutic functions.

1. They strengthen the therapeutic relationship, or *treatment alliance*.
2. They promote and sustain the patient's hope that improvement is possible.
3. They provide opportunities for cognitive and experiential learning, i.e. new ways of viewing problems and strategies for dealing with them ('cognitive mastery' and 'behavioural regulation').
4. They provide opportunities for engagement and emotional arousal, encouraging motivation for change.
5. They enhance the patient's sense of mastery (that problems can be understood and managed), and combat feelings of demoralisation and helplessness.
6. They encourage patients to act on new learnings, by means of 'working through', modelling, rehearsal and other forms of practical application.

We may note that the concepts of the treatment frame and the treatment alliance subsume most, if not all, of the common factors identified by Frank. Within the large body of process-outcome research, it is the treatment alliance that has been regarded as the most important conceptualisation of many of the key common factors.

A paradigm example of a common factor is the quality of the therapeutic relationship, variously described as the working alliance, therapeutic bond, and so on. According to this resolution, equivalent outcomes of different treatment methods are simply due to the fact that these methods pale into insignificance when contrasted with the quality of the relationship formed between client and therapist. This is an intuitively appealing idea, with seemingly overwhelming empirical support (Shapiro, 1995, p. 8)

Shapiro (2000) notes '(E)vidence continues to grow in support of the "common factors" resolution of the paradox... a common factors approach readily subsumes much if not all of the limited evidence in support of specific techniques; these may serve, for example, to provide coherent rationales that secure positive expectations and self-efficacy'.

To summarise this section: the treatment alliance is of major importance, first, because a large body of research has demonstrated its reliability as a predictor of outcome, in contrast to specific techniques; and, second, because the treatment alliance provides us with a useful way of conceptualising and researching common factors in psychotherapy. Given its importance it makes sense for all therapists to give the alliance due emphasis at the heart of their therapeutic approach.

HOW CAN THE TREATMENT ALLIANCE BE FACILITATED?

In their review of psychotherapy research Anthony Roth and Peter Fonagy (Roth & Fonagy, 1996) note that research evidence suggests four interventions in particular appear to facilitate the alliance.

1. A friendly, sympathetic attitude to the client.
2. The encouragement of a collaborative relationship.
3. Therapist intervention aimed at addressing the client's negative feelings towards the therapist.
4. Direct attention to the in-therapy relationship.

(See Roth and Fonagy, 1996, pp. 353–354 for references to relevant research.)

Roth and Fonagy point out that the outcome of therapy is most strongly associated with the capacity to identify and successfully repair 'alliance ruptures' (Roth & Fonagy, 1996, p. 352). This is a crucial point for effective therapy with patients with personality disorders, because a pattern of unstable personal relationships is so often a feature of the presentation. Therapists need to continually monitor the condition of the alliance and respond as soon as possible to any rupture. Unfortunately, evidence suggests that in general therapists are rather poor at making accurate assessments of the alliance (Orlinsky et al., 2004). Sensitivity to the condition of the alliance, and effective responses to alliance ruptures, are complex therapeutic skills that require specific attention and work.

Continuous monitoring of the alliance can be facilitated by encouraging specific feedback. We may do this through a simple process of observation such as 'We seem to be struggling today... as if we are not really connecting. . .' or through direct questions, or by means of session questionnaires, as recommended for cognitive–behavioural work (for example see Burns, 1999). Whatever the specific form of the invitation, the key factor is to give constant attention to the alliance, being sensitive to alliance ruptures and addressing these as soon as possible.

Ruptures in the alliance can occur for a wide range of reasons, and once identified should be addressed directly. A general principle for identifying alliance ruptures is to be alert to any deviations from a secure treatment frame. Pressure on what has been agreed regarding the time and place, or the tasks and relative roles of therapy, is pressure on the alliance. Some patient behaviours that may be an indication of an alliance rupture include coming late to sessions, cancellations or non-attendance, not completing homework assignments, silence, persistent disagreements, overt criticism of the therapy or therapist, sudden shifts of mood and the spontaneous production of displaced narratives that involve criticisms of other professionals, or people doing a poor job or being neglectful (for a detailed description of this aspect of unconscious communication see the work of Robert Langs, e.g. Langs, 1992).

CONCLUSION

In this chapter I have reviewed some of the theoretical and practical issues associated with the treatment frame and the treatment alliance. In conclusion, I would like to emphasise how closely connected the frame and the alliance are. The treatment frame offers the conditions under which the treatment alliance can develop and flourish. Both concepts involve an agreement and a commitment to work in therapy in a particular way. We can regard the treatment frame as a crucial aspect of the treatment alliance. The frame constitutes a formal description of the space where the alliance is to function. Attention to the treatment frame and the treatment alliance is essential if we are to work effectively with patients with personality disorders, regardless of the type of intervention or specific model of therapy that we employ.

REFERENCES

Bordin, E. S. (1979). The generalizability of the psychoanalytic concept of the working alliance. *Psychotherapy, Theory, Research and Practice, 16*, 252–260.
Bowlby, J. (1988). *A secure base: Clinical applications of attachment theory.* London: Routledge.

Burns, D. (1999). *The feeling good handbook* (2nd ed.). New York: Penguin.

Creer, T. L., Holroyd, K. A., Glasgow, R. E. & Smith, T. W. (2004). Health Psychology. In M. J. Lambert (Ed.), *Bergin and Garfield's handbook of psychotherapy and behavior change* (5th ed.), pp. 697–742. New York: Wiley.

Dawes, R. M. (1994). *House of cards*. New York: Free Press.

Elkin, I. (1994). The NIMH treatment of depression collaborative research program: Where we began and where we are. In A. E. Bergin & S. L. Garfield (Eds), *Handbook of Psychotherapy and Behavior Change* (4th ed.), pp. 114–139. New York: Wiley.

Elkin, I., Shea, M. T., Watkins, J. T., Imber, S. D., Sotsky, S. M., Collins, J. F., Glass, D. R., Pilkonis, P. A., Leber, W. R., Docherty, J. P., Fiester, S. J. & Parloff, M. B. (1989). National Institute of Mental Health Treatment of Depression Collaborative Research Program: General effectiveness of treatments. *Archives of General Psychiatry, 46*, 971–982.

Emmelkemp, P. M. G. (2004). Behaviour therapy with adults. In M. J. Lambert (Ed.), *Bergin and Garfield's handbook of psychotherapy and behavior change* (5th ed.), pp. 393–446. New York: Wiley.

Frank, J. D. (1961). *Persuasion and healing*. Baltimore, MD: Johns Hopkins University Press.

Frank, J. D. (1973). *Persuasion and healing* (revised ed.). Baltimore, MD: Johns Hopkins University Press.

Frank, J. D. (1982). What is psychotherapy? In S. Block (Ed.), *An introduction to the psychotherapies*, pp. 1–23. Oxford: Oxford University Press.

Frank, J. D. & Frank, J. B. (1993). *Persuasion and healing* (3rd ed.). Baltimore, MD: Johns Hopkins University Press.

Gaston, L. (1990). The concept of the alliance and its role in psychotherapy: Theoretical and empirical considerations. *Psychotherapy, 27*, 143–153.

Gaston, L., Piper, W. E., Debbane, E. G., Bienvenu, J. P. & Garant, J. (1994) Alliance and technique for predicting outcome in short- and long-term analytic psychotherapy. *Psychotherapy Research, 4*, 121–135.

Hollon, S. D. & Beck, A. T. (2004). Cognitive and cognitive behavioral therapies. In M. J. Lambert (Ed.), *Bergin and Garfield's handbook of psychotherapy and behavior change* (5th ed.), pp. 447–492. New York: Wiley.

Howard, K. I., Orlinsky, D. E. & Luegar, R. J. (1995). The design of clinically relevant outcome research: Some considerations and an example. In M. Aveline and D. A. Shapiro (Eds), *Research foundations for psychotherapy practice*, pp. 3–47. Chichester: Wiley.

Imber, S. D., Pilkonis, P. A., Sotsky, S. M., Elkin, I., Watkins, J. T., Collins, J. F., Shea, M. T. et al. (1990). Mode-specific effects among three treatments for depression. *Journal of Consulting and Clinical Psychology, 58*, 352–359.

Kernberg, O. F., Selzer, M. A., Koenigsberg, H. W., Carr, A. C. & Appelbaum, A. H. (1989). *Psychodynamic psychotherapy of borderline patients*. New York: Basic.

Lambert, M. J. (2004). *Bergin and Garfield's handbook of psychotherapy and behavior change* (5th ed.). New York: Wiley.

Lambert, M. J. & Ogles, B. M. (2004). The efficacy and effectiveness of psychotherapy. In M. J. Lambert (Ed.), *Bergin and Garfield's handbook of psychotherapy and behavior change* (5th ed.), pp. 139–193. New York: Wiley.

Landman, J. T. & Dawes, R. M. (1982). Psychotherapy outcome: Smith and Glass' conclusions stand up to scrutiny. *American Psychologist, 37*, 504–516.

Langs, R. (1992). *A clinical workbook for psychotherapists*. London: Karnac.

Langs, R. (1994). *Doing supervision and being supervised*. London: Karnac.

Luborsky, L., Diguer, L., Seligman, D. A., Rosenthal, R., Krause, E. D., Johnson, S., Halperin, G., Bishop, M., Berman, J. S. & Schweizer, E. (1999). The researcher's own therapy allegiances: A 'wild card' in comparisons of treatment efficacy. *Clinical Psychology: Science and Practice*, *6*, 95–106.

Luborsky, L., Singer, B. & Luborsky, L. (1975). Comparative studies of psychotherapy. *Archives of General Psychiatry*, *32*, 995–1008.

MacFarlane, M. M. (2004). *Family treatment of personality disorders: Advances in clinical practice*. Oxford: Haworth.

Martin, D. J., Garske, J. P. & Davis, M. K. (2000). Relation of the therapeutic alliance with outcome and other variables: A meta-analytic review. *Journal of Consulting and Clinical Psychology*, *68*, 438–450.

Murphy, G. E. & Guze, S. B. (1960). Setting limits: The management of the manipulative patient. *American Journal of Psychotherapy*, *14*, 30–47.

Orlinsky, D. E., Ronnestad, M. H. & Willutzki, U. (2004). Fifty years of psychotherapy process-outcome research: Continuity and change. In M. J. Lambert (Ed.), *Bergin and Garfield's handbook of psychotherapy and behavior change* (5th ed.), pp. 307–389. New York: Wiley.

Roberts, V. Z. (1994). The organization of work: Contributions from open systems theory. In A. Obholzer & V. Z. Roberts (Eds), *The unconscious at work*, pp. 28–38 London: Routledge.

Roth, A. & Fonagy, P. (1996). *What works for whom? A critical review of psychotherapy research*. New York: Guildford.

Sandler, J., Dare, C. & Holder, A. (1992). *The patient and the analyst* (revised ed.). London: Karnac.

Shapiro, D. A. (1995). Finding out how psychotherapies help people change. *Psychotherapy Research*, *5*, 1–21.

Shapiro, D. A. (2000). *Science and psychotherapy: The state of the art in 2000* (presentation to the annual meeting of Society for Psychotherapy Research, UK).

Shoham, V. & Rohrbaugh, M. J. (1999). Beyond allegiance to comparative outcome studies. *Clinical Psychology: Science and Practice*, *6*, 120–123.

Smith, M. L. & Glass, G. V. (1977). Meta-analysis of psychotherapy outcome studies. *American Psychologist*, *32*, 752–760.

Stiles, W. B., Shapiro, D. A. & Elliott, R. K. (1986). Are all psychotherapies equivalent? *American Psychologist*, *41*, 165–180.

Wampold, B. E. (2001). *The great psychotherapy debate: models, methods, and findings*. Mahwah, NJ: Erlbaum.

Winnicott, D. (1955/1992). Clinical varieties of transference. In *Through paediatrics to psychoanalysis. Collected papers*. London: Karnac.

13

The Management of Potentially Lethal Self-Harming Behaviour

MARK J. SAMPSON

GARY L. SIDLEY

INTRODUCTION

Patients who frequently engage in self-harming behaviour pose a challenge to the community mental health team (CMHT). This chapter aims to provide a model for understanding severe forms of self-harm and guidance on management. As implied in the title, the chapter focuses on self-harm that might potentially result in the patient's death. Hence, it refers to self-harming behaviours such as overdoses, severe cutting and/or suicidal expression and gestures. Self-harm that does not appear to have a risk of serious injury or death (for example, hair pulling, superficial cutting and/or head banging) is not the focus here, although it is recognised these behaviours may have similar functions.

The chapter begins by considering the function of and theory relating to self-harming behaviour. The following section then provides recommendations for short-term 'crisis' and longer-term management of potentially lethal self-harming behaviour. The final section explores the legal considerations when working with patients who frequently engage in potentially lethal self-harming behaviour.

Personality Disorder and Community Mental Health Teams: A Practitioner's Guide. Edited by M. J. Sampson, R. A. McCubbin and P. Tyrer. © 2006 John Wiley & Sons, Ltd.

THE FUNCTION OF SELF-HARM

Essentially, people self-harm because it serves a function. The function may be a desire to die (suicidal behaviour) or, alternatively, it may be seen as a way of coping.

Linehan (1993) divides self-harm into two functional categories: 'operant' (sometimes called instrumental) and 'respondent' self-harm. Operant self-harming behaviour is an act or threat that is influenced by the 'consequence' or responses in the environment. An example of this form of self-harming behaviour would be a suicidal gesture that is reinforced by services offering the patient[1] the response that she thinks she needs to help her cope (e.g. admission to hospital). Operant self-harming behaviours are sometimes referred to as 'communication', as the behaviour is trying to communicate something and elicit a response from others. In many cases of operant potentially lethal self-harming behaviour, dying is not the main driving force for the behaviour, although the patient may be ambivalent about living. This type of self-harming is driven and reinforced by the consequences of the external environment. Therefore, the CMHT's responses to this form of self-harm can potentially provide the consequence that reinforces it.

By contrast, respondent self-harm is primarily an automatic action that is driven by a specific event or intolerable internal emotional pain. The behaviour is not influenced by responses in the environment, but rather driven by a need to alleviate the intolerable feelings – for example, overdosing and/or cutting to release tension. In these incidents of self-harm the behaviour is influenced less by the consequences in the external environment and, therefore, the CMHT needs to be less concerned that their action will reinforce this type of self-harm. It is worth noting here that most acts of self-harm have varying degrees of both operant and respondent behaviour and thus have both functions simultaneously (for further discussion see Linehan, 1993).

The 'intent to die' associated with self-harm may be conceptualised as an extreme form of operant or respondent self-harm. For instance, a patient may intend to die to 'punish' another person (external intent to die), whilst for another patient suicide may be a permanent form of coping with her intense feelings of depression and despair.

It must be emphasised at the outset that self-harm can be a very effective short-term way of coping. For instance, expressing suicidal ideation is a powerful way of influencing the environment and obtaining the care and help the patient may think she needs. Overdosing on a sedative drug and cutting can be effective ways of dealing with negative feelings.

---

[1] For clarity a patient will be referred to as 'female' and a practitioner as 'male'.

THEORY RELATING TO SELF-HARM

FACTORS ASSOCIATED WITH SELF-HARMING BEHAVIOUR

Difficulties Coping with Emotion

Patients who frequently self-harm can often have difficulties managing and coping with negative emotions. These difficulties can be divided into two forms: affect modulation and affect tolerance (see Briere, 1997).

(a) *Affect modulation* refers to a patient's ability to alter her negative emotional states by internal coping methods. These are methods such as self-nurturing and/or positive self-talk, taking her mind off the painful feelings (self-distraction) and being able to put situations in perspective. A patient who has difficulties with internal modulation may find it harder to calm herself down in a stressful situation because she lacks nurturing self-talk such as 'it will be okay; I will calm down soon; this feeling will not last forever'. Alternatively, she may think in such a way as to generalise or magnify what can initially appear relatively innocuous events. Difficulties with internal modulation can lead to people experiencing more prolonged and intense distress. This may increase the need for external 'consequences' to help them cope (e.g. hospital) and therefore increases the likelihood of operant self-harming behaviour. Patients with a history of self-mutilation tend to have problems with internal modulation and rely more on external means to help them cope (Stanley, Gameroff, Michalsen & Mann, 2001).

(b) *Affect tolerance* is the patient's ability to experience and stay with negative emotions. When a patient's affect tolerance limit is reached she will need to do something to alleviate the intensity of her distress, e.g. for some patients this can be respondent self-harming behaviour.

Problem-Solving and Hopelessness

Self-harm for many patients is an 'escape from what, to them, seems like an intolerable and unsolvable life' (Linehan, 1993, p. 15). The evidence suggests that hopelessness and problem-solving abilities are key mediating factors between strong emotions and self-harm.

Hopelessness can be defined as the prediction that nothing positive will happen in the future (MacLeod, Pankhania, Lee & Mitchell, 1997). It has been associated with inflexible thinking, a lack of success in coping and an absence of credible solutions (Williams & Pollock, 2000). Hopelessness has been found to predict repetition of deliberate self-harm (see, e.g., Sidley, Calam, Wells, Hughes & Whitaker, 1999).

Difficulties with problem-solving have also been associated with self-harming behaviour. It has been consistently demonstrated that people who engage in repeated self-harm have difficulties with interpersonal problem-solving (McLeavey, Daly, Murray, O'Riordan & Taylor, 1987; Schotte & Clum, 1987). Generally, patients with a history of deliberate self-harm tend to be more 'passive' and rely more on others to help them deal with the problem (Linehan, Camper, Chiles, Strohsal & Shearin, 1987).

Axis I Disorders

Axis I disorders such as depression and/or psychosis may increase the risk of both operant and respondent self-harm and suicide. For instance, a major depressive episode may impact on a patient's ability to problem-solve as it can affect her ability to think, concentrate or make decisions. Alternatively, salient negative feelings associated with the depression (e.g. sadness) may increase a patient's affect level to a point beyond her tolerance. Psychosis may distort a patient's reality (e.g. intense paranoia) and increase her distress to an intolerable level.

Biological Factors

Impulsivity is the most scientifically robust personality variable associated with recurrent self-harming (see Williams & Pollock, 2000). It has been suggested that this personality variable is mediated by the serotonergic system and that part of the genetic risk of suicidal behaviour is associated with this system (Träskman-Bendz & Mann, 2000). This in turn suggests that treatments affecting the serotonergic system may be helpful in the management of self-harming behaviour.

An understanding of the genetic and biological mediators for self-harming behaviour is helpful as it provides practitioners with a rationale for using pharmacological treatments for self-harming behaviour. Pharmacotherapy and personality disorder is discussed further in Chapter 7.

Early Experiences

The patient's childhood experiences also appear to be associated with self-harming behaviour. It is not uncommon for patients who have a history of self-harm to report having had difficult childhoods, with many having been subjected to some form of physical, psychological (including neglect) or sexual abuse

(Zanarini et al., 1997). The impact childhood adversity has on a patient's ability to manage emotions could help explain why patients with difficult childhoods are more likely to engage in self-harm. For example, emotions associated with memories of childhood trauma may be so strong that they become too much for the patient to tolerate. The following section illustrates how early experiences can influence self-harming behaviour in more indirect ways.

USING THERAPY MODELS TO UNDERSTAND SELF-HARMING BEHAVIOUR

Therapy models can provide a framework for understanding the reasons why patients self-harm. The examples below are drawn from cognitive analytic therapy and cognitive therapy (see Chapters 4 and 5 for a more detailed review of these psychological theories and therapies).

For instance, cognitive analytic therapy (CAT) uses object relations theory to explain how a patient's early childhood could make it more difficult for her to internally modulate strong emotions. It may, for example, be because she did not have many experiences of people being kind and loving to her in her childhood. Because of this she has had fewer positive experiences of being cared for to internalise and use for herself. She may therefore find nurturing or positive self-talk more difficult. Alternatively, if the patient experienced significant abuse and punishment in her childhood, a CAT explanation might suggest that her self-harm could be a form of 'self to self' or 'self to other' punishment that is a re-enactment of the punishing and abusing experiences she received as a child. It should be noted that care should be used when inferring that self-harm is a 'complete enactment' of an abusing relationship, as this is a powerful insight which may be too overwhelming for the patient (see Pollock, 2001).

From a cognitive perspective, a patient may have difficulty dealing with emotions because of beliefs and assumptions that make it more difficult to use effective coping strategies such as nurturing and/or positive self-talk. For example, she might hold beliefs such as 'I am a bad and jinxed person who deserves to suffer'. Alternatively, a patient who has repeatedly been abused and also told that it was her fault that this happened could develop self-blaming assumptions such as 'If something bad happens to me it is my fault'. This would make it harder for her to keep events in perspective, as she will have a tendency to personalise or generalise negative events. For instance, if a male colleague touches her inappropriately, she may blame herself for this by thinking 'I elicited it'. This could then activate the unresolved trauma from her childhood and make the emotions unmanageable for her.

Explanatory models such as those described above can also provide a framework for understanding why some patients who self-harm have difficulty asking for help. From a cognitive perspective, Beck, Freeman and Associates (1990) suggest that many patients with borderline personality disorder have had childhood experiences that lead them to learn that they are weak, powerless and helpless in what they believe to be a hostile world. Thus, on the one hand, the patient may feel that they need others for help, but on the other feel it is too dangerous to ask for help. This can make it more difficult for them to seek care through verbal expressions and, therefore, may increase the likelihood of operant self-harming behaviour.

SELF-HARM AND SUICIDE

Quantifying the risk of suicide in patients with a history of self-harm is complex. As a group, patients with a history of self-harm are at a greater risk of suicide than most other clinical groups (Isometsä & Lönnqvist, 1998). When the patient also meets the diagnostic criteria for a personality disorder then the risk is even higher (Linehan, Rizvi, Welch & Page, 2000). However, the risk of dying from a suicide attempt can be smaller in patients with a history of previous attempts. For example, a study of suicides in Finland indicated that 38 per cent of women died in their first attempt, 26 per cent in their second and 15 per cent died in a suicide attempt if they had tried twice before (see Isometsä & Lönnqvist, 1998). Therefore, the risk of a *completed* suicide during a suicide attempt becomes progressively smaller with the increasing number of previous attempts. Consequently, any attempt to quantify risk of suicide during a crisis requires the CMHT to have an accurate assessment of suicidal intent and a detailed understanding (formulation) of the patient and her self-harming behaviour.

SELF-HARM AND PERSONALITY DISORDER

Many of the suggestions for the treatment and management of recurrent self-harm are drawn from the literature on borderline personality disorder (BPD). In the literature, self-harm and BPD can appear intertwined. Although not one and the same, they are closely related. A significant reason for their close relationship is, in part, to do with the diagnostic criteria of BPD. One of the diagnostic criteria required to make a diagnosis of BPD in DSM-IV is the 'recurrent suicidal behaviour, gestures, or threats, or self-mutilating behaviour' (American Psychiatric Association, 1994, p. 654). Although this chapter will be drawing heavily on the literature relating to BPD, it is important to note that many patients who engage in potentially lethal self-harming behaviour will not have BPD and the interventions suggested in the following section are aimed at managing self-harm in any patient who has complex personality difficulties, not just BPD.

SUMMARY

The reasons why somebody self-harms are complex. The points below provide a brief summary of the main factors associated with such behaviour.

- Self-harm can be seen as operant and/or respondent behaviour. Intent to die can be seen as an extreme form of either.
- There are many mediating factors for self-harm behaviour. These include the patient's ability to modulate and tolerate emotions, difficulties in problem-solving, hopelessness, whether the patient has a clinical disorder (e.g. depression), the patient's biological make-up and her past experiences.
- Therapy models are useful as they can provide the CMHT with an explanatory framework for drawing together the factors that contribute to and maintain self-harming behaviour.
- Self-harm is complex and fluid and care should be taken to avoid being drawn into assuming the self-harm is all operant or respondent.

RECOMMENDATIONS FOR THE MANAGEMENT OF POTENTIALLY FATAL SELF-HARMING BEHAVIOUR

CRISIS MANAGEMENT STRATEGIES

Assessment

The crisis management of patients who engage in potentially lethal self-harming behaviour has two simple aims: the first is to act in a way that reduces the immediate risk of suicide, and the second is to minimise the likelihood of it happening again (Linehan, 1993).

Patients engaging in self-harm who meet the criteria for a diagnosis of personality disorder frequently present to services in crisis, and practitioners have to make quick decisions about risk and how to manage this. Therefore, the first job for the assessing practitioner is to establish the patient's current intent to die, and hence risk of completing suicide. Here, we will assume that practitioners know how to carry out a standard risk assessment (e.g. paying attention to factors such as suicidal ideation, intention, access to means, lethality of method described, protective factors etc.) and recommend that they follow their employer's guidelines.

If the patient has already self-harmed, the practitioner needs to establish the level of the suicide intent. Rudd, Joiner and Rajab (2001, p. 173) suggest that the distinguishing features for intent are the following.

- Whether the patient thought the method of self-harm was lethal.
- Whether the patient took steps to prevent recovery.
- How was the patient discovered?
- How did the patient feel about surviving?
- If the intention was not death, what did the patient hope to accomplish?

An analysis of the suicidal presentation and whether the patient actively informed others or took herself to her GP or the accident and emergency department can also give the practitioner clues to the intent. Even if the patient has a long history of self-harm, the main function of which has been to influence the environment, the practitioner should always assess for intent to die.

During these early interactions, many crisis interventions such as offering support or admission risk reinforcing a function of the self-harm. This is inevitable and at times may be necessary to enable a more thorough assessment to occur. The approach we advocate with respect to early interactions is that the CMHT may need to err on the side of caution, until there is a clearer understanding of the reasons for the self-harming behaviour. The key point is that the CMHT practitioner should be *aware* that he is potentially reinforcing (or colluding with) the patient's dysfunctional patterns.

The second function of an assessment is to establish the function of the suicidal threat or self-harm. An accurate assessment will highlight the operant and respondent functions of the self-harming behaviour. Failure to consider either of these functions of the self-harming behaviour could lead to ineffective management. For instance, assuming the self-harming behaviour is 'all operant behaviour' may lead the CMHT to withhold appropriate treatments for the respondent function (e.g. antidepressant medication for clinical depression or skills training to enhance affect modulation).

In reality, it can take several presentations before a comprehensive understanding of the patient's self-harm and personality disorder is developed. Challenges for the CMHT include how to avoid being drawn into developing care plans too early, and working with patients without a clear goal. Not having a clear focus can increase the likelihood that the input from the CMHT is not going to be therapeutic, or may even contribute to the maintenance of the potentially fatal self-harming behaviour. A solution to this is to agree short-term assessment contracts that support the patient during a crisis, while a more thorough assessment can be carried out. If the patient is in extreme crisis hospital admission may be required for a more detailed assessment (see the section on hospitalisation for further discussion of admission procedures).

Assessment and crisis management in patients with a history of self-harming behaviour go hand in hand. In a sense, the first presentation is a balance between assessing risk, assessing the function of the behaviour and crisis management.

Emotional Validation

During a crisis presentation it can be helpful if the practitioner spends a significant amount of the session validating the patient's distress. This is something that many patients with personality disorders value highly and can enhance the treatment alliance (see Chapter 8 for further discussion). Allowing the patient to talk, and using responses such as 'from what you have been saying it sounds like you have been finding it really hard to cope recently', integrated with summary statements such as 'so you have had trouble with your partner over the past few weeks and last night he told you he was leaving', can be helpful with this. If the patient feels validated and understood, this can in itself be a very effective intervention, reducing the intensity of negative emotions and therefore the risk of potentially lethal self-harm. The initial aim is to help the patient feel that you understand how she is feeling and are taking her needs seriously (see Linehan, 1993; Livesley, 2003). This can be particularly valuable for patients who find it difficult to internally modulate their emotions (e.g. self nurturing/positive self-talk). In a sense they may feel they 'need' others to provide the care and/or reassurance that everything will be okay. An aim for any longer-term management would be to enhance skills in internal modulation.

Sometimes, during a crisis, the patient may be experiencing images and emotions associated with unresolved traumas, for example childhood sexual abuse. In these situations the practitioner needs to validate the patient's distress and offer reassurance if the patient is worried about the symptoms. However, further exploration may not be appropriate at this time, as it is likely to be too overwhelming or exposing for the patient. The appropriate help for such difficulties would involve longer-term therapy, in which the therapist would need to build the patient's sense of 'self' and 'identity' before they started to work on the trauma (this is based on the 'self before trauma model' of treatment; see Briere, 1997).

Problem-Solving

Problem-solving can be difficult in crisis situations. As previously discussed, the literature suggests that patients who repeatedly self-harm have difficulties with problem-solving. However, if the practitioner is too 'solution focused' the patient can feel misunderstood with respect to how difficult things are for them (thus not validating their needs). Being too solution focused may also consolidate the patient's reliance on external means (services in this case) to help her cope. Then again, validation alone may not be enough to support the patient during a crisis. Therefore, it may be necessary for the practitioner to initially act in ways that may reinforce the patient's ways of coping and at these times the practitioner may need to be more proactive during a crisis. This might involve taking an active role in helping the patient to problem-solve. The longer-term aim would be to establish a collaboratively agreed care plan that aims to increase the patient's ability to problem-solve.

The sheer number of problems patients present with can also provide a challenge, as they can often present with an overwhelming array of difficulties, past and present. It is recommended that the practitioner focus on the patient's current problems rather than being drawn into all the negative events that the patient has experienced in her life (Linehan, 1993).

Generating Hope

Most practitioners will be aware of the need to generate hope in patients with severe depression who are suicidal. In patients expressing suicidal ideation and engaging in potentially lethal self-harm, it is common to have intense feelings of hopelessness, particularly during times of crisis. It is not unusual for the mental health practitioner to also feel hopeless and at times to think that suicide might indeed be a viable solution. It is strongly recommended that the practitioner should resist this and instead consistently convey the message that suicide is not a good solution (Linehan, 1993). Initially, the practitioner may have to be very active in helping the patient feel hope, whilst being aware of the longer-term implications regarding dependency if the practitioner continues to be too active.

If the Patient Has Already Overdosed

If, during an assessment or any other appointment, the patient reports that she has recently harmed herself, medical action needs to be prioritised. In cases of overdoses it is recommended that the appointment be terminated and the patient immediately transferred to the accident and emergency department or her general practitioner (if seeing the patient in the general practitioner's practice). The message that the practitioner wants to convey to the patient is that all overdoses are potentially fatal and that there are no safe limits (this stance is recommended in the NICE guidelines for self-harm,

2004). This message may be more pertinent for patients who have a history of self-harm as they 'underestimate the lethality of their suicidal behaviour, believe they will be rescued after the attempt, and view death less finally' than patients who do not have a history of self-harm (Stanley et al., 2001, p. 430). This approach should be standard practice unless the assessment of the self-harming behaviour suggests that such a course of action would maintain the patient's high risk self-harming behaviour.

Hospitalisation

There is divided opinion as to whether hospitalisation has any value in managing potentially lethal self-harming behaviour in patients with BPD (see Paris, 2004). Although there are reservations about the effectiveness of hospital admissions, we support the position of Bateman and Tyrer (2004), who state that it would be clinically wrong to *ban* certain patients from inpatient admissions on the basis of their diagnosis or behaviour alone. To aid practitioners, Bateman and Tyrer (2004) have come up with a set of recommendations for when admissions *should* be considered:

- If there is uncertainty about risk and the patient needs a full risk assessment.
- If there is a significant escalating risk of suicide or harm to others.
- High levels of a clinical disorder such as severe depression or psychosis.
- To review medication.
- If there has been a breakdown in a significant therapeutic alliance.

If hospitalisation is required, Bateman and Tyrer (2004) also provide some guidance on management of admissions and suggest that it can be helpful if

- there is a predetermined admission and discharge date that is agreed with the patient
- the admission is informal
- the admission has a specific goal/s and is time limited.

The process of admission should, like all other treatments, be as collaborative as possible and the patient encouraged to take as much responsibility as possible for decisions. During admission it is also worth further assessing the function of the self-harm and discuss with the patient ways of managing strong emotions on the ward. A treatment plan can then be devised to help the patient manage strong emotions whilst she is in hospital. If this is not addressed, there could be a danger the patient is denied access to a very powerful way of modulating her emotions, and without this she may be driven to consider more lethal methods.

THE LONGER TERM MANAGEMENT OF POTENTIALLY LETHAL SELF-HARMING BEHAVIOUR IN PATIENTS WITH A PERSONALITY DISORDER

It can be helpful in the longer term management of patients with recurrent self-harm if the CMHT's interactions with the patient keep to a consistent strategy. This should always be formulation driven – however, it will generally involve helping to increase patients' ability to internally modulate their emotions and increase their tolerance of negative emotional states. The suggestions below aim to help the CMHT achieve these goals.

Formulation

Any effective intervention needs a thorough assessment and formulation or 'map' of the factors maintaining the patient's self-harming behaviour. Without this, the CMHT will not be aware of the factors contributing to the patient's problems and there will be no consistency in treatment. Table 13.1 contains a fictitious example of an integrative formulation of a patient who meets the criteria for having a personality disorder and has a history of self-harming behaviour.

Responsibility

Many of the ideas for the management of patients who engage in potentially lethal self-harming behaviour and who meet the diagnosis of a personality disorder are more to do with emphasis rather than anything radically new, when compared with risk management of patients with other disorders. Responsibility is an excellent example of this. It is recommended that, whenever possible, the practitioner treats the patient as a 'competent adult' and thus, unless their mental health indicates otherwise, encourages the patient to take as much responsibility as possible (including responsibility for their self-harming behaviour). As described by Krawitz and Watson (2003, p. 97), 'the clinician is responsible for carrying out clinical practice at a reasonable standard of care, however, ultimately the client is responsible for their behaviour'.

The CMHT should only take responsibility for the patient's behaviour if there is a significant Axis I clinical disorder present. Encouraging the patient to take responsibility can make it easier to avoid making clinical decisions

Table 13.1 Illustration of an integrative case formulation

Patient meets criteria for
borderline and dependent personality disorders.

Factors contributing to the personality disorders are
Significant emotional and sexual abuse. Consequently X learned that she is bad, weak and vulnerable, that people are potentially evil and that the world can be dangerous.

Difficulties with managing emotions
X copes by relying too heavily on other people, uses distraction and alcohol to cope with negative emotion and avoids putting herself in any situation where she could receive negative criticism. She has particular difficulties associated with internal modulation of emotion and relies on external help to work through a problem and put situations into perspective.

What things to consider when working with the patient
X has a tendency to see professionals as strong figures and can expect them to solve her problems for her. X may have significant fear of losing this support and can act in ways to maintain the input. X has a strong need to be cared for, which causes her to become clingy and demanding if clear boundaries are not maintained.

Dynamics to be aware of
Staff may be drawn into offering intensive support that is counter-productive for X's long-term care. For instance, X may look to elicit a special relationship with a professional to help her cope. It is also important to be aware of over-reacting and thus being cold and rejecting through a fear of X becoming dependent. There is also a danger that X could elicit controlling responses in others.

Service considerations
As X feels powerless at times and that the world is a dangerous place she can find it more difficult to ask for help. At times suicidal ideation and behaviour can be a way of influencing the environment to elicit the care that she thinks she needs.

that are in the long term unhelpful, e.g. reinforcing an operant function of the self-harming behaviour. It is also helpful if the whole CMHT discusses and agrees on the patient's care plan, particularly regarding issues of risk. In patients who frequently engage in serious self-harming behaviour, case presentations and frequent team discussion can help practitioners working with the patient to feel less burdened and reduce the risk of them acting in ways that may not be helpful to the patient.

Collaboration

The 'competent adult' approach also encourages the practitioner to work more collaboratively with the patient. Being collaborative with the patient can encourage them to take more responsibility in their care. It can help reduce the communication function of the self-harming behaviour, as it encourages patients to express their needs verbally. True collaboration can also help with developing a therapeutic relationship and reduces the risk of the CMHT being too controlling or disempowering.

Establishing Contact With Services That Is Therapeutic

A key therapeutic task for any practitioner working with a patient who has a history of potentially lethal self-harming behaviour and meets the criteria for a personality disorder is to establish a relationship with the patient that is therapeutic and does not maintain the self-harming behaviour. To do this, the practitioner may need to be clearer in his own mind as to what is the purpose and 'shape' of his relationship with the patient, as compared with work with patients who have Axis I disorders alone. The aims, structure and shape of the relationship can be referred to as the 'treatment frame' (discussed in detail in Chapter 12).

How explicit and structured the practitioner needs to be about the treatment frame will depend on the reasons for the self-harming behaviour and the practitioner's role. For instance, if the patient's self-harming behaviour is primarily operantly reinforced and associated with a 'need' for special care or intensive input that would be overburdening to services, then it may be necessary for a practitioner to explicitly discuss the limitations of what he can offer and to be clear about the boundaries and structure of their relationship (treatment frame), e.g. a very clear time, place, frequency of contact, length of and duration of appointments. It is important to emphasise that this does not mean that the patient should be excluded from accessing other services. The danger can be that patients with these types of problem draw services into providing the patient with restrictive withholding care – for example, being excluded from 24 hour on-call services. A care plan that is too withholding may increase the pressure for more lethal operant self-harming behaviour.

Patients with these types of problem should have access to the same services as other patients (to be neither 'special' or 'withholding'). The difference can be that services need to work with the patient to help them use the service more effectively. For example, if the way a patient is using the on-call service is reducing their ability to cope with emotions, by reducing their tolerance and increasing the likelihood of the self-harming behaviour happening again, then an intervention plan can be devised with the patient to address this. This could involve encouraging a patient to use the on-call service *prior* to self-harm. Supporting her through the crisis may help increase her tolerance of negative emotional states and break the association between strong emotions and self-harm. The CMHT can then devise a treatment plan to gradually reduce the patient's reliance on external means to help her cope.

Working with a patient to establish the ground rules and function of the relationship can be extremely helpful in the management of recurrent self-harm behaviour, as it often highlights the first potential area of conflict. For instance, the practitioner and the patient may have very different expectations of what each other wants from the interaction. The patient may want care and support, whilst the practitioner wants to stop the high-risk self-harming behaviour and the frequent admissions to hospital.

Practitioners and services frequently need to work harder to maintain the treatment frame for patients with certain personality disorders, e.g. Cluster B and dependent personality disorders. In particular, the practitioner will need to increase his awareness of relationship issues so he can notice when frame violations (e.g. seeking a special relationship) occur and address them as empathically as possible. Responses such as 'I get a sense that you want me to do more for you than I am doing at the moment' (addressing the pressure on the treatment frame); 'As we discussed earlier the aim of my input is to help you learn to cope with situations' (clarifying the frame); 'I am concerned that if I give you a lift to your outpatients appointment I may not be helping you meet our agreed goals'; 'As I take your needs seriously, I need to remain focused on what we are trying to achieve' can be helpful. In these examples, the practitioner is maintaining the focus of his relationship with the patient in an empathic, caring way.

It can be particularly difficult to manage boundaries in a caring way at times of crisis. Appropriate supervision can be helpful in preventing the practitioner from acting in ways that could feel very withholding, punishing and/or rejecting to the patient. It is, however, also important to highlight the need for commonsense. Therefore, although the aim is to offer consistent care with clear boundaries, there may be times when the practitioner may need to be more flexible in his boundaries to reduce the immediate risk of suicide.

Once an appropriate treatment frame is established and maintained, this may be enough for the patient's self-harming behaviour to be contained. This can then be a secure base from which the patient can explore and use help offered by other practitioners and services, e.g. help with vocational placements, assertiveness training, problem-solving or participation in a more formalised therapy. However, for some patients their difficulties are so entrenched (e.g. associated with intense feelings of loneliness and fear of abandonment) that they are unable to 'move on'. In this case, the practitioner can offer a containing role that looks to increase the time between appointments to as long as possible, if this is in line with the treatment aims.

Managing Potentially Lethal Self-Harming Behaviour That Is Driven by a Need to Influence Services' Input

As discussed previously, some patients with recurrent self-harming behaviour and a personality disorder can have difficulties establishing and maintaining boundaries. At times, their 'needs' can cause them to attempt to elicit more and more input from services. Potentially lethal self-harming behaviour and expression is often a very effective method of eliciting the response the patient thinks she needs.

When managing potentially lethal self-harming behaviour, the aim is to have an intervention that is as caring and supportive as possible, without reinforcing the dysfunctional component of the self-harming behaviour, while enhancing the patient's ability to independently modulate and tolerate affect. For example, if the main function of the self-harming behaviour is to elicit the help the patient thinks she needs from the practitioner, then the practitioner needs to establish and keep tight boundaries. During times of suicidal ideation and gestures it can be very difficult to keep these boundaries. One solution is to offer the patient alternative support (that is not as reinforcing for self-harming behaviour) – for example, offering support from a colleague or even respite or a brief admission. The key point is that the practitioner is remaining consistent with his agreed treatment frame.

Sometimes, a function of a patient's behaviour is to influence the environment to elicit an admission to hospital, as this is the help she believes she needs. As discussed earlier, it may be important to develop an intervention to break this cycle of high risk self-harming behaviour and repeated hospital admissions. Interventions for this scenario, as with any other, should be based on the individual understanding (formulation) of the patient's behaviour. For instance, if a function of the self-harming behaviour is admission to hospital and the care plan suggests that this is unhelpful (e.g. reinforcing her belief that she is weak and vulnerable), then a management plan that has a graded reduction in the intensity of input required to help the patient manage without hospitalisation could be helpful. In this case, the practitioner may need to offer *more* input (in the short term) in order to avoid admissions. The long term treatment plan would involve having a graded reduction in the intensity of support that is offered during a crisis. This is considered more beneficial than the 'cold turkey' approach that is sometimes suggested (i.e. not admitting the patient and leaving her to cope on her own), as this will probably only reinforce feelings of worthlessness, abandonment, powerlessness or hopelessness.

Another strategy that has some evidence of effectiveness in terms of reducing hospitalisation is having 'patient controlled admissions'. This is when patients themselves decide whether they need to be admitted, usually for a maximum of 72 hours (see Nehls, 1994). This strategy can help reduce the operant function of self-harm behaviour, as the admission is not dependent on this behaviour. It can also help the patient to take more responsibility for her care (empowerment). If this is not possible or practical, then alternatives such as respite care can have a similar function.

The Role of the Care Co-Ordinator in the CMHT

The care co-ordinator will be the key practitioner for the management and treatment of patients who frequently engage in potentially lethal self-harm behaviour. There are several key tasks that the care co-ordinator will need to undertake. Table 13.2 provides a list of questions that can be useful to keep in

Table 13.2 Questions to consider when developing the care plan

Do I know

- What was the trigger for this recent presentation?
- What leads the patient to cope in this way?
- What are the functions of the potentially lethal self-harming behaviour (intent to die/respondent/operant)?
- What is the sequence of the self-harming behaviour e.g. triggers, feelings, aim of self-harm, short term consequence and long term consequence of self-harm?
- Does the patient have an Axis I disorder (e.g. depression)?
- What impact is the patient's personality going to have on how she interacts with me?
- What impact has the patient's personality on how she uses services?
- What impact are services having on the patient's self-harming behaviour?
- What are the treatment aims, e.g. improving poor affect modulation/problem-solving?
- Am I and the patient working towards the same goals?
- Does the patient want to or feel able to reduce their self-harming behaviour?
- Have I discussed the focus of treatment, ground rules, boundaries of our input with the patient (treatment frame)?
- Am I adhering to the treatment frame, maintaining consistency and making sure I am not being drawn into an unhealthy relationship (e.g. special, controlling, punishing)?
- Is the care plan improving how the patient copes with emotions?
- Am I getting adequate supervision?
- Am I implementing the 'core' strategies in risk management, e.g. crisis plan, appropriate care-plan, assessed intent to die?
- Am I confident in my documentation?

mind when trying to assess, formulate and provide a care plan for a patient with enduring self-harming behaviour.

It can be helpful if the care co-ordinator also does the following.

- Clarifies with the patient what each person is responsible for. This should involve a discussion on responsibilities (ground rules) for risk management.
- Works with the patient, helping her to develop a way of communicating the severity of her distress. An example of this would be to develop a scale that can be used to indicate to services the severity of her problems. This could be a number scale (e.g. 0–10) or a coded system such as 'amber' 'I am not feeling great', 'red' indicating 'I need help' to 'black' 'I am actively suicidal' (this can help the patient communicate her distress more effectively whilst also increasing her awareness of the variations in symptoms rather than seeing a crisis in all-or-nothing terms).
- Plans with the patient what to do if there is a therapeutic breakdown between the practitioner and the patient.
- Works with the patient, helping her to verbalise how she wants services to respond during times of crisis. This can help to identify unrealistic expectations and provides an opportunity to address these.
- Explains the structure and boundaries of the service. This can include working with the patient, explaining referral pathways and reasons for exclusion criteria, for instance indicating that a respite service does not take patients who are suicidal (this can actually be helpful if a function of self-harming behaviour is to elicit care).
- Develops a crisis care plan. The crisis care plan should be individualised to the patient's needs.
- Works with the rest of the CMHT to establish a caring and consistent long-term care plan. This should include clarifying management pathways so that these are clear and predictable.

The care co-ordinator can only offer effective treatment if he is supported by the CMHT. Effective management can only occur if the CMHT is functioning well as a team.

LEGAL CONSIDERATIONS

The overwhelming feelings and confusion associated with working with somebody who is frequently overdosing and saying that she is going to kill herself can lead to mistakes in risk management. For example, practitioners may avoid performing a risk assessment because they are being drawn into colluding with the patient's feelings of being weak and fragile, and fear making her worse by asking upsetting questions. Alternatively, they may be concerned that if they do ask the patient a question about suicidal intent they will be forced to respond in a way that may be unhelpful (e.g. admission to hospital). At other times, the practitioner may not document when a patient reports she is going to kill herself because it happens so frequently and he does not want to get into trouble if the patient does kill herself. Although the relationship between suicide and the law is complex, the legal environment does acknowledge the complexity of self-harm and suicide (see Gutheil, 2004; Leenaars et al., 2000).

Krawitz and Watson (2003) note that a medico-legal investigation into a suicide would use three questions to see whether there had been any malpractice. These three questions are the following: Was there a foreseeable risk? Was there a reasonable response? Was there a reasonable standard of practice?

Was There a Foreseeable Risk?

If a practitioner does not assess for and document risk it will not only be unhelpful for the patient, but it will also be difficult for a practitioner to defend himself in court. Without a risk assessment how could he determine the nature of the risk? The practitioner has a fundamental responsibility to assess for risk and document risk. However, assessing for risk and identifying risk does not mean that the practitioner needs to act in ways that may be unhelpful for the patient. The question is whether the practitioner made a 'reasonable response'.

Was There a Reasonable Response?

A 'reasonable response' will depend on the nature of the patient's self-harming behaviour. Krawitz and Watson (2003) suggest that for patients with recurrent potentially lethal self-harming behaviour a reasonable response may require an intervention that can initially appear counter-intuitive. This could be the CMHT taking the decision not to admit a patient who is expressing active suicidal ideation, or discharging somebody from hospital who is still self-harming. The important point here is that the reasons behind the decision are documented clearly (e.g. cost/benefit analysis). If an appropriate assessment of the patient's self-harming behaviour and suicidal intent is performed and the intervention is based in a *caring therapeutic* care plan, then it is defensible from a legal point of view to take calculated risks in the treatment plan (see Krawitz and Watson, 2003).

With respect to clinical risk-taking, it can also be helpful to assess for and document whether the patient can make informed decisions. The treatment of BPD and most personality disorders encourages the patient to take responsibility for their actions (see Krawitz & Watson, 2003; Livesley, 2003;). However, there may be times when they may not be able to make informed decisions because of the nature of clinical symptoms, for example, a severe clinical depression or psychosis. As a result, it can be helpful for the practitioner to assess and document evidence that the patient has the ability to weigh up the risk and benefits of their actions.

Was There a Reasonable Standard of Practice?

Maintaining a reasonable standard of practice can be difficult in patients who frequently self-harm and who have a personality disorder. Therefore, it is recommended that any practitioner working with patients with these problems obtain appropriate supervision. This can give the practitioner greater confidence that he is offering a 'reasonable standard of practice'. CMHTs are in a good position to work with patients with these types of problem because of the support and expertise they can provide to each other.

CONCLUSIONS

This chapter has attempted to provide some ideas for CMHT practitioners to consider when working with patients who frequently engage in self-harming behaviour and who also meet the diagnosis of a personality disorder. Most of the ideas have been drawn from therapies and specialist service models aimed at the treatment of recurrent self-harming behaviour and BPD. If CMHTs are staffed and trained appropriately and offered suitable supervision, then they are in a good position to be able to help patients with these types of problem.

REFERENCES

American Psychiatric Association. (1994). *Diagnostic and statistical manual of mental disorders* (4th ed.). Washington, DC: Author.

Bateman, A. W. & Tyrer, P. (2004). Services for personality disorder: Organisation for inclusion. *Advances in Psychiatric Treatment, 10*, 425–433.

Beck, A. T., Freeman, A. & Associates. (1990). *Cognitive therapy of personality disorders.* London: Guilford.

Briere, J. (1997). Treating adults severely abused as children. The self–trauma model. In D. A. Wolfe, R. J. McMahon & R. D. Peters (Eds), *Child abuse: New directions in prevention and treatment across the lifespan* (pp. 177–204). London: Sage.

Gutheil, T. G. (2004). Suicide, suicide litigation, and borderline personality disorder. *Journal of Personality Disorders, 18,* 248–256.

Isometsä, E. T. & Lönnqvist, J. K. (1998) Suicide attempts preceding completed suicide. *British Journal of Psychiatry, 173,* 531–535.

Krawitz, R. & Watson, C. (2003). *Borderline personality disorder: A practical guide to treatment.* Oxford: Oxford University Press.

Leenaars, A., Cantor, C. H., Connolly, J., EchoHawk, M., Gailiene, D. et al. (2000). Ethical and legal issues. In K. Hawton and K. van Heeringen (Eds), *The international handbook of suicide and attempted suicide* (pp. 421–435). Chichester: Wiley.

Linehan, M. M. (1993). *Cognitive–behavioural treatment of borderline personality disorder.* London: Guilford.

Linehan, M. M., Camper, P., Chiles, J. A., Strosahl, K. & Shearin, E. (1987). Inter-personal problem solving and parasuicide. *Cognitive Therapy and Research, 11,* 1–12.

Linehan, M. M., Rizvi, S. L., Welch, S. S. & Page, B. (2000) Psychiatric aspects of suicidal behaviour: personality disorders. In K. Hawton and K. van Heeringen (Eds), *The International handbook of suicide and attempted suicide* (pp. 147–178). Chichester: Wiley.

Livesley, J. W. (2003). *Practical management of personality disorder.* London: Guilford.

MacLeod, A. K., Pankhania, B., Lee, M. & Mitchell, D. (1997). Parasuicide, depression and the anticipation of positive and negative future experiences. *Psychological Medicine, 27,* 973–977.

McLeavey, B. C., Daly, R. J., Murray, C. M., O'Riordan, J. & Taylor, M. (1987). Interpersonal problem-solving deficits in self-poisoning patients. *Suicide and Life-Threatening Behaviour, 17,* 33–49.

National Institute for Clinical Excellence (NICE). (2004). *Self-Harm: the short-term physical and psychological management and secondary prevention of self-harm in primary and secondary care.* London: NICE.

Nehls, N. (1994). Brief hospital treatment plans: innovations in practice and research. *Issues in Mental Health Nursing, 15,* 1–15.

Paris, J. (2004). Is hospitalization useful for suicidal patients with borderline personality disorder? *Journal of Personality Disorders, 18,* 240–247.

Pollock, P. H. (2001). *Cognitive analytic therapy for adult survivors of childhood abuse.* Chichester: Wiley.

Rudd, M. D., Joiner, T. & Rajab, M. H. (2001). *Treating suicidal behavior. An effective, time-limited approach.* London: Guilford.

Schotte, D. E. & Clum, G. A. (1987). Problem-solving skills in suicidal psychiatric patients. *Journal of Consulting and Clinical Psychology, 55,* 49–54.

Sidley, G. L., Calam, R., Wells, A., Hughes, T. & Whitaker, K. (1999). The prediction of parasuicide repetition in a high-risk group. *British Journal of Clinical Psychology, 38,* 375–386.

Stanley, B., Gameroff, M. J., Michalsen, V. & Mann, J. J. (2001). Are suicide attempters who self-mutilate a unique population? *American Journal of Psychiatry. 158,* 427–432.

Träskman-Bendz, L. & Mann, J. J. (2000). Biological aspects of suicidal behaviour. In K. Hawton and K. Heeringen (Eds), *The International handbook of suicide and attempted suicide* (pp. 65–78). Chichester: Wiley.

Williams, J. M. G. & Pollock, L. R. (2000). The psychology of suicidal behaviour. In K. Hawton and K. van Heeringen (Eds), *The International handbook of suicide and attempted suicide* (pp. 79–94). Chichester: Wiley.

Zanarini, M. C., Williams, A. A., Lewis, R. E., Reich R. B., Vera, S. L., Marino, M. F., Levin, A., Yong, L. & Frankenburg, F. R. (1997). Reported pathological childhood experiences associated with the development of borderline personality disorder. *American Journal of Psychiatry*, *154*, 1101–1106.

14

Community Mental Health Teams and the Assessment of Personality Functioning

LARA BENNETT

INTRODUCTION

'Clinical assessment' is the process by which essential information about the nature of an individual's difficulties is made available to the treating system. The information obtained through assessment can include details of the patients' problems, the length of time they have been experiencing these difficulties, variation in the severity of the difficulties over time and the efficacy of previous treatments. Such information helps facilitate the provision of the most effective treatment, aimed at helping the person re-establish an optimal level of functioning.

Personality difficulties are often not recognised by practitioners; partly due to lack of awareness and understanding on the part of the practitioner, but also because other psychiatric difficulties may obscure the presence of a personality disorder and appear to be the main presenting problem (Bateman & Tyrer, 2004). Consideration of the presence of a personality disorder may only occur once several treatment options have been attempted. This is unfortunate, as 'failed' treatments can further exacerbate the patient's distress and frustration with services.

In 2003, the Department of Health in conjunction with the National Institute for Mental Health in England (NIMHE, 2003) produced a document entitled *Personality Disorder: No Longer a Diagnosis of Exclusion.*

Personality Disorder and Community Mental Health Teams: A Practitioner's Guide. Edited by M. J. Sampson, R. A. McCubbin and P. Tyrer. © 2006 John Wiley & Sons, Ltd.

This document provides details of the government's plan for mental health services (both general and forensic), regarding the provision of services for people with a diagnosis of personality disorder. Prevalence rates for personality disorder of between 36 and 67 per cent in psychiatric settings are quoted, with many sufferers presenting with other co-morbid diagnoses such as anxiety, substance misuse, eating disorders and psychotic symptoms. The document was issued alongside consideration of the proposed changes in mental health law, and emphasises the importance of practitioners having skills in identifying and assessing personality disorder, in order to appropriately treat a person's difficulties. Assessment conducted in line with the principles of the Care Programme Approach (CPA; Department of Health, 1999) is advocated, with an emphasis placed on the following areas, which are likely to be triggers for referral to specialist services.

   i. The risk of harm to self and others.
  ii. The presence of other mental health difficulties and substance misuse problems and the severity of these.
 iii. The complexity of the person's personality difficulties.
  iv. The level of burden and/or distress placed on family members and other agencies.

Until now, people with personality difficulties have often been excluded from mental health services, sometimes due to beliefs that they are 'untreatable' or not a legitimate client group, due to their being viewed as 'manipulative', 'attention seeking' or 'undeserving'. It is clear, however, that in light of the recent NIMHE document people with personality disorders are increasingly becoming part of the core client group that community mental health teams (CMHTs) will be treating.

This chapter is designed to offer advice and guidance on the initial assessment of people with a possible diagnosis of personality disorder, beginning with reasons for assessment, followed by a review of the different methods of assessment and ending with some suggestions regarding the process of conducting assessment.

WHY ASSESS PERSONALITY FUNCTIONING?

As noted, current recommendations for assessment following the Care Programme Approach (CPA) advocate assessment of the person's presenting difficulties, any psychiatric diagnoses and the level of risk to self or others. Within CPA, specific assessments can cover areas of need such as psychological health, self-care, safety to self and others, language and culture, housing needs, drug and alcohol use and close relationships. Often, the practitioner is presented with someone who experiences difficulties in many of these areas – who is depressed, anxious, experiencing psychotic symptoms or exhibiting other signs of distress or emotional difficulty. Moreover, a person's inter-personal functioning and any difficulties in relationships will clearly have an impact on the levels of need in each of the areas described above. However, information sufficient to determine the presence of significant personality difficulties is generally not picked up on at the initial assessment stage.

When personality factors *are* assessed, it is usually through clinical judgement alone. However, this can be unreliable (Mellsop, Varghese, Joshua & Hicks, 1982). The assessment of personality functioning is notoriously problematic for a number of reasons, including difficulties with the classification systems, co-morbidity with other psychiatric disorders and with other personality disorders, and the accuracy of someone's self-report. Despite these difficulties, Hassiotis, Tyrer and Cicchetti (1997) emphasise that although the diagnosis of personality *disorder* remains pejorative, the accurate assessment of personality *difficulties* is extremely important in an overall assessment of every psychiatric patient's mental health. This chapter will attempt to provide guidance on how this can be achieved.

FORMAL AND INFORMAL APPROACHES TO PERSONALITY ASSESSMENT

FORMAL APPROACHES TO ASSESSMENT

Categorical Systems and Measures

The difficulties associated with categorical classification systems such as the Diagnostic and Statistical Manual of Mental Disorders (DSM; American Psychiatric Association, 1994) and the International Classification of Mental and Behavioural Disorders (ICD; World Health Organisation, 1992) are well documented and detailed in Chapter 2. They include the lack of recognition of (i) co-morbidity amongst personality disorders, (ii) co-morbidity between personality disorders and Axis I difficulties and (iii) the impact of severity on presentation (Dolan, Evans & Norton, 1995). Despite such issues, these systems continue to be widely used within mental health services. Consequently, individual categories are familiar to practitioners and therefore remain a useful system to use.

DSM-IV, the fourth revision of the *Diagnostic and Statistical Manual of Mental Disorders* (APA, 1994, p. 629) is frequently used in the UK as a classification system of psychiatric disorders. It defines personality disorder as 'an enduring pattern of inner experience and behaviour that deviates markedly from the expectations of the individual's culture, is pervasive and inflexible, has an onset in adolescence or early adulthood, is stable over time and leads to distress or impairment', and describes ten specific disorders. These ten disorders are grouped into three clusters – Cluster A, 'odd/eccentric' disorders; Cluster B, 'dramatic' disorders, and Cluster C, 'anxious/fearful' disorders.

An alternative (although very similar) system, ICD-10 (the International Classification of Mental and Behavioural Disorders, World Health Organisation, 1992, p. 202), defines personality disorder as 'a severe disturbance in the characterological constitution and behavioural tendencies of the individual, usually involving several areas of personality, and nearly always associated with considerable personal and social disruption'. It describes nine disorders with similar classifications to the DSM system.

The DSM-IV system is more widely referenced in the literature and it will be the system referred to in this chapter. In order to give the reader a sense of the types of difficulty people present with, each diagnostic category of DSM-IV is briefly described below with specific reference to the clinical presentation within each cluster.

Cluster A: 'odd/eccentric'.

(i) *Paranoid.* Some of the symptoms of paranoid personality disorder can be confused with the psychotic delusions of a paranoid psychosis. The individual may view the practitioner as wanting to harm him or her in some way, may find it difficult to form a close working relationship and appear sensitive or suspicious over comments about him- or herself. The individual can become angry when challenged or when feeling threatened.

(ii) *Schizoid.* Individuals with schizoid personality disorder are not frequently seen in services as they can find seeking help difficult and/or might not envisage any problems. They often find engagement with services difficult and any attempts at engaging in group work, day centres etc. can often be resisted. They are suspicious of people's motives and expect to be exploited, deceived or harmed in some way.

(iii) *Schizotypal.* Again, these individuals' difficulties may also be confused with a psychotic episode due to ideas of reference and strange perceptual experiences. They may wear strange clothes or act strangely, and often hold odd or different beliefs, having few friends or social contacts. They find social interactions hard to manage due to these difficulties and the associated feelings of anxiety.

Cluster B: 'dramatic'.

(i) *Antisocial*. Someone diagnosed with antisocial personality disorder may have a forensic history, can often be touchy and easily angered, with little regret for any upset or harm caused to other people, and may express pleasure at having done so. People with antisocial personality disorder are increasingly being seen in clinical populations.

(ii) *Borderline*. Often seen in services; frequent self-harming behaviour and presentations to accident and emergency departments, often in response to an interpersonal crisis. Can have a love/hate relationship with staff, experience rapid mood changes and can report hearing voices or experience other abnormal perceptual phenomena. Staff can often feel drawn into desperately trying to help or feeling annoyed and not wanting to help. Often have a history of traumatic early life experiences, e.g. childhood sexual abuse, physical abuse, emotional neglect.

(iii) *Histrionic*. Individuals can be flirtatious or provocative with staff of both sexes and come across as dramatic, where everything in their life is in a state of 'crisis'. They often want to be the centre of attention and feel uncomfortable if they are not. They may react to events in an exaggerated way, beyond what would usually be expected, and present in a dramatic and exaggerated way (e.g. clothes, speech, gestures).

(iv) *Narcissistic*. Such individuals present as superior and deserving of special treatment and can often make staff feel ineffective and incapable. Underlying the superior attitude is often a sense of worthlessness and inferiority. A person may hold staff in high regard only to feel disappointed by what is offered and feel let down, rubbishing the practitioner in the process. They may not engage with offers of help and may request specialist services, and either dismiss and criticise practitioners if they fail to provide the expected care or view them as special and someone with whom no one else can compete.

Cluster C: 'anxious and fearful'.

(i) *Avoidant*. Such individuals are avoidant of any situation requiring interpersonal contact and tend to be less frequently seen in clinical practice, due to the nature of their difficulties. They often find it difficult to open up and discuss their problems, feeling inadequate and inferior, and find engaging with services difficult, as they are hyper-vigilant for signs of rejection or criticism.

(ii) *Dependent*. Individuals with dependent personality disorder are often seen in clinical settings. Initial presentations can be of Axis I difficulties or physical health problems, but these may respond poorly to first line treatments and over time the person can be seen to be highly dependent on services and show desperate attempts to hold onto the input from a practitioner.

(iii) *Obsessive–compulsive.* Often confused with obsessive–compulsive disorder but distinguished by the difficulties being more severe, chronic, longstanding and more 'ego-syntonic', as opposed to the experience of intrusive thoughts that seem 'alien' (ego-dystonic) to the individual, as in obsessive–compulsive disorder. Individuals may shows signs of excessive perfectionism and a need for order and routine, and are often rigid in thoughts and actions, being reluctant to consider other ways of doing things.

Due to the high occurrence of co-morbidity/co-occurrence of the personality disorders, however, individuals do not fit neatly into the above categories and many people exhibit symptoms of more than one disorder. Just as we are all made up of different aspects of personality characteristics, so too are people classified with having personality disorders, in that they are combinations or 'blends' of different traits. Despite this, however, the above descriptions can be useful archetypes. In my experience, the most commonly encountered personality disorders in mental health settings tend to be borderline, dependent or histrionic. People with avoidant personality characteristics and narcissistic difficulties are less frequently seen, due to the nature of their problems and how this impacts on seeking and accepting help. With the proposed changes in mental health law and forensic services there is also a greater likelihood of people with antisocial personality disorders becoming more a part of the everyday work of CMHTs.

There are a number of user-friendly clinical assessment tools that correspond to the DSM-IV categories. The two described here are in frequent use amongst research and clinical populations.

The Millon Clinical Multiaxial Inventory (MCMI-III; Millon and Davies, 1997) is a self-report instrument consisting of 175 items requiring a true/false response. It is designed to help the practitioner assess for the presence of DSM-IV Axis II personality disorder as well as clinical syndromes such as anxiety, alcohol dependence, PTSD and so on. The instrument takes approximately 25 minutes to complete and is for use with clinical populations as the norms are based on clinical samples only.

The Structured Clinical Interview for DSM-IV Personality Disorders (SCID-II; First, Spitzer, Gibbon & Williams, 1990) is a 119-item semi-structured interview, taking up to an hour to complete and being similar to the MCMI-III in that it relates to DSM-IV Axis II difficulties. It is also available in a short version that can be used as a screening tool, taking approximately 20 minutes to complete. In this form, an indication of whether a personality disorder is present or not can be established and, if so, the practitioner can then go on to administer the full version.

Dimensional Systems and Measures

As described above, the DSM-IV and ICD-10 systems adopt a 'categorical' perspective, with the basic assumption that a personality disorder is either present or absent. Some have argued that this promotes an illogical distinction between normal and abnormal personality (see, for example, Parker and Barrett, 2000). Furthermore, such an approach is complicated by the observation that it is highly likely that if someone meets the criteria for one particular disorder she or he will also meet criteria for several others.

Dimensional models, on the other hand, view personality disorders as representing 'maladaptive variants of personality traits that merge imperceptibly into normality and into one another' (APA, 1994). These models advocate the view that features of personality disorder do not form discrete categories but are distributed along a continuum. Many studies have investigated the distinction between personality disorder and so-called 'normal' personality and have failed to identify a clear demarcation point between the two (Livesley, Jackson & Schroeder, 1992; Zimmerman & Coryell, 1990). Other authors (e.g. Clark, McEwen, Collard & Hickok, 1993) note that by using a dimensional approach patients can be rated on *several* trait dimensions relevant to personality disorder, and a more extensive and person-specific profile can be obtained.

In dimensional models, 'disordered' personality traits are thought to represent the extremes of normal personality functioning, with traits defined as consisting of 'stable internal dispositions, functional units and causal factors' (Parker & Barrett, 2000), which are consistent across a variety of situations. Investigations into the applicability of dimensional models confirm a continuous transition from normal personality to that of a personality disorder amongst individuals. As Millon, Meagher and Grossman (2001) state, there are theoretically thousands of different personality traits, and each of the associated dimensional descriptions can readily co-exist within an individual. Difficulties can occur, however, in attempting to reduce the overwhelming number of traits and organise them into clinically useful descriptions.

As with the categorical models, there are measures to assess personality disorders using a dimensional approach. The three measures described are widely used in clinical and research populations.

The Schedule for Nonadaptive and Adaptive Personality (SNAP) is a self-report inventory developed by Clark (1993). It contains 375 items requiring a true or false answer and assesses 15 traits relevant to personality disorder. The traits consist of such descriptors as mistrust, manipulativeness, aggression, self-harm, eccentric perceptions, dependency, exhibitionism, entitlement, detachment, impulsivity, politeness and workaholism. It also contains three 'temperament' dimensions. The scores generated aim to reflect the whole range of personality variation from non-pathological to severely disordered. The authors suggest that the SNAP can accurately distinguish between transient distress and difficulties that have been more stable over time.

The Dimensional Assessment of Personality Pathology – Basic Questionnaire (DAPP-BQ; Livesley & Jackson, 2002) is a 290-item instrument that assesses 18 dimensions of personality difficulty based on trait descriptions and behaviours from DSM-III and III-R axis II disorders. The 18 dimensions are affective lability, anxiousness, cognitive dysregulation, conduct problems, compulsivity, identity problems, callousness, intimacy problems, insecure attachment, narcissism, oppositionality (passive-aggressivity), rejection, restricted expression, self-harm, social avoidance, stimulus seeking, submissiveness and suspiciousness. The DAPP-BQ provides a systematic assessment of trait dimensions that encompasses the overall domain of personality disorders.

The Minnesota Multiphasic Personality Inventory-II (MMPI-II; Butcher, Dahlstrom, Graham, Tellegen & Kaemmer, 1989) is a widely known and frequently used personality measure consisting of 567 true/false items and taking approximately 60–90 minutes to complete. The profile obtained contains information regarding symptoms and interpersonal relationships and relates to 10 clinical scales referring to such descriptions as hypochondriasis, hypomania, depression and paranoia, although these do not refer to psychiatric diagnoses. Although the MMPI does not, strictly speaking, describe personality dimensions, it does describe different characteristics of personality and acknowledges their co-existence and differing severity. There is also a personality disorder version of the first version of the MMPI (Morey, Waugh & Blashfield, 1985), which consists of 11 personality disorder scales corresponding to DSM-III axis II disorders (and is therefore a categorical measure in this format).

Combined Measures (Both Categorical and Dimensional)

Some measures incorporate both the categorical and dimensional perspectives, and potentially provide a useful direction, in terms of addressing the weaknesses of categorical models (such as DSM-IV), without losing the familiarity of the diagnostic categories.

The Personality Assessment Schedule (PAS) is a trait-based instrument designed by Tyrer and Alexander (1979) which uses a semi-structured interview format covering 24 areas of personality functioning. It is the most extensively used British standardised assessment tool and has good inter-rater and test–retest reliability (Tyrer, Strauss & Cicchetti, 1983). It can be completed through interview with either the subject or an informant and takes between 30 and 45 minutes. The measure generates both a categorical diagnosis (using ICD-10) and a dimensional description of personality difficulties. It also gives an indication of co-morbidity between diagnoses.

The Inventory of Interpersonal Problems – Personality Disorder Scales (IIP-PD; Pilkonis, Kim, Proietti & Barkham, 1996) is a 47-item measure designed to assess emotional distress in interpersonal relationships. It includes five subscales covering such areas as interpersonal sensitivity, interpersonal ambivalence and aggression. Three of the five scales are based on items that indicate the presence or absence of a personality disorder and are also markers of cluster B disorders. This measure is, however, limited in the extent to which it is a categorical measure.

Informant Interviews and Measures

People with personality disorders may find it difficult to accurately describe their own difficulties due to lack of insight or awareness (Zimmerman, Pfohl, Stangl & Corenthal, 1986), and observer ratings, provided by a significant other, can be essential in the assessment process. There is also some limited evidence suggesting that there is consistent agreement when a combination of observer (carer, relative, friend) ratings are used in conjunction with each other (see Coolidge, Burns & Mooney, 1995).

Although a number of authors recommend that practitioners interview an informant (close relative, carer or friend) as well as the individual, there are also well documented difficulties with the reliability of using informants, due to apparent low subject–informant agreement (Zimmerman, Pfohl, Coryell & Stangl, 1988) and several likely possibilities have been suggested as to why this occurs.

i. Patients and informants may make different attributions concerning the same behaviour. For example, the patient may see certain behaviour as being completely reasonable under the circumstances experienced, whereas his or her informant may think he or she was over-reacting to something fairly trivial (Hill, Fudge, Harrington, Pickles & Rutter, 2000).
ii. People with personality disorders may find it difficult to identify and describe their own negative traits and are therefore likely to under-report when compared with an informant's view (Tyrer & Ferguson 1987).

iii. Depending on the measure used, there may be lack of agreement between informant and the patient over what is being assessed. For example, one individual may refer to the most severe behaviours whereas the other refers to behaviours in general, sampling different situations. Additionally, the patient may base answers on their own feelings while the informant bases theirs on the behaviours they observe (Hill et al., 2000).

iv. Informants may have personal grudges against the patient and therefore may make exaggerated claims about behaviour and may also have their own mental health difficulties (Mann et. al., 1999).

Despite these inconsistent findings, interviewing an informant (where possible) is recommended and viewed as a potentially important source of additional information regarding the individual. Several structured assessment measures have been devised to routinely interview informants regarding the person's problems.

The Standardised Assessment of Personality (SAP; Mann, Jenkins, Cutting & Cowen, 1981) is an informant-only interview that can be conducted face to face or via the telephone, has good psychometric properties and enables either ICD-10 or DSM-IV diagnoses to be made. The informant needs to have known the person for at least five years and some researchers have found that female informants who have known the person for a long time show the highest reliability between comparisons of informant and individual ratings (Pilgrim, Mellers, Boothby & Mann, 1993). The authors suggest that this measure can be used as an effective and time-efficient screening tool to assess the presence of personality difficulties prior to assessing further with a more detailed measure.

As mentioned above, the Personality Assessment Schedule (PAS; Tyrer and Alexander, 1979) can also be used with informants, and a recent development – the Personality Assessment Schedule – Document Derived Version (PAS-DOC) (Tyrer, 2005), has been found to be a reliable and simply completed assessment from written records above.

Conclusions About Formal Measures

While Clark and Harrison[1] (2001) argue that interview formats (such as the SCID-II) are generally seen to be the 'gold standard' when it comes

---

[1]For further information about formal assessment measures see Clark, L. A. & Harrison, J. A. (2001). Assessment instruments. In W. J. Livesley (Ed.), *Handbook of personality disorders; theory, research and treatment.*

to diagnosing someone with a personality disorder, there can be clear psychometric weaknesses that should be taken into account depending on the measure used. They further state that while self-report measures (e.g. the MCMI-III) may have less utility in formally diagnosing a personality disorder, they clearly have something to offer in the wider view of the impact of a personality difficulty on the individual and can often be more user friendly.

Despite their limitations, the usefulness of self-report information as provided in questionnaires or interview schedules should not be under-rated. Work conducted on so called 'normal personality' assessment, most notably by Funder (1993), indicates that individuals can comment on their own personality characteristics fairly accurately and individual–informant agreement is generally high, especially when informants know the individual well and reliable measures are used. However, a note of caution must be sounded: further studies have assessed the impact of Axis I difficulties on the accurate identification of a personality disorder and found that responses given by patients can vary depending on whether the individual is depressed, anxious or psychotic (Widiger, 1993). The person's current mental state always needs to be taken into account.

INFORMAL APPROACHES TO ASSESSMENT

Although this may seem obvious, important information can easily be gained from reviewing the patient's psychiatric notes, as people with personality difficulties can often be heavy users of services and already well known within the mental health system. Details of Axis I difficulties, information regarding previous admissions, co-morbidity with drug/alcohol misuse, presentations to accident and emergency departments and dependency issues indicated through difficulties in being discharged from services can be easily identified. Although not always clearly documented, other information regarding family history and details regarding the circumstances surrounding previous attempts at self-harm can also be established.

In an assessment interview, certain descriptions given by the individual need to be listened out for, as these can indicate the longstanding, pervasive nature of someone's problems, suggestive of the presence of a personality disorder. These can include describing a long history of similar difficulties beginning in mid- to late childhood and continuing throughout the individual's life, and experiencing intense emotions and reactions in response to repeatedly being on the receiving end of actual or perceived abuse, rejection or conditional care.

When it comes to the assessment interview, it has been suggested that the primary personality dimensions, along with the usual general psychiatric domains, should routinely be assessed (Bateman & Tyrer, 2004) and that the practitioner should enquire about four domains affecting the person's functioning:

i. symptoms
ii. interpersonal functioning
iii. social functioning, including work history
iv. the patient's inner experience (as opposed to how an observer may have viewed a situation).

It is also recommended that an interview is conducted with an informant (e.g. a close friend, carer or relative) to verify the information already gained and give additional information regarding the individual's impact on others and the quality of her or his relationships. As well as being concerned with a person's difficulties in relation to personality characteristics and the existence of Axis I problems, it is also extremely important to identify the presence of any strengths and adaptive coping mechanisms that have enabled her or him to survive and can be worked with during treatment.

Interpersonal Processes in Clinical Situations

A further important source of information can be obtained through the overall impression made by the individual on the practitioner conducting the assessment. A simple process of self-reflection can provide details about the individual's interactions with others in their lives, by paying close attention not only to the *content* of someone's verbal responses but also to the emotional expression in the *way they are talking* and any *non-verbal communication*, as well as the *feelings engendered in the practitioner.*

These constructs relate to the ideas of 'transference' and 'counter-transference', which some practitioners may have dismissed as belonging exclusively in the realms of psychotherapy and not relevant in their day to day clinical practice. These observations, however, can be invaluable in providing first hand experience of the difficult and overwhelming emotions often faced by people with a personality disorder and help enhance the practitioner's understanding and empathy in working with someone with such a diagnosis. Supervision can also often help with identifying and clarifying such responses.

A survey conducted by Westen (1997) found that practitioners' judgements regarding the presence of a personality disorder are primarily based on their observations during the assessment process of the individual's behaviour and the individual's description of their interactions with significant others. Parker and Barrett (2000) suggest that this approach, with an emphasis on 'signs' (defined as phenomena observed by the practitioner) as opposed to 'symptoms' (descriptions given by the individual), can assist in avoiding some of the limitations seen to be inherent in the self-report of personality characteristics, for example, contamination by Axis I difficulties, defensiveness, lack of insight and so on. Other issues to take into account in clinical work include the individual's level of co-operation with the assessment process, his or her willingness to share personal information and the degree of response exaggeration (Butcher & Rouse, 1996). It is helpful to consider not just the detail of the responses given but also the way the questions are received and answers communicated.

Interviews and commonly used self-report measures are often restricted to enquiring about a person's current functioning and the recent history of their presenting problems. They tend to be symptom focused, with little attention paid to a person's earlier developmental history and past experience. A good assessment will not only cover the current difficulties but also attempt to gain a clear understanding about the possible origins of these problems and how they have developed over time. Emphasis on early trauma, including experiences of abuse and neglect, are often particularly relevant, and details about how the individual coped and survived can add to the overall formulation and understanding.

Some of these issues can be seen in the fictitious description of Jane's difficulties below.

Jane, a 34 year old woman, was assessed in her home, on two occasions, by a community psychiatric nurse (CPN) following a referral by her GP. She reported feeling low in mood, was frequently tearful and having difficulty sleeping. She gave details of the current difficulties with her partner, with whom she would often feel incredibly angry, for not providing her with the care she wanted. She also became angry with her young children (aged 7 and 5) for not noticing when she needed time on her own and constantly demanding her attention. Jane coped with her angry feelings by lashing out at times, hitting the doors and walls, or at other times she would take the feelings out on herself by cutting her arms with a piece of broken glass. She also drank heavily and had been known to use amphetamines in the past. Jane disclosed details of her childhood; her mother had raised her after her father died when she was 6 years old, and she had five younger siblings. Her mother was often out of the house working and expected Jane to cook, clean and take care of her younger siblings on a daily basis. No matter what Jane did, she was criticised and berated and at times physically beaten. Jane also described ongoing sexual abuse by an uncle between the ages of 4 and 10 and said she began drinking alcohol excessively at the age of 12.

In terms of previous contact with services, Jane had a long history of involvement with both medical and psychiatric services. Her notes revealed frequent investigations for non-specific physical symptoms and input from a counsellor spanning two years, which had ended when the counsellor retired. Jane had also had four admissions to the in-patient psychiatric ward and a colleague of the CPN's remembered that it had been difficult for Jane to be discharged because as soon as she began to improve and discharge was mentioned her mental state deteriorated. Jane described her previous experience of psychiatric care as a 'joke' and that nothing had ever made any difference to her difficulties apart from the counsellor, who she described as an 'angel in disguise'. She had been devastated when the counsellor retired.

Throughout the assessment, Jane described her difficulties in a cold and detached way with little emotional content, almost as if she were describing her weekly shopping rather than immensely distressing events. She sat in a chair, hunched over her knees and continually wringing her hands. The CPN found he doubted the reliability of Jane's history and felt bored and irritated during the assessment. In reflecting on these feelings later and in supervision, he recognised that Jane had perhaps had to disconnect from her earlier experiences in order to cope and the way she talked about her past events reflected this (with the distress and ongoing difficult feelings being expressed through her non-verbal communication) rather than the legitimacy of what she was saying. He also recognised that he had identified with Jane's 'cut-offness' in his own boredom and irritability. The CPN further felt that Jane met the criteria for borderline personality disorder with dependent and narcissistic elements.

HOW TO PRESENT THE PROCESS OF ASSESSMENT TO PATIENTS

Any form of clinical contact for someone with mental health difficulties can be distressing and difficult for that individual, and people with personality disorders are no exception to this. Alternatively, the experience of participating in the process of assessment can be enlightening and positive for the individual. Clearly, there are a number of considerations to incorporate into the assessment process, which include such issues as the manner and environment in which the assessment is conducted, how the information is shared, who has access to the information gathered and how the information will help to inform future care.

What needs to be obtained from an assessment is a clear sense of the *function* of someone's behaviours – an understanding of why they feel as they do and why they react in certain ways – rather than placing someone in a particular diagnostic category that says little about their day-to-day interpersonal functioning, the history of their difficulties and the severity of distress they are experiencing.

The authors of the NIMHE document *Personality Disorder: No Longer a Diagnosis of Exclusion* (NIHME, 2003) consulted service users on their views of service provision and reported that often the diagnosis of a personality disorder carried a great deal of stigma and negativity with it. They also noted, however, that the sharing of a diagnosis could potentially be a useful process if done in a non-judgemental way, but that it needed to be backed up with the provision of reliable information, and that assessment/treatment links were made clear to people with personality disorders. Although DSM-IV diagnoses have, at times, been used pejoratively, especially with regard to personality disorder, the sharing of a diagnosis can often be met with a sense of relief and understanding that can be therapeutic in itself.

The selection of any formal measures used to assess personality disorder should be given careful consideration, including ideas of how the measure is introduced to the individual (which can be crucial for enhancing compliance and the legitimacy of responses obtained) and the impact of participating in the process, along with any likely distress caused by completing it (MacKenzie, 2001). MacKenzie suggests that a clear explanation is given for the purpose of using a questionnaire or structured measure and an explanation of how the results obtained from the measure will be used, as well as an opportunity for the individual to ask any questions or seek further clarification. In feeding back results obtained from assessment measures, it is further recommended that information should be given in a tentative manner using real life examples and the individual's own language as far as possible, without using technical jargon. It can also be helpful to link in the results with the corresponding treatment or care plan.

CONCLUSIONS

The assessment of personality factors can be readily incorporated into the assessment procedures currently used by community mental health teams. Self-report assessment measures that provide information regarding diagnosis and interpersonal functioning can be used and, where possible, the interviewing of a relative, carer or close friend can also provide additional useful information. Specific details regarding the individual's early childhood experiences and means of coping can be invaluable in understanding the development and maintenance of his or her interpersonal difficulties. Consideration of the practitioner's own feelings towards the individual and vice versa is also useful in informing the assessment process. In undertaking these assessments and sharing the results, it is important to be aware of the impact on the individual and the need for the process to be conducted in a sensitive and non-judgemental manner, in order to establish a good working alliance between the practitioner and the patient.

The process of assessment is not a discrete task with a clear beginning and end; it is an ongoing and flexible process, important throughout a person's involvement with mental health services, which enables the practitioner to monitor and identify changes in his or her mental health over time. With the points raised in this chapter, it is hoped that staff working in CMHTs will feel able to routinely consider and incorporate personality functioning into their assessment process, in order to allow for the recognition of difficulties in this area and to inform the most appropriate interventions for the patient.

REFERENCES

American Psychiatric Association (APA). (1994). *Diagnostic and statistical manual of mental disorders* (4th ed.). Washington, DC: Author.

Bateman, A. W. & Tyrer, P. (2004). Services for personality disorder: Organisation for inclusion. *Advances in Psychiatric Treatment, 10,* 425–433.

Butcher, J. N., Dahlstrom, W. G., Graham, J. R., Tellegen, A. & Kaemmer, B. (1989). *Manual for the restandardized Minnesota multiphasic personality inventory: MMPI-II.* Minneapolis, MN: University of Minnesota Press.

Butcher, J. N. & Rouse, S. V. (1996). Personality: Individual differences and clinical assessment. *Annual Reviews Psychology, 47,* 87–111.

Clark, L. A. (1993). *Manual for the Schedule for Nonadaptive and Adaptive Personality (SNAP).* Minneapolis, MN: University of Minnesota Press.

Clark, L. A. & Harrison, J. A. (2001). Assessment instruments. In W. J. Livesley (Ed.), *Handbook of personality disorders; Theory, research and treatment* (pp. 277–306). New York: Guilford.

Clark, L. A., McEwen, J. L., Collard, L. M. & Hickok, L. G. (1993). Symptoms and traits of personality disorder; two new methods for their assessment. *Psychological Assessment,* 5(1), 81–91.

Coolidge, F. L., Burns, E. M. & Mooney, J. A. (1995). Reliability of observer ratings in the assessment of personality disorders: A preliminary study. *Journal of Clinical Psychology,* 51, 22–28.

Department of Health. (1999). *Effective Care-Co-ordination in mental health services – modernising the care programme approach.* London: Author.

Dolan, B., Evans, C. and Norton, K. (1995). Multiple axis II diagnoses of personality disorder. *British Journal of Psychiatry, 166,* 107–112.

First, M. D., Spitzer, R. L., Gibbon, M. & Williams, J. B. W. (1990). *Structured Clinical Interview for DSM-IV Personality Disorder (SCID-II).* Washington, DC: American Psychiatric Press, Inc.

Funder, D. C. (1993). Judgements as data for personality and developmental psychology: Error versus accuracy. In D. C. Funder, R. Parke, C. Tomlinson-Keasey and K. Widamen (Eds), *Studying lives through time: Personality and development* (pp. 121–146). Washington, DC: American Psychological Association.

Hassiotis, A., Tyrer, P. and Cicchetti, D. (1997). Detection of personality disorders by a community mental health team: a study of diagnostic accuracy. *Irish Journal of Psychological Medicine, 14,* 88–91.

Hill, J., Fudge, H., Harrington, R., Pickles, A. & Rutter, M. (2000). Complementary approaches to the assessment of personality disorder: The Personality Assessment Schedule and Adult Personality Functioning Assessment compared. *The British Journal of Psychiatry, 176,* 434–439.

Livesley, W. J. & Jackson, D. N. (2002). *Manual for dimensional assessment of personality pathology – basic questionnaire.* Port Huron, MI: Sigma.

Livesley, W. J., Jackson, D. & Schroeder, M. L. (1992). Factorial structure of traits delineating personality disorders in clinical and general population samples. *Journal of Abnormal Psychology, 101,* 432–440.

MacKenzie, K. R. (2001). Personality assessment in clinical practice. In W. J. Livesley (Ed.), *Handbook of personality disorders; Theory, research and treatment* (pp. 307–323). New York: Guilford.

Mann, A. H., Jenkins, R., Cutting, J. C. & Cowen, P. J. (1981). The development and use of a standardised assessment of personality. *Psychological Medicine, 11,* 839–847.

Mann, A. H., Raven, P., Pilgrim, J., Khanna, S., Velayudham, A., Suresh, K. P., Channabasavanna, S. M., Janca, A. & Sartorius, N. (1999). An assessment of the Standardised Assessment of Personality as a screening instrument for the International Personality Disorder Examination: A comparison of informant and patient assessment for personality disorder. *Psychological Medicine, 29*(4), 985–989.

Mellsop, G., Varghese, F., Joshua, S. & Hicks, A. (1982). The reliability of axis II of DSM-III. *American Journal of Psychiatry, 139,* 1360–1361.

Millon, T. & Davies, R. D. (1997). The MCMI-III: Present and future directions. *Journal of Personality Assessment, 68,* 69–85.

Millon, T., Meagher, S. E. & Grossman, S. D. (2001). Theoretical perspectives. In W. J. Livesley (Ed.) *Handbook of personality disorders; Theory, research and treatment* (pp. 39–59). New York: Guilford.

Morey, L. C., Waugh, M. H. & Blashfield, R. K. (1985). MMPI scales for DSM-III personality disorders: Their derivation and correlates. *Journal of Personality Assessment, 49,* 245–251.

National Institute for Mental Health in England (NIMHE). (2003). *Personality disorder: No longer a diagnosis of exclusion.* London: Department of Health.

Parker, G. & Barrett, E. (2000). Personality and personality disorder: Current issues and directions. *Psychological Medicine, 30,* 1–9.

Pilgrim, J. A., Mellers, J. D., Boothby, H. A. & Mann, A. H. (1993). Inter-rater and temporal reliability of the Standardised Assessment of Personality and the influence of informant characteristics. *Psychological Medicine, 23*, 779–786.

Pilkonis, P. A., Kim, Y., Proietti, J. M. & Barkham, M. (1996). Scales for personality disorders developed from the Inventory of Interpersonal Problems. *Journal of Personality Disorders, 10*, 355–369.

Tyrer, P. (2005). Personality Assessment Schedule – Document Derived Version (PAS – DOC). Department of Psychological Medicine, Imperial College, London.

Tyrer, P. & Ferguson, B. (1987). Problems in the classification of personality disorder. *Psychological Medicine, 17*, 15–20.

Tyrer, P. & Alexander, J. (1979). Classification of personality disorder. *British Journal of Psychiatry, 135*, 163–167.

Tyrer, P., Strauss, J. & Cicchetti, D. (1983). Temporal reliability of personality in psychiatric patients. *Psychological Medicine, 13*, 393–398.

Westen, D. (1997). Divergences between clinical and research methods for assessing personality disorders: Implications for research and the evolution of Axis II. *American Journal of Psychiatry, 154*, 895–903.

Widiger, T. A. (1993). The DSM-IIIR categorical personality disorder diagnoses: A critique and an alternative. *Psychological Inquiry, 4*, 75–90.

World Health Organisation. (1992). *The ICD-10 classification of mental and behavioural disorders. Clinical descriptions and diagnostic guidelines.* Geneva: Author.

Zimmerman, M. & Coryell, W. H. (1990). DSM-III personality dimensions. *Journal of Nervous and Mental Disease, 178*, 686–692.

Zimmerman, M., Pfohl, B., Coryell, W. & Stangl, D. (1988). Diagnosing personality disorder in depressed patients: A comparison of patient and informant interview. *Archives of General Psychiatry, 45*, 733–737.

Zimmerman, M., Pfohl, B., Stangl, D. & Corenthal, C. (1986). Assessment of DSM-III personality disorders: The importance of interviewing an informant. *Journal of Clinical Psychiatry, 47*, 261–263.

15

Involving Family, Friends and Carers

REMY McCUBBIN

INTRODUCTION

Difficulties in relationships are central to personality disorders. Section One of this book summarises ideas about the ways in which past relationships may have influenced the development of such disorders, and current relationships can maintain a person's difficulties. Chapters 11 and 12 consider the relationship between those seeking help and those in the community mental health team (CMHT) attempting to help them, acknowledging that there can often be frustration on both sides as particular difficulties emerge.

While it is important for those working in CMHTs to continually reflect upon the quality of the relationships they build with patients, there are clearly other relationships that will also be important influences on the patient's well-being. A person referred to psychiatric services is likely to have significant existing relationships, with a range of people. These may be members of their family, friends or people who have come to be involved in some informal 'caring' role. This chapter will attempt to summarise ideas about how the CMHT can best work with these people, to improve the well-being of the patient and to reduce any burden experienced by those they are in close contact with.

Most consideration in this area has been given to work with the families (parents, siblings, spouses and children) of personality-disordered patients, and so this chapter will refer to 'patients' and their 'family', although many of the observations might equally apply to anyone in close contact with the patient, even if they are not related.

Personality Disorder and Community Mental Health Teams: A Practitioner's Guide. Edited by M. J. Sampson, R. A. McCubbin and P. Tyrer. © 2006 John Wiley & Sons, Ltd.

It is clear that the family environment of personality-disordered patients can be significantly disrupted. Fieldman et al. (1995) compared the families of procreation of 9 mothers with borderline personality disorder and 14 mothers with other personality disorders. Two semi-structured interviews were used to evaluate family history, and it was found that the families of borderline mothers scored significantly lower in terms of 'cohesion' and 'organisation', although not in terms of 'conflict'. Nichols (2004) considers the *impact* of living with someone with dependent personality disorder, noting that intense feelings of frustration, bitter disagreements (for example, between parents) and high levels of criticism are common when relatives encourage the individual to manage more independently.

While such observations are commonplace in the literature, it should be noted that not all studies support the idea of there being significant difficulties in patients' families. Gunderson and Lyoo (1997) compared ratings of the family environment made by patients with borderline personality disorder with those made by their parents. They found that while patients rated the family environment significantly more negatively than did a non-clinical control group, parents tended to agree with each other, and rated the family in ways that were similar to the non-clinical control group. While the authors concluded that this was likely to have followed from 'defensive responding' on the part of the parents, alternative explanations are clearly possible. It may indeed be that the family environment is *not* particularly abnormal, but is perceived as such by patients. These are complicated issues. This chapter will attempt to provide an introduction to some of the key ideas in trying to understand when and how difficulties arise within the family environment, and their relevance to the work of CMHTs.

Consideration will be given to five different aspects of work with the family:

- the rationale for working with the family
- family interventions described in the literature
- evidence regarding the effectiveness of family intervention
- obstacles to working with families, and how to overcome them
- the practical and ethical considerations of working with family members.

Generally, it should be acknowledged that this is not an area that has been studied in great detail, and conclusions are based as much on theoretical grounds and expert consensus as on robust empirical findings. It does, however, deserve special attention for a number of reasons, not least of which is the professional obligations faced by CMHT members to work with families (for example, under the recommendations of the Care Programme Approach; Department of Health, 1990). However, as we shall see, there are other arguments for seeking involvement with the people who are significant in patients' lives.

Ruiz-Sancho, Smith and Gunderson (2001) note several reasons for clinicians and researchers to have had reservations about working with the families (in particular) of personality-disordered clients. First, there has been a lack of consensus regarding the concept of 'personality disorder' itself, and what the key factors in the development of such difficulties are. As a result, it was far from clear what perspective on the clients' difficulties might be used as the basis for such contact – what CMHT staff might *say* to relatives, friends and carers. Second, there has been a reluctance to use a diagnostic 'label' that has been seen as stigmatising. Third, the suggestion that relationships with other people (especially family) play a significant part in the development of patients' difficulties leads to professionals having to strike a difficult balance: while families are not 'to blame', they may be seen as having contributed to the difficulties experienced. Related to this, the observation that family members often experience social and mental health difficulties of their own (see below) has been suggested as a factor contributing to therapeutic pessimism (Gunderson, 2001). Finally, the heterogeneity of a 'personality-disordered' group of patients is such that it has been difficult to develop clearly defined family interventions.

Together, these factors resulted in little being published on working with families through the 1980s and 1990s. However, there has been increasing interest in this area (illustrated by the publication of books dedicated specifically to family interventions, e.g. MacFarlane, 2004) and the litera-ture does now contain some useful observations to guide the clinician working in the CMHT.

THE RATIONALE FOR FAMILY INTERVENTIONS

There are three main reasons for considering the involvement of family members in interventions for personality-disordered clients: their role in assessment, the opportunity to reduce the distress experienced by the family members themselves and the potential to enhance the effects of treatment programmes developed for the patient.

INVOLVING CARERS IN ASSESSMENT

(Fictitious) case illustration: a young woman of 24 is referred to the CMHT, following her reports to her GP that she is regularly cutting herself while under the influence of alcohol. When seen for assessment, she goes on to describe her

life as empty and unrewarding. She lives with her parents, has no siblings or friends and rarely leaves the house as she feels people are looking at her, because she is ugly (a concern which in the clinician's view is unfounded). She describes her childhood as unremarkable, saying that she had a few friends at school but has lost touch with them since leaving at 16. She describes her parents as both being obsessed with their work, and never having had time for her. The clinician conducting the assessment begins to consider whether the young woman is best understood in terms of body image difficulties, or more general social anxiety. Possible goals for therapy are discussed, including individual therapy for key aspects of her self-image, and referral to a day centre, to assist with attempts to increase her social confidence.

By chance, the clinician speaks to the patient's mother the following week, when she phones to cancel an appointment for her daughter. In the course of attempting to re-schedule, it emerges that some of the impressions gained by the clinician are inaccurate. The young woman does indeed leave the house regularly – she is working part-time at a health food shop, is actively involved with an amateur theatre group, and has a large number of friends who regularly phone her and always call round to accompany her when she goes out. The mother describes a good deal of concern in the family and among friends that her daughter is 'immature' and 'fragile'.

It seems that the young woman has misled the clinician and greatly exaggerated the severity of her difficulties, in terms of the impact on her day-to-day functioning. Moreover, this is something she appears to do with other people in her life. The clinician realises that he now has to understand why she has done this, and how he can let her know what he has learned. Clearly, the interventions he was considering carry a danger of reinforcing her interpersonal behaviour, which might in turn maintain a view of herself as someone 'unable to cope without intensive support from others'.

While the suggestion that patients may not report their difficulties accurately is frequently made in the literature on personality disorder assessment (Bernstein et al., 1997; Zimmerman, 1994), there have in fact been few empirical studies examining this in detail.

What can be said, however, is that patients with significant personality pathology *may* at times give a misleading impression to professionals as to the extent of their difficulties, their ability to cope, the support available to them or almost any aspect of their life that is being assessed. Previous chapters have described ideas about how such misunderstandings can arise, and often put emphasis on the patient's powerful needs for others to respond towards them in a certain way. For example, it is possible that someone desperate to seek the protection of others will (as in the example above) emphasise or exaggerate the extent to which he or she neglects basic self-care, is unable to manage social encounters and so on. This might, if the misunderstanding continues, lead to a response from the CMHT that is an 'over-reaction', in the sense that they are over-protective and undermine the patient's confidence in his or her ability to manage situations independently.

While such dynamics can be formulated and understood, they nevertheless introduce a potentially significant obstacle to effective clinical work. Therapists may become irritated, despondent or even feel flattered, when the objective reasons for such reactions are far from clear. Patients may feel that they have to behave in certain ways in order to maintain the relationship, for example by being either 'reasonable', 'agreeable' or 'incapable'.

The first and most obvious reason for attempting to involve carers in the assessment of a patient's presenting problems is therefore the gathering of all available *accurate* information. This can prevent misunderstandings and serve to orient the CMHT practitioner towards interventions that are genuinely helpful. Involving carers can also 'extend' the assessment, by giving staff a much better understanding of their patient's interpersonal environment, and the capacity for this to change. For example, it can be difficult when hearing one person's account of her or his spouse's lack of empathy to feel clear whether this is broadly accurate, or a reflection of a powerful need for others to show concern. The significant people in patients' lives might well have difficulties of their own, and do not always share the values held by the CMHT, or wish for the patient to make the kinds of change being proposed. By meeting with the family, some of these aspects of the patient's circumstances become clearer.

These arguments for involving the family apply to all stages of contact the CMHT has with the patient. A carer's account can also give useful information regarding the patient's progress, and any impact upon their difficulties that services are having. They may, for example, be able to alert staff to an increase in self-harming behaviour in the course of psychotherapy, which would otherwise be overlooked.

Certain formal assessment measures do include so-called 'collateral' (or 'informant') versions for use with carers. For example, the Personality Diagnostic Questionnaire (Hyler, Skodol, Oldham, Kellman & Doidge, 1992), the Schedule of Nonadaptive and Adaptive Personality (Clark, 1993) and the Coolidge Axis II Inventory (Coolidge & Merwin, 1992) all have such versions. However, there have been no studies using such measures looking at the degree of convergence between the accounts of patients and those of an informant. As such, it is yet to be established empirically that obtaining a second account by such means does, for example, increase diagnostic accuracy – let alone lead to better outcomes.

Clearly, these are questions for future research to address. For immediate and practical purposes, however, there seems to be enough expert consensus and anecdotal evidence to suggest that involving carers in assessment should be considered, and that clinical interview can be sufficient. Issues to be considered in such interviews would include the following.

- The carer's understanding of the patient's 'symptoms', in terms of levels of depression, anxiety and so on.
- Their understanding of the patient's history, including early relationships, past social and occupational functioning, any forensic history and so on.
- What they observe in terms of the patient's coping mechanisms – self-harm, alcohol and illegal substances.
- The support available to the patient (from family, through work and through statutory and non-statutory organisations) and whether he or she makes use of it.

In some cases, significant observations will emerge, which usefully inform the formulation of the patient's difficulties.

REDUCING FAMILY DISTRESS

(Fictitious) case illustration: a woman goes to her GP, saying that she is worn out after years of trying to manage her 19 year old daughter's behaviour. The GP, who also knows the daughter, is sympathetic – over the years, he has referred the daughter to the CMHT on several occasions, on each occasion receiving a letter some weeks later saying that she has failed to attend after one or two sessions. The daughter continues to attend her GP surgery, however, asking for further trials of new medication and complaining of intolerable side-effects on each occasion. At the same time, he has observed the mother becoming increasingly run down and has had to sign a number of sick notes for her, to allow her time off work.

On this occasion, the mother describes the burden of looking after her daughter in more detail. At home, the daughter refuses to help with any of the housework, which is considerable as there is another child (her brother) who has severe physical and learning difficulties. If her mother or father do ask her to contribute, she complains bitterly that they have never given her enough attention, have always put her second and are responsible for her misery. This leaves them feeling guilty, and has led to arguments between them on many occasions. Much of the parents' time is spent in giving their daughter lifts to and from social events, which they subsidise as she has never worked. This is leading them into significant amounts of debt.

Under the Care Programme Approach (CPA) there is a requirement for CMHTs to assess and address the distress caused to carers of all patients, regardless of diagnosis. As already noted, it is inherent to the concept of personality disorder that the condition often places a burden on others. This is readily understandable, when looking at the kinds of behaviour associated with personality pathology – self-harming, substance abuse, social withdrawal and explosions of anger. All are likely to cause considerable distress to carers. One can readily imagine family and friends feeling intense frustration, guilt, anxiety or helplessness when faced with such behaviour.

However, relatively few studies have been carried out that attempt to describe and quantify this distress. In a study by Schulz et al. (1985) families indicated that having a relative with borderline personality disorder was more burdensome than having one with a serious physical illness. Antisocial behaviour (drunkenness, promiscuity) caused the greatest difficulty, although unemployment and dependency were also significant burdens. With regard to the help available from services, many families felt excluded or in some way blamed for the patient's difficulties.

Gunderson and Lyoo (1997) surveyed 40 families of patients with borderline personality disorder, and noted that the most common problems were with minimal/poor communication, hostile behaviour and fears about suicide. In addition, Ruiz-Sancho et al. (2001) note from clinical experience that family members often have to deal with intense feelings of grief as they come to terms with their relative's difficulties, while Gunderson (2001) highlights the potential for parents of borderline patients to feel extremely guilty, as they are often explicitly blamed by their children.

Mitton and Links (1996) carried out a survey of the needs of 15 family members of patients attending a specialist personality-disorder outpatient clinic. All of the relatives said they would want more information about the patient's illness, while two-thirds wanted support for themselves and expressed an interest in a family support group. As an indication of their lack of information, it is notable that 80 per cent thought their relative was being treated for depression.

While the research literature relating to the needs of family members is sparse, there is a general recognition among those who have worked with relatives of personality-disordered patients that the burden placed on them can be very heavy indeed. This leads to the argument for interventions targeted directly at alleviating this distress through working not just with the patient, but with family members as well. Such an approach is clearly something which is possible, even when the patient is refusing support, or when the support they receive is not effective. The approaches that might be considered are summarised in the section on 'interventions' and certainly extend beyond what might strictly be termed 'education'.

IMPROVING PATIENTS' WELL-BEING THROUGH WORK WITH THE FAMILY

(Fictitious) case illustration: following referral to the CMHT, a middle-aged female patient attends for initial assessment. She insists upon her husband sitting in on the session, and is generally silent, saying that she prefers for him to answer questions on her behalf. It emerges that he is her second husband, and that they met when he was getting over a difficult, acrimonious divorce. She has two children from her previous marriage. Her husband has always run the household, as he is aware she suffers with intense low moods. She has never explained these moods to him in detail, and he has come to worry that they may be because of him. Certainly, she appears to have functioned much better before their relationship, having looked after the children and even held down a fairly senior job.

In recent years, however, she has come to spend large parts of each day in silence, while he looks after the home and children. In the session, she acknowledges that she is spending much of this time ruminating about events in her childhood. While she does not describe these events in any detail, she does say that she has never felt 'grown up' and able to cope. When working, she always felt that her life was on the verge of 'total collapse', and she drank heavily to try and feel calm. She dislikes herself intensely, saying that she is 'useless' and will never amount to anything. She feels guilty for how much she relies on her husband.

Over the next two assessment sessions, it was possible to develop with the couple a formulation highlighting the way in which the high levels of support he provided actually reinforced her sense of inadequacy. An intervention built around attempts to break up her rumination and increase her involvement in esteem-enhancing activities was developed. Within this, it was made clear that the husband would have to resist any temptation to do things for her, even if she made strident demands for him to do so. This was something about which he felt very apprehensive, being extremely keen to avoid a second, distressing divorce.

It is commonly held that the family is influential in the development and maintenance of the kinds of difficulty leading to a diagnosis of personality disorder. Given this role in maintenance, it is perhaps surprising that treatment approaches focused on the individual have dominated the literature to the extent they have. Some authors have argued that there is little prospect of significant change in the patient's behaviour without some corresponding change in the family system (Magnavita, 2000; Magnavita & MacFarlane, 2004). The third aim of working directly with families is to try and facilitate such change.

This can happen in a number of ways. In addition to attempts to influence relatives' behaviour 'directly' (for example, through instruction, education and advice), family members are potentially able to provide patients with reminders of ideas and strategies discussed in sessions. Finally, it may be possible to change the family's appraisals of patients' behaviour, and hence their behaviour towards them. The interventions described in the following section illustrate some of the many ways in which these ideas have been developed.

Some studies suggest specific ways in which family interventions might be designed, in order to improve a patient's situation. For example, Guttman and Laporte (2000) studied empathy in the families of 27 women with borderline personality disorder (BPD), as compared with 28 women with anorexia nervosa and a control group of 27 women with no clinical diagnosis. Parents of the BPD group had the lowest scores on an instrument measuring four dimensions of empathy. Furthermore, both participants with BPD and their parents agreed that there had been a relative lack of empathic parenting during the patient's childhood (based on family interview). This suggests that patients with BPD might well be living in an interpersonal environment lacking in emotional support, and that this has often been the case for a very long time. While it is hard to tease out causal relationships in the development of such a situation, it also indicates a potential focus for interventions. Efforts to enhance accurate empathy in family members might prove to be beneficial.

Evidence of this kind relating specifically to personality disorders is at present fairly limited. It is to be hoped that as this evidence builds up such ideas can be refined, leading to specifically targeted interventions designed to address those aspects seen to have the greatest role in the *maintenance* of patients' difficulties. It will be important to move beyond studies that are merely 'descriptive', highlighting associations but no causal relationships, and to look at current maintaining factors rather than historical factors, which cannot be influenced.

FAMILY INTERVENTIONS DESCRIBED IN THE LITERATURE

The first attempts to provide family interventions for personality disorder were reported in the 1970s. These programmes were designed for adolescent patients with borderline personality disorder and based on psychodynamic formulations, which emphasised a 'conflict' model in which parental over-involvement was seen to foster dependency and abandonment fears in the child. In this view, the family 'system' is seen as pathogenic, with the patient as the primary 'symptom carrier'. Attempts are made to enhance family closeness and mutual understanding through self-disclosure and the recognition and acceptance of individual differences. Gunderson (2001) reviews such programmes, noting that while they could on occasion be helpful, they were difficult to deliver in most settings and often resisted by families.

A number of developments led to a revision of these early interventions. Studies began to question whether families of borderline patients were indeed over-involved. Instead, the more typical finding was that most families were insufficiently involved and either perpetrated or did not help with patients' traumatic experiences (Frank & Paris, 1981; Gunderson, Kerr & Englund, 1980; Millon, 1987). The subsequent shift towards a 'deficit' model of borderline personality disorder (emphasising the patients' difficulties with, for example, affect regulation and tolerance of being alone) has been significant, as it has given rise to much of the research and theorising relating to family interventions for personality-disordered patients.

Within this literature, the concept of expressed emotion (EE) suggested a new focus for interventions. Originally developed in relation to schizophrenia, expressed emotion (EE) is a term used to describe the family environment of patients, in terms of the extent to which their relatives are critical, hostile or over-involved. Families can be described as either 'high' or 'low' EE, based on their responses to an instrument called the Camberwell Family Interview (Vaughn & Leff, 1976). On the hypothesis that it would be helpful for families to reduce the levels of EE in the patient's home environment, interventions were designed in order to do just this. These were termed 'psycho-educational' (PE) interventions. They were primarily 'didactic' in nature, based on information giving and the premise that families could be trained to create an environment in which the risk of relapse was reduced.

While the focus in these PE interventions is on the behaviour of family members, they are still based on a view that there are key difficulties (deficits) being experienced by the *patient*, which must be coped with, rather than suggesting that the difficulty is with the family as a whole. In relation to schizophrenia, such interventions have been shown to be effective in preventing relapse (McFarlane et al., 1995), and there have been attempts to adopt similar approaches with other Axis I disorders including depression, bipolar affective disorder and post-traumatic stress disorder.

With regard to personality disorder – and borderline personality disorder in particular – similar 'psycho-educational' interventions have been developed. However, these interventions have typically combined the aims of helping patients and helping their families in the same programme. As such, they have a broader set of aims than interventions focused solely on expressed emotion. Also, it is apparent that 'systemic' ideas have not been abandoned altogether. While the idea of 'parental over-involvement' as a central difficulty in borderline personality disorder has been largely abandoned, many of the interventions described still conceptualise much of the 'problem' as being in the patient's interpersonal environment, rather than solely residing in the patient themselves.

Of course, it is perfectly possible to conceptualise both 'intrinsic' and 'environmental' deficits as co-existing (Villeneuve & Roux, 1995) and it is notable that many of the treatment approaches described in the literature that involve the family are based on an 'integrated' approach (various chapters in MacFarlane, 2004). These not only combine ideas of intrinsic and environmental deficits, but various treatment approaches/models within the same intervention. At the beginning of this chapter, three arguments for involving the family were presented separately, but it is clear that when it comes to the actual interventions being provided these goals are often combined.

The literature now contains reports of many, varied attempts to deliver such interventions to single families, as well as multiple family groups. In addition to PE interventions, there are reports of dialectical behaviour therapy (DBT)-based family interventions for borderline personality disorder, the application of ideas from family and couple therapy, various forms of self-help literature and family support groups. Many of the interventions reported in the literature are hard to 'classify', because of the way in which several approaches have been integrated. This chapter will, however, attempt to briefly illustrate some of these treatment programmes. They are described here as an indication of the range of ideas being discussed in the literature, rather than to serve as endorsements or to suggest that such approaches are established, empirically founded interventions. As will be apparent in the following section, evidence of effectiveness is unfortunately often lacking.

PSYCHO-EDUCATIONAL INTERVENTIONS

Ruiz-Sancho et al. (2001) review the common elements of psycho-educational interventions, as well as ways in which programmes have differed from each other. Common goals of such interventions include:

- the provision of a theoretical framework for families to understand patients' behaviour
- allowing families to have their feelings expressed and validated
- increasing family members' understanding of the particular stressors that may trigger a crisis for the patient

- helping the family to find better coping strategies
- helping families to tolerate difficult behaviour, while at the same time setting limits on disruptive, abusive behaviour.

Programmes vary in terms of the extent to which they include ideas taken from 'systems' models, whether they are focused on a particular personality disorder and which family members are invited.

One highly structured intervention described in the literature is the McLean psycho-educational multi-family group (so called because it was developed at McLean University in Massachusetts, USA; Berkowitz & Gunderson, unpublished manuscript). This programme is designed for patients/families with borderline personality disorder and has two phases. The initial 'joining' phase consists of between one and five sessions with a single family, followed by a half day workshop at which they meet with other families. There is then the more substantial multi-family group (MFG) phase, which can last for 18 months or more.

DBT INTERVENTIONS INVOLVING THE FAMILY

Hoffman, Fruzetti and Swenson (1999) propose a short-term family inter-vention, based on dialectical behaviour therapy (DBT) and conceptualised as 'skills training'. Within the aims of this approach are attempts to improve all family members' emotional regulation skills and to increase their under-standing of the patient in a clear, non-judgmental way. As such, there are significant elements of a 'psycho-educational' approach within the wider framework of a DBT approach. Again, the intervention is directed towards borderline personality disorder in particular.

Woodberry, Miller, Glinski, Indik and Mitchell (2002) review the literature relating to the inclusion of families in the treatment of adolescents, finding support for a dialectical framework to be applied as a way of synthesising individual and systemic approaches. While they go on to outline the implications for a DBT family therapy model, it is again a theoretical paper and the authors do not report any conclusions from the actual provision of such an approach.

FAMILY THERAPY APPROACHES

MacLean and MacLean (2004) describe a short-term, structured family therapy intervention for avoidant personality disorder, conceptualised as existing within a traditional 'family systems' perspective, with consideration given to concepts such as family structure, power, alignments and boundaries. However, what is notable is the degree to which approaches taken from cognitive and behavioural therapies have been integrated. A good deal of time is given to behavioural experiments addressing particular beliefs, graded exposure programmes and interpersonal skill training for the patient with avoidant personality disorder. This exemplifies the way in which therapies are becoming increasingly 'integrative'; much of what they describe might elsewhere be provided to patients on an individual basis, but is here integrated into working with the family as a whole.

COUPLE THERAPY

Links and Stockwell (2001, 2002) emphasise the potential for couple therapy to be helpful for patients with both borderline and narcissistic personality disorders, and provide clinical examples to support their proposals. With regard to borderline patients, they suggest developing the therapy around three behavioural clusters ('impulsive', 'identity' and 'affective'), while for narcissistic patients they suggest three factors that indicate the appropriateness of attempting couple therapy (the ability to curtail acting out, the individual's narcissistic defensiveness and vulnerability, and the 'complementarity of gratification' within the couple). Both forms of therapy are based on the premise that stable, intimate relationships have an intrinsic healing influence.

SELF-HELP LITERATURE AND FAMILY SUPPORT GROUPS

In addition to support available through statutory services such as CMHTs, it should be emphasised that there is a range of alternatives for family members, in the form of books, websites and non-statutory support groups. A quick search of the internet will highlight the enormous amount of information readily available, although the quality of this information is sometimes poor and, of course, the content liable to change over time. The potential for relatives (and indeed patients themselves) to be misled must be recognised. However, some suggestions for 'starter' websites include: borderlinepersonalitytoday.com; borderlineuk.co.uk; mind.org.uk. While there is a predominance of sites relating to borderline personality disorder, links are available to sites addressing other disorders. Some sites contain bulletin boards and chatrooms, allowing relatives to discuss difficulties with each other. Books for relatives of people with borderline personality disorder that receive widespread support include *Stop Walking on Eggshells: Taking Your Life Back When Someone You Care About Has Borderline Personality Disorder*

(Mason & Kreger, 1998), *New Hope For People With Borderline Personality Disorder: Your Friendly, Authoritative Guide to the Latest in Traditional and Complementary Solutions* (Bockian, Villagran & Porr, 2002) and *I Hate You – Don't Leave Me: Understanding the Borderline Personality* (Kreisman & Straus, 1989). Finally, in larger cities, there are often support groups, established to provide support and information to relatives, through a variety of organisations. All of these should be considered when discussing ways to involve families, friends and carers.

EVIDENCE OF EFFECTIVENESS

The first observation to make about the evidence for the effectiveness of these interventions is that it is very sparse indeed (Clarkin, Marziali & Munroe-Blum, 1991; Ruiz-Sancho et al., 2001). Very few systematic investigations have been carried out, and the literature used to support their delivery mainly consists of 'descriptive' studies (investigating those factors that interventions *aim* to address), a large number of single case studies (see, for example, various chapters in McFarlane, 2004) but just one study presenting grouped data relating to actual treatment. While this is clearly unsatisfactory, it does highlight the need for further studies to clarify which interventions should be routinely offered.

Interestingly, some of the 'descriptive' studies have produced findings that *contradict* widely held beliefs and the interventions that follow from them. For example, 'psycho-educational' approaches to working with carers are based on the premise that carers who understand the difficulties the patient experiences will feel more sympathetic towards them and less self-critical and be more supportive of the values inherent in the CMHT's approach. It is therefore interesting to note the findings of a study carried out by Hoffman and colleagues in the USA, involving 32 family members of patients with borderline personality disorder (Hoffman, Buteau, Hooley, Fruzetti & Bruce, 2003). In this study, greater knowledge about BPD was found to be associated with *higher* levels of burden, distress, depression and *greater* hostility towards patients. This highlights the importance of carefully considering what kinds of information should be provided, and how this will interact with relatives' existing beliefs. It should not be assumed that giving information is necessarily always helpful.

Similarly, the findings reported by Hooley and Hoffman (1999) contradict another commonly held belief about families. Thirty-five patients with a diagnosis of borderline personality disorder were followed up a year after they left hospital, and outcome (assessed through interviews with patients and families) related to expressed emotion in the patient's relatives at the time of their index admission. Contrary to expectations, 'criticism' and 'hostility' were not related to outcome or rates of re-admission. Moreover, it was observed that patients whose relatives scored highly on 'emotional over-involvement' had *better* clinical outcomes. Such observations are obviously important when designing the content of specific interventions, before proceeding to investigations of their efficacy and effectiveness.

The one study presenting grouped data is that by Gunderson, Berkowitz and Ruiz-Sancho (1997), who report on preliminary indicators of the effectiveness of the McLean psycho-educational approach. After one year, parents reported feeling more knowledgeable, less burdened and less concerned regarding suicidality and unpredictability. Patients felt less angry towards their parents, less troubled by their parents' efforts to control them and more aware of their own separation anxieties. Outcome was also considered in relation to levels of expressed emotion (EE). Five of eleven parents decreased in levels of 'criticism', while two increased. As in other studies, high initial levels of EE did not predict poor outcome, and the authors again note that high levels of over-involvement seem to be a positive predictor.

As already noted, the effective interventions described in the literature very often contain a mix of approaches, intended to achieve a number of goals. It is therefore difficult to draw conclusions as to what the 'active ingredient' of the intervention is. This is something that has complicated the literature with regard to other mental disorders, and needs to be considered in the design of any future studies looking at family interventions. Also, while the rationale for involving families is not only to do with benefiting patients – there is also the contribution they make to assessment, and the obligation on services to attempt to minimise their distress – these are sometimes overlooked when assessing outcome. While no-one has attempted to specifically evaluate the benefits of involving relatives in assessment, for example, it remains something for which a case can clearly be made but that would benefit from greater empirical support.

OBSTACLES TO WORKING WITH FAMILIES, AND HOW TO OVERCOME THEM

Descriptions of the families of personality disordered patients frequently report significant levels of psychological and social difficulties among the patient's relatives. For example, Gunderson (2001) describes parents of patients with borderline personality disorder as often having mental health difficulties – commonly, depression, substance abuse or personality disorder.

While they can be very difficult to distinguish, there are clearly problems encountered by family members as a *consequence* of a close relationship with a personality-disordered individual (for example, the distress caused and attempts to cope with this, as discussed earlier in this chapter) and difficulties that are present 'independently' of the patient. The latter might be the result of stressors *shared by* patients and their families, or reflect the relative's own mental health difficulties. Both potentially contribute to the difficulties experienced by patients.

The difficulties experienced by family members are, of course, additional to the patient's own interpersonal difficulties, which colour *their* perceptions of what aspects of the family situation it is possible or desirable to change. Taken together, there is clearly the potential for interventions involving the family to run into difficulty. While it is not possible to provide anything approaching a 'comprehensive list' of such obstacles, the following suggestions give an indication of what might be expected.

Patients' reservations may include

- a reluctance to 'blame' family members
- a concern that involving the family will invite (further) criticism from them
- anger towards their family members
- a desire to be viewed by their family as 'ill' or requiring special care
- embarrassment or shame.

Relatives' concerns might relate to

- a perception that they are being blamed for causing the patient's difficulties
- resentment towards the patient for the distress caused to the family
- the belief that the primary problem is 'depression', substance abuse, etc.
- guilt, after many years of having blamed themselves for the difficulties
- concern that the patient might become too 'independent' and leave them.

Several authors have commented on such matters. For example, Gunderson (2001) notes that parents who have been abusive may seek to deny the impact of their parenting, or avoid the shame that acknowledgement might bring. He goes on to say that in his experience with borderline patients whose parents are still married there is very often a split between the parents with regard to getting involved in treatment. In such cases, it can be hard to proceed as to do so would threaten their relationship. Fonagy (1995) notes that parents of borderline patients frequently have their own difficulty in recognising, tolerating and expressing negative emotions (in particular, sadness and anger) and goes on to suggest this may be one of the factors contributing to their child's difficulties. It also clearly impedes the kinds of intervention typically advocated by CMHTs.

Rather than conclude that family interventions will inevitably be ineffective when such features are observed, however, it may sometimes be possible to 'work around' or overcome such difficulties. In the following section, the restrictions on what teams can offer due to professional guidelines and legislation are considered. First, however, it is necessary to outline some of the responses that might be considered on purely clinical grounds, if the opportunity to work in this way is to be realised. Clearly, there is potential 'resistance' on both sides, to be addressed and if possible overcome. The alternative might be that the patient's progress becomes 'stuck' in some way. For example, without the explicit support of his or her family for a particular endeavour, a patient may be less likely to commit to personal change, if they believe they may risk losing the most important relationships they have (Young, 1991). Overcoming obstacles in relation to the family may at times be essential to moving forward.

Gunderson (2001) suggests general 'principles' for engaging families of borderline patients, which can be used to help establish a working relationship with most families, including those of patients with other disorders. They are also useful when considering how to present the idea of family work to patients. Some of these ideas are outlined below.

- Be prepared to have to 'sell' the advantages, to both the patient and their family – for example, emphasising that it will help you to understand them better.
- Be clear about what you are doing: what the intended goals are and how you hope to achieve them.
- Be prepared to adapt: to alter the treatment focus or modality in order to maintain the alliance.
- Emphasise the need for consistency and a collaborative approach – where appropriate, try to avoid anyone being characterised as the 'bad guy'.
- Work around questions of guilt by expressions of sympathy, provision of information about temperament and so on.

Regarding the use of the term 'personality disorder' (potentially a concern for both patients and their relatives), Gunderson suggests being prepared to sidestep disagreements about the validity or usefulness of the diagnosis. Instead, he advocates focusing on specific issues (such as intense anger or role functioning) and the provision of information relating to these difficulties.

In summary, there are numerous potential difficulties, objections and reservations regarding family work, in the minds of both patients and their relatives. These should be anticipated, explored and addressed, through discussion that is in many ways similar to the work conducted with the patient on their own. Patients and their relatives may benefit simply from ventilating their feelings, from receiving information, or through some process that is in keeping with one or other of the psychotherapeutic approaches. For example, if working within a cognitive framework, patients and families might be encouraged to undertake certain 'experiments', with the aim of challenging a particular belief that constitutes an obstacle to progress. In such ways, the task of 'overcoming obstacles' merges with the intervention itself.

In some cases, it will be possible to establish a useful working alliance with the family, as well as the patient. However, it should be recognised that there are limitations to what is possible. The obstacles described in this section can be major difficulties, and CMHT staff should not expect things to always run smoothly. Also, there are clearly limits to when it would be considered advisable to even attempt to involve a family member, depending on factors such as the severity of any mental illness or substance abuse in the relative, the degree of abusive behaviour on the part of the relative, and so on. CMHT staff need to be confident in their judgements with regard to this, and to not feel under pressure to involve the family in all cases.

THE PRACTICAL AND ETHICAL CONSIDERATIONS OF WORKING WITH THE FAMILY

In addition to the obstacles noted above, there are certain obligations placed on CMHT staff by legislation and their professional roles, which can also influence the process of trying to engage patients and families in interventions. The following checklist summarises some of the main considerations:

- consent
- confidentiality
- information sharing within the team and with outside agencies
- the need for close supervision
- the keeping of casenotes.

In the UK, patients do have the right to have personal information kept confidential from their family – but they cannot prevent their family from seeking support from mental health services for difficulties of their own. As such, a formal 'family intervention' (or any approach that goes beyond what might be considered a 'discrete' and separate intervention specifically for family members) can only proceed with the patient's consent.

However, there is also a requirement in the United Kingdom under CPA to assess and address the needs of patients' main carers. While it is within a patient's rights to prevent the details of their treatment being shared with anyone (unless there is judged to be a significant risk of harm to either the patient or other members of society) it remains possible to talk to the family about the difficulties they experience, and *their* perspective on the patient's problems, but not to unite this with information gathered through other parts of the service.

Within the team, there are obviously arguments for the sharing of information, and for staff to receive regular clinical supervision. Again, patients can request that information not be shared between staff, and it is for individual staff and local policy to decide the extent to which they will agree to consent to such restrictions. Provided such limitations are made clear to the patient at the outset, this allows them to make an informed choice regarding whether to engage with the intervention being proposed.

Clearly, it is helpful to record in the notes precisely what arrangement was agreed upon with regard to confidentiality. The issue of keeping records also raises the question of whether casenotes relating to a family intervention should be kept in the patient's file, or in a separate file. Again, it is worth seeking guidance from local managers regarding policies on this matter, as there appears to be a degree of uncertainty in and variability between different services.

These considerations obviously apply to all of the work undertaken by CMHTs, with any client group. With regard to family interventions for personality disorder, however, the importance of attending to such matters is perhaps of greater importance. Difficult situations can arise, either if the purpose of the sessions is unclear or if multiple therapeutic aims are being targeted.

SUMMARY AND CONCLUSIONS

This chapter has outlined some of the ways in which CMHTs might seek to understand and influence aspects of the interpersonal environment of the patient, in order to reduce the distress experienced by patients and their relatives, as well as to minimise the impact of the patient's personality difficulties on their day-to-day functioning. Gunderson (2001) uses the term 'sociotherapy' for such approaches – i.e. therapeutic approaches addressing the individual's social adaptation.

Working with carers is not something that can ever replace attempts to work directly with patients themselves. However, the observations made in this chapter do hopefully make a case for considering it as an option. As has been noted, the potential benefits are many and varied, and are not restricted to gains for the patient alone. They can also be justified in terms of the benefit to carers themselves.

As has been emphasised, it is not an approach that will always be easy – there are a variety of significant obstacles that might arise. However, to ignore the patient's social environment completely might result in greater difficulties being encountered in the course of interventions focused solely on the individual. Hopefully, this chapter has made the case for attempting to involve families, friends and carers where possible.

It must nevertheless be acknowledged that this chapter has very much focused on the reasons *for* working with families – as noted, there are situations in which it would be unadvisable to do so. The potential to make a situation worse must always be recognised, and at times the conclusion following assessment will be that there is unlikely to be any clear benefit.

A note of caution should also be sounded given the state of the literature relating to such interventions, and the relative lack of empirical evidence supporting work with families. What descriptions are contained in the literature focus heavily on borderline personality disorder, and also relate to interventions that are 'manualised' rather than truly 'formulation driven'. Given the general consensus of opinion in favour of individualised treatment plans, it is hard to draw conclusions from the literature as to which components of the interventions described should be incorporated into any individual patient's care. Recent reviews of psychological treatments for personality disorder (e.g. Bateman & Tyrer, 2004) have overlooked family/carer interventions, and for the time being this is perhaps understandable.

This is, however, a growing field and one that is already uncovering interesting information about the social environments in which patients live. Some of the orthodoxies built up from talking only to patients are being questioned. Coherent theoretical arguments for attempting to intervene are being put forward. It is to be hoped that further information will be added to the academic literature, and that this will be of use to those involved directly with delivering services. In addition to the need for formal investigations of such interventions, there is the possibility of 'practice-based evidence' making a significant contribution to the knowledge base. This will require practitioners such as those working in CMHTs to become involved with attempts at providing such interventions. Working with family, friends and carers might at times be difficult, but in some cases it will either be an essential feature of the care plan as a whole, or something that can greatly enhance the effects of other elements of treatment.

REFERENCES

Bateman, A. W. & Tyrer, P. (2004). Services for personality disorder: Organisation for inclusion. *Advances in Psychiatric Treatment, 10*, 425–433.

Bernstein, D., Kasapis, C., Bergman, A., Horvarth, T., Klar, H., Silverman, J. & Siever, L. (1997). Assessing axis II disorders by informant interview. *Journal of Personality Disorders, 11*, 158–167.

Bockian, N. R., Villagran, N. E. & Porr, V. (2002). *New hope for people with borderline personality disorder: Your friendly, authoritative guide to the latest in traditional and complementary solutions.* New York: Prima.

Clark, L. A. (1993). *Manual for the schedule for non-adaptive and adaptive personality.* Minneapolis, MN: University of Minnesota Press.

Clarkin, J. F., Marziali, E. & Munroe-Blum, H. (1991). Group and family treatments for borderline personality disorder. *Hospital and Community Psychiatry, 42*, 1038–1043.

Coolidge, F. L. & Merwin, M. M. (1992) Reliability and validity of the Coolidge Axis II Inventory: a new inventory for the assessment of personality disorders. *Journal of Personality Assessment, 59*, 223–238.

Department of Health. (1990). *The care programme approach for people with mental illness referred to specialist psychiatric services.* London: HMSO.

Fieldman, R. B., Zelkowitz, P., Weiss, M., Vogel, J., Heyman, M. & Paris, J. (1995). A comparison of the families of mothers with borderline and nonborderline personality disorders. *Comprehensive Psychiatry, 36*, 157–163.

Fonagy, P. (1995). Playing with reality: the development of psychic reality and its malfunction in borderline personalities. *International Journal of Psychoanalysis, 76*, 39–44.

Frank, H. & Paris, J. (1981). Recollections of family experience in borderline patients. *Archives of General Psychiatry, 38*, 1031–1034.

Gunderson, J. G. (2001). *Borderline personality disorder: A clinical guide.* Washington, DC: American Psychiatric Publishing.

Gunderson, J. G., Berkowitz, C. & Ruiz-Sancho, A. M. (1997). Families of borderline patients: a psychoeducational approach. *Bulletin of the Menninger Clinic, 61*, 446–457.

Gunderson, J. G., Kerr, J. & Englund, D. W. (1980). The families of borderlines: a comparative study. *Archives of General Psychiatry, 37*, 27–33.

Gunderson, J. G. & Lyoo, I. K. (1997). Family problems and relationships for adults with borderline personality disorder. *Harvard Review of Psychiatry, 4*, 272–278.

Guttman, H. A. & Laporte, L. (2000). Empathy in families of women with borderline personality disorder, anorexia nervosa and a control group. *Family Process, 39*, 345–358.

Hoffman, P. D., Buteau, E., Hooley, J. M., Fruzetti, A. E. & Bruce, M. L. (2003). Family members' knowledge about borderline personality disorder: correspondence with their levels of depression, burden, distress and expressed emotion. *Family Process, 42*, 469–478.

Hoffman, P. D., Fruzetti, A. E. & Swenson, C. R. (1999). Dialectical behaviour therapy – family skills training. *Family Process, 38*, 399–414.

Hooley, J. M. & Hoffman, P. D. (1999). Expressed emotion and clinical outcome in borderline personality disorder. *American Journal of Psychiatry, 156*, 1557–1562.

Hyler, S. E., Skodol, A. E., Oldham, J. M., Kellman, H. D. & Doidge, N. (1992). Validity of the Personality Diagnostic Questionnaire – Revised (PDQ-R): a replication in an outpatient sample. *Comprehensive Psychiatry*, *33*, 73–77.

Kreisman, J. J. & Straus, H. (1989). *I hate you – Don't leave me: Understanding the borderline personality*. New York: Avon.

Links, P. S. & Stockwell, M. (2001). Is couple therapy indicated for borderline personality disorder? *American Journal of Psychotherapy*, *55*, 491–506.

Links, P. S. & Stockwell, M. (2002). The role of couple therapy in the treatment of narcissistic personality disorder. *American Journal of Psychotherapy*, *56*, 522–539.

MacFarlane, M. M. (Ed.). (2004). *Family treatment of personality disorders: Advances in clinical practice*. Binghampton, NY: Haworth.

MacLean, P. D. & MacLean, C. P. (2004). Family therapy of avoidant personality disorder. In M. M. MacFarlane (Ed.), *Family treatment of personality disorders: Advances in clinical practice* (pp. 273–304). Binghampton, NY: Haworth.

Magnavita, J. J. (2000). *Relational therapy for personality disorders*. New York: Wiley.

Magnavita, J. J. & MacFarlane, M. M. (2004). Family treatment of personality disorders: Historical overview and historical perspectives. In M. M. MacFarlane (Ed.), *Family treatment of personality disorders: Advances in clinical practice* (pp. 3–40). Binghampton, NY: Haworth.

Mason, P. T. & Kreger, R. (1998). *Stop walking on eggshells: Taking your life back when someone you care about has borderline personality disorder*. Oakland, CA: New Harbinger.

McFarlane, W. R., Lukens, E., Link, B., Dushay, R., Deakins, S. A., Newmark, M., Dunne, E. J., Horen, B. & Toran, J. (1995). Multiple-family groups and psychoeducation in the treatment of schizophrenia. *Archives of General Psychiatry*, *52*, 679–687.

Millon, T. (1987). On the genesis and prevalence of the borderline personality disorder: a social learning thesis. *Journal of Personality Disorders*, *1*, 354–372.

Mitton, J. M. & Links, P. S. (1996) Helping the family: a framework for intervention. In P. S. Links (Ed.), *Clinical assessment and management of severe personality disorder. Clinical practice* (No. 5, pp. 195–218). Washington, DC: American Psychiatric Press.

Nichols, W. C. (2004). Integrative family and marital treatment of dependent personality disorders. In M. M. MacFarlane (Ed.), *Family treatment of personality disorders: Advances in clinical practice* (pp. 173–204). Binghampton, NY: Haworth.

Ruiz-Sancho, A. M., Smith, G. W. & Gunderson, J. G. (2001). Psychoeducational approaches. In W. J. Livesley (Ed.), *Handbook of personality disorders* (pp. 107–123). New York: Guilford.

Schulz, P. M., Schulz, S. C. H., Hamer, R., Resnick, R. J., Friedel, R. O. & Goldberg, S. C. (1985). The impact of borderline and schizotypal personality disorders on patients and their families. *Hospital Community Psychiatry*, *36*, 879–881.

Vaughn, C. E. & Leff, J. P. (1976). The influence of family and social factors on the course of psychiatric illness. *British Journal of Psychiatry*, *129*, 125–137.

Villeneuve, C. & Roux, N. (1995). Family therapy and some personality disorders in adolescence. *Adolescent Psychiatry*, *20*, 365–380.

Woodberry, K. A., Miller, A. L., Glinski, J., Indik, J. & Mitchell, A. G. (2002). Family therapy and dialectical behaviour therapy with adolescents: Part II: a theoretical review. *American Journal of Psychotherapy*, *56*, 585–602.

Young, D. W. (1991). Family factors in the failure of psychotherapy. *American Journal of Psychotherapy*, *45*, 499–510.

Zimmerman, M. (1994). Diagnosing personality disorders. A review of issues and research methods. *Archives of General Psychiatry*, *51*, 225–245.

16

Personality Disorder in other Healthcare Settings

DAWN BENNETT

IAN B. KERR

INTRODUCTION

Patients with personality disorders or features of them, whether or not they have been formally diagnosed as such, present to healthcare professionals in diverse ways and in various settings. Some may cope with psychological distress by reverting to substance misuse or self-harm, some may have difficult and sometimes abusive and violent relationships and others may neglect or damage their own health in various ways. Some may find it difficult or 'fail' to co-operate in treatment of possibly genuine physical illnesses or present with somatisation-type disorders as a result of under-lying psychological distress or difficulty. Others may finish up in the prison system, where it is well recognised that large numbers suffer from diagnosable personality disorder (Coid, 2003), a setting that is more likely to exacerbate than ameliorate their condition. Although the latter group is beyond the scope of this chapter, as is the field of learning disability, many of the problems relating to treatment and management of patients in the broader healthcare system apply similarly to such settings (Pollock, 2001; Pollock, Stowell-Smith & Goepfert, in press). Many do not ever present to the healthcare system but may suffer considerable distress in their lives, also

Personality Disorder and Community Mental Health Teams: A Practitioner's Guide. Edited by
M. J. Sampson, R. A. McCubbin and P. Tyrer. © 2006 John Wiley & Sons, Ltd.

causing distress in those around them, frequently at considerable human and economic cost.

It will be clear from other chapters in this volume that the concept of personality disorder is nosologically questionable and complex. It is increasingly recognised that such patients represent one end of a spectrum of severe and complex, non-psychotic, disorders. Inevitably, a range of problems and symptoms are characteristic of such disorders, usually (although misleadingly) described as 'co-morbidity'. Many patients suffering from personality difficulties will have suffered a history of developmental deprivation, trauma or abuse, which lead to the distressing, disabling and hard-to-help difficulties encountered clinically. These are also characterised by interpersonal difficulties, which may, amongst other things, make 'rational' and co-operative involvement in treatment of health problems (whether physical or psychological) difficult. As such, they can be seen to fall under the more general rubric of the 'difficult' patient. This is not a diagnostic category but one that may helpfully illuminate discussion and consideration of such patients, many – but by no means all – of whom would qualify for a formal diagnosis of personality disorder. A major issue in work with such patients is that staff behaviours or enactments in reaction to such 'difficulty' assume critical importance, and may well frequently contribute to the difficulty. Although any approach to such disorders requires a robust and coherent model to address all of their various aspects, it is the latter area of disordered interpersonal relations that is a major focus of this chapter, given its importance in working with this patient group.

This chapter, in considering these general issues and their impact on healthcare systems, is of general importance for CMHT workers for two reasons. First, they themselves face exactly the same issues in their day-to-day work with this group. Second, they will be asked to liaise or provide psychiatric consultation to other professionals across the healthcare system. We review the settings and ways in which such personality disordered or 'difficult' patients may present and the impact they may have. We consider treatment and management approaches, focusing especially on what in our view are the key systemic or contextual dimensions of such difficulties. We finally attempt to offer CMHT workers guidance for a consultation approach for this work. Such developments are of relevance and importance in working with all kinds of patient in all kinds of setting. We are, however, mindful that this broadening of the CMHT worker role and the emphasis on coherent models to inform formulation-led care has implications for further training.

PSYCHOLOGICAL PROBLEMS IN OTHER HEALTHCARE SETTINGS

Given the severe and complex nature of the difficulties experienced by people with personality disorders, it is not surprising that patients present with a range of symptoms in different settings. The diagnosis of personality disorder is associated with high morbidity and significant mortality (Perry, 1993) and has been reported in association with eating disorders, somatisation disorders, schizophrenia, bipolar disorders, sexual disorders, obsessive–compulsive disorders and dissociative disorders (Zimmerman, 1999). There are high rates of suicide, self-harm, substance misuse, panic, depression and severe relationship difficulties. In addition, there are patients whose physical disorders are complicated by psychological factors and poor self-care and those with unexplained medical symptoms. In this section, we consider some of these 'disorders', highlight the challenges they pose to the healthcare system and outline some approaches that have made major contributions in helping staff respond helpfully. We suggest that psychological understandings should play a major role in their management and, whilst generic (CMHT) workers may not be offering psychological therapy, they have important therapeutic responsibilities in informing the care of these patients across the broader healthcare system. Throughout this chapter, we will primarily explain such ideas with reference to cognitive analytic models, as this is the model with which we are most familiar. However, it is clear that there are many alternative psychological approaches that address similar phenomena, with reference to similar ideas, albeit using different terminology.

PRIMARY CARE

Personality disorder represents a significant source of burden in primary care. Studies have found around a quarter of consecutive attenders fulfil diagnostic criteria (Moran, Jenkins, Tylee, Blizard & Mann, 2000), often presenting with difficulties characteristic of common mental disorder. One-third of general practitioner (GP) consultations have a substantial mental health component, but studies have consistently found that GPs often fail to detect such difficulties in approximately half of these patients (see, e.g., Goldberg and Bridges, 1987). This may reflect the way patients present mental health problems in primary care: presenting with somatic symptoms, attributing their physical symptoms to physical illness; hesitating to disclose psychological symptoms through fear they will seem trivial; finding that psychological problems are not as easy to talk about and potentially stigmatising.

Understanding and managing psychological problems differs in primary care from specialist services – defining problems is often more difficult as the patient presents earlier with symptoms that are less developed. The nature of primary care consultation means that GPs 'tune into' patients' problems over the course of several consultations, exploring psychological problems in the context of containing patients' health problems, following the patient's pace and readiness to explore, which may also involve some degree of intervention (Balint & Norell, 1973). However, consultations may become dysfunctional if the GP is unable to identify the patient's 'true' reason for attending. This may relate to the problem of 'frequent attenders' (Little et al., 2001).

Although some patients will be attending frequently for appropriate medical management of acute or chronic diseases, there are others who have no apparent mental or physical health problem accounting for the consultation pattern. They may include those presenting with psychosocial difficulties, medically unexplained symptoms, somatisation disorder and health anxiety. Frequent attending is classed as 11 or more visits per year and the workload generated by these patients can be considerable (Neal, Heywood, Morley, Clayden & Dowell, 1998). Similarly, some patients attend accident and emergency departments frequently (seven or more visits per annum). This group has poorer general health and higher levels of psychiatric disorder, more GP visits, and more general and psychiatric hospital admissions (Williams et al., 2001). While there may be many factors that influence attendance, their difficulties will vary. There will be factors in the professional–patient relationship that are likely to maintain frequent attendance. For example, doctors can unwittingly contribute to the exacerbation of medically unexplained symptoms, through such reactions as over-treatment, multiple investigations and ineffective reassurance (Page & Wessely, 2003).

'Frequently attending' patients in primary care are often significantly psychologically distressed (Katon et al., 1991), so making reduced attendance a 'goal' in itself would be inappropriate. It would be more important to recognise the problem and consider ways to influence dysfunctional patterns of service use. We will describe three promising interventions. In the first, a specialist multi-disciplinary community team undertook a comprehensive bio-psychosocial consultation followed by presentation of a formulation, offering an understanding of symptoms in terms of the patient's life history. This was followed, if required, by short term psychological therapy (10 sessions), pharmacotherapy for anxiety, depression or panic and in some cases referral for specialist psychological treatment. This approach was found to reduce treatment costs substantially in an uncontrolled study (Matalon, Nahmani, Rabin, Maoz & Hart, 2002). There is pilot data showing encouraging efficacy of cognitive analytic therapy (CAT) in reducing psychological difficulties and frequency of attendance for patients with a range of difficulties (see Baker et al. in Ryle & Kerr, 2002). Pickvance, Parry and Howe (2004) report using a cognitive analytic model to enable a primary care team to formulate the phenomenon of frequent attendance. They identified 'reciprocal roles' in doctor–patient interactions and identified patterns characterising unhelpful but self-maintaining patterns of consulting. Teaching inputs and consultancy supervision helped to alert practitioners to these patterns and they influenced their responses, which led to increased understanding, team co-operation and changes in practice.

UNEXPLAINED MEDICAL SYMPTOMS AND SOMATISATION

A small but significant number of patients undergo extensive investigation for physical symptoms for which no cause is found. For example, patients having more than ten admissions over eight years (Fink, 1992) and a third of patients in neurology, cardiology and gastrointestinal clinics have medically unex-plained symptoms at discharge (Hamilton, Campos & Creed, 1996). Chronic pain associated with no somatic pathology, where different psychological factors are thought to play an important role, is also an unresolved problem. One study has reported that almost half of a large group of patients referred to a behavioural medicine clinic met personality disorder criteria (Emerson, Pankrantz, Joos and Smith, 1994).

Psychosomatic conditions and medically unexplained symptoms have been characterised by concepts such as alexithymia (an inability to put feelings into words), emotional inhibition and negative affectivity. These conceptualisations sometimes imply that physical symptoms either serve as a defence against psychological symptoms or are the result of emotional disorder. A large number of studies have observed the defence mechanisms of 'somatisation' and 'denial' in patients with medically unexplained long-lasting pain disorder (e.g. Monsen & Havik, 2001), indicating a tendency to deny psychological distress and to transform personal conflicts into more socially acceptable problems such as pain and somatic complaints. The relationship between these symptoms and interpersonal style has been investigated, suggesting that chronic pain patients are overly submissive, with problems in self-identity, e.g. trying hard to please and difficulties in feeling and expressing anger and being assertive (Pither and Nicholas, 1991; Monsen and Havik, 2001).

In our view, unexplained somatic symptoms can often reflect problems in patterns of relating and self-management, notably internalised prohibitions on the expression of anger or assertion and associated anxious and submissive roles in relationships. One feature of the patterns enacted in somatisation is commonly an inability to communicate anxious feelings, often in relation to a belief that one ought to cope alone. Although this inability may be partly constitutional and represent temperamental factors referred to as alexithymia, it may also reflect the difficulties in self-reflection and self-expression that are often experienced by those subjected to childhood adversity or abuse. A pattern of conforming to others may be formed by repeated early experiences, in which focusing on others' experiences, wishes, needs and renouncing their own subjectivity was the best way to ensure the availability of significant others. When such internal processes interact with a person's interpersonal situation, they can produce chronic physiological changes, causing or exacerbating psychosomatic 'illness'. The person's non-validated self-experiences and emotion are transformed into bodily worries and pain. The situation would become more complex when this influences interpersonal responses, such that the consequence of pain is eliciting care from others.

A focus on the patient within his or her current relationships – on awareness, tolerance and expression of affects and on interpersonal problems – is therefore necessary. The good outcomes from brief psychodynamic–interpersonal therapy in 'functional' gut disorders (Hamilton et al., 2000) support the importance of such a focus. However, not all patients would agree on the presence of psychological problems or accept a referral. In these situations, patients with somatisation syndrome may benefit from frequent consultation with a small number of primary care clinicians who know the patient, and can avoid invasive medical procedures or surgery (Kashner, Rost, Cohen, Anderson & Smith, 1995).

DIFFICULTIES IN MANAGING CHRONIC MEDICAL CONDITIONS

Even if given full explanations and support, a considerable proportion of patients with chronic medical conditions do not adhere to treatment regimes. Some may act in ways that contradict advice offered by medical staff and put themselves at physical risk. Two conditions in which this has serious consequences are asthma and diabetes. They are complex conditions placing a remarkable amount of responsibility on patients, so problems with self-care are not surprising. In each, there is some research support for the value of psychological models, in understanding these conditions and improving self-management. Again, we will describe applications using a cognitive analytic model (Walsh, Hagan & Gamsu, 2000; Fosbury, Bosley, Ryle, Sonksen & Judd, 1997), although it is clear that this is not the only theoretical framework that can be applied.

Failing to adhere to treatment regimes can be thought about in terms of destructive patterns of self-care, which the patient may be largely unaware of. In diabetes, Fosbury et al. (1997) have identified reasons for failing to adhere to diets, attend for blood tests and take an appropriate dose of insulin, and shown that these are not specific to the condition but are manifestations of more general patterns of self-management. These included depressive self-neglect and passive resistance to authority in general, but importantly to clinic staff. Walsh et al. (2000), in relation to asthma, explored factors that influenced self-care regimes, specifically non-compliance. Their findings are particularly valuable in understanding the influence of healthcare relationships for patients' illness self-management. They identified three specific non-compliance 'procedures' – denial, avoidance and depression – with overlaps to those in diabetes. These procedures had clear short- and longer-term health risks for the patient (e.g. crisis-driven management of asthma attacks and higher levels of medication) and the service (reduction in morale from the effects of non-compliance). These studies offer an understanding of how and why roles within the healthcare relationship left the patient and helper stuck and unable to find alternative ways to manage life-long illness.

While not clearly indicative of personality *disorder*, these observations suggest how early experiences and subsequent coping strategies may explain how these patients struggle to be self-caring or accept care from others, and how this may be one aspect of their personal difficulties. Damaging and neglecting care in childhood can prevent the integration of healthy ways of caring for oneself, or trusting or eliciting care from others. It may not be the diagnosis of a chronic medical condition that results in emotional difficulties, but that pre-illness life dilemmas can affect self-care. In simplistic terms, a child may learn to respond by protesting to a controlling parent and later be sensitised to respond in the same way when faced with the restricted controls of an illness and the advice of professionals. The condition can therefore become a vehicle through which unresolved relationship difficulties can be channelled. In order to treat these problems effectively, the work needs to address the ways in which the individual's way of construing or coping with the situation affects her or his illness management. A psychological conceptualisation would be used to recognise these self-destructive patterns. We would argue that the recognition and treatment of damaging self-care is not only a humane response, but cost effective (see below).

Equally important is the need to consider the healthcare relationship and for workers to examine their own emotional and behavioural responses, particularly around care and nurturance (Walsh et al., 2000). Illness, particularly if it is of a chronic nature, may generate powerful emotions concerning personal vulnerability, the need for care or longing for rescue. Workers need to be alert to their own responses, such as feelings of power and a desire to rescue and how we are pulled to relate to patients. A clear implication of this recognition is that 'difficulty' is always a *systemic* phenomenon and requires ways of thinking and acting that offer systemic understandings of staff reactions and also of the pressure they in turn experience.

DISTRESS AND DISTURBANCE EXPRESSED THROUGH SELF-DESTRUCTIVE TENDENCIES: SUBSTANCE MISUSE, EATING DISORDERS AND DELIBERATE SELF-HARM

There is a high prevalence of personality disorder among drug and alcohol misusers in treatment and custodial settings. Antisocial and borderline personality disorder are the most common categories, with prevalence being lower among alcohol abusers, compared to those with other drug use disorders (Seivewright and Daly, 1997; Verheul, 2001). However, the validity of the personality disorder diagnoses can be questioned for people whose behaviour is characteristic of the diagnosis, but may be secondary to the effects of a dependence syndrome – for example, engaging in criminal activity to fund drug addiction. Disturbances in relationships may also be due to a dependence syndrome. These concerns are important, but similar difficulties are present in considering co-occurrence of many psychiatric disorders. Staff in substance misuse treatment services are highly accustomed to managing patients with personality difficulties in their day-to-day work, although they may not routinely use diagnoses in their assessment and treatment planning. For many patients, misusing substances serves to keep at bay memories and feelings from disturbed early experiences. Withdrawal may leave them with a sense of emptiness and unmanageable feelings. Other common patterns may be that substances may provide a state of 'blissful fusion' and an absence of conflict and need. Assessment should aim to identify the role of the substance within the patient's self-management (intra-personal) and interpersonal relationship patterns.

Eating disorders similarly may represent a covert means of communicating or coping with feelings, commonly feelings of not being heard or being pressurised to perform. These inter- and intrapersonal problems can be expressed through an abnormal preoccupation with weight and food. Ryle and Kerr (2002) suggest that they are always associated with, but may serve to obscure, problems at the level of 'self-processes'. These are then expressed mainly around issues of control, submission, pleasing others and perfectionism. Severe cases may meet criteria for a personality disorder diagnosis and can be associated with problems of substance abuse.

Only a small proportion of those who self-harm have a formal psychiatric illness but a considerable proportion have borderline traits or meet the full borderline personality disorder (BPD) criteria. Self-harm often occurs in the xt of interpersonal problems and has been understood as a (problematic) of communication, help-seeking and management of difficult emotions. cal approaches have previously predominantly understood it as a form of logy or disorder, requiring intervention to stop it. Self-harm is now more nonly viewed as a way of coping in a harmful environment and a visible of internalised pain and abuse in environments where this may have been et. Many patients are ambivalent about addressing self-harm as it can be gnificant coping mechanism and many, especially those who repeat, experienced by healthcare professionals as 'difficult' patients. They [uently provoke indifferent or hostile reactions and poor or even abusive care (Hemmings, Donaldson & Reval, 1996). This reflects the lack of an adequate psychological understanding and the power with which collusive responses, such as 'rejection' or 'inappropriate concern', are elicited. Such reactions may reflect a replication of the patient's problematic relationships (past and present) and become a maintaining factor. They also make more difficult the complex task of assessing suicide risk. There have been some effective interventions aimed at attempting to reduce repeated self-harm that specifically address patterns of relating to self and others (Guthrie et al., 2001; Sheard et al., 2000). These emphasise understanding the meaning behind self-harm, validating the significant emotional issues involved and allowing the person power, control and responsibility.

OLDER ADULTS: THE RISK OF OVERLOOKING PSYCHOLOGICAL PROCESSES

Later life can be a time when coping mechanisms are challenged by losses, disability and changes in social role. Pre-existing trauma and low self-esteem can surface to produce anxiety, depression and self-destructive behaviours. Wesby (2004) offers a useful framework, which moves from 'personality' to 'personality vulnerability' to 'personality disorder', i.e. normality through vulnerabilty to disorder. It offers a way to understand how some older people fail to withstand the vicissitudes of life if they have depended upon external sources of esteem. These are challenged in later life through the various losses, leading to some form of distress or 'feeling unwell', expressing distress somatically. There is a tendency to label 'difficult' older people as confused and beyond therapeutic help, so creating a false belief that personality disorders in older people are rare (Hepple & Sutton, 2004). Clinicians in this field argue for this to be understood in terms of the person's whole life story. Sutton (1997) illustrates how a client's challenging behaviour towards her family and care staff could be understood in terms of her past abuses. Older adults are able to work on their relationships with others and there are promising extensions to psychological approaches for later life that are countering negative attitudes in this area (Hepple & Sutton, 2004; Laidlaw, Thompson, Dick-Siskin & Gallagher-Thompson, 2003).

SUMMARY

The above review focuses on patients presenting in various settings with distressing, disabling and hard-to-help difficulties. Their care becomes 'difficult' as there is often a failure of 'rational' attempts to help them. These patients would not all qualify for a diagnosis of personality disorder but they may be experienced as 'difficult' and their health outcomes may be poor. Some of the work reported lends support to our view that there is a need for a 'whole person', high level understanding as opposed to a focus on the symptoms or illness. An understanding of the function of the symptoms and the patient's specific damaging behaviours would offer a new perspective and a way of more fully engaging the patient in appropriate forms of care. In the approaches reviewed above there are two general principles that stand out as likely to be necessary features for this task: a conceptual framework (or 'case formulation') and an interpersonal focus. We will now consider these two principles.

PSYCHOLOGICALLY INFORMED MANAGEMENT IN OTHER HEALTHCARE SYSTEMS

CONCEPTUAL FRAMEWORK OR CASE FORMULATION

In the cited approaches, a conceptual framework or case formulation was used to understand the healthcare problem or the patient's engagement with the service (the patient–helper/team relationship). This then informed treatment and management strategies. There are competing or contradictory paradigms for understanding such disorders. Along with other authors, we suggest that a fully adequate understanding of an individual patient needs to take into account genetic and biological factors and the effects of early experience on development, which can be explained within psychodynamic, attachment or cognitive theories. In addition, the current life circumstances and their impact on the individual's sense of self and ability to act need to be considered. This information would be constructed into a case formulation, the central aim of which is to set the patients' problems and distress in the context of an understanding of their lives. A comprehensive, individualised bio-psychosocial formulation should be a minimum prerequisite for working

conversational style and emphasis on developing a close working relationship with the patient was considered particularly helpful in engaging patients who were ambivalent or wary of psychiatric treatment and had been resistant to previous therapeutic endeavours.

We would see these two principles as essential features of any model that aims to account for the difficulties experienced by these patients and any approach that offers ways of working effectively with them. We propose that such a *formulation-based theoretically coherent* management approach is crucial for a consistent and coherent approach to their management. The various treatment models (which might include dialectical behaviour therapy, cognitive therapy, psychoanalytically informed day hospital, cognitive analytic therapy, therapeutic communities or others) would each have contributions to make, particularly those models that can inform indirect working.

THE ROLE OF SPECIALIST MENTAL HEALTH SERVICES IN PSYCHOLOGICALLY INFORMED MANAGEMENT IN OTHER HEALTHCARE SYSTEMS

The specialist mental health services have important therapeutic responsibilities in informing the care of psychologically disturbed patients who present across the broader healthcare system. They may be approached to offer assessment for individual patients, or to liaise with primary care or medical teams in the management of patients with such difficulties. We offer some guidelines based on the principles outlined above.

Whether offering direct or indirect care, such workers would ideally be able to offer specialist skills of psychological assessment, formulation and intervention. Indirect work may take one of two forms but is most likely to be indirect patient work or consultancy focusing on helping other health professionals or staff groups to work with a patient. This may include facilitating enhanced multi-disciplinary team assessment, formulation and care planning change through practice development. The aim would be to offer a conceptual framework to help the patient and/or referrer/key worker (who may be a nurse, general practitioner or someone from any of a range of professions) to construct a new meaning to the problematic situation (A. Carradice, personal communication). We have found the following steps a useful framework to such indirect working. These ideas are clearly relevant to a wide range of problems, in addition to – but including – personality disorders.

UNDERSTANDING THE SITUATION

Initially, specialist workers would listen to and help to contain the reactions of the key worker(s). They would tune into and start to identify patterns in what they are describing with regard to the patient and the difficulties they present. A central aim is to view the patient as a 'patient with a problem' and not a 'problem patient'. The intended emphasis is on a collaborative approach to decision-making and sharing of responsibility. Flynn and Bartholomew (2003) emphasise these elements in their consultancy model in in-patient settings as helping to 'break a cycle of conflict' that can become active between a patient and the system, often reinforcing the patient's problematic behaviours.

PROVISIONAL CONCEPTUALISATION

Specialist workers offering consultancy would help to develop a conceptual framework that facilitates reflective practice, gives greater insight and can inform management. The resulting formulation needs to be a concise account of the patient's difficulties and damaging repetitive patterns of relating. It would use a coherent theoretical framework and use the patient's personal history and the key worker's experiences, e.g. counter-transference responses to working with the patient.

Once a provisional formulation has been developed, the specialist worker would agree with the key worker(s) an appropriate assessment period to test and refine the formulation. For example, in CAT one may draw a partial sequential diagrammatic reformulation (SDR) that captures the problem and agree to spend a period of time observing to see if the SDR is a helpful way of understanding what is going on. As an illustration, the aim in consultation for a 'frequent attender' would be to help the clinical team to understand the patterns of interpersonal relating that the patient was enacting in the consultation and to help him or her to avoid reciprocating the problematic 'reciprocal role' patterns, which were leading to stuck, unproductive or unnecessary consultations.

REFINING UNDERSTANDING

The key worker and specialist worker would then refine the formulation through additional information, both from the patient's life and from the experience of the therapeutic relationship with the key worker(s). The formulation would need to make sense of repeated patterns and be able to account for the problems in healthcare relationships and management to date. Responsibility for developing the formulation would be shared between patients and the service they interact with. By providing a model or philosophy, the team may be able to develop a 'shared language' which can only enhance understanding and cohesion.

TEACHING AND SKILLS INPUTS

The above approaches may help staff to identify the gaps in their skills. Specialist workers may also provide some teaching relating to the case formulation or psychological processes. They may need to educate and inform about transference and counter-transference and assist the key worker(s) to process their own reactions and understand them in reference to the formulation.

FUTURE CARE AND PSYCHOLOGICALLY INFORMED CARE PLANS

The formulation aims to be a non-blaming and containing framework to assist in developing an effective care plan. Specialist workers would aim to identify whether the consultancy had enabled the key worker(s) to feel more confident about their work with the patient and whether they feel less anxious, which in turn should allow a more empathic but less collusive response to the patient. In attending to the working relationship, they would aim to make sense of patients' difficulties alongside professional responses and consequently help the key worker(s) to reflect on and negotiate their therapeutic engagement, possibly informing new ways of relating with the patient. They would agree a way forward to address the patient's needs and the level of consultation or support required by the key worker(s).

There are a range of consultancy models but we suggest that if possible, the specialist worker be someone who is part of or can be attached to the team, who is viewed as a resource rather than an expert, who works collaboratively and is willing to get involved. We would stress an informal consultative stance, using opportunities, for example in informal discussions, to promote dialogue and psychological thinking.

THE ECONOMIC COSTS OF PERSONALITY DISORDER

The economic costs of personality disorder and the burden on healthcare, social and criminal justice agencies have yet to be accurately quantified. Coid (2003) describes borderline personality disorder as 'the clinical face of personality disturbance' in mental health services because of its affective components but also because this group is characterised by tendencies to seek help. However, it is the antisocial group that has the biggest public health impact. Some of the traits associated with the Cluster B personality disorders, such as impulsivity and recklessness, may contribute to high rates of physical morbidity, due to drug and alcohol use, violence, self-harm and risk-taking behaviours.

There is some promising evidence for the impact of specialist psychosocial treatment on healthcare service use costs by patients with personality disorder. Research has been stimulated by the need to demonstrate the cost-effectiveness of psychotherapies, particularly focusing on the use of therapeutic communities as a treatment option. This compares service utilisation indices, usually relating to psychiatric services, for the year before and after treatment. Studies from three groups report a reduction in costs for the year after treatment in comparison to the year before (Chiesa et al., 2002, Cassel Hospital, London; Davies, Campling & Ryan, 1999, Francis Dixon Lodge, Leicester; Dolan et al., 1996, Henderson Hospital, London). The Leicester service found reduction in acute bed occupancy was maintained at three year follow-up (Davies & Campling, 2003).

There have been similar findings for less intensive treatments. Bateman and Fonagy (2003) assessed healthcare costs associated with psychoanalytically oriented partial hospital treatment for borderline personality disorder compared with treatment as usual within general psychiatric services. Their treatment included individual and group psychoanalytic psychotherapy and other components (community meeting, medication, case co-ordinator meeting) all delivered in accordance with a theoretically informed approach. Costs of partial hospital treatment were offset by less psychiatric inpatient care and reduced A and E treatment. The authors state that less structured and less intensive programmes are inadequate treatments and fail to reduce medical risks, suicide, symptoms or numbers and duration of hospital stays. However, Guthrie et al. (1999), offering brief out-patient psychodynamic–interpersonal therapy to patients (with complex and enduring non-psychotic symptoms and interpersonal difficulties) who had found it difficult to engage in or respond to other kinds of conventional psychiatric treatment, found it cost-effective relative to usual care.

SOME POTENTIAL DIFFICULTIES FOR PSYCHOLOGICALLY INFORMED MANAGEMENT IN OTHER HEALTHCARE SYSTEMS

The central aim of a formulation-based approach is to extend the benefit of psychological approaches to patients who might not otherwise be considered suitable for or be asking for psychotherapy, but whose presentation is impairing the ability of staff to think or work effectively. There are clear challenges to such work. Psychologically informed approaches drawing on the models outlined in this book assume the role of developmental and social issues in the formation of the patient's difficulties. This may represent a new way of understanding symptoms. In focusing on the worker/health system–patient relationship, we are asking workers to pay attention to their own responses to patients. Many staff will find this unfamiliar, whilst some will see it as unprofessional, going against earlier training, which may have emphasised 'objectivity'.

IMPLICATIONS FOR TRAINING

The widespread nature of such complex difficulties and the proposal of models of consultation have important training implications. Training will need to address the widely differing professional and multi-agency groups who in one way or another work with such patients, and the contexts in which they work. It is probably unreasonable to expect a large input of resources for specialist training and appointment of dedicated therapists. A gradually increasing awareness of and skills in robust and coherent models of psychotherapy and case formulation among 'front-line' workers, certainly in mental health, will probably deliver the most overall benefit. In addition, some form of less intensive skill training across other healthcare fields and 'awareness training' could usefully be extended to those who do not necessarily have direct therapeutic contact with individuals with personality disorder.

CONCLUSIONS

Patients with personality disorders (or features of them) are encountered commonly in a variety of healthcare settings, whether they are recognised formally as such or not. They may present in many ways but are almost always characterised by relational and interpersonal difficulties, in addition to various focal symptoms or problems, which complicate and confound attempts to work with them. These attempts are also frequently complicated by unhelpful systemic reactions and enactments by staff, who may in addition be subject to institutional and other pressures as well as their own personal motivational issues or 'roles'. Clear and coherent models of such disorders and their attendant difficulties are needed, to provide a 'common language' which will enable joint working with patients on the basis of agreed formulations. This will help to develop workers' clinical skills and reflective practice. Such models should also help to provide conceptual support and containment to staff, to help them to effectively address (rather than colluding with or exacerbating) patients' problems and also to prevent staff stress and 'burn-out'. These ideas have major policy implications in particular around training and more general reconsideration of the aims of services (currently greatly preoccupied with supportive interventions directed at overt symptoms) and also in terms of fostering the general aims of greater understanding of the nature and origins of mental disorders in the emerging field of public mental health.

REFERENCES

Balint, E. & Norell, J. (1973). *Six minutes for the patient: Interactions in general practice consultation.* London: Tavistock.

Bateman, A. & Fonagy, P. (2003). Health service utilization costs for borderline personality disorder patients treated with psychoanalytically oriented partial hospitalization versus general psychiatric care. *American Journal of Psychiatry, 160*, 169–171.

Chiesa, M., Fonagy, P., Holmes, C., Drahorad, C. et al. (2002). Health service use costs by personality disorder following specialist and nonspecialist treatment: A comparative study. *Journal of Personality Disorders, 16*, 160–173.

Coid, J. (2003). Epidemiology, public health and the problem of personality disorder. *British Journal of Psychiatry, 182*, 3–10.

Davies, S. & Campling, P. (2003). Therapeutic communities treatment of personality disorder: A service use and mortality over 3 years' follow-up. *British Journal of Psychiatry, 182*, 24–27.

Davies, S., Campling, P. & Ryan K. (1999). Therapeutic community provision at regional and district levels. *Psychiatric Bulletin, 23*, 79–83.

Dolan, B., Warren, D., Menzies, D. et al (1996). Cost-offset following specialist treatment of severe personality disorders. *Psychiatric Bulletin, 20*, 413–417.

Emerson, J., Pankrantz, L., Joos, S. & Smith, S. (1994). Personality disorders in problematic medical patients. *Psychosomatics, 35*, 469–473.

Fink, P. (1992). The use of hospitalizations by persistent somatizing patients. *Journal of Psychosomatic Research, 36*, 439–447.

Flynn, S. & Bartholomew, D. (2003). Personality disorders: the challenge of acute in-patient management. *Clinical Psychology*, 22, 17–21.

Fosbury, J. A., Bosley, C. M., Ryle, A., Sonksen, P. H. & Judd, S. L. (1997). A trial of cognitive analytic therapy in poorly controlled Type 1 patients. *Diabetes Care*, 20, 959–964.

Goldberg, D. & Bridges, K. (1987). Screening for psychiatric illness in general practice: The general practitioner versus the screening questionnaire. *Journal of the Royal College of General Practitioners*, 37, 15–18.

Guthrie, E. (2000). Psychotherapy for patients with complex disorders and chronic symptoms: The need for a new research paradigm. *British Journal of Psychiatry*, 177, 131–137.

Guthrie, E., Kapur, N., Mackway-Jones, K., Chew-Graham, C., Moorey, J., Mendel, E., Marino-Francis, F., Sanderson, S., Turpin, C., Boddy, G. & Tomenson, B. (2001). Randomised controlled trial of brief psychological intervention after deliberate self poisoning. *British Medical Journal*, 323, 135–138.

Guthrie E., Moorey J., Margison F., Barker H., Palmer S., McGrath G., Tomenson, B. & Creed F. (1999). Cost-effectiveness of brief psychodynamic–interpersonal therapy in high utilizers of psychiatric services. *Archives of General Psychiatry*, 56, 519–526.

Hamilton, J., Campos, R. & Creed, F. (1996). Anxiety, depression and the management of medically unexplained symptoms in medical clinics. *Journal of the Royal College of Physicians of London*, 30, 18–20.

Hamilton, J., Guthrie, E. Creed, F. et al. (2000). A randomised controlled trial of psychotherapy in patients with chronic functional dyspepsia. *Gastroenterology*, 119, 661–669.

Hemmings, A., Donaldson, L. & Reval, K. (1996). *The management of suicide and self harm: A three stage study of policies, attitudes, training and staff support.* University of Sussex Trafford Centre for Medical Research, Brighton.

Hepple, J. & Sutton, L. (2004). *Cognitive analytic therapy and later life.* Hove: Brunner-Routledge.

Kashner, T. M., Rost, K., Cohen, B., Anderson, M. & Smith, G. R. (1995). Enhancing the health of somatization disorder patients. *Psychosomatics*, 36, 462–470.

Katon, W., Lin, E., Von-Korff, M., Russo, J., Lipscom, P. & Bush, T. (1991). Somatization: A spectrum of severity. *American Journal of Psychiatry*, 148, 34–40.

Laidlaw, K., Thompson, L. W., Dick-Siskin, L. & Gallagher-Thompson, D. G. (2003). *Cognitive behavioural therapy with older people.* Chichester: Wiley.

Little, P., Somerville, J., Williamson, I., Warner, G., Moore, M., Wiles, R. et al. (2001). Psychosocial, lifestyle and health status variables in predicting high attendance among adults. *British Journal of General Practice*, 51, 987–993.

Matalon, A., Nahmani, T., Rabin, S., Maoz, B. & Hart, J. (2002). A short-term intervention in a multidisciplinary referral clinic for primary care frequent attenders: Description of the model, patient characteristics and their use of medical resources. *Family Practice*, 19, 251–256.

Monsen, K. & Havik, O. E. (2001). Psychological functioning and bodily conditions in patients with pain disorder associated with psychological factors. *British Journal of Medical Psychology*, 74, 183–196.

Moran, P., Jenkins R., Tylee, A., Blizard, R. & Mann, A. (2000). The prevalence of personality disorder amongst UK primary care attenders. *Acta Psychiatrica Scandinavica*, 101, 1–6.

Neal, R. D., Heywood, P. L., Morley, S., Clayden, A. & Dowell, A. (1998). Frequency of patients' consulting in general practice and workload generated by frequent attenders: Comparisons between practices. *British Journal of General Practice*, 48, 895–898.

Page, L. A. & Wessely, S. (2003). Medically unexplained symptoms: Exacerbating factors in the doctor–patient encounter. *Journal of the Royal Society of Medicine*, 96, 223–227.

Perry, J. C. (1993). Longitudinal studies of personality disorders. *Journal of Personality Disorders, 7,* 63–85.

Pickvance, D., Parry, G. & Howe, A. (2004). A cognitive–analytic framework for understanding and managing problematic frequent attendance in primary care. *Primary Care and Mental Health, 2,* 165–174.

Pither, C. E. & Nicholas, M. K. (1991). Psychological approaches in chronic pain management. *British Medical Bulletin, 47,* 743–761.

Pollock, P. H. (2001). *Cognitive analytic therapy for adult survivors of childhood sexual abuse: Approaches to treatment and management.* Chichester: Wiley.

Pollock, P. H., Stowell-Smith, M. & Goepfert, M. J. (in press). *Cognitive analytic therapy for offenders: A new approach to forensic psychotherapy.* Hove: Brunner-Routledge.

Ryle, A. & Kerr, I. (2002). *Introducing cognitive analytic therapy: Principles and practice.* Chichester: Wiley.

Seivewright, N. & Daly, C. (1997) Personality disorder and drug use: A review. *Drug and Alcohol Review, 16,* 235–250.

Sheard, T., Evans, J., Cash, D., Hicks, J., King, A., Morgan, N., Nereli, B., Porter, I., Rees, H., Sandford, J., Slinn, R., Sunder, K. & Ryle, A. (2000). A CAT derived one to three session intervention for repeated deliberate self-harm: A description of the model and initial experience of trainee psychiatrists in using it. *British Journal of Medical Psychology, 73,* 179–196.

Sutton, L. (1997). 'Out of the silence': When people can't talk about it. In L. Hunt, M. Marshall and C. Rowlings (Eds), *Past trauma in later life: European perspectives on therapeutic work with older people* (pp. 155–170). London: Kingsley.

Verheul, R. (2001). Comorbidity of personality disorders in individuals with substance use disorders. *European Psychiatry, 16,* 274–282.

Walsh, S., Hagan, T. & Gamsu, D. (2000). Rescuer and rescued: Applying a cognitive analytic perspective to explore the 'mis-management' of asthma. *British Journal of Medical Psychology, 73,* 151–168.

Wesby, R. (2004). Inpatient dynamics: Thinking, feeling and understanding. In S. Evans and J. Garner (Eds), *Talking over the years. A handbook of dynamic psychotherapy with older adults* (pp. 101–116). Hove: Brunner-Routledge.

Williams, E. R., Guthrie, E., Mackway-Jones, K., James, M., Tomenson, B., Eastham, J. & McNally, D. (2001). Psychiatric status, somatisation, and health care utilization of frequent attenders at the emergency department: A comparison with routine attenders. *Psychosomatic Research, 50,* 161–167.

Zimmerman, M. M. (1999). Axis I diagnostic comorbidity and borderline personality disorder. *Comprehensive Psychiatry, 40,* 245–252.

17

Clinical Supervision

MARY SHINNER

DAWN BENNETT

> By three methods we may learn wisdom: First, by reflection, which is the
> noblest; second, by imitation which is easiest; and third, by experience, which
> is the bitterest. Confucius (551–479 B.C.)

INTRODUCTION

In this chapter we aim to help community mental health team (CMHT)
practitioners[1] think about the need for, and the nature of, regular clinical
supervision[2] for their work with patients with a diagnosis of personality
disorder. We also aim to assist the practitioner with the development of the
quality of their own supervision, and that of their team.

CMHTs play a significant role in the delivery of care for people with this
diagnosis (Hall, 2000; Tyrer, 2000), and offer many potential benefits; their
multi-disciplinary nature facilitates access to a wide range of skills, and
there is the potential for mutual support amongst team members (Chalk,
1999). People with a diagnosis of personality disorder are identified as needing
a multi-disciplinary approach (NIMHE, 2003a). However, in our experience,
CMHT practitioners are often unsure about their role with this group of patients.

---

[1] The focus of this chapter will be on the regular practice of post-qualification professionals and non-
registered practitioners, rather than those in training.
[2] The term 'clinical supervision' is used to refer to supervision focused on clinical issues associated with
patient contact, as distinct from other forms, such as line management or case management supervision.
All subsequent references to supervision in this chapter should be taken to refer to clinical supervision.

Personality Disorder and Community Mental Health Teams: A Practitioner's Guide. Edited by
M. J. Sampson, R. A. McCubbin and P. Tyrer. © 2006 John Wiley & Sons, Ltd.

In addition, despite supervision being generally regarded as a 'good' thing, shortcomings in its provision have been identified (Morrall, 1997), as well as difficulties in maintaining the quality of the therapeutic work of teams (Holmes, 1998; Morrall, 1997). These difficulties are in the context of current guidelines for working with people with a diagnosis of personality disorder, which promote the development of 'reflective practice', and state that all practitioners, whatever their role, need access to supervision in order to work effectively with this group (NIMHE, 2003a, 2003b). 'Access to supervision' is one of the defining features of a 'capable organisation' (NIMHE, 2003b) with respect to services for people with a diagnosis of personality disorder.

We hope this chapter will provide practitioners with greater clarity of thinking about the essential role of supervision in maintaining and developing their skills in working positively and effectively with this group of patients. Our hope is that this will, in turn, enable them to work towards ensuring that their supervisory needs are met.

In the first section, we think about what supervision is and how it has developed, and review the supervision models and frameworks available in mental health. In the second section, we consider why supervision is a necessary component of our work with patients with a diagnosis of personality disorder, particularly in terms of its role in helping us meet the challenges presented by the complex and interpersonal nature of their difficulties. In the third section, we review the blocks at individual, CMHT and organisational levels that might be preventing us from getting our supervisory needs met. In the fourth and final section of this chapter, practitioners are asked to assess their supervisory needs for their work with patients with a diagnosis of personality disorder, and whether these needs are being met. Some ways of overcoming blocks to supervision are suggested, at individual, CMHT and organisational levels, and consideration is given to ways of enhancing the quality of supervision.

DEFINITIONS AND MODELS OF SUPERVISION IN MENTAL HEALTH

WHAT IS 'SUPERVISION'?

A broad definition of supervision, relevant to the range of practitioners working in CMHTs, is as follows:

> a formal process of professional support and learning which enables practitioners to develop knowledge and competence, assume responsibility for their

own practice and enhance consumer protection and safety of care in complex clinical situations (Department of Health, 1993, cited by Wheeler, 2004, p. 15).

The term 'complex clinical situations' and the emphasis on safety of care seem particularly relevant to the management and treatment of patients with a diagnosis of personality disorder within CMHTs. Another definition is as follows:

> Supervision is a working alliance between a supervisor and a worker or workers, in which the worker can reflect on herself in her working situation by giving an account of her work and receiving feedback and where appropriate guidance and appraisal. The object of this alliance is to maximise the competence of the worker in providing a helping service (Inskipp & Procter, 1988, cited by Scaife, 2001, p. 2).

These definitions seem to capture some key components of what we mean by supervision: it involves at least one other person; it provides formalised and structured time for reflection on work-related experiences and practices; it allows for constructive and purposeful input by the supervisor; it has as its desired outcomes the maintenance and development of the skills of the worker, and the quality of services provided to the recipients of the service.

HOW DID SUPERVISION COME ABOUT?

Supervision of practice in mental health began in the early 20th century, as the followers of Freud utilised their personal analysis to discuss their patients' problems. Wheeler (2004) describes how, as this happened more and more, their own analysts became frustrated, and demanded that their patients' problems be discussed in an alternative forum! Since then, the main models of supervision have been derived within counselling, psychological therapy and social work frameworks. As the roles of the various mental health professions have developed, there has been a demand for a higher complexity of clinical decision-making, and for a broader range of skilled interventions. This has resulted in an increasing need for supervision across all professions, and in all mental health settings. It is now common for the registering and accrediting bodies of the mental health professions to make statements about the need for supervision at all levels of practice and experience.

MODELS AND FRAMEWORKS OF SUPERVISION

The models or frameworks available to help us think about supervision tend to fall into two categories: 'theory-specific' models and 'general' models.

Theory-specific supervision models are those that are intrinsically linked to specific theoretical approaches (such as psychodynamic, cognitive–analytic, cognitive, behavioural, interpersonal, systemic, dialectic–behavioural and integrated approaches). These theory-specific frameworks are not incompatible with the general models and can be used in conjunction with them. A common *aim* of these different models is to facilitate in the supervisee the application of the specific theory into clinical practice. A common *feature* is that the nature of the supervision model reflects aspects of the application of the specific theory in clinical practice with patients. So, for example, supervision based on a theory that places interpersonal relationships at the centre will be likely to focus on relationship issues, including the relationship between the supervisor and supervisee. Supervision related to a more problem-focused model will be likely to spend more time developing an understanding of the problem of focus from within that framework.

These theory-specific frameworks will not be described here, and the interested reader should refer to the seminal volumes available on this topic, such as those of Watkins (1997) and Bernard and Goodyear (1992). It is, however, likely that the supervision offered to practitioners working with patients with a diagnosis of personality disorder in CMHTs will be influenced by one of the theories of mental health, according to the theoretical orientation of whoever is providing it, as well as the practitioner's own personal preference. Indeed, in the next section, we consider how the presence of a theoretical framework for understanding personality disorder is essential if supervision is going to be of maximum benefit.

The second category is 'general' models: supervisory models and frameworks that are not specifically linked to a theoretical model of mental health problems. These frameworks do not imply that there is no need for a theoretical model of mental health to guide supervision; rather, they reflect a way of thinking about supervision that can be applied to any such theoretical framework. It is not possible to give an exhaustive account here of all the models available, but two types of model will be selected that we consider to be potentially useful for practitioners in CMHTs working with patients with a diagnosis of personality disorder. These are 'functional' models, and 'knowledge and learning' models. For a more comprehensive overview of general models, the reader can consult a range of excellent texts available (e.g. Beinart, 2004; Hawkins and Shohet, 2000; Scaife, 2001).

Functional Models

General models include those that focus on the function of supervision, such as those of Inskipp and Procter (1993) and Kadushin (1992), summarised by

Hawkins and Shohet (2000). Three main functions are described: educative/ formative; supportive/restorative; managerial/normative. The first of these includes an attempt to understand the patient better, to become more aware of our own reactions to patients, to understand the dynamics of the interaction, to look at the interventions used and the consequences of these and to explore other ways of working with these and other similar patient situations.

The second function, supportive/restorative, is described by Hawkins and Shohet (2000) as primarily involving attending to our emotional responses to our patients. They emphasise that failing to attend to these inevitably leads to us being less effective workers, either over-identifying with patients, or using strategies to defend ourselves from further emotional reactions, such as by rejecting them. This can lead to a build-up of stress, leaving us at risk of burnout.

The third, managerial/normative, function addresses issues of 'quality control'. This might be more of an emphasis in training environments, where a supervisor is involved in assessing whether someone is fit to practice in a given profession. However, it is inevitable, Hawkins and Shohet (2000) claim, that however qualified or experienced we are, we bring our own 'failings', blind spots, areas of vulnerability and prejudices with us to work. We have a responsibility to ensure that the impact these might have on the quality of our working practices is minimised. Supervision can provide a reflective space in which to identify our personal responses and explore their impact, giving us an opportunity to think about how we can contain and manage these.

We believe this functional model is helpful because it provides a framework for considering the range of our supervisory needs, and for understanding the supervisory process as it happens. It is also helpful in that it increases the likelihood that there is an opportunity for all these functions to take place, avoiding emphasis on one at the expense of the others.

Models of Knowledge and Learning

Theories about how people learn and develop knowledge have been used to assist supervision, focusing primarily on the 'educative/formative' function of understanding and skill development (reviewed by Scaife and Scaife, 2001). Experiential learning theory (Kolb, 1984) is one such model, and can be used to provide a framework for the inclusion and tracking of some essential components of supervision. The 'learning cycle' that is associated with it is illustrated in Figure 17.1, and represents a continuous process, which can be entered at any point.

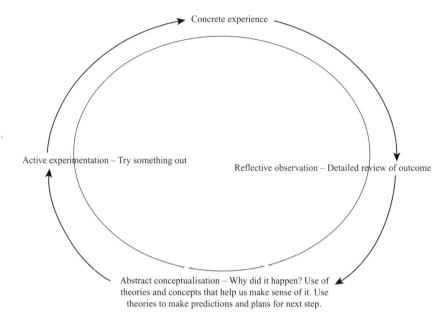

Figure 17.1 Learning cycle (Kolb, 1984). Supervision and learning. In J. Scaife (Ed.), *Supervision in the mental health professions: A practitioner's guide* (p. 28). Hove: Brunner-Routledge)

The different stages are followed in sequence, and include the 'active experimentation' component of trying something out. This leads to the 'concrete experience' of what actually happened, which provides information for further 'reflective observation'. This, in turn, leads to further 'abstract conceptualisation', within which theoretical ideas are developed, and on their basis plans are made for 'active experimentation', leading to further 'concrete experience' and so on. When this model is used in supervision, the emphasis is very much on supervisees being active participants in their development and learning. It requires both supervisor and supervisee to be open to considerable reflection, and Scaife and Scaife (2001) make the point that this requires supervision to feel 'safe' and supportive.

This emphasis on reflection and conceptualisation, in addition to the experience of 'trying things out', will be particularly relevant to our work with patients with a diagnosis of personality disorder. The complexity of these patients' difficulties, and the potential for our actions somehow 'feeding' their difficulties (see the next section) makes it even more vital that supervision provides space for these functions. The clarity of the different stages identified in the framework is helpful for reflection both in and out of supervision, to ensure that learning is maximised.

WHY WE NEED SUPERVISION AND HOW IT CAN HELP

PARTICULAR CHALLENGES POSED

Personality Disorders are Complex Problems that are Difficult to Understand

As has been discussed elsewhere in this volume, many patients with a diagnosis of personality disorder have suffered a history of trauma, abuse and developmental deprivation, leading to highly complex difficulties. It is often hard to make sense of their problems or to know how to help. Consider the following examples: the patient who appears to have made great improvements and to be functioning well, but reacts desperately when there is the remotest prospect of losing any aspect of services; the patient who appears quite calm, in control and motivated to improve things, but who chaotically self-harms soon afterwards; the patient who seems to want and need help, but is insulting, belittling and undermining of our efforts; the patient who constantly suspects our motives, holds back, and tests us, when our motives seem to us good, and our attempts to engage sound; the patient who tells us they have done something we consider unethical, but calmly rationalises it.

On the face of it, these are perplexing actions, and indeed they reflect the very real complexity of difficulties that have developed over a lifetime, as a result of a complicated and unique interaction of biological, psychological, social and environmental factors.

The Interpersonal Nature of Personality Disorder Impacts on Practitioners and Teams

In the above examples, practitioners will inevitably *react* to these kinds of behaviour; feeling angry, anxious, frustrated, outraged and perplexed are all predictable responses. Along with these inevitable emotional responses comes a 'pull' to act in accordance with them; to be aggressive, become over-involved, avoid, dismiss or even punish.

We would experience these emotional responses, and a 'pull' to act in these ways, even if we were extremely psychologically resilient, exceptionally well functioning people. In fact, we all have our own personal psychological vulnerabilities and idiosyncrasies, based on our own histories, and our current lives. At times, these might serve to magnify our emotional responses and enhance the 'pull' to act in accordance with them.

If we experience our patients' extreme, difficult and sometimes risky behaviours *without any way of making sense of them*, there is a risk that we may personalise their responses, which may, for example, lead us to feel critical and reduce our empathy. This may result in ruptures in the working relationship and poor outcomes for any form of intervention we may attempt. We may become demoralised and doubtful of our skills. Even if we can resist being 'pulled' to act in accordance with our emotions initially, over time, we might find ourselves starting to behave in some of the ways listed, in an attempt to protect ourselves from difficult emotions. Unfortunately, some of these reactions may reinforce our patients' problematic interpersonal patterns of relating to others, and may maintain or exacerbate them.

To add yet another level of complexity, it is common for patients with a diagnosis of personality disorder to be involved with more than one practitioner, often because of issues to do with risk, but also because of the range of interventions being offered by CMHTs. Each person in the care team, as well as the patient, will have their own understanding of what the patient's problem is, and based on this a view of what the care team should be doing for progress to be made. Practitioners may not have much opportunity to discuss their views amongst themselves or with their patients, they may avoid this or they may actively disagree (Henneman, Lee & Cohen, 1995; Norman & Peck, 1999). All these scenarios potentially lead to fragmented, inconsistent and incoherent service provision (Heginbotham, 1999). A service compromised in this way is likely to be less helpful, which can be anxiety provoking and frustrating for all parties.

Given these challenges, it really is no wonder that CMHT practitioners can struggle to provide high quality services to this group, and that patients with this diagnosis can be left feeling that their needs are not being met (NIMHE, 2003b).

HOW SUPERVISION CAN HELP MANAGE AND OVERCOME THESE DIFFICULTIES

Developing Understanding

The educative or formative function of supervision provides an opportunity to help us to make sense of our patients' difficulties. Supervision provides a space in which to reflect on our knowledge of the patient, what they have told us, our own responses to them, what has been attempted and the outcome of this. It enables us to draw on a wider body of knowledge about these problems, and begin to develop ideas and plans about what to try next. It is this cyclical process of reflection, understanding, hypothesising and planning that facilitates the development of our clinical skills, and our ability to apply learning to novel situations.

As our understanding of someone's difficulties develops, we can begin to work out what might be the most helpful thing to do. If our contact is actively psychotherapeutic (such as the delivery of skill training, the provision of insight or change-oriented psychological therapy), this might include assisting the patient in developing their own understanding of their difficulties, and working with them towards helpful changes based on this understanding. If we have another specific role or combination of roles (such as crisis management, supportive, medical or care co-ordination roles), it might help us work out the most productive way of delivering services, and supporting and reacting to the patient in specific circumstances.

Incidentally, although we have distinguished here between the concepts of psychotherapeutic and other management-type roles (in that the former tends more explicitly to promoting change, whilst the latter tends to supporting and optimising the status quo), they are not entirely distinct; good management may contribute to change and conversely reactive or unhelpful management approaches may undermine any attempt at treatment. Additionally, many patients will choose not to seek formal therapy, feel unable to engage in it, or be unable to make productive use of it at times, leaving CMHTs providing predominantly 'management' oriented services. The complexity of the characteristics of personality disorder, and its challenging interpersonal nature, render supervision a necessity for all practitioners engaged in work with this group, regardless of their role.

In order to utilise supervision for the purposes described, we need reference to some kind of framework for understanding the concept of personality disorder. The dominant theoretical models of personality disorder are psychological, and despite their variations what they have in common is an internal theoretical coherence, which enables the practitioner to reflect in a focused way, to hypothesise and to plan in accordance with it. At a basic level, they provide us with a way of 'making sense' of someone's difficulties, by putting them in their historical context, and providing a means of understanding what is happening currently. This is what is known as a psychological formulation or conceptualisation, and is a vital tool for providing effective, individualised packages of care to this patient group.

A second reason for having a model of personality disorder within supervision is to help foster consistency and coherence amongst practitioners involved with the same patient. An individualised formulation, which is shared and accepted by all those involved, will help the team move forward together with the patient. Practitioners are more likely to perceive each other, and be perceived by the patient, as supportive and helpful if they have a shared understanding and agreement about why they are doing what they do.

Managing and Utilising the Interpersonal Impact

Given the nature of our patients' problems, the supportive or normative function of supervision is vital; the interpersonal features of their difficulties, the inevitable impact these will have on us, the reality of our own vulnerabilities, and the interpersonal complexity of a CMHT render an opportunity to reflect on our own responses essential. This helps to prevent the build-up of stress and frustration that can put us at risk of burnout.

The presence of a theoretical framework for understanding personality disorder allows us to reflect on our responses in a focused way. They can help us further to understand patients' difficulties, to maintain an empathic and non-judgmental stance, and ultimately give us a better chance of keeping our relationships with our patients helpful, rather than falling into behaving in ways that might be counterproductive. This is consistent with the third function of supervision, the managerial or normative function. If we assume that we as practitioners have a responsibility to reflect on our own contribution to the therapeutic process and minimise the impact of our own vulnerabilities on our work, we need to ensure that we have opportunities to do so.

Another aspect of the managerial or normative function of supervision might be to assist the practitioner, and provide a theoretical framework for assessing whether there are aspects of the system of care itself that might be inadvertently serving to maintain or exacerbate the patient's difficulties. Many services have genuine problems in terms of resources, skill levels, organisation and communication between various agencies, all of which may present particular problems to this patient group (NIMHE, 2003a). Supervision provides an ideal opportunity to examine the impact of the wider network of care, in order to plan how to address issues around the quality of services to support the practitioner and patient in promoting recovery.

POTENTIAL BLOCKS TO SUPERVISION IN CMHTs

INDIVIDUAL FACTORS

In their seminal text on supervision, Hawkins and Shohet (2000) identify a range of potential blocks to supervision, including four that can reside in the individual practitioner.

Previous Experience of Supervision

Good or bad, our previous experience of supervision will impact on our motivation to seek out more, and our attitude to any we receive.

Personal Inhibition

A practitioner's personal history may lead to experiences of discomfort within a supervisory relationship, or avoidance of it altogether, due to oversensitivity to criticism or defensiveness.

Difficulties with Authority

Hawkins and Shohet (2000, p. 2) draw on psychodynamic concepts when they talk about the possibility of the supervisee 'projecting... critical or uncontaining parental images' on to the supervisor, and also the possibility of 'sibling rivalry' between the two in terms of who can manage the patient more effectively.

Difficulty in Receiving Support

Work cultures can often serve to reinforce a wider cultural notion that needing help equates to some kind of 'weakness', or implies 'dependency' on others. Although we may be comfortable working with our patients and *their* needs, acknowledging our own may be much more difficult. This may prevent us seeking the support and supervision that we need. For some of us, our professional culture and training may have given great value to objectivity, and a lack of personal involvement. A need for supervision, which at least suggests some focus on our own responses, may therefore feel to some to be professional failure. Additionally, in a busy CMHT providing a 'front-line' service, there can be high expectations of resilience in ourselves and in our colleagues. The experience of powerful emotions such as anxiety or anger can be seen as at best an inconvenience, and at worst a sign of failure, weakness or an indication that someone is not coping. Requesting regular supervision where this is not the norm may be viewed by oneself or by others in this way.

CMHT FACTORS

Conflict of Roles

In a CMHT, it can often be the case that a practitioner's clinical supervisor is also their manager or involved in some way in their appraisal. Many authors writing about supervision (e.g. Hawkins & Shohet, 2000; Scaife, 2001) identify this kind of 'dual role' as a potential block to supervision, because it might result in some reluctance to be entirely open about what is being struggled with. Alternatively, knowing all too well the pressures that their manager is under, a practitioner may feel obliged to 'protect' them from the perceived extra burden of their own difficulties, preventing their own needs from being met. Scaife (2001, p. 5) proposes that, ideally, the supervisory relationship should 'preclude the simultaneous existence of other role-relationships between participants (friendships, managerial relationships)'. Another role-related block highlighted by Hawkins and Shohet (2000) is a mismatch in expectations on the part of supervisor and supervisee. They go on, as we do later in this chapter, to highlight the importance of a clear supervisory contract, and a willingness for open discussion about expectations.

Practical Blocks

Hawkins and Shohet (2000) highlight financial and geographical factors as potential blocks, as well as the lack of availability of an appropriate supervisor. Although not all of these might apply in a CMHT, it is a reality of practice that there is limited choice and availability of supervisors. There is also limited time to obtain or provide supervision; a request for more formal, structured supervision, in the face of the enormous workload of the team and its 'crisis management' role, may seem unmanageable, difficult to prioritise or even self-indulgent. The supervision we do manage to deliver and receive is required to cover an enormous range of patient problems, making it hard to obtain or provide specialist supervision for a particular patient group such as this one. It tends to be the case that what is available will depend on the expertise and enthusiasm of particular individuals, and provision will depend to an extent on who 'shouts the loudest' (a situation also reflected in relation to training, e.g. Duggan, 2002), a distinctly unsatisfactory state of affairs.

Multiple Practitioners Involved

Various practitioners may be involved with the care of one patient, and this may have implications for the way supervision structures are designed and utilised. As we have already stated, we believe that patients and practitioners alike benefit from the multiple practitioners involved having a shared understanding of their patient. A rigorous supervisory framework is a necessary part of achieving this aim, although it is unlikely to be sufficient; other aspects, such as formal structures (for example, regular meetings) for sharing psychological formulations of the patient's difficulties and the provision of training are also likely to be necessary.

Understanding of Personality Disorder

We have alluded to the fact that a CMHT may not have a unified frame-work for understanding and intervening with this group of patients. Indeed, some practitioners may feel they have no framework at all for understanding patients with a diagnosis of personality disorder (NIMHE, 2003b). Different professional training and training in different models of mental health problems may result in a range of values, beliefs and approaches to these patients within a team. This poses a challenge to all aspects of service delivery (and, indeed, to the care of all our patients), including the nature and structure of supervision. We believe that it is desirable for the practice of a team to be consistent and unified, and that a unified framework is necessary if this is to be achieved (Fahy, 2002). Although supervision alone may be insufficient in achieving this end (as has been stated, the sharing of psychological formulations and the provision of training may also be required), it will be a vital means of reinforcing and developing such a unified perspective.

Variety in Attitudes to Supervision

Different professionals and practitioners have different attitudes to super-vision. This can be in terms of their understanding of what it is and what it is for, which will affect their judgement regarding their need for it, and their motivation to obtain it. For some people it might seem like a low-priority luxury, whilst for others it is an essential requirement for their practice. Another variation might be the autonomy and confidence individuals have to seek out and make time for supervision. Factors such as seniority, profes-sional background and the perceived role of an individual in the team structure may contribute to such variations. We hope that the content of this chapter will help any practitioner who works with patients with a diagnosis of personality disorder to develop a clearer understanding of the nature and purpose of supervision, and if necessary assist in building their resolve to ensure that their supervisory needs are met.

ORGANISATIONAL FACTORS

Hawkins and Shohet (2000) highlight organisational factors, which will interact with the other factors listed earlier, and either serve to overcome them or to reinforce them. They identify a number of problematic 'cultural dynamics' that serve negatively to affect supervision. These include cultures within which the message is given that if you wish to be successful you need to demonstrate that you do not need supervision. The tendency will be, within this dynamic, to provide regular supervision to only the most junior staff, with there being no provision for more senior practitioners. Another problematic cultural dynamic is characterised by a focus on task completion, with written policies for every eventuality. Supervision within this cultural dynamic is likely to be a 'checklist' of tasks, at the expense of personal reflection and reflection on relationships.

In a cultural dynamic within which battles for power exist between competing subgroups, Hawkins and Shohet (2000) suggest supervision could become conspiratorial, and negative about other parties. A crisis-driven cultural dynamic will tend not to prioritise supervision, and will result in a general lack of time for reflection. A final problematic cultural dynamic identified is characterised by high degrees of dependency and over-work being elicited from staff, the covert message being that success is defined as not taking breaks, and staying late.

DEVELOPING SUPERVISION FOR YOU AND YOUR CMHT

ASSESSING YOUR SUPERVISORY NEEDS AND YOUR CURRENT SUPERVISION

Following the preceding discussion in this chapter, particularly the issues raised in the second section, and in the light of national guidelines for good practice, it can be assumed that *if you are in clinical contact with this group of patients, you should have access to regular supervision*. This would be regardless of whether your contact is actively psychotherapeutic, or if you have another specific role or combination of roles.

In thinking about your supervision needs, you may want to use the supervision models and frameworks outlined in the first section to devise a series of questions, such as the following.

- Do you get sufficient, supportive, 'safe' (i.e. non-judgmental, non-evaluative) space to discuss your emotional reactions to these patients?
- Do you have (and does any current supervision promote) a framework for understanding the nature of personality disorder, which enables you to develop with your patients an understanding of their experiences, and to help make sense of how they interact with the system of care?
- Does supervision allow you to utilise this framework to reflect upon your own and others' responses, and to guide your practice, to maximise the helpfulness of the relationship, in order to promote recovery?

- Do you have the opportunity to reflect on your own responses in a way that would help you identify where your personal issues are impacting on your work?
- Can you reflect on the wider system of care in a way that allows you to identify (and possibly remediate) any problems within it?

If you have no formal access to supervision currently, you may want to consider the evidence you need to take to your manager (of which, we hope, this chapter will be a part) in order to establish some provision. If you are already receiving regular supervision associated with this work, you may want to use the models and frameworks to consider, perhaps together with your supervisor, how to develop the quality and effectiveness of the supervision you receive.

OVERCOMING BLOCKS TO SUPERVISION

In the third section the potential blocks to supervision were considered: those residing in the individual; those in the system of a CMHT; and those that might be more cultural or organisational.

Overcoming Individual Blocks

Based on the work of various authors (e.g. Inskipp & Procter, 1993), and the review in the third section of potential individual blocks to supervision, the following are some suggestions to help you identify and understand any resistance you might feel to or within the supervisory context.

- Monitor how open you are to feedback and criticism. Consider what might underlie any lack of openness.
- Monitor any tendencies to justify your actions or be defensive in supervision. Consider whether this reflects the specific supervisory relationship, or whether it is a more personal characteristic.
- Consider how easy you find it to accept support, in or out of supervision. Do you tend to minimise your own responses, or deflect attention away from these? Try to establish whether this tendency is entirely personal, a product of specific relationships (such as a need you feel to protect particular people), or reflects the working culture of your CMHT.
- Evaluate whether any supervisory relationship that you have is open to two-way feedback. If not, are any constraints you feel in giving feedback internal (for example, your own fears) or external (for example, due to a dual relationship with your supervisor that includes performance evaluation)?

Having identified any personal blocks, and what might underlie them, it will be important to devise a plan to overcome these. This might entail identifying a series of steps to test out different responses (including arranging supervision for yourself, if you have no current access to it), in order to find out whether any fears you have are justified. It might also require you to revisit any supervisory relationship you have, to clarify whether it is able to meet your needs.

Overcoming Blocks in CMHTs

Overcoming the *conflict of roles* of supervisors (for example, when someone is both manager and supervisor), which is common in CMHTs, ideally requires the allocation of an alternative supervisor. This is not always possible, however, and Scaife (2001) suggests that 'where dual relationships pertain this should be acknowledged and the implications addressed'. The most effective way of achieving this is through the use of an explicit supervision contract (see later in this section for a description of contracts).

Overcoming *practical blocks* in CMHTs often requires support, permission and facilitation from managers. As has been stated, we hope that this volume, and this chapter in particular, will provide practitioners with confidence and the necessary evidence to approach managers to help them identify the necessary resources (in terms of legitimised time, access to appropriately skilled people, and funding, if necessary) for supervision arrangements to be made. Regular formal and informal discussions with your colleagues are likely to be invaluable in overcoming the difficulties associated with *multiple practitioners* being involved with the same patients, in overcoming the fact that those practitioners may not have a *shared framework* for understanding personality disorder, and in overcoming the presence of a *variety of attitudes to supervision*.

Sharing your experiences of working with this patient group, discussing your and others' frameworks for understanding these kinds of problem, and finding out what support and supervisory input others are getting will all assist you in building up a picture of where you and your team are up to in working with this patient group. It may also be helpful in terms of generating interest in the possibility of accessing some training for team members, and perhaps the development of some structures, informal or otherwise, for developing and sharing psychological formulations of individual patients by those involved in their care. If a gradually developing consensus can be reached that these aspects are all vital in improving the quality of services provided to this patient group, team members will be in a stronger position to seek support from management for further team development along these lines. To assist

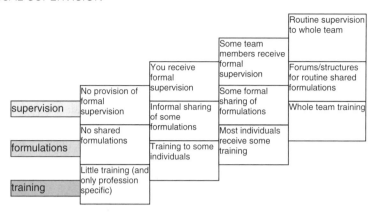

Figure 17.2 Sequence of 'steps' representing practitioner development

with this, we have devised a sequence of 'steps' which we believe represent a gradual increase in the quality of the development of practitioners within teams, and therefore the quality of the services they deliver. You may want to locate your team on the diagram in Figure 17.2 for the three factors identified, and observe what the next step might be to achieve these ends.

Overcoming Organisational Factors

If you recognise any of the problematic cultural dynamics described in the third section, you may want to think about how you could participate in overcoming these. Hawkins and Shohet (2000) identify seven steps for developing supervision policy and practice, which would assist in moving an organisation towards what they term a 'learning developmental culture'. This, they propose, is the kind of context within which supervision is most likely to flourish (for an extensive description of this kind of cultural dynamic, and ideas for moving towards it at an organisational level, see Hawkins and Shohet, 2000). They suggest that any such developmental process should be cyclical in nature.

1. 'Appreciatively enquire' into what supervision already takes place. This avoids the mistaken assumption that no good practice exists, and engages those demonstrating good practice in a process of change.
2. 'Awaken interest' in the development of supervision policies and practices. Work to demonstrate the benefits, such as in relation to meeting existing good practice guidelines, and the potential positive impact on staff morale and attitudes. Hawkins and Shohet (2000) emphasise that the impetus for change needs to come from within, and be 'owned' by team members.

3. Initiate experiments, by engaging a small group with the interest and enthusiasm to take forward such a process. This kind of process can generate interest beyond the boundaries of the team, potentially facilitating further support for the initiatives.
4. Manage resistance to change by attending to its source, rather than by pushing harder. There will be reasons why change is resisted, often related to personal fears, perceived threats and strong norms in the peer group. Engaging in meeting these needs will increase the chances of resistance being overcome.
5. Develop supervision policies, including a description of purpose and focus, minimum requirements, and explicit statements about the priority that supervision should be given in relation to other tasks.
6. Develop an ongoing learning and development process for supervisors and supervisees. This should include training supervisees how to make best use of supervision, as well as supervisor training.
7. Have an ongoing audit and review process, including measuring staff satisfaction and illustrating examples of best practice.

IMPROVING THE QUALITY OF SUPERVISION

Qualities of a Supervisor

It may be worth considering the qualities that research has shown to be indicative of a 'good' supervisor in relation to your current or any potential supervisor. Wheeler (2004) reviews the available literature and identifies qualities that practitioners have highlighted as valuable in supervisors, such as promoting equality in the relationship, a sense of safety, a degree of challenge, skills in forming supportive relationships, having relevant skills and knowledge, being committed to the supervisory process, and having good listening skills. It is likely that you will have your own ideas about what makes a good supervisor, and you could devise your own list of evaluation criteria. One such criterion may be the theoretical orientation of a prospective supervisor. If this is the case for you, it is important to note that there is likely to be huge variation between supervisors within the same theoretical framework, related to their personal style, and that the latter may be the major determinant of whether your supervisory needs are ultimately met. This could be seen to reflect the research findings that the patient's judgement of the quality of the therapeutic relationship is the best predictor of outcome of therapy (see, e.g., Martin, Garske & Davis, 2000), this being a better predictor than the theoretical orientation of the therapist.

Supervision Contracts

Along with many authors who have written on the subject of supervision, Scaife (2001, p. 5) suggests that supervision should be based on a written agreement or contract which specifies the purposes, aims, methods, terms, frequency, location, etc. of the supervision. This is to assist with clarifying this unique relationship, and is particularly important when the supervisory relationship exists in parallel with other relationships between the individuals involved. The presence of a negotiated contract facilitates the development of a collaborative supervisory relationship, and promotes some of the most valued qualities in supervisors (equality, safety, commitment and so on). Although supervision contracts do not need to be exhaustive, basic information such as the purpose, aims and methods, the expectations and roles of the people involved and the terms and conditions of supervisory sessions should be included. This allows all parties the opportunity to express their expectations of supervision, in order for any discrepancies in these to be addressed.

Format of Supervision

You may want to consider the potential advantages and disadvantages of different supervision formats: whether you receive supervision as an individual or as part of a group (in a group the person benefits from hearing about the work of others and from contributing to the learning of others, and helping the development of a shared consensus in understanding, but may have less time spent on their individual cases); whether supervision is with peers or with those you consider to be senior practitioners in this area (easier to arrange, and more 'ownership' of learning and development with peers, but possibly less access to expert knowledge); whether supervision is provided from within or outside the team (useful objectivity associated with external supervisors, but supervision within teams contributes to consensus). Of course, practical considerations will influence the decisions you and your team make, but it is worth highlighting and maximising the potential value that any particular format presents, as well as identifying and attempting to compensate for any disadvantages.

Your Use of Supervision

Once supervision is established, a big factor in determining the quality and utility of the supervision you receive is likely to be how you make use of that time. As a supervisee, you will need to take responsibility for preparing thoroughly: identifying key issues you wish to discuss; deciding how to describe the patient and your work succinctly; deciding how to summarise key events; identifying the specific issues that prompted you to bring a patient; considering whether you want help with content or process, theoretical, technical or relationship issues (which may link with the role you play with the patient). Whilst in supervision, it will be important to articulate your needs clearly, whilst remaining open to issues you may have overlooked. As has been mentioned, self-monitoring in terms of any reluctance to receive feedback, excessive self-justification and defensiveness, and an openness to addressing these, will be likely to enhance your experience of supervision. It will also allow you to participate with your supervisor in moderating the supervisory relationship, so that it maximises the chances of your needs being met.

CONCLUSION

In the first section, we summarised some of the frameworks developed to help us think about supervision. They provide us with some concrete ideas about what needs to be included in supervision, and frameworks to evaluate what we get out of it. In the second section we considered two of the main challenges for practitioners working with patients with a diagnosis of personality disorder: the problems are complicated and difficult to understand; the interpersonal nature of the problems has an inevitable impact on individual practitioners and teams. We considered how supervision is well placed to assist us with overcoming these challenges, by providing a forum for reflection, learning, reference to a wider body of theoretical knowledge and planning what to do next. Supervision also provides opportunities for expressing our own responses, reflecting on the nature of these, and where necessary, determining how our own needs may best be met. It provides an opportunity to consider the wider system of care, how it may need modification and how we can participate most productively within it for the benefit of our patients.

In our experience, CMHTs readily provide informal opportunities to 'offload' about our reactions to and difficulties with patients, usually in the context of strong and supportive personal relationships. Although there is a need for such a supportive peer group, particularly when working with patients with complex and severe needs, we do not see this as sufficient; all staff working with this group need formal, regular and effective supervision. Due to various blocks, some of which were outlined in the third section, CMHTs do not tend to be places where this occurs, leaving practitioners and patients vulnerable.

In the final section, we considered ways of assessing supervisory needs and whether these are being met, for you and for your CMHT. We suggested some ways in which blocks to supervision at all levels may be addressed, and eventually overcome. We consider it vital that practitioners develop a clear rationale for supervisory input, and the confidence to push for its provision, regardless of any existing blocks. We believe that all practitioners in CMHTs should be striving to obtain skilled and appropriate supervision, particularly for this patient group: as we argued in the second section, the complexity and emotional impact of working with these patients, the high risk of falling into problematic traps with them and the potential value of understanding the patient's intra- and interpersonal functioning render supervision a necessity if safe and effective services are to be provided.

REFERENCES

Beinart, H. (2004). Models of supervision and the supervisory relationship and their evidence base. In I. Fleming & L. Steen (Eds), *Supervision and clinical psychology: Theory, practice and perspectives* (pp. 36–51). Hove: Brunner-Routledge.

Bernard, J. M. & Goodyear, R. K. (1992). *Fundamentals of clinical supervision*. Boston: Allyn and Bacon.

Chalk, A. (1999). Community mental health teams: Reviewing the debate. *Mental Health Nursing, 16*, 12–14.

Department of Health. (1993). *A vision for the future*. London: HMSO.

Duggan, M. (2002). Developing services for people with personality disorder: The training needs of staff and services. Supporting paper to National Institute for Mental Health in England. (2003). *Personality disorder: No longer a diagnosis of exclusion*. London: Author.

Fahy, T. (2002). Organisation of personality disorder services in general adult psychiatry services. Supporting paper to National Institute for Mental Health in England. (2003). *Personality disorder: No longer a diagnosis of exclusion*. London: Author.

Hall, P. (2000). Effective community mental health services for people with serious mental illness: A critical review. *Mental Health Care, 31*, 299–303.

Hawkins, P. & Shohet, R. (2000). *Supervision in the helping professions* (2nd ed.). UK: Open University Press.

Heginbotham, C. (1999). The psychodynamics of mental health care. *Journal of Mental Health, 8*, 253–260.

Henneman, E. A., Lee, J. L. & Cohen, J. I. (1995). Collaboration: a concept analysis. *Journal of Advanced Nursing, 21*, 103–109.

Holmes, J. (1998). The psychotherapy department and the community mental health team: Bridges and boundaries. *Psychiatric Bulletin, 22*, 729–732.

Inskipp, F. & Procter, B. (1993). *The art, craft and tasks of counselling supervision*. Twickenham: Cascade.

Kadushin, A. (1992). *Supervision in social work*. New York: Columbia University Press.

Kolb, D. A. (1984). *Experiential learning: Experience as the source of learning and development*. Englewood Cliffs, NJ: Prentice-Hall.

Martin, D., Garske, J. P. & Davis, M. K. (2000). Relation of the therapeutic alliance with outcome and other variables: A meta-analytic review. *Journal of Consulting and Clinical Psychology, 68*, 438–450.

Morrall, P. A. (1997). Lacking in rigour: A case study of the professional practice of psychiatric nurses in four community mental health teams. *Journal of Mental Health*, *6*, 173–180.

National Institute for Mental Health in England (NIMHE). (2003a). *Personality disorder: No longer a diagnosis of exclusion. Policy implementation guidance for the development of services for people with personality disorder*. London: Author.

National Institute for Mental Health in England (NIMHE). (2003b). *Breaking the cycle of rejection. The personality disorder capabilities framework*. London: Author.

Norman, I. J. & Peck, E. (1999). Working together in adult community mental health services: An inter-professional dialogue. *Journal of Mental Health*, *8*, 217–230.

Scaife, J. (2001) *Supervision in the mental health professions: A practitioner's guide*. Hove: Brunner-Routledge.

Scaife, J. & Scaife, J. (2001). Supervision and learning. In J. Scaife (Ed.), *Supervision in the mental health professions: A practitioner's guide*. Hove: Brunner-Routledge.

Tyrer, P. (2000). The future of the community mental health team. *International Review of Psychiatry*, *12*, 219–225.

Watkins, C. E. (1997). *Handbook of psychotherapy supervision*. New York: Wiley.

Wheeler, S. (2004). A review of supervisor training in the UK. In I. Fleming and L. Steen (Eds), *Supervision and clinical psychology: Theory, practice and perspectives* (pp. 15–35). Hove: Brunner-Routledge.

Index

Note: page numbers in *italics* refer to figures or tables. CAT = cognitive analytic therapy; CMHTs = community mental health teams; DBT = dialectical behavioural therapy; PIT = psychodynamic-interpersonal therapy.